THE WORLD IS CHANGING...

No experience required books help you learn the industry's most important software without ANY previous experience. Real-world examples, skills-based discussions, and compact lessons give you the practical skills that will enable you to succeed in today's marketplace.

ISBN: 0-7821-2170-5
Joe Schmuller
$29.99

ISBN: 0-7821-2157-8
Erik Strom
$29.99

ISBN: 0-7821-2078-4
Steven Holzner
$29.99

ISBN: 0-7821-2115-2
Bill Bercik, Sylvia Percupile
$29.99

ISBN: 0-7821-2171-3
Steven Holzner
$34.99
2nd Edition
CD included

ISBN: 0-7821-2150-0
Celeste Robinson
$29.99

ISBN: 0-7821-2143-8
Stephen Mack, Janan Platt
$29.99

ISBN: 0-7821-2135-7
John Zukowski
$29.99

ISBN: 0-7821-2081-4
Robert Cowart, Boyd Waters
$29.99

ISBN: 0-7821-2111-X
Paulo Franca
$29.99

© 1997 Sybex Computer Books

WINDOWS® 95

No experience required.™

Sharon Crawford

SYBEX®

San Francisco • Paris • Düsseldorf • Soest

Associate Publisher: Gary Masters
Acquisitions Manager: Kristine Plachy
Acquisitions & Developmental Editor: Sherry Bonelli
Editor: Kim Wimpsett
Technical Editors: Dean Denno, Jim Bonelli
Book Designers: Patrick Dintino, Catalin Dulfu
Graphic Illustrator: Patrick Dintino
Electronic Publishing Specialist: Kate Kaminski
Production Coordinator: Anton Reut
Proofreaders: Duncan Watson, Katherine Cooley
Indexer: Ted Laux
Cover Design: Ingalls + Associates

Screen reproductions produced with Collage Plus and Collage Complete.

Collage Plus and Collage Complete are trademarks of Inner Media Inc.

SYBEX is a registered trademark of SYBEX Inc.

No experience required. is a trademark of SYBEX Inc.

ISBN: 0-7821-2249-3

Manufactured in the United States of America

10 9 8 7 6 5 4 3 2 1

To the Sybex editorial team—the best in the business.

Acknowledgments

As with any book, the effort is widely collaborative—so I have plenty of people to thank.

First, thanks to Gary Masters without whom this book wouldn't have been possible—or necessary.

I also appreciate the labors of Acquisitions & Developmental Editor Sherry Bonelli and Editor Kim Wimpsett, who performed admirably under the considerable stress of a very short schedule.

Special gratitude to the entire production team: Electronic Publishing Specialist Kate Kaminski worked with her usual professional grace, Production Coordinator Anton Reut conscientiously monitored the book's progress, and Proofreaders Duncan Watson and Katherine Cooley meticulously checked page after page of galleys.

Thanks to Barbara Gordon and Chris Meredith for putting together the editorial team that continues to shine, book after book.

A virtual bouquet to David Rogelberg, an agent who far transcends that mundane description. A friend indeed.

And of course, to Charlie who keeps on being the best.

Contents at a Glance

Table of Contents

Introduction

Windows 95 is rapidly becoming the leading operating system on the desktops of home and corporate users in North America (and is making big strides in the rest of the world as well). Many millions of DOS and Windows 3.1 users have already converted to Windows 95, leaving millions more to come. Every month thousands and thousands of people are facing Windows 95 for the first time—and you're no doubt one of them.

Some conversions are involuntary. You've bought a new PC and Windows 95 is the installed operating system. Or perhaps your company is making the move to Windows 95 and its presence on your work machine is a *fait accompli*. On the other hand, many people convert because they're attracted to the new features in Windows 95 or they want to use a particular piece of software that requires Windows 95.

It doesn't matter why you've come to Windows 95. What is apparent at once is that this operating system is *new*, not an update to something you already know. So you are going to need some help—preferably help that is smooth, painless, and easily digestible.

Why This Book?

As you've no doubt noticed, the bookstores have plenty of Windows 95 titles—everything from massive and esoteric tomes on programming to books with names like *I'm a Fool, You're a Fool, Let's Do Windows 95!* The problem with many of these books is that they assume you aspire to become an expert's expert, no matter how painful. Others are written in a style that in the past was reserved for the village idiot. If neither of these approaches appeals to you, keep reading.

This book is different. It's meant for the person who has already used a PC but is a novice in the particular area of Windows 95. You will not be talked down to in this book. The assumption is that you're new to Windows 95—not that you're stupid.

So there's no chapter telling you what a mouse is—but there *are* 25 essential skills designed to get you proficient in Windows 95 in the shortest possible time (including one on the *new* mouse functions available in Windows 95).

How to Use the Book

As you can see from the Table of Contents, this book covers a wide range of Windows 95 topics. Some you will have more interest in than others, so I've divided the book into separate and discrete skills. The first few skills will introduce you to the interface and the basic concepts built into Windows 95. After that, each skill can be read independently without a lot of cross-referencing.

Use the book as a Windows 95 directory, if you wish. Get what you need and put the book aside. When the day comes that you need to learn about remote access or faxing or building your own network, just turn to the relevant skill and get going right away.

Elements in This Book

At the beginning of each skill, you'll see a list of the topics covered. And at the end of a skill, you'll see a list of the intended results. Here and there you'll see certain elements designed to draw your attention:

- ➤ designates choosing a command from a menu. For example, "choose File ➤ Exit" means you should open the File menu and then choose Exit.

- + signs indicate key combinations. For example, "press Ctrl+Alt+Del" means that you should hold down the Ctrl and Alt keys, and press the Del key.

- **Boldface** indicates items that you want to type in exactly as they are printed.

- A monospaced font is used to denote URLs.

- *Italics* are used to introduce new terms or information that may not be exactly the same from computer to computer, such as drive letters. (See the Glossary for definitions of key terms.)

 NOTE   Notes are pulled out of the text to make a specific point. It may be to highlight some point of information that might escape notice in a regular paragraph. Notes can also be specific advice and pointers to other resources.

TIP

Tips are time and labor savers. They're not-so-obvious shortcuts or approaches that have been discovered over time. They're *always* worth reading.

 WARNING

Warnings fall into the category of you-can't-be-too careful. Although Windows 95 is extraordinarily forgiving of errors, it's always better to stay out of trouble. So you'll see a few of these icons, but many fewer than in a comparable Windows 3.1 book.

DISCUSSIONS IN SIDEBAR BOXES

When you see text set off in a box like this, it indicates a "side issue" or technical point to which I want to draw your attention. You'll probably find them of interest even when they don't directly relate to the topic at hand.

In case you care, these boxes are called "sidebars" even though they're never at the side. The term that probably arose in magazine publishing when sidebars were set off to the left or right of a page instead of smack in the middle as these are. (This paragraph is an example of the "side issue" nature of sidebars.)

Moving Onward

I hope you enjoy your introduction to Windows 95 and find this book useful. I'd appreciate feedback on any errors or omissions you discover. Just drop a note to me at:

NoExp@scribes.com

And, of course, if you like the book, it would be an act of mercy to let me know about that, too.

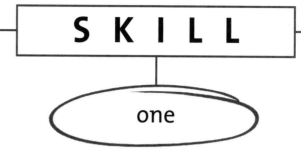

S K I L L

one

Getting Your Bearings

- ❑ Using the Taskbar
- ❑ Learning new mouse skills
- ❑ Navigating menus
- ❑ Identifying Desktop components
- ❑ Recognizing shortcuts

Whether or not you've used a previous version of Windows, the look (or *interface*) of Windows 95 will look pretty unfamiliar. The intent of the design is, of course, to make everything easier—but it may not seem that way at first—especially for those who are accustomed to the various Windows 3.*x* operating systems. In general, it's easier to learn Windows 95 if you're not *unlearning* Windows 3.1 at the same time. So forget what you know about Windows and try to look at Windows 95 afresh.

In this skill, you'll get a quick tour of the opening screen and a couple of key concepts so you can identify the parts of your new virtual Desktop and begin to use them immediately.

Using the Taskbar

The opening screen in Windows 95 is mostly blank with two or more icons in the upper-left corner and a Taskbar at the bottom of the screen. Every open program (or folder) will have a button on the Taskbar. This is extremely handy because it means you don't have to close windows or move them aside to find other ones. Click the button that represents a program, and the corresponding open item will become active. Figure 1.1 shows the Taskbar with Microsoft Word open.

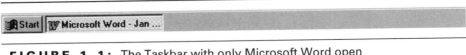

FIGURE 1.1: The Taskbar with only Microsoft Word open

You can change the Taskbar's screen location easily. Just click the Taskbar and drag it to the top of the screen or to either side. To make it wider, position the mouse pointer at the top edge of the Taskbar. When you see a double-headed arrow, click and drag the border to where you want it.

Making the Taskbar Disappear

If you have a smallish monitor, you may want the Taskbar to disappear when you don't need it. To try this look, take these steps:

1. Click the Start button and select Settings ➢ Taskbar; the Taskbar Properties dialog box will appear.

2. On the Taskbar Options tab check Auto Hide.

3. If you want to be able to get at the Taskbar even when you're running a program full-screen, select Always on Top as well.

4. Click OK.

Now when you move the mouse pointer away from the Taskbar, the Taskbar will fade away. When you move the mouse pointer back, the Taskbar will pop up.

Recognizing Other Features on the Taskbar

The right corner of the Taskbar is interesting as well. That's where you'll find active bits of hardware. If you have a sound card and it's working, you'll see a little speaker icon on the Taskbar. Also, when you're printing or faxing, a miniature printer appears in the same area. Position the mouse pointer over the time display and a box showing the day and date will pop open.

 If you have an internal modem, sometimes it's hard to tell if the modem is still connected to the phone line. Just look at the Taskbar and if you see the icon shown here next to the time display, the modem is still operating (it may not be operating correctly, but that's another matter).

 NOTE   The modem icon will only appear when you're using the Microsoft Network, HyperTerminal (the version included with Windows 95), or another 32-bit communications program.

Mastering the Newly Talented Mouse

The key to using Windows 95 efficiently is right on your Desktop—namely, your mouse or trackball pointer. Windows 95 is very mousy compared to any other operating system. In fact, you scarcely have to touch the keyboard at all for most basic operations.

NOTE   You can still use the keyboard if you like. A list of keyboard commands and shortcuts is included in Skill 7.

But your old familiar mouse works quite differently now in two important ways.

Mouse Trick #1   First, the right mouse button is used just about *everywhere*. You can place the pointer almost anywhere, press the right mouse button, and something will happen. Usually, you'll see a pop-up menu like one of these shown here.

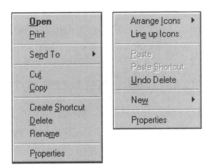

The contents of the menu will vary depending on whether you're pointing at a file, a folder (Windows 95's term for a directory), a Windows 95 element, or an icon representing hardware of some type.

Then there are those occasions when you'll be looking at a dialog box full of settings—most of which you don't understand. Place your pointer on the text and click the right mouse button. If you see a "What's This?" box, like the one shown here, you can click it for a window of explanation.

Mouse Trick #2   Here's another way the mouse behaves differently. To open a menu, you click the menu title only once. Slide the mouse pointer to the item you want to select and (only then) click one more time.

Holding the mouse button down as you move the pointer is limited to those times you're actually dragging and dropping an object. However, there's different behavior depending on whether you're using the left or right mouse button.

Click and Drag Object with	Location	Result
Left mouse button	Within a drive	Object is moved
Left mouse button	Across drives	Object is copied
Right mouse button	Anywhere	Menu allowing choice between moving the object, copying the object, or creating a shortcut

As you can see from the previous list, the right mouse button is by far the easiest to use. The left mouse button requires you to remember where the object is relative to your hard drive(s). If you get in the habit of using the right mouse button, you can be saved from that silliness.

Throughout this book "click" refers to pressing the left mouse button and "right-click" means pressing the right mouse button. (Unless you're using a left-handed mouse in which case everything is reversed!)

You'll be using the mouse a lot in Windows 95 so you might as well start practicing now.

NOTE   In Windows 95, the mouse has even more talents; read about them in Skill 2.

Getting Started with the Start Button

Fortunately, in all the empty expanse of the screen, you have a clear signal of where to begin in the form of the Start button in the lower-left corner.

Click the Start button once to open a menu of choices. Initially only a few basic items will be present, but they're enough to get you going. Starting from the top, the following sections show you what you'll see.

Programs

Slide the mouse pointer to Programs and you'll get a cascading menu that includes all the programs currently installed plus access to a DOS prompt (more about this in Skill 9) and Windows Explorer (talked about here and in Skill 4, among other places).

You can add programs to the Start menu and change what's on the Programs menu quite easily. Look at Skill 8 for the steps to do just that.

Documents

Windows 95 remembers the files you recently worked on and puts them on the Documents menu. This makes it really easy for you to click the document you want to open. To clear the Documents menu, follow these steps:

1. Right-click the Taskbar and select Properties.

2. Select the Start Menu Programs tab in the Taskbar Properties dialog box.

3. In the Documents Menu area, click the Clear button.

To clear the Documents menu *selectively*, follow these steps:

1. Click the Start button once, and then slide the pointer to Programs ➤ Windows Explorer.

2. Find your Windows folder and double-click it.

3. Double-click the Recent folder. Inside the folder are shortcuts to the documents on which you've been working. Delete the ones you don't want to appear in the Documents menu.

Settings

Branching off the Settings item, you'll find the Control Panel, the Printers folder, and another way to get at the Taskbar settings. The Control Panel is similar to the one in Windows 3.1. For information on elements in the Control Panel, look them up individually. Printers and their settings are covered in Skill 13.

Find

This neat little program will let you search for files or even for a particular piece of text. You can search your whole computer or just a particular drive. If you're on a network, you can search for a particular computer by name. Skill 6 has more on using Find to search for almost anything.

Select Find and then Files or Folders to open the window shown in Figure 1.2.

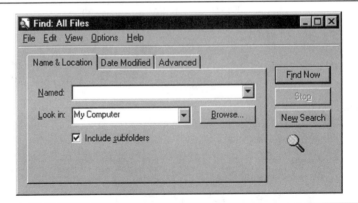

F I G U R E 1 . 2 : The start-up window for the Find program

As you can see from the tabs, you can search by name, location, or by the date modified. The Advanced tab has an option for searching for a particular word or phrase. The menus include options to make your search case sensitive or to save the results of a search.

The really nice thing about Find is that once you locate the file you want, you can just double-click the file to open it or you can drag it to another location. In other words, the file or list of files displayed at the end of a search is "live" and you can act on it accordingly.

TIP   To launch a search of the current file or folder, press the F3 key.

Help

The help files in Windows 95 are much improved over those in the past. They're a lot more searchable, for one thing. When you first select Help you'll a get a window like the one shown in Figure 1.3.

FIGURE 1.3: Looking for help in all the right places

The Contents and Index tabs are pretty straightforward. However, the Find tab contains a nice new feature. With the Find tab you can search all or part of the help files for a particular word or phrase. This can be really nice when you know the term you want but haven't a clue as to what the authors of the documentation might have filed it under. The first time you use this tool, Windows 95 builds a database of help files for future searching. You choose from one of three options:

Minimize Database Size   With this option you don't get every single help file but all the ones likely to have useful information.

Maximize Search Capabilities   This means every help file is included. It's the most thorough approach but may make searches a little slower depending on the speed of your processor and hard drive.

Customize Search Capabilities   Select this option and you can decide which help files go into the database.

After the database is built you can use the Find tab to make very sophisticated searches.

Run

Those who love the command line will find succor here. Select Run and you can type in the name of any program you want to launch. You'll have to include the path, but if you like this kind of hands-on operation, you won't mind at all.

 NOTE   You can also use the Browse button to look around for the program you want. And if you click the downward arrow, you get a drop-down list of all the recent programs you've run from this box.

Using My Computer

The My Computer icon is on every Windows 95 Desktop. Double-click it to see icons for all your drives, plus a folder for the Control Panel and a Printers folder. This isn't the only way to get at your drives, but the My Computer icon does have a number of features you can't get any other way:

- Right-click the My Computer icon, and select Properties for a look at your hardware. (Look to Skill 13 for more on accessing this to get reluctant hardware to work properly.)

- Double-click the My Computer icon, and select Options from the View menu. On the Folder tab you can select whether you want single window or separate window browsing. Single window means as you go from folder to subfolder to subsubfolder, with only one window is open at a time. Separate window means the parent folders also stay open.

TIP   If the name "My Computer" is just too, too cute for your tastes, right-click the icon and select Rename from the menu. Type in a new name that's less annoying.

Introducing the Recycle Bin

The Recycle Bin, as you might imagine, is where old deleted files go to die. Despite the name, the deleted files aren't actually recycled unless you rescue them from the bin before they're deleted permanently.

Nevertheless, the Recycle Bin gives you a nice margin of safety that wasn't available in Windows 3.1 (unless you had another program that provided it). Now when you delete a file you have days or even weeks (depending on how you set things up) to change your mind and retrieve it.

Skill 3 describes how to configure and use the Recycle Bin. In the meantime, here are two important facts about the Recycle Bin:

- The Recycle Bin icon cannot be renamed or deleted.

- Files that are deleted using programs other than Windows 95 are not sent to the Recycle Bin. They're just deleted. Be careful.

NOTE   Other icons that may be on your Desktop, depending on the installation, may include the Inbox and Microsoft Network. These are covered in Skill 15.

Discovering Property Sheets

In Windows 3.1 it was a real pain sometimes to find out how to change the settings for something. Depending on whether it was a file, a program, or a piece of hardware, you had to memorize where to find the critical settings. In Windows 95 this has all changed, so now there's only one rule to remember: Right-click the object and select Properties.

When you select Properties, you open what's called a property sheet. Property sheets vary, of course. Some types of files will have multiple pages in the property sheet; others will have only one page and very few options. Figure 1.4 shows a property sheet for a simple text file.

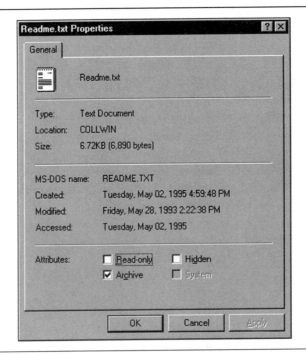

FIGURE 1.4: A property sheet for a text file

Property sheets are valuable repositories for information about files, programs, and devices. So when you find yourself with a program or a piece of hardware that isn't working the way you want to, refer to the rule above. In fact, you might apply that rule to just about every aspect of Windows 95. When you want to know more about *anything* in Windows 95, right-click the item you're interested in and see what appears.

How to use various property sheets is discussed in later skills. For example, the property sheets for DOS programs are covered in Skill 9, the property sheets for printers are covered in Skill 13, and so forth.

Introducing Shortcuts

If you're to use your Desktop as a workplace, you want to be able to organize everything you need in one place and be able to access it instantly. And even when documents aren't involved—as in, say, using a calculator or phone dialer— you'd like immediate access to necessary programs without searching for them.

Shortcuts are one of the leading benefits of Windows 95, and yet they're not an *obvious* feature like multitasking or long file names. Shortcuts are mentioned here so you can learn a little about what they are and the part they play in Windows 95.

A shortcut is a little file that acts as a pointer to a file, folder, or program. For example, a shortcut lets you have as many "copies" of your printer as you want— in as many locations as you want. Of course, a shortcut to a printer isn't really a copy of the printer, just a pointer to that printer. With shortcuts you can have your word processor in as many locations as necessary and only use a little hard disk space for each instance. Another advantage of shortcuts is that when you're done with one, you can delete it with impunity. Deleting the shortcut has no effect on the original object.

Shortcuts are identifiable by the little arrow in the lower-left corner of the icon as shown here. When you create shortcuts they'll also have a label: "Shortcut to..." followed by the name of the object. You can rename shortcuts to make the label more manageable. The Create Shortcut option is available:

- On objects' pop-up menus

- From various drop-down menus

- On the Desktop (see Figure 1.5)

For more on shortcuts and their many talents, see Skill 7 where you'll find information on how to make the most of these useful tools.

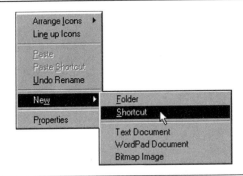

FIGURE 1.5: You can find the Create Shortcut command on many menus.

Are You Experienced?

Now you can...

☑ move and adjust the Taskbar

☑ use the mouse to its best advantage

☑ navigate through menus

☑ identify Desktop components

☑ recognize a shortcut

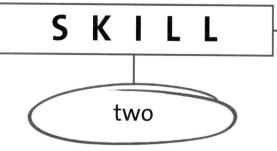

SKILL

two

Using Your Mouse

- ❑ Double-clicking and single-clicking

- ❑ Using the right mouse button

- ❑ Configuring your mouse

- ❑ Changing mouse pointers

The Windows user interface has always depended on a mouse or other pointing device, and with Windows 95 that reliance is even more pronounced. You can still administer most commands from the keyboard (Skill 7 includes a whole list of key combinations), but everything is much easier when you're using a mouse. Fewer steps are required and there's no memorization, as there is when you use the keyboard.

NOTE   In this skill the term "mouse" is used, but all devices that perform point-and-click actions (such as trackballs and pens) are included.

Everywhere you go in Windows 95, you can click with the mouse to produce an action—whether it's opening a file or just getting helpful information. In this skill you'll discover how the mouse works and how you can customize most functions for your own use.

Learning When to Double-Click or Single-Click

It's not always easy in Windows 95 to know whether to double-click or single-click the mouse button. The double-click (two rapid clicks in succession) with the left mouse button serves to open icons on the Desktop. If the icon represents a program, the program is started. If the icon represents a folder, the folder expands into a window on the Desktop so you can see and get at what's inside.

A single-click with the left mouse button serves to highlight the item you clicked. So if you're choosing a file in Windows Explorer or other folder with the idea of moving it or acting on it in some other way—other than opening it—a single-click will do the job.

Windows 95 attempts to reduce the number of clicks needed by making use of the right mouse button. Use the right mouse button to click a file or folder, and you'll have an array of choices on the menu that pops up. The top choice on this menu is usually Open, so you can open a program, file, or folder with the right mouse button as easily as double-clicking with the left. Other functions are just as direct.

Using the Right Mouse Button

You can right-click everything on the Desktop as well as the Desktop itself. As mentioned in Skill 1, you can right-click almost anywhere to provide some helpful result. All the programs that come with Windows 95, as well as programs written specifically for Windows 95, will use the right mouse button extensively. Bear in mind that programs written for Windows 3.1 will not use the right mouse button in the same way, though quite a few have some right mouse button functionality built in.

Right-Clicking a File

Right-click a file and you're presented with a menu of multiple options, including opening the file with its associated program.

If there's a Quick Viewer associated with the file, you can get a look at the contents by choosing Quick View from the menu.

If the file is of a registered file type, you can get still another option. Hold down the Shift key while right-clicking and you get Open With—an option that lets you open the file with a different application.

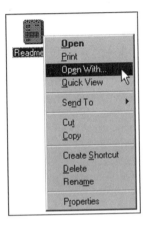

A number of programs will add other entries to the right mouse button menu. For example, the archiving program WinZip puts the item Add to Zip on the menu so you can select files to be added to an archive.

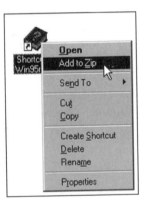

Right-Clicking a Folder

The menu that opens when you right-click a folder is similar to the one for a file. If you chose Open, you'll see the contents of the folder. The Explore option does much the same thing, except the folder will be shown in Explorer view—two panes, with the left one showing the folder and its placement on the hard drive and the right pane detailing the folder's contents.

You can also select Find to search the folder for a particular file either by name or by contents. (For more information on using Find, see Skill 6.)

Right-Clicking the Start Button

Place your pointer on the Start button and right-click to bring up three choices:

- Open will open the Start Menu folder. This folder contains the programs you've dropped on the Start Menu and the Programs folder, which contains all the shortcuts that make up the Programs menu that cascades off the Start Menu.

- Explore will open the Start Menu folder in Windows Explorer view.

- Find is a shortcut to finding a file in the Start Menu folder.

The first two choices on the menu are quick ways to get at the items on the Programs menu so you can move a program up a level or two or remove one from the menu entirely. If you choose Explore, the window that opens will have two panes, the left one showing the folder and its place in the file system, the right pane showing the files inside whatever folder is chosen on the left. If you choose Open, the view is of a single window. When you double-click a folder, another window opens showing the contents.

Right-Clicking the Taskbar

When you right-click a blank spot on the Taskbar, a menu pops up with options to:

- Cascade the windows that are currently open on the Desktop.
- Tile the open windows horizontally.
- Tile the open windows vertically.
- Minimize all the open windows to the Taskbar.
- Access the Taskbar properties.

Right-Clicking Taskbar Icons

Open programs and folders will each have an icon on the Taskbar. Right-click the icon and, if the item isn't open on the Desktop, you'll get the option to Restore (in other words, open a window on the Desktop), Maximize (restore it full screen), or Close.

For items that have a window open on the Desktop, left-clicking the icon will bring that window to the front. A right-click will bring the window to the front, plus open the same menu.

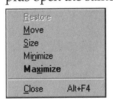

Move and Size are keyboard options. Select one of them and you can move the window or change its size using the arrow keys.

Right-click other icons in the far right corner of the Task-bar, and you'll get a chance to adjust the date and time or adjust the volume on your sound card. Other icons may appear in this section of the Taskbar depending on the hardware and software you have installed. As in other places, try right-clicking and see what you get!

Right-Clicking My Computer

Right-click the My Computer icon on the Desktop, and you have the option of opening My Computer in a regular window or in Windows Explorer view. You can also connect or disconnect network drives, find files or computers, or open the properties sheets for your system.

Adjusting Mouse Settings

Because the mouse (or other pointing device) is used so often in Windows 95, it's important to have it set up comfortably. To change how your mouse operates, you can manipulate the mouse settings in the Control Panel.

Switching to a Left-Handed Mouse

To change your right-handed mouse to a left-handed one, double-click the Mouse icon in the Control Panel. On the Buttons page, click the left-handed button to swap left and right mouse buttons. On a three-button mouse, these are the two outside buttons.

Setting That Middle Mouse Button

If you have a Logitech pointing device, it probably has three buttons. The software that came with the device includes the Mouse Control Center. If you run this program after Windows 95 is installed, you can set the middle mouse button to Double Click (see Figure 2.1).

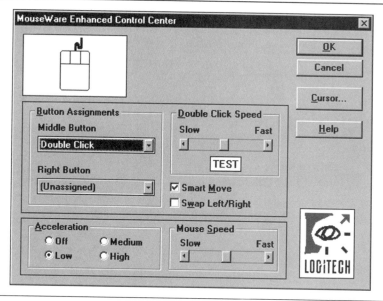

FIGURE 2.1: Set the middle mouse button of a Logitech mouse or trackball to Double Click.

After you click OK, the program is minimized to your Taskbar.
Right-click the minimized icon and select Hide Icon to make it invisible.

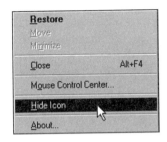

Changing the Double-Click Speed

You can adjust the amount of time allowed between two mouse-clicks for them to
be counted as a double-click. Open the Mouse icon in the Control Panel. On the
Buttons page, move the slider under Double-Click Speed toward Slow or Fast.
Double-click in the Test area to try out a different setting.

TIP If you have a three-button mouse with the middle button set to Double Click,
move the Double Click Speed all the way to Fast. It will make all the menus in
Windows 95 open much faster, even though it won't change the double-click
speed for your mouse's middle button.

Adjusting the Pointer Speed

As you move the pointer around the Desktop, perhaps you find you have to
move the device too much to get a small result on the screen. Or, vice versa,
you move the mouse just a little and the pointer moves too far. To adjust this,
double-click the Mouse icon in the Control Panel. Then follow these steps:

1. Select the Motion tab.

2. Move the slider under Pointer Speed one notch to the left or the right.

3. Click the Apply button, and try the new setting.

4. Repeat until you have a speed you like, and click OK.

Making the Pointer More Visible

If you're working with a smaller screen—particularly the kind on a laptop, you may find the pointer "disappearing" sometimes. To make the pointer more visible, open the Mouse icon in the Control Panel and select the Motion tab.

Click the box next to Show Pointer Trails. Use the slider to adjust for long or short trails. You can see the results as you move the slider, without having to use the Apply button.

Picking Mouse Pointers

Windows 95 comes with an assortment of new mouse pointers, so you can choose ones you like. You'll probably find them a big improvement on the default pointers. A few of the pointers included with Windows 95 are animated, and many more animated cursors come with the Plus! package.

Animated cursors are on their way to becoming the kind of cottage industry that icons were with earlier versions of Windows. Animated cursors can be downloaded from many online services and are also distributed as shareware.

 NOTE   Your display must be set to at least 256 colors for the animated cursors to work. To check your settings, open the Display icon in the Control Panel and click the Settings button. The color palette must be set for 256 colors, High Color, or True Color.

Figure 2.2 shows the Pointers page under Mouse Properties. These default pointers are described in Table 2.1. Once you understand what each pointer represents, you're better able to select appropriate substitutes. For example, you wouldn't want an animated pointer for Text Select because the animation would make it very difficult to make a precise selection.

TABLE 2.1: Mouse Pointers in Windows 95

Pointer	What It Does
Normal Select	The regular pointer for selecting items
Help Select	Click the ? button and move the pointer to the area you want information about and click again
Working in Background	Something is going on in the background, but you can often move to another area and do something else

TABLE 2.1 (CONTINUED): Mouse Pointers in Windows 95

Pointer	What It Does
Busy	Just hang in there. Windows 95 or an application is doing something and can't be disturbed
Precision Select	Cross-hairs for very careful selection
Text Select	The I-beam that's seen in word processors and used to select text
Handwriting	When you're using a handwriting input device
Unavailable	Sorry, you can't drag a file to this location, either because the area is unacceptable or the application won't accept drag and drop
Resizing	Cursors that appear when you're moving a window border
Move	Select Move from the system menu or a right-click menu and you'll get this cursor, allowing you to move the window using the arrow keys
Alternate Select	Used in the FreeCell card game. Probably other uses to come

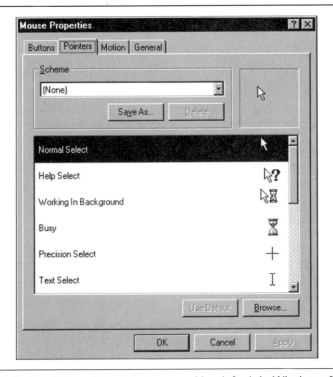

FIGURE 2.2: The pointers that are used by default in Windows 95

Changing Pointers

You can change one or more pointers and even have more than one set of pointers that you can switch among. To change one or more pointers on your system, follow these steps:

1. Double-click the Mouse icon in the Control Panel, and select the Pointers tab.

2. In the middle of the screen you'll see a display of the pointers with their functions. Highlight a pointer you want to change, and click the Browse button.

3. The window shown in Figure 2.3 will open. When you click a selection (files with the .ANI extension are animated), it will be displayed in the Preview box.

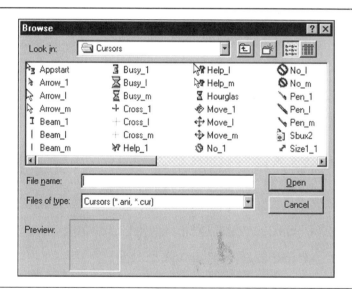

FIGURE 2.3: The Cursors folder contains the cursor images that come with Windows 95.

4. Click the Open button when you've selected the one you want.

If you accumulate a large number of animated cursors, you may want to gather them together in a subfolder inside the Cursors folder.

TIP   The animated cursors that come with Plus! are located in the Program Files\Plus!\Themes folder. Copy them over rather than moving them. If you move them, your Plus! themes may not work properly.

To save a selection of pointers as a set, click the Save As button and enter a name for the scheme. After you save it, the set will be listed in the Scheme drop-down list and you can select it any time.

Using the DOS Mouse

DOS programs that use mouse movements and button presses should work fine in Windows 95. Windows 95 passes the mouse information along without the need to install special DOS mouse drivers.

However, if you have occasion to run a program in the special MS-DOS mode (described in Skill 9), you'll have to load a mouse driver for that program. The mouse driver is a program that came with the mouse when you bought it. Or if you upgraded by installing Windows 95 over Windows 3.1, it's probably still on your machine. Consult the mouse documentation to find the name of the driver file.

Are You Experienced?

Now you can...

- ☑ **choose when to single-click or double-click**
- ☑ **use your right mouse button**
- ☑ **configure your mouse**
- ☑ **change mouse pointers**

based telefundraising. Minimum of 7 years experience in similar field. 4 year degree preferred. Proficient computer skills incl. Windows-based software applications required. Salary commensurate w/skills & exp. plus benefits. Send letter and resume to Well-Being Clinic, 543 Spring Ave., Daytonville, VA.

Executive Secretary
OfficePlus, an office supply & furniture company is looking for administrative support to VP. Requires 5 years min. of secretarial experience, proficiency with MS Word and Excel and excellent communication skills. Must be willing to learn database & desktop software. Fax: OfficePlus, Personnel 665-555-9122.

FACILITIES PLANNER Training Centers Inc. seeks individual to study & develop infrastructure requirements and capital improvement projects. Req's BA in Planning, Engineering, Architecture or rel. field w/7 years exp & knowl of Windows (Word, Excel) & graphics programs. 4 yrs' exp w PC's planning arch/eng or facilities mgmt & exp w/CAD, database mgmt & project scheduling pref'd. Fax: HR. 885-555-2398.

MANAGEMENT REPORTING ANALYST

Join the team that maintains the purchasing and logistics information systems that support order entry, provide product and contract information, track product utilization, and manage operating budget and inventory systems. Must be proficient in a high-level database system and Excel, Lotus 1-2-3, or similar applications. Fax resume to Data Systems Placement Services 444-555-9998.

MANAGER, ASSET MODELING

This worldwide logistics company is expanding it's transportation network. The successful candidate will have a Bachelor's degree in Economics, Finance or Business Mgmt, with a MBA degree preferred; a solid foundation in Mathematics, and excellent analytical skills. Knowledge of PC applications in Excel, Word, PowerPoint & Visio essential. Competitive benefits and compensation plan. Fax: 966-555-2298/

Manager, Business Analysis You will direct a team of Business Analysts and oversee timely completion of all projects in accordance with departmental policies & procedures. Requires BA/BS Behavioral Health Sciences, Business Administration, MIS, or equivalent experience, system development/analysis and software testing; strong project management and team building skills, and software development experience. Hart Corporate Services. Call J. Thornton 243-555-9583.

Market Research Project Manager SuperHouse Designs is creating a new research division. You will provide research consulting services to internal clients and manage external research providers. A BA/BS degree or equivalent with 4-6 years' experi-

---

send cover letter, resume & salary req's to: Sommes Communications, Attn: HR/Job 85, 776 Bowser Lane, Bowtown, MA.

MARKETING ASSISTANT
Supporting 2 Marketing Mgrs. you'll handle a variety of admin. responsibilities, direct mail coordination, desktop publishing, and ad space coordination. Require 1-2 years admin. exper. and strong computer skills, esp. desktop pub., HTML, Office & Windows. Fax. R. Smith 365-555-8844.

OFFICE MANAGER

Join a growing firm that offers competitive salaries & benefits for a take-charge type. Responsible for all office purchases & operations, including a quarterly newsletter. Windows & MS Office experience req'd. Call 973-555-4545.

PC Support Specialist High-end catalog company and specialty retailer has opening in MIS Dept. Support corporate associates with PC and network systems. Extensive PC hardware installation and configuration experience is required. Must be able to communicate effectively and determine cause of problems, & develop solutions. Requires network admin. & multiple PC operating systems experience. (Windows, UNIX) Fax resume & salary reqs to: High Profile Images 388-555-9634.

PROJECT ASST. Serve as a point person in HR office of fast growing biotech firm. Requires creative thinking and up-to-date office computer skills, esp. Word, PowerPoint & Excel. Fax resume to TruPoint Systems 689-555-1298.

PROJECT MANAGER

Public agency seeking environmental project manager to oversee 18-month marsh preservation project. Develop, analyze, organize & summarize planning data and financial info. Windows computer skills essential. Send resume to Public Planning Services, Attn: HR., 34 Marsh Lane, Willowdale, CA.

Sales/Computer Expanding computer software & hardware store is looking for more qualified sales associates to staff our busy downtown location. Windows software experience required. Send resume and salary/commission requirements to General Manager, Computers for You, 433 Main St., Ontario, MN.

Sales Support Associate Work with customer service, account managers, marketing & brand management. You will handle distribution of sales materials and internal correspondence. You will need 1-2 years in sales admin. and basic office functions (mail, fax, phones etc.), plus PC skills. Computer troubleshooting skills a plus.

Sales: Sr. Account Coordinator Looking Good, a national clothing chain is looking for seasoned sales pros to oversee sales operations. Qualified candidates must have 4-5 years sales mgmt exp. and strong

---

pros to oversee sales operations. Qualified candidates must have 4-5 years sales mgmt exp. and strong PC skills. A college degree, working knowledge of Excel, PowerPoint, Word and database software req'd. Fax resume and cover letter to: Looking Good, Attn: K. Ferkovich, 877 Goody Ave., Reno, NV.

SALES/COMPUTER

Expanding computer software & hardware store is looking for more qualified sales associates to staff our busy downtown location. Windows software experience required. Send resume and salary/commission requirements to General Manager, Computers For You, 433 Main St., Ontario, MN.

SALES SUPPORT ASSOCIATE

Work with customer service, account managers, marketing & brand management. You will handle distribution of sales materials and internal correspondence. You will need 1-2 years in sales admin. and basic office functions (mail, fax, ph)

Senior Calendar Clerk Large international law firm is seeking qualified candidates with strong organizational and data entry skills, and extremely high level of service orientation and excellent oral and written communication skills. Applicants must possess a BA/BS degree, have knowledge of computer databases and Word or WordPerfect. Send resume and salary requirements to HR, Jackson Madison Madison Teller & Pewter, 1001 Main Street, Atlanta, GA

Sr. Financial Analyst JJO Enterprises seeking senior member of financial team. Requires a degree in Finance/Econ/Acctg; minimum 3 yrs' public acct. exp. (CPA), Lotus/Excel, MS Word/WordPerfect proficiency. P&L/cashflow statement exp is preferred. Competitive salary/benefits pkg. Fax: Mr. Rogers, JJO Enterprises 442-555-1267.

SENIOR LAW CLERK

Large international law firm is seeking qualified candidates with strong organizational and data entry skills, and extremely high level of service orientation and excellent oral and written communication skills. Applicants must possess a BA/BS degree, have knowledge of computer databases and Word or WordPerfect. Send resume and salary requirements to HR, Madison Madison Teller & Pewter, 1001 Main Street, Atlanta, GA

Senior Secretary Bolan Lumber Co. looking for add'l office support staff. Type 60 wpm. Word/Excel/ Windows and some desktop publishing experience. Call Ron 336-555-9944.

TECHNICAL COMMUNICATOR Biotech Systems is expanding and is seeking someone to develop & maintain user documentation/training materials and on-line help systems. Requires a BA/BS in Technical Communication or equiva-

---

Group. Req. a BA/BS with 4 years' experience in financial analysis or system implementation or development. Attention to detail & time and resource mgmt. abilities are vital. Excel and PowerPoint req'd. Contact Financial Resources Executive Search at 443-555-2398.

Clerical Receptionist F/T position available in a fast paced HR dept. You must be a self-starter, organized, and dependable. Excellent customer-service, written and verbal communication skills required. Computer experience a must! Norwell Medical Center, 100 Front St. Allentown, MD

Computer Operator/PC Technician Large software retailer looking for someone to assist in tech dept. as well as to give seminars for customers looking to upgrade. Successful candidate must have 3-5 years' technical experience and 2-3 years in customer service. Teaching experience a plus. Fax resume to Best Systems: 545-555-6677.

COMPUTERS

Immediate openings! Computer technicians with PC hardware and Windows experience. Send resume to: Delta Plus, 1200 Sutter St. San Francisco, CA.

Corporate Human Resources Mgr

Specialized background in Employment or Compensation & Benefits, and general knowledge of all other HR functions. PC skills essential. Fax resume to 334-555-9112.

Editorial Researcher Business publication seeking researcher responsible for weekly business lists, etc. Computer/Internet skills required. Must be fast, accurate & thorough. Salary DOE. Write: Researcher, 9106 Shasta Blvd., Pittsburgh, PA.

Editor/Reporter

National financial journal seeks experienced writer to cover the brokerage/financial services industry. Must have strong writing/editing skills and background in business reporting. Computer/word processor experience a must!. Fax resume and clips to JIT 887-555-2256.

Engineering Senior Industrial Engineer needed for large wholesale buyers club, to help reduce operating costs and increase revenues. A BS degree and at least 6 years in the distribution/transportation field are required. Strong business writing skills, PC proficiency using Microsoft Office and electronic communications is essential. Send cover letter and resume to HR/Job 445, AB Industries, 4498 Howard Blvd, Kansas City, MO

Executive Assistant You'll need strong organizational, interpersonal, and analytical skills, coupled with good computer knowledge in applications such as Access, PowerPoint, Excel and Word. Send resume & salary history

---

based telefundraising. Minimum of 7 years experience in similar field. 4 year degree preferred. Proficient computer skills incl. Windows-based software applications required. Salary commensurate w/skills & exp. plus benefits. Send letter and resume to Well-Being Clinic, 543 Spring Ave., Daytonville, VA.

FACILITIES PLANNER
Training Centers Inc. seeks individual to study & develop infrastructure requirements and capital improvement projects. Req's BA in Planning, Engineering, Architecture or rel. field w/7 years exp & knowl of Windows (Word, Excel) & graphics programs. 4 yrs exp w PC's planning arch/eng or facilities mgmt & exp w/C database mgmt & project scheduling pref'd. Fax: HR. 885-555-2398.

Management Reporting Analyst Join the team that maintains purchasing and logistics information systems that support order entry, provide product and contract information, track product utilization, manage operating budget and inventory systems. Must be proficient in a high-level database system and Excel, Lotus 1-2-3, or similar applications. Fax resume to Data Systems Placement Services 444-555-9998.

MANAGER, ASSET MODELING
This worldwide logistics company is expanding it's transportation network. The successful candidate will have a Bachelor's degree in Economics, Finance or Business Mgmt, with a MBA degree preferred; a solid foundation in Mathematics, and excellent analytical skills. Knowledge of PC applications in Excel, Word, PowerPoint & Visio essential. Competitive benefits and compensation plan. Fax: 555-2298/

Manager, Business Analysis You will direct a team of Business Analysts and oversee timely completion of all projects in accordance with departmental policies & procedures. Requires BA/BS Behavioral Health Sciences, Business Administration, MIS, or equivalent experience, system development, analysis and software testing; strong project management and team building skills, and software development experience. Hart Corporate Services. Call J. Thornton 243-555-9583.

MARKETING ASSISTANT
Supporting 2 Marketing Mgrs. you handle a variety of admin. responsibilities, direct mail coordination, desktop publishing, and ad space coordination. Require 1-2 years admin. exper. and strong computer skills, esp. desktop pub., HTML, Office & Windows. Fax. R. Smith 365-555-8844.

MARKET RESEARCH PROJECT MANAGER
SuperHouse Designs is creating a new research division. You will provide research consulting services to internal clients and manage external research providers. A BA/BS degree or equivalent with 4-6 years' experience with full service

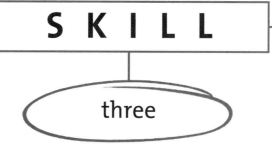

SKILL

three

3

Customizing the Desktop

❑ Choosing wallpaper and a background pattern

❑ Using a screen saver

❑ Changing display resolution

❑ Setting up the Recycle Bin

❑ Recovering deleted files

The default Windows 95 screen is not one likely to induce little cries of joy unless you're a hard-core minimalist—in which case you won't want to change a thing. Fortunately, in Windows 95 you can have your Desktop as plain or fancy as you want.

Remember that you can use the entire area of your monitor's screen in Windows 95. You can have many folders, a few, or none. You can have all your programs on menus that fold out of the Start button's menus, or you can have program icons on the Desktop where you can open them with a double-click. (For everything on files and folders, see Skill 5, "Managing Files and Folders.")

Accessing the Desktop's Properties

To add even more flexibility, you can have colors, fonts, and Desktop wallpaper of many types. Here's how to get at all the settings that affect the Desktop.

Move the pointer to a blank spot (of which there's a muchness) and click the right mouse button. Select Properties from the pop-up menu and you're there (see Figure 3.1).

Each tab covers one aspect of the display, and in the next sections, we'll cover each page.

Background

Here you set the wallpaper and background pattern much like the Desktop settings in Windows 3.1. Use the Browse button to locate files you can use as wallpaper.

Any files that are bitmaps (.BMP) or device-independent bitmaps (.DIB) can be used as wallpaper.

TIP   The Apply button lets you see how a setting will work without having to close the Display Properties dialog box.

Screen Saver

If you installed screen savers—either the ones that come with Windows 95 or some other package—you can adjust the settings on this page. All the installed screen savers are in the Screen Saver drop-down list.

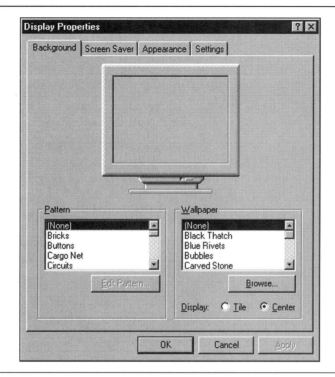

FIGURE 3.1: The property sheets for display

Click the Preview button to get a full-screen view of the selected screen saver. Move your mouse or press any key on the keyboard to return to the display properties.

Appearance

This page is also similar to Desktop settings in Windows 3.1. Use one of the many color combinations listed under Schemes or make your own.

Click any of the elements in the window at the top of the Appearance page and a description appears in the Item box. Change the size or color, or both. If there's a font that can be changed, the current one will show in the Font box.

Settings

Of all the pages in the Display properties, this page has the most going on (see Figure 3.2). Here's where you can change how your screen actually looks (as well as what Windows 95 knows about your display hardware).

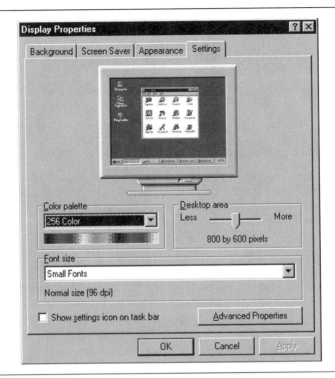

FIGURE 3.2: The page for changing display settings

Changing Resolutions

Displays are described in terms of their resolution—the number of dots on the screen and the number of colors that can be displayed at the same time. The resolutions you can choose using the slider under Desktop Area are determined by the hardware you have. You can't make your monitor and video card do any more than their built-in capacity.

Here are the most likely possibilities:

- **640x480** A standard VGA display that's 640 pixels wide by 480 pixels high.

- **800x600** A typical SVGA display (super VGA).

- **1024x768** This is the upper limit of SVGA and the beginning of more advanced systems such as 8514/A and XGA. This is a very fine (that is, non-grainy) resolution but if your monitor is 15 inches or smaller, you'd better have very good eyes.

- **1280x1024**   A very fine resolution, but one that requires a large monitor. Even with a 17-inch screen, you'll need good eyes.

You'll notice as you move the slider toward higher resolutions that the number of colors displayed in the Color Palette box changes. As resolution numbers go up, color numbers go down because they're both competing for the same video memory. That's why, if you want the most realistic color represented on your screen, you'll need a video card (also called a *display adapter*) with 2, 4, or more megabytes of its own memory.

TIP   If you change resolutions or video settings frequently, check the box next to Show Settings Icon on Task Bar. You'll be able to click this icon and change resolutions on the fly, or go to the video settings directly.

Resolution choices are based on what you like to look at—constrained by the capabilities of your monitor and video card. At the lowest resolution, you may not be able to see all the elements of some programs, so try the next higher resolution. At the highest resolutions, screen elements are very small, so you may want to try Large Fonts from the Font Size box. That will make the captions on the Desktop easier to see.

Most of the time you'll have to reboot to see the effect of these changes.

WARNING   If you change your screen resolution, you may end up with some very peculiar arrangement of your icons. They may be way too far apart or so close together that they're difficult to use. The Appearance page has controls for the spacing of icons. Pull down the Item drop-down list and select one of the Icon Spacing choices. You can also select Icon and change both the size of your icons and their font. However, I strongly recommend that you make note of the original settings because it's fairly easy to make a hash of your Desktop and not remember where you started.

Changing the Display Type   Also on the Settings tab is a button labeled Advanced Properties. Click the Advanced Properties button and you'll see a window like the one shown in Figure 3.3. The first two tabs, Adapter and Monitor, show the hardware you currently have installed. To change information about the adapter or monitor or to install new video hardware, click the Change button and follow the instructions.

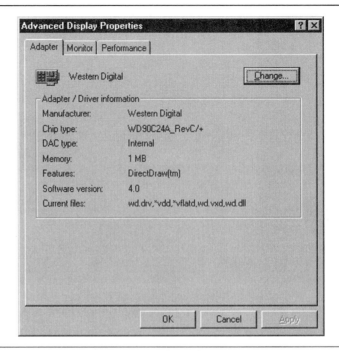

FIGURE 3.3: Information about your video system

Improving Video Performance   The third tab on the Advanced Display properties sheet is labeled Performance (see Figure 3.4). If you're having video-related problems, you may be able to fix them here.

And what are the symptoms of video problems? Here are a few of the symptoms that may be helped by using the settings on this page:

- Changed screens are very slow to redraw.

- Programs frequently stop responding.

- Mouse pointer "disappears" or reacts slowly as you drag it across the screen. (First check the mouse settings described in Skill 2.)

- Unexpected program errors and faults.

Set the Hardware Acceleration slide at the highest setting that can be managed without problems. If you have to set the slider all the way down to None, you'd be advised to switch to a newer, more compatible video card.

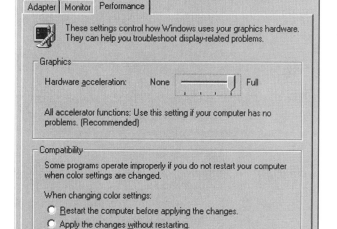

FIGURE 3.4: Troubleshooting video problems

 TIP   If you have the Plus! for Windows 95 package, there will also be a property sheet tab for Plus! that lists various visual enhancements that Plus! provides. Choices that are gray are not available because your hardware can't deliver them. To configure Desktop themes using Plus! use the Themes icon in the Control Panel.

Using the Recycle Bin

In the bad old days of computing, it was far too easy to accidentally delete a file from your system—and all you could do was wave bye-bye because there was no going back. You could buy a package of tools like the Norton Utilities that included a utility to retrieve deleted files—providing you acted quickly enough. And DOS itself, starting with version 5, included a program to undelete files. The weakness of both approaches was if you didn't undelete right away, your file could easily be overwritten by another file and then there was *no way* to recover.

The Recycle Bin will retain all your deleted files for as long as you want, and you can adjust the amount of security from "just a little" to "all I can get" to match your own personal comfort level.

What It Is

The Recycle Bin is a reserved space on your hard drive. When you delete a file or drag it to the Recycle Bin icon, the file is actually moved to that reserved space. If you have more than one hard drive, each drive has its own reserved space.

There's an icon that represents the Recycle Bin on each drive—though the contents displayed when you double-click any icon will be the same as the Recycle Bin on any other drive. If you want a deleted file back you can double-click the Recycle Bin icon to open it and retrieve any file.

The Recycle Bin functions as a first-in, first-out system. That is, when the bin is full, the oldest files are the first ones deleted to make room for the newest ones.

As configurable as the rest of Windows 95 is, this is one place where Microsoft draws the line. The Recycle Bin cannot be:

- Deleted

- Renamed

- Removed from the Desktop

though there are a number of settings you can change to make the Recycle Bin suitable for your use.

 NOTE   See "Changing Recycle Bin Settings" later in this skill for information on how to determine the amount of disk space used by Recycle Bin as well as other settings.

Sending Files to the Recycle Bin

By default, Windows 95 is set up to deposit all deleted files in the Recycle Bin. When you right-click a file and select Delete, or highlight a file and press the Del key, you'll be asked to confirm if you want to send the file to the Recycle Bin.

After you click Yes, that's where the file is moved. Deleted shortcuts are also sent to the Recycle Bin.

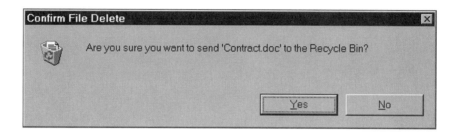

 TIP   If you delete an empty folder, it isn't sent to the Recycle Bin, but you can recover it by immediately selecting Undo Delete from the Recycle Bin's Edit menu. If the folder came from the Desktop, just right-click a blank spot on the Desktop and select Undo Delete from the pop-up menu.

Sending a Floppy Disk's Files to the Recycle Bin

Normally, files you delete from a floppy drive are *not* sent to the Recycle Bin. They're just deleted. However, if that strikes you as just a little too impetuous, you can easily make sure that the files on your floppy do go to the Recycle Bin:

1. Open Windows Explorer. Use the scroll bar for the left pane to move up so you can see the entry for your floppy drive.

2. Click with the left mouse button on the floppy drive icon. In the right pane, select the file(s) you want to delete but still want in the Recycle Bin.

3. Right-click the file(s) and select Cut. Right-click the Desktop and select Paste.

4. Highlight the file on the Desktop. (If there's more than one, hold down the Shift key while you click each one in turn.) Right-click a highlighted file and select Delete. You'll be prompted to confirm that you want to send the file(s) to the Recycle Bin.

There's not a more direct way to do this function because the Recycle Bin stubbornly refuses to see any files that are sent directly from a floppy.

TIP   You can also use this method when you're deleting files from any external drive (such as a Zip drive) and you want the security of having the files safely stashed in the Recycle Bin for a while.

Bypassing the Recycle Bin

If you've got a file that you know for sure you want to delete and you don't want it taking up space in the Recycle Bin, just hold down the Shift key when you select Delete. But be sure that's what you want to do because Windows 95 can't recover a deleted file that's bypassed the Recycle Bin.

NOTE   If you have the Norton Utilities for Windows 95, you can use their Unerase program to recover deleted files that are not in the Recycle Bin—again, you must do this very quickly before another file overwrites the one you want to recover.

Files That Won't Go Willingly

Some older programs (not written specifically for Windows 95) allow you to delete files from within the program. Files deleted this way will not be sent to the Recycle Bin. Similarly, files you delete at the DOS prompt will also disappear into never-never land rather than the Recycle Bin.

Therefore, you should make all your deletions through Windows Explorer or My Computer, or on the Desktop. If Windows 95 knows about the deletion, the file will automatically go to the Recycle Bin.

NOTE   Using the DOS prompt is covered in Skill 9.

Recovering a Deleted File

Retrieving a file from the Recycle Bin is remarkably easy. Just double-click the Recycle Bin icon. The Recycle Bin window can be set up in any of the usual choices on the View menu. The most useful are probably Large Icons (as shown in Figure 3.5) and Details.

FIGURE 3.5: In the Large Icon view you can quickly identify files that were made by a particular program.

The Details view is the best view if you're looking for a file recently deleted (see Figure 3.6). Just click the Date Deleted bar to arrange the files in date order. A second click will reverse the order. Similarly, if you know the name of the file, a click on the Name bar will list the files in alphabetical order.

To retrieve a single file, click it with either the left or right button and drag it to a folder or the Desktop. If you just want to send it back to its original location, right-click the file name and select Restore from the pop-up menu.

Recovering More Than One File

To recover more than one file at a time, hold down the Ctrl key while selecting the file names. Then right-click one of the highlighted names and select Restore. Or cut and paste to send the whole bunch to a different location. And of course, you can click and drag (with either the right or left button) and drag the files to your Desktop or another open folder.

To retrieve a number of files all in a series, click the first one and then hold down the Shift key while selecting the last one in the series.

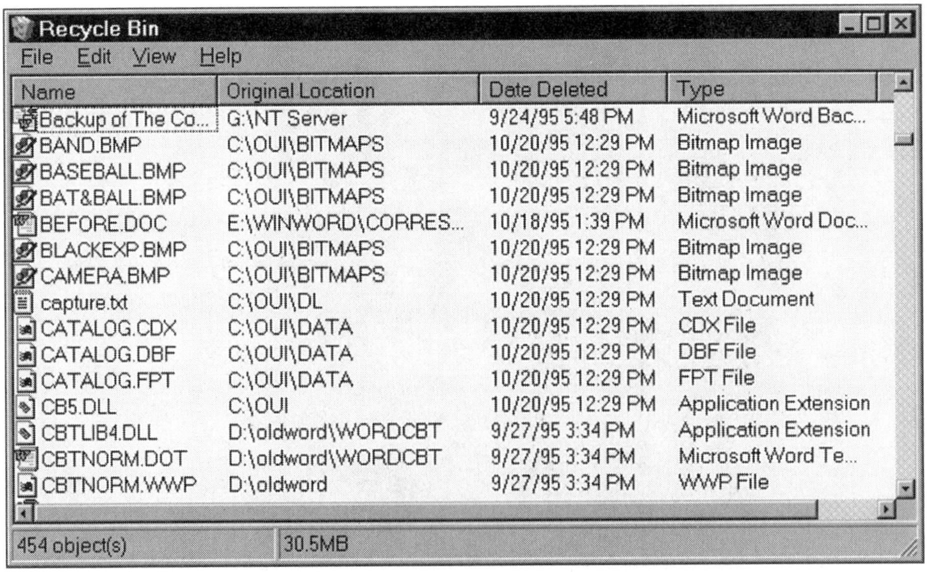

FIGURE 3.6: The Details view is useful if you're searching by date or name.

Let's say you deleted a whole folder and the only thing all the parts of the folder have in common is that all were deleted at the same time. Here's how to recover them:

1. Open the Recycle Bin by double-clicking the icon.

2. Select Details from the View menu.

3. Click the Date Deleted button. Use the scroll bar to move through the list until you find the group of files you want to retrieve.

4. Click the first one's name. Then, while holding down the Shift key, click the name of the last one you want. All the files in between the first and last click will be highlighted.

5. Right-click one of the highlighted files and select Recover from the pop-up menu.

All the files will be returned to their original home, and even though the original folder is not listed in the Recycle Bin, the files will be in the original folder.

Changing Recycle Bin Settings

You can adjust the amount of space the Recycle Bin claims and change other settings that affect how the Recycle Bin works. Mostly you have to decide just how much safety you want and are comfortable with.

Determining How Much Space Is Used

Right-click the Recycle Bin icon and select Properties. The Recycle Bin's property sheets will open as shown in Figure 3.7.

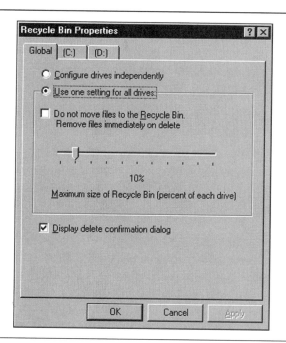

FIGURE 3.7: The Recycle Bin's property sheets

As you can see, you can set the amount of space reserved for the Recycle Bin for each hard disk drive individually, or make a global setting. By default, 10 percent of each driver is set aside for the Recycle Bin. On a large drive, that's a lot of megabytes, so you may want to reduce the size a bit.

Click Configure Drives Independently and then click each drive tab in turn. Click the sliding arrow and move it up or down until the space reserved is to your liking.

NOTE   There's also a field below the slider, showing the percentage of the drive that is reserved. If your drives are different sizes, you might want to make things easier for yourself by just reserving the same percentage on each drive.

Remember that the Recycle Bin is first-in, first-out, so if you make the reserved space very small, deleted files may pass into oblivion faster than you might want.

Getting Rid of Confirmations

☑ Display delete confirmation dialog   On the first page of the Recycle Bin property sheet, you can check a box if you don't want to be questioned every time you delete a file.

If there's a check in the box, you won't see any messages when you select Delete. If you like the comfort of being consulted about every deletion, leave this box clear.

Doing Away with the Recycle Bin

Well, you can't exactly do away with the Recycle Bin completely. As mentioned before, you can't delete it or remove it from the Desktop. However, you can check

☐ Do not move files to the Recycle Bin. Remove files immediately on delete   the box on the Recycle Bin property sheet shown here. If you have the Recycle Bin space configured separately for each drive you can pick to which drives you want this to apply. Checking this box is a *very bad* idea unless you have another program for undeleting files. Files that are deleted and not sent to the Recycle Bin are gone forever.

Even if you do have a program that rescues files deleted in error, it's still not a good idea to bypass the Recycle Bin completely because most of these programs are dependent on you getting to the deleted file before it is overwritten by something else. And that can easily happen in Windows 95 where there's almost always something going on behind the scenes.

TIP   If you begrudge large portions of your hard drive, make the reserved space on the hard drive very small—maybe 5 or 10 megabytes. Check the box on the property sheet to disable the confirmation requests. Then the Recycle Bin will be quite unobtrusive, but you'll still have some margin for safety.

Emptying the Recycle Bin

To get rid of everything in the Recycle Bin, right-click the Recycle Bin icon and select Empty Recycle Bin. There's also an option to Delete Recycle Bin under the File menu.

To remove just *some* of the items in the Recycle Bin, highlight the file names, right-click one of them and select Delete from the pop-up menu. You'll be asked to confirm the deletion (assuming you have the confirmation option turned on) and when you say Yes, the files will be deleted permanently.

Are You Experienced?

Now you can...

☑ change the appearance of your Desktop

☑ change video resolutions and other settings

☑ configure and use the Recycle Bin

☑ recover deleted files from the Recycle Bin

Skill 3

based teleundraising. Minimum of 7 years experience in similar field. 4 year degree preferred. Proficient computer skills incl. Windows-based software applications required. Salary commensurate w/skills & exp. plus benefits. Send letter and resume to Well-Being Clinic, 543 Spring Ave, Daytonville, VA.

Executive Secretary

OfficePlus, an office supply & furniture company is looking for administrative support to VP. Requires 5 years min. of secretarial experience, proficiency with MS Word and Excel and excellent communication skills. Must be willing to learn database & desktop software. Fax: OfficePlus, Personnel 665-555-9122.

FACILITIES PLANNER Training Centers Inc. seeks individual to study & develop infrastructure requirements and capital improvement projects. Req's BA in Planning, Engineering, Architecture or rel. field w/7 years exp & knowl of Windows (Word, Excel) & graphics programs. 4 yrs' exp w PC's planning arch/eng or facilities mgmt & exp w/CAD, database mgmt & project scheduling pref'd. Fax: HR. 885-555-2398.

MANAGEMENT REPORTING ANALYST

Join the team that maintains the purchasing and logistics information systems that support order entry, provide product and contract information, track product utilization, and manage operating budget and inventory systems. Must be proficient in a high-level database system and Excel, Lotus 1-2-3, or similar applications. Fax resume to Data Systems Placement Services 444-555-9998.

MANAGER, ASSET MODELING

This worldwide logistics company is expanding it's transportation network. The successful candidate will have a Bachelor's degree in Economics, Finance or Business Mgmt, with a MBA degree preferred; a solid foundation in Mathematics, and excellent analytical skills. Knowledge of PC applications in Excel, Word, PowerPoint & Visio essential. Competitive benefits and compensation plan. Fax: 966-555-2298/

Manager, Business Analysis You will direct a team of Business Analysts and oversee timely completion of all projects in accordance with departmental policies & procedures. Requires BA/BS in Behavioral Health Sciences, Business Administration, MIS, or equivalent experience, system development/ analysis and software testing, strong project management and team building skills, and software development experience. Hart Corporate Services. Call J. Thornton 243-555-9583.

MAPLE RESEARCH PROJECT MANAGER SuperMouse Designs is creating a new research division. You will provide research consulting services to internal clients and manage external research providers. A BA/BS degree or equivalent with 4-6 years' experi-

---

send strong Word & Excel skills, and cover letter, resume & salary req's to: Sommes Communications, Attn: HR/Job 85, 776 Bowser Lane, Bowtown, MA.

MARKETING ASSISTANT

Supporting 2 Marketing Mgrs., you'll handle a variety of admin. responsibilities, direct mail coordination, desktop publishing, and ad space coordination. Require 1-2 years admin. exper. and strong computer skills, esp. desktop pub., HTML, Office & Windows. Fax. R. Smith 365-555-8844.

OFFICE MANAGER

Join a growing firm that offers competitive salaries & benefits for a take-charge type. Responsible for all office purchases & operations including a quarterly newsletter. Windows & MS Office experience req'd. Call 973-555-4545.

PC Support Specialist High-end catalog company and specialty retailer has opening in MIS Dept. Support corporate associates with PC and network systems. Extensive PC hardware installation and configuration experience is required. Must be able to communicate effectively, and determine cause of problems, & develop solutions. Requires network admin. & multiple PC operating systems experience. (Windows, UNIX) Fax resume & salary reqs to High Profile Images 388-555-9634.

PROJECT ASST. Serve as a point person in HR office of fast growing biotech firm. Requires creative thinking and up-to-date office computer skills, esp. Word, PowerPoint & Excel. Fax resume to TruPoint Systems 689-555-1298.

PROJECT MANAGER

Public agency seeking environmental project manager to oversee 18-month marsh preservation project. Develop, analyze, organize & summarize planning data and financial info. Windows computer skills essential. Send resume to Public Planning Services, Attn: HR, 34 Marsh Lane, Willowdale, CA.

Sales/Computer Expanding computer software & hardware store is looking for more qualified sales associates to staff our busy downtown location. Windows software experience required. Send resume and salary/commission requirements to General Manager, Computers For You, 433 Main St., Ontario, MN.

SALES SUPPORT ASSOCIATE Work with customer service, account managers, marketing & brand management. You will handle distribution of sales materials and internal correspondence. You will need 1-2 years in sales admin. and basic office functions (mail, fax, phones etc.), plus PC skills. Computer troubleshooting skills a plus.

Sales: Sr. Account Coordinator Looking Good, a national clothing chain is looking for seasoned sales pros to oversee sales operations. Qualified candidates must have 4-5 years sales mgmt exp. and strong

---

pros to oversee sales operations. Qualified candidates must have 4-5 years sales mgmt exp. and strong PC skills. A college degree, working knowledge of Excel, PowerPoint, Word and database software req'd. Fax resume and cover letter to: Looking Good, Attn: K. Ferkovich, 877 Goody Ave., Reno, NV.

SALES/COMPUTER

Expanding computer software & hardware store is looking for more qualified sales associates to staff our busy downtown location. Windows software experience required. Send resume and salary/commission requirements to General Manager, Computers For You, 433 Main St., Ontario, MN.

SALES SUPPORT ASSOCIATE

Work with customer service, account managers, marketing & brand management. You will handle distribution of sales materials and internal correspondence. You will need 1-2 years in sales admin. and basic office functions (mail, fax, ph)

Senior Calendar Clerk Large international law firm is seeking qualified candidates with strong organizational and data entry skills, and extremely high level of service orientation and excellent oral and written communication skills. Applicants must possess a BA/BS degree, have knowledge of computer databases and Word or WordPerfect. Send resume and salary requirements to HR, Jackson Madison Madison Teller & Pewter, 1001 Main Street, Atlanta, GA

SR. FINANCIAL ANALYST JJO Enterprises seeking senior member of financial team. Requires a degree in Finance/Econ/ Acctg, minimum 3 yrs' public acct. exp. (CPA), Lotus/Excel, MS Word/WordPerfect proficiency. P&L/cashflow statement exp is preferred. Competitive salary/ benefits pkg. Fax: Mr. Rogers, JJO Enterprises 442-555-1267.

SENIOR LAW CLERK

Large international law firm is seeking qualified candidates with strong organizational and data entry skills, and extremely high level of service orientation and excellent oral and written communication skills. Applicants must possess a BA/BS degree, have knowledge of computer databases and Word or WordPerfect. Send resume and salary requirements to HR, Jackson Madison Madison Teller & Pewter, 1001 Main Street, Atlanta, GA

SENIOR SECRETARY Bolan Lumber Co. looking for add'l office support staff. Type 60 wpm, Word/Excel/ Windows and some desktop publishing experience. Call Ron 336-555-9944.

TECHNICAL COMMUNICATOR Biotech Systems is expanding & is seeking someone to develop & maintain user documentation/training materials and on-line help systems. Requires a BA/BS in Technical Communication or equiva-

---

Group. Req. a BA/BS with 4 years' experience in financial analysis or system implementation or development. Attention to detail & time and resource mgmt. abilities are vital. Excel and PowerPoint req'd. Contact Financial Resources Executive Search at 443-555-2398.

Clerical Receptionist F/T position available in a fast-paced HR dept. You must be a self-starter, organized, and dependable. Excellent customer-service, written and verbal communication skills required. Computer experience a must. Norwell Medical Center, 100 Front St. Allentown, MD

Computer Operator/PC Technician Large software retailer looking for someone with expert computer skills to assist in tech dept. as well as to give seminars for customers looking to upgrade. Successful candidate must have 3-5 years' technical experience and 2-3 years in customer service. Teaching experience a plus. Fax resume to Best Systems: 545-555-6677.

COMPUTERS

Immediate openings! Computer technicians with PC hardware and Windows experience. Send resume to: Delta Plus, 1200 Sutter St. San Francisco, CA

Corporate Human Resources Mgr

Specialized background in Employment or Compensation & Benefits, and general knowledge of all other HR functions. PC skills essential. Fax resume to 334-555-9112.

Editorial Researcher Business publication seeking researcher responsible for weekly business lists, etc. Computer/internet skills required. Must be fast, accurate & thorough. Salary DOE. Write: Researcher, 9106 Shasta Blvd. Pittsburgh, PA.

Editor/Reporter/

National financial journal seeks experienced writer to cover the brokerage/financial services industry. Must have strong writing/editing skills and background in business reporting. Computer/word processor experience a must. Fax resume and clips to JIT 887-555-2256.

Engineering Senior Industrial Engineer needed for large wholesale buyers club, to help reduce operating costs and increase revenues. A BS degree and at least 6 years in the distribution/transportation field are required. Strong business writing skills. PC proficiency using Microsoft Office and electronic communications is essential. Send cover letter and resume to HR/Job 445. AB Industries, 4498 Howard Blvd., Kansas City, MO

Executive Assistant You'll need strong organizational, interpersonal, and analytical skills, coupled with good computer knowledge in applications such as Access, PowerPoint, Excel and Word. Send resume & salary history

---

and experience in direct marketing based teleundraising. Minimum of years experience in similar field. year degree preferred. Proficient computer skills incl. Windows-based software applications required. Salary commensurate w/skills & exp. plus benefits. Send letter and resume to Well-Being Clinic, 5 Spring Ave. Daytonville, VA.

FACILITIES PLANNER

Training Centers Inc. seeks individual to study & develop infrastructure requirements and capital improvement projects. Req's BA in Planning, Engineering, Architecture or rel. field w/7 years exp & knowl of Windows (Word, Excel) & graphics programs. 4 yrs' exp w PC's planning arch/eng or facilities mgmt & exp w/CAD, database mgmt & project scheduling pref'd. Fax: HR. 885-555-2398.

Management Reporting Analyst Join the team that maintains purchasing and logistics information systems that support order entry, provide product and contract information, track product utilization, and manage operating budget and inventory systems. Must be proficient in a high-level database system and Excel, Lotus 1-2-3, or similar applications. Fax resume to Data Systems Placement Services 44 555-9998.

MANAGER, ASSET MODELING This worldwide logistics company is expanding it's transportation work. The successful candidate have a Bachelor's degree Economics, Finance or Business Mgmt, with a MBA degree preferred; a solid foundation Mathematics, and excellent analytical skills. Knowledge of PC applications in Excel, Word, PowerPoint Visio essential. Competitive benefits and compensation plan. Fax: 9 555-2298/

Manager, Business Analysis You will direct a team of Business Analysts and oversee timely completion of all projects in accordance with departmental policies & procedures. Requires BA/BS Behavioral Health Sciences, Business Administration, MIS, or equivalent experience, system development/ analysis and software testing, strong project management and team building skills, and software development experience. Hart Corporate Services. Call J. Thornton 243-5 9583.

MARKETING ASSISTANT

Supporting 2 Marketing Mgrs., you handle a variety of admin. responsibilities, direct mail coordination, desktop publishing, and ad space coordination. Require 1-2 years admin. exper. and strong computer skills, esp. desktop pub., HTML, Office & Windows. Fax. R. Smith 365-555-8844.

MARKET RESEARCH PROJECT MANAGER SuperMouse Designs is creating a new research division. You will provide research consulting services internal clients and manage external research providers. A BA/BS degree or equivalent with 4-6 years' experience with high service

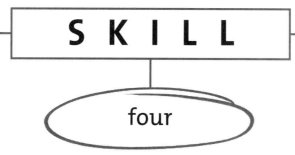

S K I L L

four

4

Using Windows Explorer

- ❏ Learning about Windows Explorer

- ❏ Setting individual window options

- ❏ Displaying file names and extensions

- ❏ Connecting files with programs

- ❏ Using My Computer

Windows 95 is set up so you can get at most things in more than one way. This is initially a little confusing because you may think you're looking at different places—when only the view has changed. In this skill we'll talk about Windows Explorer and the My Computer icon and the differences between what they offer.

TIP   For some reason, Microsoft saw fit to name their operating system's navigational tool "Windows Explorer" while naming their Internet browser "Internet Explorer." We'll try and use the full name of each in this book so as to minimize the confusion.

What Is Windows Explorer?

Windows Explorer is the heir to File Manager in Windows 3.1. It's the main tool for viewing the files and folders on your hard drive. Everything you see in the My Computer window is also in Windows Explorer.

NOTE   Shortcuts are the best tool for launching programs. See Skill 7 for all the information on creating and using shortcuts.

When you install a program on your computer, the program's folders are placed on the hard drive—usually in the form of a main folder and one or more subfolders (folders inside the main folder). Sometimes there are even subsubfolders. Figure 4.1 shows an open Windows Explorer window with the hierarchy of folders on the left. If you look closely, you can see that the Paint Shop Pro folder in the left column is shown as "open." The contents of that folder are displayed in the right-hand pane. You use the scroll bars on either side to move up and down through the listing.

In the left pane, folders may have either a plus or minus sign next to them. A plus sign (+) means there are subfolders—click directly on the plus sign to expand the view. When expanded, the plus sign turns into a minus sign (–).

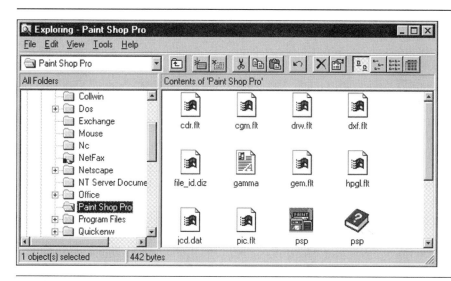

FIGURE 4.1: One view of Windows Explorer

TIP Want to see every branch of folder and subfolder on a drive? Highlight the drive in Windows Explorer and press the asterisk key (*) on your numeric keypad. Or highlight a single folder and press the asterisk key to open the contents of the folder to view. When you're ready to close everything again, don't bother with all those minus signs (-). Simply click the plus sign next to the top of the branch and press F5.

To open Windows Explorer, click the Start button and select Programs ➤ Windows Explorer.

Understanding Windows Explorer

Slide the scroll bar for the left pane all the way to the top. Note that the hard drive C: and the floppy drive A: have dotted lines going to My Computer. This indicates their connection to My Computer. But even further up is the top folder called Desktop.

In Windows Explorer terms, the Desktop is the top of the hierarchy (see Figure 4.2) with My Computer and all its pieces connected to it.

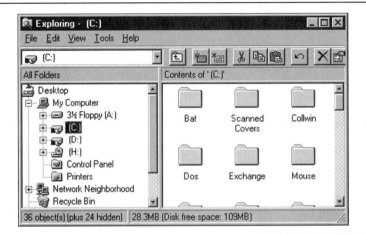

FIGURE 4.2: How your system is viewed in Windows Explorer

The dotted lines show the connections, like in a flow chart. Lines that come from the bottom of an icon and connect horizontally to other icons indicate that the destination items are contained inside the object represented by the top icon. For example, you can see that floppy drive A: and drive C: are all part of My Computer. Inside drive C: are numerous folders. The ones with plus signs to the left of them have subfolders (click the plus sign to see them). Folders without plus signs have no other folders contained within them.

Looking further down the "tree" in the left pane in Figure 4.2 you can see that the Network Neighborhood is connected to the Desktop on the same level as My Computer. And why not? Other computers on the network are equivalent to your machine. The Recycle Bin is also on the same level—it spans all drives and can't be moved or deleted.

Special folders such as the Control Panel and the folder for printers are displayed on the same level as the disk drives so they're easier to find.

Folders you have placed directly on the Desktop will also show up in the left pane. Shortcuts to folders aren't in the left pane because shortcuts are only pointers to the actual folders. The original folders are found along with other folders on your hard drive. To see the shortcuts on your Desktop, click the Desktop icon in the left pane. The shortcuts will then be displayed—along with the rest of the stuff on the Desktop—in the right pane.

NOTE Other items that don't appear in the left pane are the Inbox for Microsoft Messaging, the icon for the Microsoft Network, and any individual files on the Desktop. However, all these are visible in Windows Explorer's right pane when you click the Desktop icon in the left pane.

Exploring a Folder

Right-click any folder—including My Computer or Network Neighborhood—and select Explore. The folder will open in Windows Explorer view, with the hierarchy of folders shown in the left pane and the content of an open folder shown in the right pane.

Making a Shortcut to Windows Explorer

To put Windows Explorer at the top of your Start menu, open Windows Explorer and find the EXPLORER.EXE file in your Windows folder. Drag and drop it on the Start button. Similarly, you can put Windows Explorer on your Desktop. Right-click EXPLORER.EXE and drag it to the Desktop. When you release the mouse button, select Create Shortcut(s) Here.

Making a Shortcut to the Desktop

Try as you may, you can't drag the Desktop icon from Windows Explorer's left pane and create a shortcut that way. But you can create a shortcut to the Desktop following these steps:

1. Click the Windows folder in Windows Explorer.

2. In the right pane, right-click the Desktop folder and drag it to the Desktop.

3. Release the right mouse button and select Create Shortcut(s) Here.

Or, instead of dragging it to the Desktop, drag and drop on the Start button to put the Desktop folder on the top of your Start menu.

When opened, this shortcut will contain all the folders and files and other icons on the Desktop—except the system-type folders like My Computer, the Microsoft Network, and Recycle Bin.

Skill 4

Opening Two Explorers

If you're moving around a number of files or folders, it's simpler if you can have two instances of Windows Explorer open. It's certainly easy enough to have more than one Windows Explorer window open. All you have to do is select Explore whenever you right-click a folder.

To arrange the Windows Explorer windows so you can access them easily, right-click the Taskbar and select Tile Horizontally or Tile Vertically. Figure 4.3 shows two instances of Explorer tiled vertically.

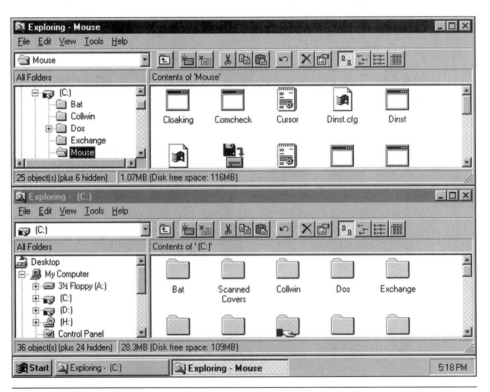

FIGURE 4.3: Tile the Explorer windows so you can move back and forth between them easily.

Navigating in Windows Explorer

As mentioned before, when you see a plus sign next to an icon in Windows Explorer, it means that at least one subfolder is inside. Click the plus sign to expand the view. Click the minus sign and the subfolders will be collapsed inside the main folder. You can slide the scroll boxes to view items that are outside the pane view.

TIP   Scroll boxes are proportionate in Windows 95. That is, the scroll box shows how much of the window's contents is being displayed. A scroll box that fills half the bar tells you that you're looking at half of what there is to see (in that particular window).

There are several ways to get at folder contents using your mouse:

- Click a folder in the left pane of Windows Explorer and the contents are displayed in the right pane.

- Right-click a folder in the left pane and select Open. A new folder will open on the Desktop displaying the contents of the folder you clicked on.

- Double-click a folder in the left pane and you expand that branch and display the folder contents in the right pane.

Getting Quick Access with the Toolbar

The toolbar in Windows Explorer is a standardization of a visual device that's been used in most Windows applications. It's a collection of icons that provide quick access to the functions on the menus. Position the mouse pointer over a button and a small window opens telling you what the button does. The toolbar is not on by default, so you'll need to select Toolbar from the View menu to make it visible.

From left to right, the functions on the toolbar are:

- Move to another folder by selecting the folder from this drop-down list.

- Move up one level in the folder hierarchy.

- Map a network drive. In other words, assign a letter to a drive on another computer on the network so your computer can access it.

- Disconnect a network drive (un-map it).

- Cut the highlighted item(s).

- Copy the highlighted item(s).

- Paste what you've just cut or copied.

- Undo the last operation.

- Delete the highlighted item(s).

- View the properties sheet for the highlighted item.

- Change the view to Large Icons.

- Change the view to Small Icons.

- Change the view to a list.

- Change the view to a list with details about file size, date, and so forth.

Recognizing Other Tools and Buttons

Windows Explorer, like the other folder windows, has a number of additional tools and buttons—many of them new in Windows 95.

Minimize, Maximize and Restore

 The Minimize and Maximize/Restore buttons have new icons, and a Close button has been added.

Click the rightmost button and the window will close. The button on the left will minimize the window to the Taskbar. The middle button maximizes the window. If the window is already at its maximum size, the middle button will restore the window to its normal size.

Sizing Handles

 The odd little graphic effect in the bottom-right corner of some windows is called a sizing handle.

Click and drag a sizing handle to change the size of a window. A Windows 95 window without a sizing handle can't be resized. Application windows can be resized as they always have been—by dragging a corner or border.

Sort Buttons

A folder that's being displayed in the form of a detailed list will have several sort buttons at the top of the display.

Click a button to get the following results:

Name   Contents will be sorted in alphabetical order. A second click will sort the files in *reverse* alphabetical order.

Size   Files will be sorted in order of their ascending size. A second click will reverse the size order.

Type   Files will be sorted alphabetically by type with folders first, then files. A second click will reverse the order.

Modified   Files will be sorted by the date they were last changed—most recent to oldest. A second click will reverse the order.

All of the above sort methods are also available on the View menu under Arrange Icons.

Setting the Display of a Folder's Contents

The contents of folders can be viewed as large icons, small icons, a list, or a detailed list. Pull down the View menu in any folder window to try out different looks.

If you use large or small icons, you can select View ➤ Arrange Icons and toggle Auto Arrange on or off. Remove the check mark from in front of Auto Arrange and you can drag the icons around inside the folder. With Auto Arrange selected, the icons snap to an invisible grid and can't be moved about arbitrarily.

If you turn off Auto Arrange and have moved your folder icons every which way until you've made a mess, you can select Line Up Icons from the View menu and the file icons all snap to an invisible grid.

Understanding File Extensions

If you have ever used any version of DOS or Windows, you know the file-naming conventions used. A file name can have a maximum of eight characters plus a three-character extension. This has historically been one of the more irritating facts about using a PC. Not because naming a file is especially hard—but because six months later you're probably going to have a hard time remembering what CZMLHTL.DOC is all about.

With Windows 95, long file names are finally permitted, so you can give that file a name like LETTER TO HOTEL IN COZUMEL. But because the underlying file structure is unchanged, the actual name of that file will be LETTER TO HOTEL IN COZUMEL.DOC.

By default, Windows 95 hides most file extensions. If Windows 95 knows what program *made* the file, the extension doesn't need to be seen. All you have to do is click the file and Windows 95 will open the associated application.

Seeing Extensions

If you want the file extensions displayed, follow these steps:

1. Select Options from the View menu.

2. On the View page, remove the check from Hide MS-DOS File Extensions for File Types That Are Registered.

3. Click OK.

Note that the reference is to all registered file types. If Windows 95 doesn't know what program is associated with a particular file extension, the extension will continue to be displayed even when the Hide MS-DOS File Extensions box is checked.

Seeing All Files

Windows 95 also hides from normal view a whole assortment of files, including system files and various kinds of device drivers. These are hidden for two reasons.

First, because most users don't need to see these files and they just clutter up the Desktop. Second, if you were to accidentally change or delete one of these files, it might cause a particular program—or even your whole system—to stop working.

However, there's certainly no harm in displaying them, so if you really want to see all the files on your system, you can do so easily. Just select Option from the View menu, and on the View page of the properties sheet (Figure 4.4), select Show All Files.

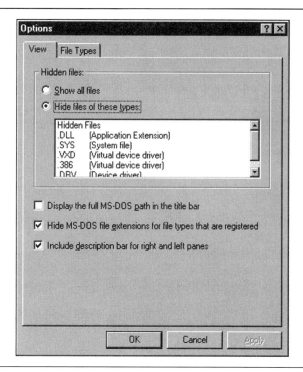

FIGURE 4.4: Hidden files can be un-hidden using the View menu.

Unfortunately, there's no way to pick and choose among the files that are designated as hidden. Either they're all displayed or none are.

Connecting Files with Programs

Windows 95 does a pretty good job of determining which files go with which programs. Once Windows 95 knows that a certain type of file is associated with a particular program, you can double-click *any* file of that type and the program will start.

 NOTE Connecting a file type with a program used to be called "associating" a file with a program. Now Windows 95 calls it "registering," but the terms mean the same thing.

Making a New Connection

Most of the time, merely installing a program is enough to teach Windows 95 which files go with that program, but not always. If a file is of a registered type, when you right-click it the first option on the menu is Open. If it's not registered, the first option will be Open With. Select Open With and you can select from the list of applications as shown in Figure 4.5.

FIGURE 4.5: Choosing the program to connect to an unregistered file

If you want to have all your files of a particular type to be always open with a particular application, you need to tell Windows 95 about it by checking the box next to Always Use This Program.

To register a file type, follow these steps:

1. Open Windows Explorer and from the View menu, select Options.

2. Select File Types and click New Type.

3. In the Description of Type box, enter how you want this type of file to be shown in windows that display in Details view. This is for your information, so you can describe it in any way you choose.

4. In the Associated Extension box, enter the three letters that make up this file type's extension (see Figure 4.6). These three letters *are* important because all files with the same extension will display a particular icon and will be acted on in the same way as far as the operating system is concerned.

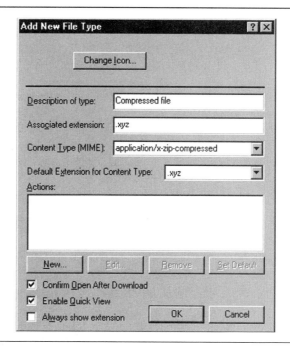

FIGURE 4.6: Fill in a description of the file type.

5. For files that will be sent via the Internet, you can include a Content Type.

6. Click the New button. In the New Action box, type in the action you want performed when you double-click files of this type and the application used to perform the action (see Figure 4.7).

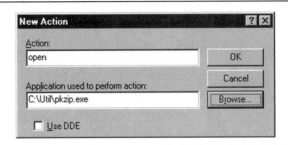

FIGURE 4.7: Defining what you want the associated program to do

7. Use the Browse button to find the exact location of the application you want used. Click OK.

8. Back in the Add New File Type box, you can click the Change Icon button to select a different icon for the associated files. Click OK when you're done.

 NOTE   Almost all the time, you'll want the program to open the file. That is, the program will start and then load a file with the specified extension.

Having One File Type and Multiple Programs

Most file types are associated with a single program—but there are exceptions. For example, when confronted with bitmapped files (extension .BMP) you may want to open some in Microsoft Paint, others in Collage Plus, still others in Paint Shop Pro or another program.

To have multiple associations, follow these steps, substituting the file types and programs you want to use:

1. Open Windows Explorer and from the View menu, select Options.

2. Click the File Types tab. In the Registered File Types window, find the file type you want to add another association for and highlight it.

3. Click the Edit button. (Figure 4.8 shows the default actions for text documents with a .TXT extension.) If you double-click a .TXT file, it will open (the action in bold type). The print action is available from the menu that pops up when you right-click a .TXT file.

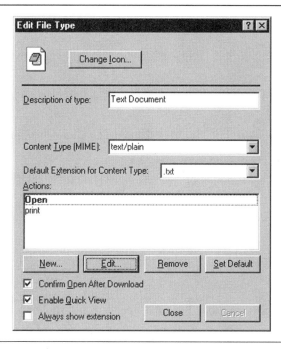

FIGURE 4.8: Default actions for documents with the TXT extension

4. Click the New button to add an action. In the New Action window, enter the action you want performed as well as the application to perform the action. In Figure 4.9 we're adding the option to open the file in Word for Windows.

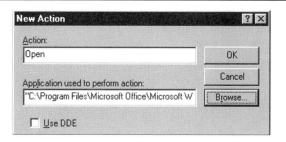

FIGURE 4.9: Adding Open in Word for Windows as an association for text files

5. Click OK. Back in the Edit File Type window, all the actions will be listed. To change the default (the action that occurs when you double-click a file of the type in question), highlight the one you want and click the Set Default button. Click OK again when you've finished.

Now a right-click on a text file gives you the additional option of opening the file in Word for Windows.

You can clutter up your right-click menu with as many associations as you want.

Changing Connections

To change a connection between a file type and a program, follow these steps:

1. Open Windows Explorer and select Options from the View menu.

2. Under File Types, highlight the type you want to change and click the Edit button.

3. Highlight the Action you want to change.

4. Click Edit to make a change and make the change in the Editing action box.

5. When you're finished, select OK several times until you're back on the Desktop.

Deleting Connections

To delete a connection, open Windows Explorer and select Options from the View menu. Under File Types, highlight the file type you want to unregister and click Remove.

Using File Manager

If you're a convert from a previous version of Windows, you're probably missing File Manager about now. Fortunately, it's still included with Windows 95.

To open File Manager, open Windows Explorer and then open the Windows folder. Inside, you'll see a file called WINFILE (or WINFILE.EXE if you have the display extensions turned on). Double-click WINFILE and File Manager will open.

You can create shortcuts to File Manager so they can be available in areas where you're likely to need them. The advantages of File Manager are:

- It's faster than Windows Explorer.

- You can rename a group of files (as long as the file names are in the old-style eight characters/three characters form).

The disadvantages stem from File Manager's origins in older versions of Windows:

- Long file names aren't recognized, only the shortened versions are.

- Right-clicking doesn't work.

Nevertheless, there are times when using File Manager can be more efficient; so a shortcut on the Desktop or the Start menu may be in order.

Using My Computer

When you first set up Windows 95, there'll be several icons on the left side of your screen. The number will vary, depending on the options you chose when installing. One of them—in fact, the first one—is called My Computer. Double-click it and you'll see a window like the one shown in Figure 4.10. It may not be exactly the same because computers vary.

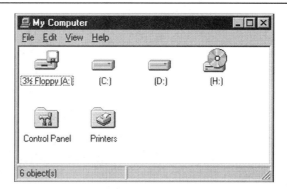

FIGURE 4.10: The folder named My Computer

The items displayed in the window are symbols for the physical contents of your computer, including the floppy drives, hard drives, and CD-ROM drives. There'll also be a folder labeled Printers (even if you have only one or none) and one for the Control Panel.

 NOTE   Because so many settings are accessed through the Control Panel, it makes sense for them to be available in a variety of locations: off the Start menu, in My Computer, and in Windows Explorer. Plus you can make shortcuts to the Control Panel and put them wherever you like.

Click a drive once and the disk's capacity and free space appear in the status bar at the bottom of the window. Double-click one of the icons and a window will open displaying the contents. For example, double-click the hard drive labeled C: and you'll see all the folders contained on the C: drive.

CHECKING OUT THE SIZE OF FOLDERS

One valuable service that Windows Explorer does not offer is the ability to see the amount of space individual folders and their contents take up on your hard drive. However, a nice freeware program called TreeSize will do exactly that.

You can find it on the World Wide Web at http://www.informatik .uni-trier.de/CIP/marder/software.html.

To download this useful program, point your Web browser at the address above and select TreeSize in the list. After it's downloaded, unzip the file to the location you choose. Right-click the file Treesize.inf and select Install from the menu.

After it's installed, you can start TreeSize from Start ➤ Programs ➤ TreeSize. Open the File menu and choose Select Directory. Navigate your way to the folder you'd like to view. Click OK, and TreeSize creates the hierarchy, complete with sizes. Double-click any folder to display all the folders inside.

Even handier, use the right mouse button to click a folder in Windows Explorer or on the Desktop, select TreeSize from the menu, and TreeSize opens showing the folder's contents.

Setting My Computer's Properties

Right-click the My Computer icon and select Properties. You can find a great deal of information in these properties sheets. Of particular interest is the Device Manager page (see Figure 4.11). Double-click any of the hardware items in the list to see exactly what's installed on your system.

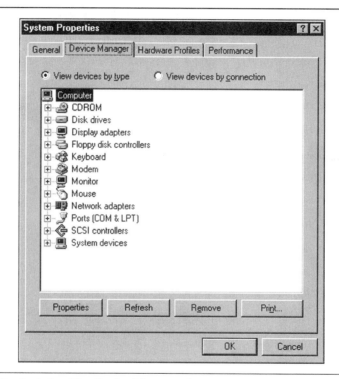

FIGURE 4.11: The Device Manager lists all your hardware either by type or by connection.

Highlight a specific piece of hardware and click the Properties button to see some of what Windows 95 knows about it. There are a number of other settings—particularly under the Performance tab—that you may want to take a look at. Most of these settings *never* need to be changed, but you should know where they are.

 TIP   To create a shortcut to the Device Manager, right-click the Desktop and select New ➤ Shortcut. In the Command line box, type this exactly: **c:\windows\control .exe sysdm.cpl,system,1**

Setting Disk Properties

Right-click one of the disk drives and select Properties. You'll get a properties sheet (see Figure 4.12) that reports the used space and free space in detail. You can also supply a name (what the dialog box calls a Label) for the hard drive.

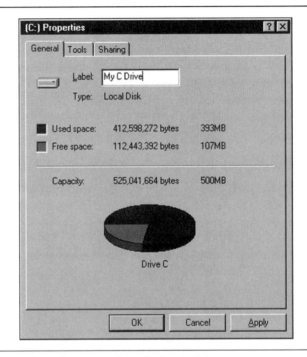

FIGURE 4.12: The properties of a hard disk

The Tools tab will let you check the disk for errors, back it up, or defragment it. If you're on a network, the Sharing tab lets you share this drive with others on the network.

Viewing One Window or Many

Click the View menu and select Options when you're in a window (like My Computer) and you can choose one of two ways to open folders:

- Separate window. With this choice, every double-click on a folder will open a new window, leaving open all previous windows. This will fill up your screen pretty quickly, but it will give you a clear indication of where you are and how you got there.

- Single window. This means that as you double-click through multiple layers of folders, the contents of the current folder fill the window.

You can experiment to see which one you prefer.

 TIP Select the single window option, and you'll be able to make some view settings permanent. Using single window browse, if you select (let's say) Large Icons for the parent window, all the child windows will also display Large Icons. For another parent window, another view setting can be selected and all the sub-folders will retain that setting.

It's possible to keep the clutter to a minimum using the multiple window option. Open folder windows until you get to the one you want. Then hold down the Shift key and click the Close box of the parent folder of the folder you want left open. This will close all windows leading down to the current folder.

If you like the multiple window option most of the time, you can switch to a single window on occasion. Instead of a simple double-click on a folder to open a new window, hold down the Ctrl key as you double-click. This will open the contents of the clicked folder in the current folder.

Hold down the Shift key as you double-click a folder and the folder will open in Windows Explorer view. Make sure the focus is on the folder you want to open this way, otherwise Windows 95 will open all the folders between where you clicked and the folder where the focus actually was.

In a folder where none of the objects are highlighted, the focus is on the object that has a dotted line around the name. If an item is highlighted, that's the focus object. Every open folder has an item that is the focus.

Are You Experienced?

Now you can...

- ☑ **use Windows Explorer**
- ☑ **configure file extensions**
- ☑ **connect (register) a file type with a program**
- ☑ **use the My Computer folder**

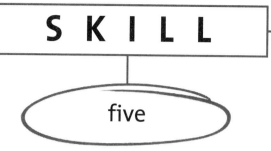

Managing Files and Folders

- ❏ Selecting files and folders

- ❏ Making new files and folders

- ❏ Moving, copying, and deleting files and folders

- ❏ Undoing a mistake

- ❏ Using long file names

- ❏ Formatting and copying floppy disks

In this skill we'll continue some of the discussion from Skill 4 with an emphasis on the basics of making and manipulating files and folders, and getting them organized in ways you find comfortable and useful.

Selecting Files and Folders

You can select a single file or folder by clicking it once. As soon as you click, you'll see that the object is highlighted. You can do this with the left mouse button and then move, rename, or copy the object as described later in this skill. Or you can click the object with the right mouse button and a menu will open with possible actions.

Selecting Everything

To select a bunch of files or folders, open the window where the objects in question are, and then click the Edit menu and click Select All. Everything in the window will be highlighted. Right-click one of the highlighted icons and choose the action you want from the pop-up menu (see Figure 5.1).

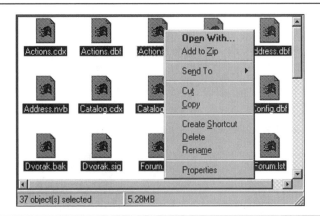

FIGURE 5.1: All the files are selected, and the right mouse menu lets you choose what you want to do with them.

Selecting Some but Not All

There are lots of ways to select some of the objects in a window. The easiest way often depends on how you have the files and folders displayed.

If you have large icons displayed, you might want to simply lasso the items in question. Right-click an area near the first item and, holding the mouse button down, draw a line around the icons you want to select. When you're finished drawing the box, the icons will be highlighted and the pop-up menu will appear, giving you a choice of actions. Figure 5.2 shows some icons selected in this way.

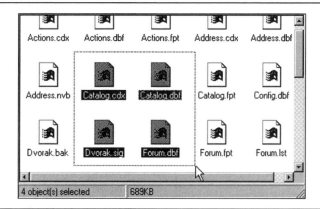

FIGURE 5.2: Icons captured by lassoing

You can also draw the box using the left mouse button, but when you go to grab the icon group you must click one of the highlighted icons with the right mouse button. Otherwise, the highlighting will disappear and you'll need to start over.

If you have the icons displayed as a list or in the details view, it's probably easier to select them using Ctrl+click. In other words, hold down the Ctrl key while clicking the items you want.

If you want all the files in a series, click the first one, then hold down the Shift key while clicking the last one. All the objects in between the two clicks will be selected.

Making a New Folder

Folders are the Windows 95 equivalent of DOS and Windows 3.1 directories. Differences exist in that Windows 95 folders can contain shortcuts, can be short-cuts to *real* folders in other locations, and can be placed right on the Desktop.

Creating a New Folder on the Desktop

To create a new folder on the Desktop, right-click the Desktop in some unoccupied space and select New ➤ Folder from the menu. A folder will appear with the cursor already placed for you to type in a name.

This folder is actually located on your hard drive in the Desktop folder inside the Windows folder. Figure 5.3 shows this new folder as it appears in Windows Explorer.

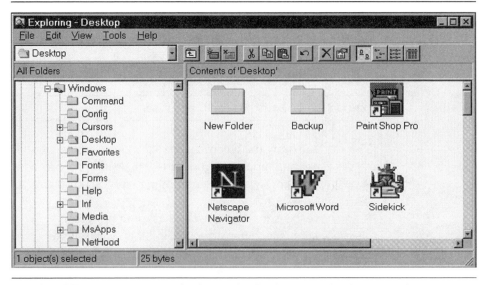

FIGURE 5.3: The new folder on the Desktop can also be seen when you open the Windows Explorer.

TIP   If you can't see the Desktop folder, it's because Hide Files of These Types is checked under View ➤ Options. Check Show All Files instead and the Desktop folder will appear.

Making a Folder Inside Another Folder

To make a folder inside another folder, follow these steps:

1. Open Windows Explorer. Use the scroll bars to locate the folder where you want to place the new folder.

2. Expand the existing folder by double-clicking it.

3. Move your pointer to a blank spot in the right pane, and click once with the right mouse button.

4. Select New ➤ Folder from the menu.

5. Type in the name for the new folder.

You can do this with a folder on the Desktop. Just open the folder where you want to place the new folder and right-click once in a blank spot inside the open window.

 TIP   Make a folder in the wrong place? Just right-click the errant folder and select Delete. You'll be asked to confirm that you want to send the folder to the Recycle Bin.

Looking at Folder Properties

Since everything else has Properties sheets, it should come as no surprise that folders do too. Right-click a folder and select Properties from the menu. You'll see a window like the one shown in Figure 5.4.

General Page

The General page provides information about the folder including its size and the number of files and other folders to be found inside. As with properties sheets for individual files, there are also check boxes for setting attributes:

Read-Only   Set this attribute and the folder cannot be written to. This is not a security measure except in that it makes it harder to accidentally change something. A determined person can easily figure out how to change this attribute.

Archive   A check in this box means that all the files in the folder have been backed up by a program that sets the archive bit. If the box is filled, it means that some of the files are backed up but others are not.

Hidden   Folders and files that are hidden will disappear from the Windows 95 interface. They'll still work as usual, but just won't be visible to the Windows Explorer or other programs.

System   System files are required by Windows 95. You don't want to delete them. In any case, a whole folder cannot be designated as System, so this box is always grayed out when you're looking at a folder.

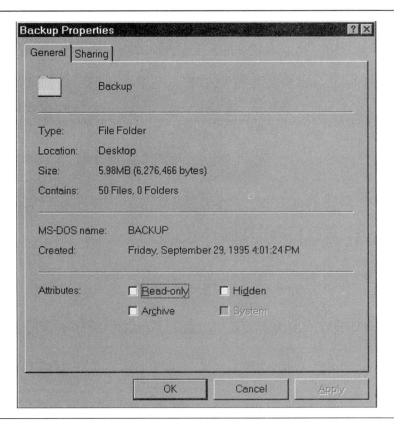

FIGURE 5.4: The properties of a folder

TIP   To change a file or folder from hidden to visible, go to View ➤ Options on a window's toolbar and select Show All Files. Find the file you want to change and open its properties page so you can change the Hidden attribute.

Sharing Page

You can share your folder with others on the network by selecting the Sharing page. You can give other users read-only or read-write access. You can require a password from other users. You can also allow sharing at the drive level or the individual file level. If you set drive C: as shared on the network, you can't *un*-share anything on drive C:. Everything will be accessible. Similarly, if you share a folder, all files in that folder are shared.

 TIP   If there's no Sharing tab on the properties sheet, you'll need to go to the Network icon in the Control Panel and activate File and Printer Sharing on the Configuration page. This will make the Sharing tab visible.

Making a New File

As long as you're using older software not specifically made for Windows 95, you'll probably make new files as you always have: by opening the application and selecting New from the File menu. However, a number of applications do place themselves on a New File menu and you can make new files from there.

Creating a New File on the Desktop

To create a new file on the Desktop, right-click the Desktop in some unoccupied space and select New from the menu. Select the type of file you want to make. A file will appear with the cursor already placed for you to type in a name.

This file is located on your hard drive in the Desktop folder inside the Windows folder. Figure 5.5 shows this new file as it appears in Windows Explorer.

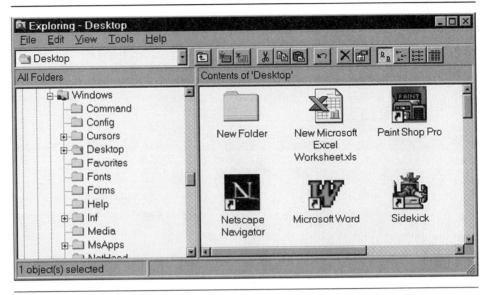

FIGURE 5.5: The new file on the Desktop can also be seen in Windows Explorer.

 TIP If you can't see the Desktop folder, it's because Hide Files of These Types is checked under View ➤ Options. Check Show All Files instead and the Desktop folder will appear.

Making a File Inside Another Folder

To make a file inside another folder, for example in Windows Explorer, open the folder that'll be the outside folder. Right-click a blank spot and select New from the pop-up menu. Then select the type of file from the list and type in the name for the new file.

 TIP Make a file in the wrong place? Just right-click the errant file and select Delete. You'll be asked to confirm that you want to send the file to the Recycle Bin.

Identifying File Properties

As a rule, most properties sheets for files are a single page like the one shown in Figure 5.6. It will include some information about the file's location, size, and creation date. There will also be boxes for setting and removing attributes as described in "Looking at Folder Properties" earlier in this chapter.

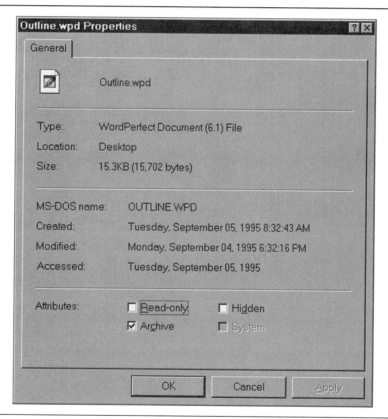

FIGURE 5.6: A file's property sheet

A few programs include other pages on the properties sheets for files. For example, Word for Windows files include a page of statistics about the file and another page of summary information about the file. As more programs are written specifically for Windows 95, this trend toward including ever more data on the properties sheets is bound to continue.

Moving and Copying Files and Folders

There are at least three different methods for moving and copying files or folders. You can adopt one method and use it all the time, or you can pick and choose from the various methods, depending on the circumstances.

Moving or Copying Using Right Drag and Drop

This is my personal favorite because it requires a minimum of thought:

1. Locate the file or folder using Windows Explorer or My Computer.

2. Click the file or folder using the right mouse button.

3. Hold the button down and drag the object to its new location.

4. Release the mouse button and choose Move or Copy from the pop-up menu.

For the shortest distance between two points, you may want to open a second instance of the Windows Explorer so you can drag and drop directly. Or you can move or copy the object to the Desktop, and then open the destination folder or drive and drag the object a second time.

Moving or Copying Using Left Drag and Drop

This method requires a bit more mental attention because when you use the left mouse button to drag and drop, the result is a move—only if the source and destination are on the same hard drive. If they are on different drives, the result will be a copy. If you're dragging a program file (one with the extension .EXE, .COM or .BAT), Windows 95 will create a shortcut to the original file at the destination. You can tell a shortcut is going to be made because a shortcut arrow can be seen in the transparent icon that you're dragging (shown here).

 If you see a black plus sign in the transparent icon as you drag (shown here), that means a copy will be made when you release the left mouse button.

In both cases you can force a move by pressing and holding the Shift key before you release the left mouse button.

TIP   If you decide while dragging to cancel the move or copy, just hit the Esc key before you release the mouse button. This stops the drag but leaves the files or folders highlighted.

Moving or Copying Using Cut/Copy and Paste

Using the right mouse button menu to move or copy files and folders is very efficient because you don't need to have both source and destination available at the same time.

To move or copy a file, follow these steps:

1. Locate the file or folder you want to move or copy, using My Computer or Windows Explorer.

2. Right-click the object and select Cut (to move) or Copy from the pop-up menu.

3. Find the destination folder and open it.

4. Right-click a blank spot inside the folder and select Paste from the pop-up menu.

NOTE   There are a few objects, such as disk icons, that you can't move or copy. If you try to move these objects you'll get a message informing you of this fact and asking if you want a shortcut instead.

Deleting Files and Folders

The easiest way to delete a file or folder is to click it once with the right mouse button and select Delete from the pop-up menu. Or you can click the object with the left mouse button and then press the Del key on your keyboard.

Another method is to drag and drop the object on the Recycle Bin icon. A plus of this method is that you won't be asked to confirm that you want to delete the file.

Skill 5

In any of the previous methods, the Recycle Bin protects the user from over-hasty deletions because the data is not instantly deleted. It can be retrieved from the Recycle Bin if you later decide you want it back. There's much more on the Recycle Bin in Skill 3.

 TIP   To delete a file or folder without sending it to the Recycle Bin, press the Shift key while you select Delete from the pop-up menu or while pressing the Del key.

Renaming Files and Folders

There are two easy ways to change the name of a file or folder.

- You can click the name twice (with about a second between each click), and the name will be highlighted so you can type in a new one.

- Or you can right-click the file once and select Rename from the pop-up menu.

Unfortunately, there's no provision for renaming a group of files. For that you'll need to use File Manager (discussed in Skill 4).

Using the Undo Command

When you move, copy, or rename something, the command to undo that action gets added to a stack maintained by Windows 95. The stack is built up as you move, copy, and rename, with the most recent action on top.

To undo an action you can click the Undo button on the window's toolbar or you can right-click the Desktop or in a free area of a folder, and the Undo command will be on the pop-up menu.

The unwieldy thing about Undo is that it's a big and global stack. You can merrily undo dozens of commands, but you may not be able to see where the Undo is taking place and just what moves, copies, and renames are being undone. (Particularly if you've been working in a variety of folders.) So it's best to use Undo quickly and to do it in the folder where you performed the original action. That way you can see the results of Undo.

TIP   If you don't remember what you did last, and therefore don't know what Undo will undo, rest your mouse pointer on the button and the pop-up help will tell you whether it was a move, copy, or rename.

Utilizing Long File Names

One of the most attractive features in Windows 95 is the ability to give files and folders long file names. In fact, a name can be as long as 250 characters. However, you don't want to get carried away because the full path, including folder and subfolder names, can't exceed 258 characters.

File names can now include spaces as well as characters you couldn't use before like the comma, semicolon, equals sign (=) and square brackets ([ ]). However, the following characters are still not allowed in either file or folder names:

\ / * < > : ? " |

File and folder names can also have both upper- and lowercase letters and the system will preserve them. However, this is for display purposes. When you type in the name, you don't need to remember whether you capitalized some part of it. Windows 95 will find it as long as the spelling is correct.

NOTE   Passwords in Windows 95 are case-sensitive—as they are everywhere.

What Happens to Long File Names in DOS

The DOS commands that come with Windows 95 also know how to handle long file names. Figure 5.7 shows some files and shortcuts as they appear in an open window in Windows 95.

Newsletter
File Edit View Help
Newsletter
Corel Gallery
Fotoman Camera
Scanner
Screen Capture Program
WordPerfect
November Board Meeting
November Finances
7 object(s)
30.9KB

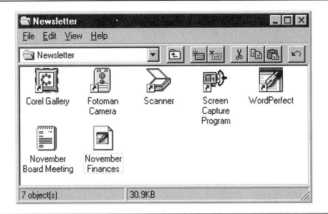

FIGURE 5.7: The contents of a folder called Newsletter

Figure 5.8 shows those same items in a DOS window.

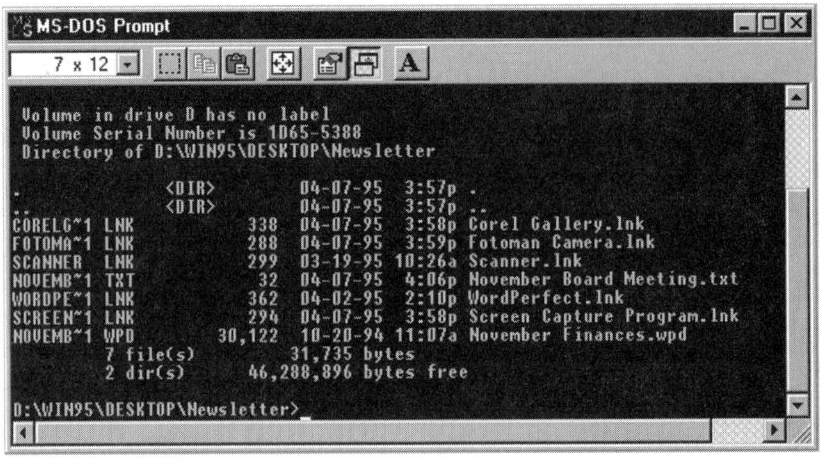

MS-DOS Prompt
7 x 12
Volume in drive D has no label
Volume Serial Number is 1D65-5388
Directory of D:\WIN95\DESKTOP\Newsletter
. <DIR> 04-07-95 3:57p .
.. <DIR> 04-07-95 3:57p ..
CORELG~1 LNK 338 04-07-95 3:58p Corel Gallery.lnk
FOTOMA~1 LNK 288 04-07-95 3:59p Fotoman Camera.lnk
SCANNER LNK 299 03-19-95 10:26a Scanner.lnk
NOVEMB~1 TXT 32 04-07-95 4:06p November Board Meeting.txt
WORDPE~1 LNK 362 04-02-95 2:10p WordPerfect.lnk
SCREEN~1 LNK 294 04-07-95 3:58p Screen Capture Program.lnk
NOVEMB~1 WPD 30,122 10-20-94 11:07a November Finances.wpd
7 file(s) 31,735 bytes
2 dir(s) 46,288,896 bytes free
D:\WIN95\DESKTOP\Newsletter>_

FIGURE 5.8: The same objects displayed in a DOS window

As you can see, the long file names are preserved on the right while shortened versions appear on the left. As a rule, DOS will make the short file name by taking the first six letters of the long file name and appending a tilde (~) and a number. So if you have a series of files called Chapter 1, Chapter 2, and Chapter 3, they'll show up in a DOS window as Chapte~1, Chapte~2, and so forth.

WARNING Numbers added to make short file names are used in the order that the files are created. So if you create Chapter 3 first, it will be named Chapter 1, not Chapter 3 as you might expect.

Understanding the Limitations of Long File Names

Unless you're running all Windows 95 programs (and few of us are), long file names will be truncated when you view them from inside the program. For example, if you've made a file in WordPad called Luisa's Party Invitation and then want to open it in Word for Windows 2.0 (which predates Windows 95), you'll see that the file name has changed to luisas~1.

After you modify and save the file, though, and return to WordPad, the long name will be intact.

Similarly if you copy some files to a disk and take those files to a computer running DOS or some previous version of Windows, you can edit the files on the floppy disk and, when you return to the Windows 95 machine, the long file names will be intact. However, if you copy those files to the other machine's hard drive and edit them, later copying them back to the floppy, when you return to your Windows 95 machine the long names will be replaced by short names.

Dealing with Floppy Disks

Floppy disks remain part of the computing arsenal even for people on networks. Sooner or later, you have to put something on a floppy or take it off (by formatting). Windows 95 includes tools to do all the floppy tasks, though some may not work exactly as you may expect.

Formatting a Floppy

To format a floppy disk, put the disk in the drive and follow these steps:

1. Open Windows Explorer.

2. Use the scroll bars to move up to the point where you can see your floppy drive in the left window.

3. Right-click the floppy drive and select Format.

4. The window shown in Figure 5.9 will open. Make sure the choices selected are the ones you want. If not, change them.

Skill 5

5. Click the Start button. When the formatting is complete (you'll see a progress bar at the bottom of the window), click the Close button.

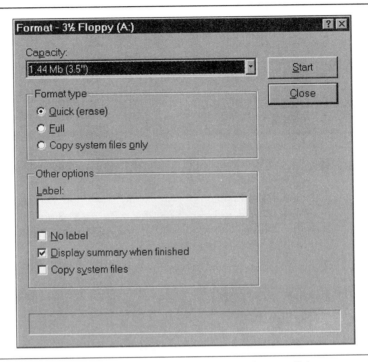

FIGURE 5.9: The dialog box used to format a floppy disk

 TIP   Make sure you right-click the floppy drive. If the contents of the floppy are displayed in the right panel of Windows Explorer, you won't be allowed to format it because Windows 95 will see the floppy as "in use." This is true even if the floppy has no files on it.

Cloning a Floppy

To make an exact copy of a floppy disk, put the floppy in the drive and follow these steps:

1. Open Windows Explorer.

2. Use the scroll bars to move up to the point where you can see your floppy drive in the left window.

3. Right-click the floppy drive and select Copy Disk.

4. If you have more than one floppy drive, you'll have to specify the Copy From drive and click Start. With only one floppy drive, just click Start.

The system will read the entire disk and then prompt you to insert the disk you want to copy to.

Copying Files to a Floppy

Put the floppy disk in the drive and use one of these approaches:

- Highlight the file or folder and then right-click and select Send To ≻ and then the specific floppy drive.

- Drag and drop the items to the floppy drive icon in Windows Explorer or My Computer.

- If you have a shortcut to a floppy drive on your Desktop or in a folder, drag and drop the items there.

You may even find other ways to copy files over time.

Are You Experienced?

Now you can...

- ☑ select files and folders
- ☑ make new folders and files
- ☑ move, copy, and delete files and folders
- ☑ undo a wrong move
- ☑ use long file names
- ☑ copy and format floppies

Skill 5

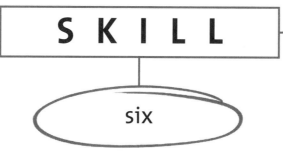

S K I L L

six

6

Finding What You Need

- ❏ Searching for files on your computer

- ❏ Finding computers on your network

- ❏ Searching other computers on your network

- ❏ Finding information on the Microsoft Network

Windows 95 comes with a very sophisticated file-finding tool that makes it possible to find any file or folder on your hard disk, even if you know very little about it. It's also useful for finding data on your network or on the Microsoft Network.

Searching When You Know the Name

To find a file or folder when you know the name (or even part of it), follow these steps:

1. Click the Start button, slide the pointer to Find, and then click Files or Folders.

2. Type in the file name, either whole or in part. Unlike previous Find tools, you don't need to know how the file begins or ends. For example, a search for files with "part" in their names yielded the results shown in Figure 6.1.

3. The Look In box tells the program where to search. If you haven't a clue, use the drop-down list or the Browse button to select My Computer, and the program will look everywhere on your system.

4. Click Find Now to start the search.

NOTE Selecting Save Results from the Options menu can save the results of file and folder searches. The search results will be saved in the form of an icon on your Desktop. Double-click the icon to open the Find window with the search criteria and results displayed.

Searching When You Know Something Else

And then there are the times when you don't know *any* part of the file name. If you have an idea of when the file was last worked on, you can use the Date Modified tab. You can specify a search between specific days or just look for files created or modified in some previous months or days, as shown in Figure 6.2.

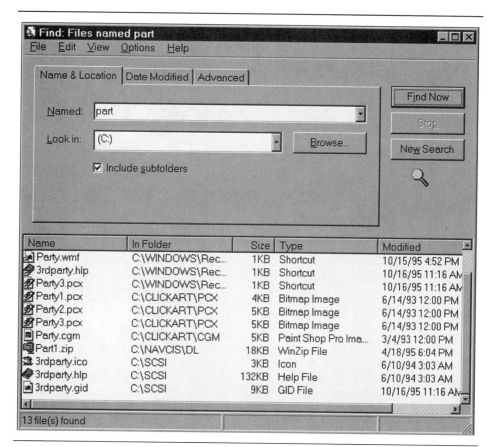

FIGURE 6.1: Searching with only a part of the name

Maybe all you know is that the document you want is a letter written in Microsoft Word and that it was addressed to a branch office in Poughkeepsie. Click the Advanced tab, select the file type from the Of Type drop-down list, and enter **Poughkeepsie** in the Containing Text box (see Figure 6.3).

Searches can be based on even skimpier information. You can have the program search All Files and Folders (look in the Of Type drop-down list) for files containing a certain word or phrase. Of course, the more information you can tell the program, the faster the search will be.

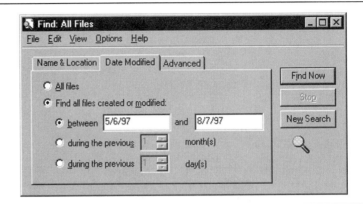

FIGURE 6.2: Searching for files by date

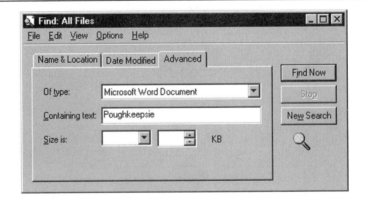

FIGURE 6.3: Searching for a type of file and a word it contain

TIP

Once you find the file you want, you can drag it to the Desktop or into another folder. You can double-click program files to open the program. If a file is connected to a program (as discussed in Skill 4), double-click the file and the program will open with the file loaded.

Finding a Computer on a Network

You can use Find to locate a particular computer on your network. Again, you don't have to know the entire name of the computer. Just click the Start button, slide the pointer to Find, and select Computer. Type in what you know of the name and click the Find Now button. Figure 6.4 shows the result of a search for computers with "ci" in their names.

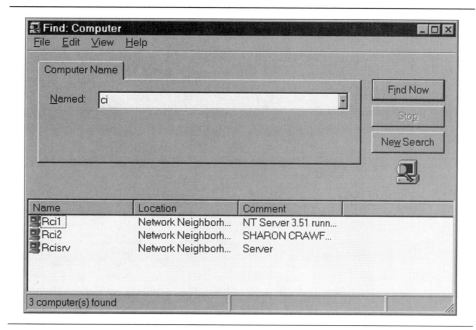

FIGURE 6.4: Searching for computers on a network

Searching Other Computers on a Network

There are occasions when you need to locate a file that resides on another person's computer. This can be done provided the following conditions are met:

- The drive on the other computer must be *shared*.
- The drive on the other computer must be mapped to your computer.

All you have to do is open Find ➤ Files or Folders. Select the mapped drive in the drop-down list and specify what you're searching for. Figure 6.5 shows the result of a search for .TXT files on another computer's I: drive.

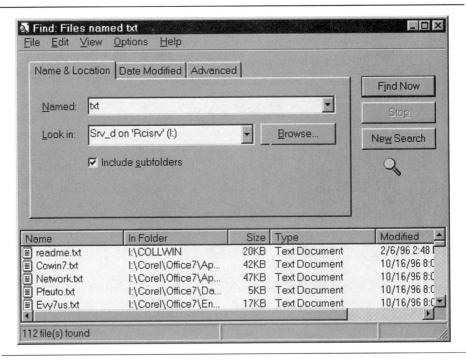

FIGURE 6.5: Searching for text files on another computer

 NOTE   Sharing and mapping drives are both covered in one short section in Skill 18.

Finding Items on the Microsoft Network

Another function in Find is the ability to search the Microsoft Network. Click Find and then click the Microsoft Network. Your usual connection to MSN will be made, and the Search window will open. Type in the topic or name of the place you want to find and select Enter. Figure 6.6 shows the results of a search for places or articles with "tech" in their names.

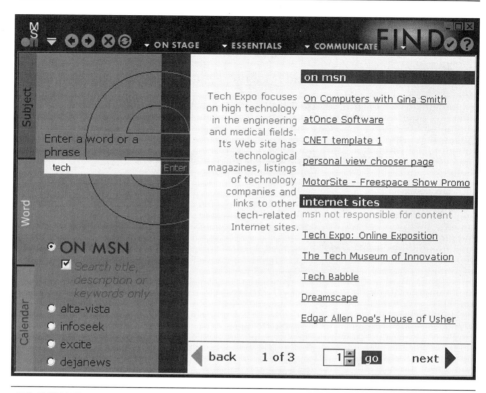

FIGURE 6.6: Searching on the Microsoft Network

Move your pointer to the name of any of the found items and a description will appear. Double-click an item and you'll be sent there. Or right-click and, in addition to the Open option, you get the choice to open the object in question, create a shortcut to the place, or add it to the MSN Favorite Places folder.

NOTE To find what you want on the Internet, see Skill 21, where you'll learn about using the World Wide Web with Internet Explorer. For more on joining and using the Microsoft Network, see Skill 15.

Are You Experienced?

Now you can...

- ☑ find files and folders on your computer
- ☑ find computers on your network
- ☑ search for files on other network computers
- ☑ find what you want on the Microsoft Network

Making and Using Shortcuts

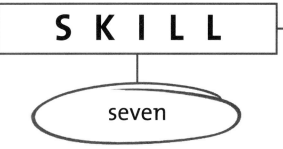

❏ Making, naming, and moving shortcuts

❏ Putting shortcuts where you want them

❏ Viewing shortcut settings

❏ Using keyboard shortcuts

Shortcuts introduce a new level of convenience and customization to Windows. They are convenient ways to get at all the items on your computer or network: documents, applications, folders, printers, and so on. They're most likely to be placed on your Desktop, on the Start menu, or in the Send To folder. In this skill, we'll cover all the ways to make and modify a shortcut and how to place the shortcuts you want in the places you want them.

The small arrow in the lower-left corner of an icon identifies a shortcut. The arrow isn't just there to be cute. It's important to know (particularly before a deletion) whether something is a shortcut or a real object. You can delete shortcuts at will. You're not deleting anything that you can't re-create in a second or two. But if you delete an actual program or other file, you'll have to rummage around in the Recycle Bin to retrieve it. (And if it's a while before you notice it's missing, the Recycle Bin may have been emptied in the meantime and the object is *gone*.)

 NOTE   Configuring and using the Recycle Bin is covered in Skill 3.

Here's an example. I have a folder on my hard drive called No Experience Required. On my Desktop, I have a shortcut to that folder. If I delete the shortcut folder on my Desktop, the folder on the hard drive remains untouched. If I delete the folder on the hard drive, the shortcut on the Desktop is still there, but there's nothing for it to point to. And if I were to click the shortcut, I get a dialog box like the one shown in Figure 7.1.

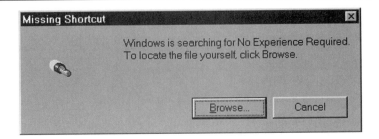

FIGURE 7.1: If you delete or move the original object, you'll see this when you click the shortcut.

You'll find the Create Shortcut option in a lot of places, including:

- On objects' pop-up menus (see Figure 7.2)

- From various drop-down menus

- On the Desktop pop-up menu as New ➤ Shortcut

FIGURE 7.2: Create Shortcut is an option on most of the menus that pop up when you click the right mouse button.

Shortcuts are an excellent tool for customizing your Desktop to suit you. You can make shortcuts to folders, to programs, and to individual files. Arrange them any way you want on the Desktop, inside other folders, or on menus.

NOTE Until Windows 95, the term "shortcut" always referred to a keyboard shortcut—in other words, a combination of keys that would produce some action on the screen. But now we have the term "shortcuts" referring to pointers. In this book, "shortcut" will always mean a pointer and "keyboard shortcut" will mean a key combination.

Creating a Shortcut

Shortcuts are pointers to objects. So you need to either find the object you want to point to or be able to tell the system where the original object is located. The easiest way to make a shortcut to a program is to right-click the Start button and select Explore. The contents of your Start menu, including the Programs folder, will be in the right pane of the window that opens. Click your way down through the tree until you find the program you want.

You can also open Windows Explorer and similarly find the program. Windows Explorer (or My Computer) is where you'll need to look to find drives, printers, or folders when you want to make shortcuts to them. Windows Explorer (or My Computer) will also be needed for a DOS program or any other program that doesn't manage to install itself off the Start menu.

Creating a Shortcut with the Original in View

To make a shortcut when you have the original object in view inside Windows Explorer or My Computer, follow these steps:

1. Point to the object and click it once with the right mouse button.

2. Holding the button down, drag the object to the Desktop.

3. When you release the mouse button, you'll see a menu like the one shown below.

4. Select Create Shortcut(s) Here.

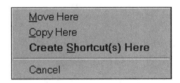

Here's a shortcut to the Word for Windows program on the Desktop. This shortcut, when double-clicked, will open the Word for Windows program.

TIP If you use the method of right-clicking the Start button described previously, you'll be using a shortcut to make another shortcut, without having to go back to the original object. Just right-click the shortcut and select Make Shortcut from the menu that opens.

Cutting and Pasting a Shortcut

Another way to make a shortcut is to right-click the program or file, and select Create Shortcut from the pop-up menu. A shortcut to the object you clicked will appear in the same folder. You can then move the shortcut by right-clicking it and choosing Cut from the menu. Then right-click where you want the shortcut to be and choose Paste. (Or you can drag it from the folder and drop it in a new location.)

Creating a Shortcut to Objects You Don't See

If the original object isn't handy or you don't want to go find it, you can still create a shortcut as follows:

1. Right-click the Desktop and select New ➤ Shortcut.

2. In the dialog box that opens, type in the location and name of the original object. If you don't know the path (and who ever does?), click the Browse button.

3. Using the Browse window, mouse around until you find the file or object to which you want to link. You may have to change the Files of Type item in the Browse window to read All Files. Highlight the file with the mouse (the name will appear in the File Name box) and click Open.

4. The Command line box will now contain the name and location of the object. Click Next to accept or change the name for the shortcut.

5. Click Finish and the shortcut appears on your Desktop.

Skill 7

Renaming a Shortcut

When you create a shortcut, the system always gives it a name that starts with "Shortcut to" and then names the object to which the shortcut is pointing. To rename the shortcut, you can right-click the icon and select Rename from the menu that opens.

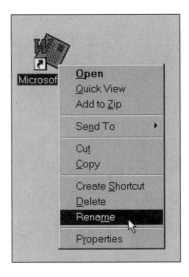

Type in the name you want. Click a blank spot on the Desktop when you're through.

You can also rename a shortcut (or most other icons for that matter) by clicking the name once, waiting a second or two, and clicking again. That'll highlight the name and you can edit it as you wish.

Choosing a Name

When you rename a shortcut, take full advantage of long file names to give it a name that's meaningful to you. No need to get carried away, but you might as well call a folder March Budget Reports rather than MARBUDGT, as you might have previously. Certain characters aren't allowed in shortcut names:

/ \ < > | : " ? *

but you ought to be able to live without those few.

TIP   On some systems, particularly multiplatform networks, you may be stuck with using the old 8.3 naming convention. Of course, any files you don't need to share can still have long names.

Putting Shortcuts Where You Want Them

Obviously, the point of shortcuts is to save you time and energy. Merely placing a bunch of shortcuts on your Desktop may help you or it may not. So here are a number of other ways shortcuts can be made useful.

Putting a Start Menu Item on the Desktop

As you've seen, when you click the Start menu and follow the Programs arrow, you get a hierarchical display of all the programs installed on your system. All those menu items are just representations of shortcuts. To find them and put the ones you want on your Desktop, you'll need to (if you'll pardon the expression) go exploring:

1. Right-click the Start button and select Open or Explore.

2. Double-click the Programs icon.

3. Find the programs you want or you may have to go down another level by clicking one of the folders.

4. Right-click the shortcut you want and drag it to the Desktop, selecting Create Shortcut(s) Here from the menu that opens when you release the mouse button.

Adding a Program to the Start Menu

You undoubtedly have some programs that you'd like to get at without having to go through the menus or without searching around the Desktop. To add a program to the top of the Start menu, just click a shortcut, drag it to the Start button, and drop it on top. Then when you click the Start button, the program will be instantly available (as shown in Figure 7.3).

Skill 7

FIGURE 7.3: For instant access to your favorite programs, add them to the top of your Start menu.

Remove programs from the Start menu by selecting Start ➢ Settings ➢ Taskbar. Click the Start Menu Programs and then the Remove button. Highlight the program you want to remove and then click the Remove button.

As you can see in Figure 7.4, you can also use this page to add programs to the Start menu, though it requires more steps than the simple drag-and-drop method.

 TIP   This page is also where you can clear the Documents menu that branches off from the Start menu.

Adding a Shortcut to Send To

When you right-click most things in Windows 95, one of the choices on the menu is Send To. By default, the Send To menu includes shortcuts to your floppy drive (or drives) and also may include (depending on your installation) shortcuts to mail and fax recipients.

To add a shortcut to Send To, follow these steps:

1. Click the Start button and select Programs ➢ Windows Explorer.

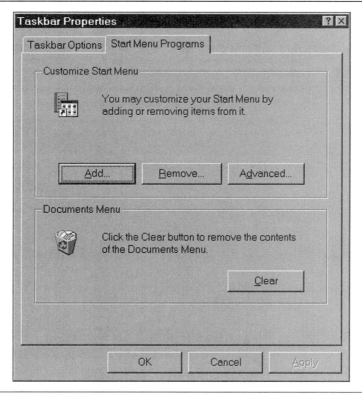

FIGURE 7.4: Use the Taskbar Properties dialog box to add and remove programs from the Start menu.

2. In Windows Explorer, find your Windows folder in the left pane and double-click it.

3. Under the Windows folder, find the Send To folder and double-click.

4. Use the right mouse button to drag and drop shortcuts into this folder to add them to the Send To menu.

You may have to open a second instance of Windows Explorer to get at other folders if the shortcuts you want are not on the Desktop. Or you can use Copy and Paste on the right mouse button menu.

 TIP   When you use Send To, you're actually performing the equivalent of drag and drop. The item you've highlighted will be dropped on the selection you make in Send To.

Setting a Shortcut's Properties

Every shortcut has a properties sheet that you can get at by right-clicking the shortcut icon and selecting Properties from the pop-up menu. For shortcuts to Windows objects (as opposed to DOS programs), the more interesting tab is the one labeled Shortcut (shown in Figure 7.5).

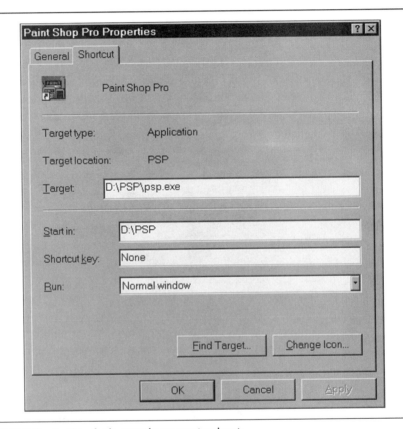

FIGURE 7.5: A shortcut's property sheet

Finding the Target

Click the Find Target button to find out just where the shortcut is pointing. When you click this button, a window opens into the folder containing the application or file the shortcut is for.

Changing a Shortcut's Icon

Shortcuts to programs will display the icon associated with that program. However, shortcuts to folders and documents are pretty dull. In any case, you can change the icon for a shortcut by following these steps:

1. Right-click the icon and select Properties from the pop-up menu.

2. Select the Shortcut tab and click the Change Icon button.

3. Select an icon from the default SHELL32.DLL file (see Figure 7.6) or use the Browse button to look in other files (WINDOWS\MORICONS.DLL has a bunch).

4. Click OK twice to display the new icon.

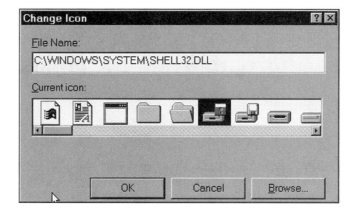

F I G U R E   7 . 6 : The SHELL32.DLL has many icons to choose from.

Many icons are available from icon libraries distributed as shareware. Icons are often included in executable files, so if you have a shortcut to an application (a file with an .EXE extension) you can pick from those icons as well.

Adding a Shortcut Key

If you're fond of opening certain applications with keystrokes, you can still do so in Windows 95—with some limitations. Toward the end of this skill, you'll find Table 7.1, a list of the keyboard shortcuts used to move around the screen.

However, you can also set up a key combination to open a shortcut to a program or folder:

1. Right-click the shortcut and select Properties.

2. On the Shortcut page click in the Shortcut key field.

3. Type in a letter and Windows will add Ctrl+Alt. (So if you enter a W, the keyboard combination will be Ctrl+Alt+W.)

4. Click OK when you're finished.

To remove a keyboard shortcut, you need to click in the Shortcut key field and press the Backspace key.

It's best to limit keyboard shortcuts to just a few programs or folders because these shortcuts have precedence in Windows. So if you define a keyboard combination that's also used in a program, that program loses the ability to use the key combination.

Using a Shortcut When the Linked Object Is Moved or Renamed

As I've said, the shortcut is only a pointer to the original object—a pretty smart pointer, but it has limitations. If you move the original object, the shortcut can almost always find it. (It may take a few seconds the first time for the search to be made.) Even renaming the original object doesn't thwart Windows 95.

However, if you move the original object to a different drive or both move and rename the original object, the system will offer you a chance to Browse for the original object. If that doesn't appeal to you, just let the search continue. Windows 95 will come up with a suggestion.

If the proposed solution is correct, click Yes. If it's not, select No. Click the shortcut with the right mouse button and select Properties. In the properties sheet, provide the correct path for the shortcut.

 WARNING   Shortcuts to DOS programs will not be so forgiving. So if you move your game to another drive or rename a batch file, plan on making new shortcuts.

Creating Shortcuts to Other Places

Shortcuts quickly become a normal way of accessing files and programs on your own computer, but they're a much more powerful tool than you'd suspect at first.

DOS Programs

Shortcuts to DOS programs are made in the same way as other shortcuts. Find the program file in Windows Explorer and do a right-mouse drag to the Desktop. However, the properties pages for a DOS program are more complex to allow for individual configuration of older programs. Skill 9 covers these settings in some detail.

Disk Drives

Right-click a disk drive in Windows Explorer or My Computer and drag it to the Desktop to create a shortcut to the contents of a drive. When you click the shortcut, you'll see its contents almost instantly—it's much quicker than opening the entire Windows Explorer.

Other Computers

You can put a shortcut to another computer—or part of it—on the Desktop. It can be a computer you're connected to on a network or even a computer you connect to using Dial-Up Networking. Just use Network Neighborhood to find the computer or part of it or even a single file, right-click it and drag it to your Desktop (or another folder) and create a shortcut there.

HyperTerminal Connections

After you've used HyperTerminal to make a connection, you can drag the connection out of the folder onto your Desktop. Double-click it and the call will be made.

 NOTE HyperTerminal is a communications applet that comes with Windows 95 and is covered in Skill 10.

Skill 7

In E-mail and Other Documents

Shortcuts can even be dropped into your e-mail or other documents. This still has limited use, but if you're communicating with someone who's also using, say, the Microsoft Network, you can send a shortcut to a location on MSN or the Internet. The recipient has only to double-click the shortcut and the appropriate connection will be made.

As you can see, shortcuts are a valuable tool now and have even more potential in the future. As you experiment, you'll find even more ways to use shortcuts that are specific to your needs and work habits.

Using Keyboard Shortcuts

Even though Windows 95 is much mousier than earlier versions of Windows, you can still do practically everything from the keyboard. Of course, you probably can't be bothered to memorize all these keyboard combinations, but you may want to consider a few for your memory bank (the one in your head), particularly if there are actions that you do repeatedly that you find the mouse too clumsy for.

Table 7.1 includes the most useful (and in many cases, undocumented) keyboard shortcuts.

TABLE 7.1: Helpful Keyboard Shortcuts

Key	Action
F1	Opens Help
F2	Renames the file or folder that's highlighted
F3	Opens Find
F4	Opens the drop-down list in the toolbar. Press F4 a second time and the drop-down list will close
F5	Refreshes the view in the active window
Tab or F6	Each time you press this key, the focus will move from the drop-down window in the toolbar to the left pane to the right pane and back again
F10 or Alt	Puts the focus on the menu bar. To move between menus, use the left ($\leftarrow$) and right ($\rightarrow$) arrow keys. The down arrow ($\downarrow$) key will open the menu
Backspace	Moves up one level in the folder hierarchy

TABLE 7.1 (CONTINUED): Helpful Keyboard Shortcuts

Key	Action
Right arrow (→)	Expands the highlighted folder. If the folder is already expanded, goes to the subfolder
Left arrow (←)	Collapses the highlighted folder. If it's already collapsed, moves up one level in the folder hierarchy
Alt+Esc	Switches between open applications. Hold down the Alt key and each press of Esc will take you to another application. Applications on the Taskbar, once highlighted, can be activated by then clicking Enter once or twice.
Alt+Tab	Opens files and folders (see Figure 7.7 after this table). Hold down the Alt key and press Tab to move the cursor from item to item
Alt+Shift+Tab	Moves the cursor through the open items in the opposite direction from Alt+Tab
Ctrl+Esc	Opens the Start menu
Alt+F4	Closes the current application. If no application is open, activates the Shut Down window
Alt+Spacebar	Opens the Control menu (same as clicking the icon at the extreme upper-left corner of the application or folder window)
Spacebar	When the selection cursor in a dialog box is selected, toggles the choice
Tab	Moves the selection cursor to the next choice in a folder or dialog box
Shift+Tab	Moves the selection cursor in the opposite direction from Tab
PrintScreen	Copies the current screen to the Clipboard from which it can be pasted into Paint or another graphics application
Alt+PrintScreen	Copies the active window to the Clipboard

 NOTE   The Clipboard is a special place in the memory and not a specific application. However, there is a Clipboard Viewer (available under Accessories) that can see whatever you copy. If it's not installed, go to Add/Remove Programs in the Control Panel. Select Windows Setup and then Accessories.

In addition to the above shortcuts, there are a number of key combinations that have a special effect when you're starting up your machine. Listed in Table 7.2, these keys are used as soon as you see this message: Starting Windows 95.

Skill 7

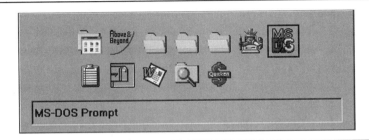

FIGURE 7.7: Using Alt+Tab to switch among active folders and programs

TABLE 7.2: Keyboard Shortcuts during Start Up

Key	Action
F4	Starts the previous operating system. In other words, if you have Windows 95 installed on a computer that also has a directory for DOS 6.x or earlier, this key will force the loading of DOS
F5	Starts Windows 95 in safe mode. Safe mode is a sure-fire way to get your system to boot. If you have, for example, accidentally changed something that causes your whole system to go south, use safe mode to change it back. Safe mode bypasses your AUTOEXEC.BAT and CONFIG.SYS files, if you have them
Shift+F5	Starts at the DOS 7 command line. Also bypasses AUTOEXEC.BAT and CONFIG.SYS files
Ctrl+F5	Starts at the DOS 7 command line without compressed drives. Any Doublespaced or Drivespaced drives will not be available
F6	Starts Windows 95 in safe mode but includes network connections
F8	Goes to the following menu before starting Windows 95: 1. Normal 2. Logged (BOOTLOG.TXT) 3. Safe mode 4. Safe mode with network support 5. Step-by-step confirmation 6. Command prompt only 7. Safe mode command prompt only 8. Previous version of MS-DOS
Shift+F8	Goes through CONFIG.SYS and AUTOEXEC.BAT one line at a time, letting you choose which commands to accept
Shift	Bypasses all the programs in the Startup folder

Are You Experienced?

Now you can...

- ☑ make, move, and name shortcuts
- ☑ put shortcuts where they're convenient
- ☑ change a shortcut's icon and settings
- ☑ use keyboard commands

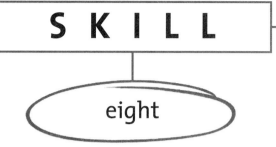

Running Programs

❑ Adding and removing programs from the Start menu

❑ Arranging the order of the Start menu

❑ Starting programs using the right mouse button

❑ Changing the Start ➤ Programs menu

❑ Putting programs in the Startup folder

❑ Finding and using Program Manager

In this skill we'll cover the essentials of launching programs. There are lots of ways to get programs started, and also lots of places to start them *from*: The more frequently used programs can be placed in the most easily accessible spots, and the infrequently used ones can be accessible but still out of the way.

Starting a Program

As you might suspect by now, there are a lot of different ways to start a program. For instance, you may prefer the approach of clicking on shortcuts that are on your Desktop or on the Start menu. The previous skill, "Making and Using Shortcuts," already covered the basic steps for creating both kinds of shortcuts, but in this section I'll show you more options for starting programs, and I'll describe how to arrange the order of the programs within the Start menu to your own liking.

Putting a Program on the Start Menu

In the previous skill, I described how if you've already created a shortcut on the Desktop, you could drag it to the Start menu so that you can launch it from either place, as shown in Figure 8.1. As you may have discovered, you don't *have* to create a shortcut on the Desktop first—I only showed you that approach because it offers the easiest way of giving your shortcut a name of your own choosing. You can drag a program directly to the Start button from Explorer, as described here:

1. Open Explorer (Start ➤ Programs ➤ Windows Explorer).

2. Using the scroll bars in the left pane, find the folder for the program you want to put on the Start menu. Double-click the folder to display its contents.

3. In the right pane, click the Type button at the top of the list to arrange the folder's contents by file type. The file that runs the program will be listed as an Application-type file.

4. If there's a single application file, right-click the file and drag it to the Start button. When the pointer is on the Start button, release the mouse.

TIP

If there's more than one file listed as an Application-type file in your program's folder, you may have to guess which one is the actual main program file—you can usually judge it from the name or from the icon. If worse comes to worse, double-click a file you think might be "it." If the program opens, you've hit the jackpot. If it doesn't, just close whatever did open and try another one.

FIGURE 8.1: The Start menu with programs and a folder added

 TIP

Like the idea of having a shortcut to the Desktop itself on your Start menu? Open Windows Explorer and look inside your Windows folder for the Desktop subfolder. Right-click the Desktop subfolder, drag it to the Start button, and drop it. Now you don't have to have a clear view of the Desktop to see its short-cuts—you can "open" the Desktop directly from the Start menu.

Forcing the Order on the Start Menu

Programs on the Start menu are listed in alphabetical order, so if you're feeling creative you can rename them solely to affect their position in the list (changing

Microsoft Word to *Word*, for instance, to move it toward the bottom), but suppose you're already satisfied with the names you've got. You can still choose which programs appear at the very top of the list using the following trick:

1. Right-click the Start button and select Explore.

2. In the window that opens, you'll see a Programs folder (whose contents are what you see when you select Start ➤ Programs) and shortcuts for any programs you've placed on the Start button (see Figure 8.2).

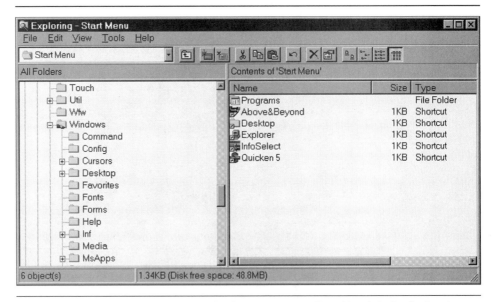

FIGURE 8.2: Programs on the Start menu are listed in alphabetical order.

3. Right-click the program you want to move to the top of the list, and choose Rename from the menu that pops up.

4. Insert an underscore (_) as the first character in the program's name.

5. Click the Start button and you'll see that the name that begins with an underscore has been moved to the top (see Figure 8.3).

If you use the underscore trick just described, you can also control which program appears *second* on the list. Just rename the program you want to appear second by using a tilde (~) as the first character.

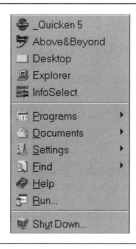

FIGURE 8.3: The underscore character moves a program to the top of the list.

  TIP   You can rename several files using the underscore as the first character and they'll be listed together at the top of the menu, in alphabetical order. You can also rename several with the tilde as the first character and they'll also be listed together in alphabetical order but *after* the group with the underscore.

Launching Programs with the Right Mouse Button

In addition to all its other talents, the right mouse button is, not surprisingly, useful for launching programs. You can just right-click a program in Windows Explorer or on the Desktop and select Open from the menu.

If the top item on the menu is Open With, however, instead of Open, and you haven't a clue as to what program might be able to handle the file, make a shortcut to the file viewers by following these steps:

1. Click the Start button and select Find.

2. Search for QUIKVIEW.EXE (note the spelling!). Or you can open Windows Explorer and look in the following folders: Windows\System\Viewers. You'll find QUIKVIEW.EXE in the last folder.

Skill 8

3. Right-click QUIKVIEW.EXE and drag it to the Desktop, selecting Create Shortcut(s) Here when you release the mouse button.

4. Next open Windows Explorer and open the folder Windows\SendTo. Drag the QUIKVIEW.EXE shortcut to the SendTo folder and drop it inside.

Now when you right-click an object, one of the options under SendTo will be Quikview. From then on, whenever you see a file that you don't recognize, you can always send it to Quikview for a fast look.

Launching from the Start ➤ Programs Menu

Click the Start menu once, slide the pointer up to Programs, and then select the program you want. This is a relatively easy way to find and start up just about any program on your system, because by default most Windows programs place their shortcuts in the Start ➤ Programs menu. However, you may dislike its multilevel nature—first there's a folder for each application and then another menu for all the stuff inside (see Figure 8.4). This is the default setup for Windows 95, but you can change almost all aspects of it.

Many of the menus in Windows 95 contain just a series of shortcuts that are easily accessible through Windows Explorer. Once you find the window that represents the menu, you can add to it or subtract from it. To change the Programs menu, follow these steps:

1. Right-click the Start button and select Explore.

2. Double-click Programs and you'll see a listing of folders and shortcuts that correspond to the Start ➤ Programs menu.

3. Double-click a folder to see the program inside. To move a program up a level, right-click the shortcut and select Cut from the pop-up menu.

4. Click the up-one-level icon on the toolbar.

5. Right-click in the right pane and select Paste from the menu. Remember that these are all shortcuts, so you can rename them or delete them without worry. You can also drag new shortcuts to any level of the menu.

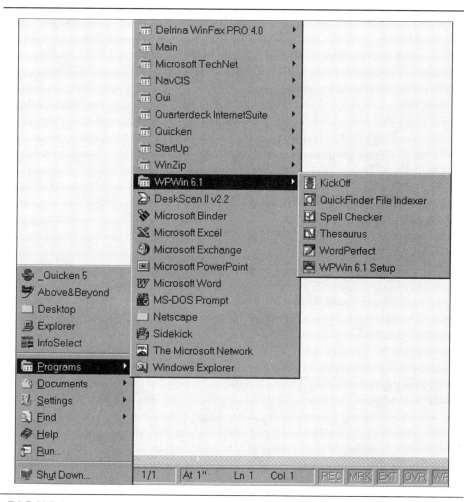

FIGURE 8.4: Maybe this degree of cascading menus is more than you want.

Adding a Program to the Start ➢ Programs Menu

You can add a program to the Start ➢ Programs menu quite easily. Just follow these steps:

1. Find the program you want (or a shortcut to the program), either by searching Windows Explorer or by using Start ➢ Find.

2. Once you locate the program or shortcut, right-click it and drag it to the Desktop, creating a new shortcut when you get there.

3. Right-click the Start button and select Explore. Double-click the Programs icon.

4. You can drag and drop your newly made shortcut to this window. That will put it on the first level of the Programs menu.

If you want, you can create a new folder in Programs (right-click a blank spot inside the folder and select New ➤ Folder). Then you can put other shortcuts in this folder—which will then be on the second level of the Programs menu.

Removing a Program from the Start ➤ Programs Menu

Removing stuff from the Programs menu is equally easy:

1. Right-click the Start button and select Explore.

2. Double-click the Programs icon.

3. Right-click anything you want to get rid of and select Delete from the pop-up menu.

WARNING All the items in the Programs folder and any subfolders *should* be shortcuts, though the icons are too small in many cases to verify this at a glance. If you have any doubts, right-click the object and select Properties. If there isn't a Shortcut page with the properties sheet, don't delete the file until you're sure it's not the *only* copy.

Starting a Program When Windows Starts

You may have programs you want to have started and ready to run when you start Windows—for example, your calendar or other application that you want to be able to launch immediately. Windows 95 includes a Startup folder for such programs. To put a shortcut in the startup folder, follow these steps:

1. Right-click the Start button and select Open or Explore from the pop-up menu.

2. Double-click Programs and then Startup.

3. Drag shortcuts to the programs you want launched into the Startup folder. If you want to leave the original shortcut where it is, drag with the right mouse button and choose Copy Here from the menu that pops up when you release the button.

To specify how the programs should look when Windows 95 starts:

1. Right-click the shortcut and select Properties.

2. Click the Shortcut tab.

3. In the Run window, select Minimized (or Normal or Maximized).

4. Click OK when you're done.

The choice you made in step 3 affects the size of the program. A minimized program appears as a button on the Taskbar after the system starts. Selecting Maximized in Step 3 causes the program to appear full-screen. Selecting Normal means the program will start in whatever is the normal-sized window for that particular application.

Using Program Manager

If you really miss Program Manager from Windows 3.1, there's good news for you. It's still around and, in fact, included with Windows 95. Look in your Windows folder for a file called PROGMAN.EXE. Right-click it and drag it to the Desktop and make a shortcut.

 TIP While you're looking for PROGMAN.EXE, it might be useful to learn that the fastest way to locate a file, at least when you already know the name of the file, is usually by using Find from the Start menu. Once Find locates the file, you can right-click the file and make a shortcut or a copy, or even move it from its folder.

Even if you don't miss Program Manager, sometimes you'll still need to use it. Some older programs that work perfectly well in Windows 95 have a devil of a time *installing* in Windows 95. If you run into one of these uncooperative programs, try installing it from Program Manager:

1. Use Find to locate PROGMAN.EXE in Windows 95.

2. Right-click it and drag it to your Desktop and make a shortcut there.

3. Double-click the shortcut to PROGMAN.EXE.

4. Select Run from Program Manager's File menu.

5. If you've been prudent enough to check the program's floppy disk for the name of the install program (usually INSTALL.EXE or SETUP.EXE), type in the full path and file name in the Command line box. Otherwise, click Browse and check the floppy drive for the install file, and select it.

6. Click OK twice and the program should install.

The program will still be available to Windows 95, though if you want to put it in the Start ➤ Programs menu, you may have to do it by dragging a shortcut to the Programs folder (described in the section "Adding a Program to the Start ➤ Programs Menu" earlier in this skill).

Are You Experienced?

Now you can...

☑ add a program to the Start menu

☑ launch a program using the right mouse button

☑ add and remove programs from the Start ➤ Programs menu

☑ find and use Program Manager for troublesome installs

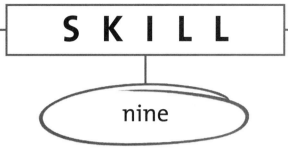

S K I L L

nine

9

Using DOS

❏ Fine-tuning DOS settings

❏ Making even unruly DOS programs work perfectly

❏ Putting a DOS prompt on the Desktop

❏ Knowing which DOS commands are available

Windows 95 comes with a set of DOS commands called DOS 7. They aren't referred to very often because you don't need to have much to do with them. If you have DOS programs, most of them can be run in a window on the Desktop or full screen. Only the most aggressive DOS programs (games for the most part) require any fiddling with settings. In this skill we'll talk about the simple way to run DOS programs, and how you can cajole even the most poorly behaved DOS program into running without complaint.

Running DOS Programs Easily

DOS programs aren't automatically placed on your Programs menu the way Windows programs are when you first install them. But you can create a shortcut to a DOS program and put the shortcut either on your Desktop or in one of the folders that make up the Programs menu (as discussed in Skill 8).

The steps will be familiar to you by now: Open Windows Explorer and find the folder with your program in it. Right-click the program name and drag it to the Desktop to make a shortcut. Put it on your Start menu or in a folder. In other words, you can handle DOS programs like Windows programs. The vast majority of DOS programs will open with a simple double-click. But what about one that won't? Or a program that opens in a window and you'd like it to run full screen? Fortunately, every DOS program has an extensive collection of *properties sheets* that you can use to tweak your DOS performance.

Tweaking Performance with DOS Properties Sheets

When you run a DOS program, whether from the Desktop or off the Start menu, you can set a variety of properties for the program. As elsewhere in Windows 95, you get to those properties by right-clicking the icon for the program or its shortcut in any of three places:

- Highlight the program's executable file in Windows Explorer or My Computer, and right-click it.

- Right-click a shortcut to the program.

• Open a DOS window and click the little icon in the upper-left corner once.

In all cases, you'll select Properties from the menu that opens. This will open a properties sheet for the DOS program like the one shown in Figure 9.1.

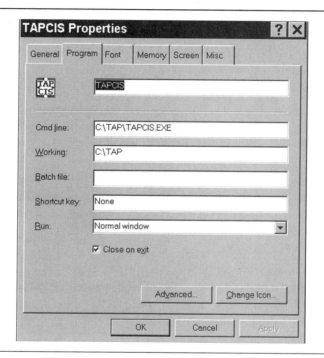

FIGURE 9.1: A DOS program's multi-tabbed properties sheet.

There are five or six pages on the properties sheet:

General   Shows information about the file and file attributes. (You won't see this sheet if you examine the properties of a running DOS program.)

Program   Sets command line options and sets the program's icon.

Font   Sets the font to be used when you run the program in a window.

Memory   Sets how much and what kind of memory is made available to the DOS program.

Screen   Changes whether the program runs full screen or in a window, and the characteristics of the window.

Misc   Like miscellaneous files everywhere, Misc sets stuff that doesn't fit in any other category.

The default settings are usually adequate for most programs, but if you need to fuss with one or more of these pages, the following sections contain some guidance.

General Properties

The General tab shows information about the program, as well as allowing you to set the attributes of the underlying file. (If you are looking at an open DOS window or program, you won't see this page.) As you can see in Figure 9.2, this tab shows you the type of program or file, its location and size, the DOS file name associated with it, and when the file was created, modified, and last accessed.

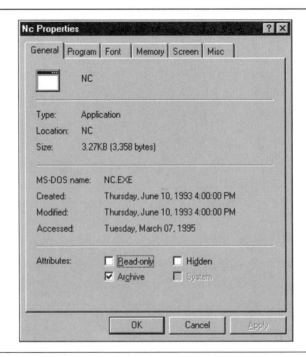

FIGURE 9.2: Control the attributes of the program file with the General tab of the DOS properties sheets.

If you're looking at a shortcut, the information about the file size, location, and type will refer to the shortcut and not to the original object (the file itself).

On this tab you can change the MS-DOS attributes of the program, including whether the archive bit is set, whether the file can be modified (the read-only bit), and whether the file is a hidden or system file. Generally you won't want to change these bits except in special circumstances. And then only if you're sure you know why you're making the change.

Program Properties

The Program tab of the properties sheet (see Figure 9.3) lets you change the running parameters of the program as well as the name and icon associated with it.

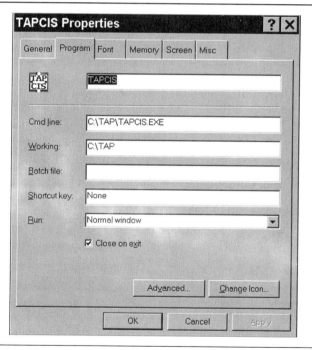

FIGURE 9.3: Control the command options of a DOS program from the Program tab.

Setting Basic Program Properties

Here's what the settings in the Program properties sheet mean:

Cmd Line   This box shows the actual command line executed. Here you can add any command line parameters you need. (If you want to be able to add parameters each time you run the program, add a question mark as the only command line option and Windows 95 will prompt you for parameters.)

Working   If your program has a favorite working directory, set that here. This isn't common anymore, but some older programs need to be told this information. If there's already an entry in this box, Windows 95 and the program have figured out that it's necessary, so don't change this setting unless you're sure you know why.

Batch File   If you want to run a batch file either before or as part of the program, place the name (and full path, if necessary) for that batch file in this box.

Shortcut Key   This box lets you add a shortcut key. (Some DOS programs may not work well with this option, but there's no harm in trying.)

Run   You can decide whether the program will run in a normal window, maximized, or minimized. Some DOS programs may pay no attention to this setting.

Close on Exit   When this box is checked, the DOS window will close when you close the program.

There are also the two buttons at the bottom of the Program tab: Advanced and Change Icon. We'll discuss these next.

Advanced Settings

Use the Advanced button of the Program tab only if you have an extremely ill-behaved or aggressive application—such as a game or other specialized, hardware-dependent program. Click Advanced to open the Advanced Program Settings dialog box shown in Figure 9.4.

Here is where you can keep the program from knowing it's even running in Windows. (Many games like to think they have your system all to themselves.) If really drastic measures are required, you can set the program to run in MS-DOS mode, which is required of any program that needs its own configuration files to run correctly. In fact, if you need to set up a specialized configuration for the program, you can type in new CONFIG.SYS and AUTOEXEC.BAT files in this dialog box. Changing to MS-DOS mode closes all your applications, restarts your computer in MS-DOS mode, and may even reboot your computer.

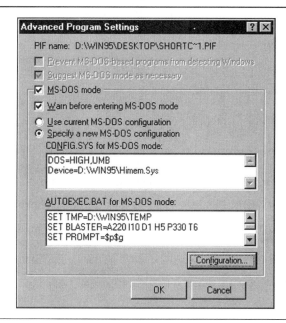

FIGURE 9.4: The Advanced button of the Program tab provides precise control over the relationship of your DOS program and Windows.

 NOTE   If you need to set your program to run in MS-DOS mode, you'll also need to load your 16-bit (pre-Windows 95) drivers in order to have access to your mouse, CD-ROM, and sound card while it's running.

Always keep the Suggest MS-DOS Mode As Necessary option checked. That way, it's not necessary for you to guess whether your game needs MS-DOS mode to run. Just go ahead and run the game; Windows will suggest MS-DOS mode if the program requires it. So except in the most unusual situations, the system will let you know when a particular program needs MS-DOS mode to run.

In MS-DOS mode you can only run a single program, and when you exit from it, the system starts Windows 95. Again, this may mean another reboot, so don't be startled.

 TIP Unless Windows suggests it, you should only consider running programs in MS-DOS mode as a last resort. Almost every DOS program should run fine in a full-screen DOS session or a DOS window without having to run in MS-DOS mode—even Flight Simulator or DOOM. (A primary reason for avoiding MS-DOS mode is that you lose the multitasking advantages of Windows 95. Plus, since a reboot may be required, the whole process takes a substantial amount of time.)

Changing the Icon

Click the Change Icon button on the Program page to change the program icon. You can accept one of the icons offered or use the Browse button to look elsewhere.

Font Properties

The Font tab of the properties sheet (see Figure 9.5) lets you set which fonts will be available when the program is running in a window on the Desktop. You can select from either bitmapped or TrueType fonts or have both available.

In general, bitmapped fonts look better on high-resolution displays and are easier to read. If you want to be able to scale the window when it's open on your Desktop, set the font size to Auto, and the fonts will change as you resize the open window.

Resizing a DOS Window

To change the size of a DOS window, go to the program's properties sheet and try setting the font size to Auto and then clicking and dragging the edge of the DOS window. Sometimes setting the font to a fixed size and then dragging the edge of the window will work as well. Different programs have different abilities to shrink and expand.

Memory Properties

The Memory tab of the properties sheet (see Figure 9.6) lets you control how much and what kind of memory DOS programs have available when they run.

On this tab you can make sure your program has a specific amount of conventional, expanded, and extended memory. You can also let Windows 95 automatically determine how much to make available. Generally, you'll want to leave the settings here on Auto, but if you know you have a program that requires a specific amount of expanded memory to run well, you can set that here.

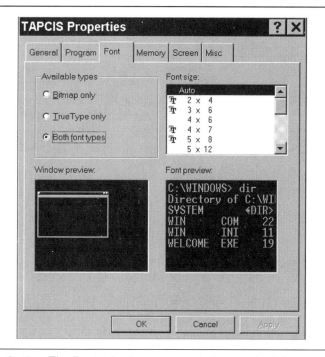

FIGURE 9.5: The Font tab gives you control over which fonts are used for the DOS program when it's running in a window.

And Memory Problems

If you have a program that has a habit of crashing occasionally, and you want to be sure it doesn't cause problems for the rest of the system, check the Protected box in the Conventional Memory section. This may slow the program a little but will provide an additional layer of protection.

Some programs can actually have a problem with too much memory. Older versions of Paradox, for example, have difficulty coping with unlimited extended memory. If you leave the Expanded and Extended sections set to Auto, programs like this may not run reliably. Try setting expanded and extended memory to some reasonable maximum number, such as 8192, which should be enough for most programs.

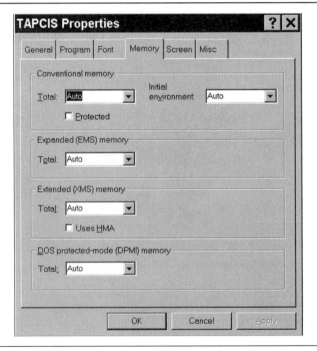

FIGURE 9.6: Use the Memory page to specify the various types of memory your DOS program uses.

Screen Properties

The Screen tab of the properties sheet (shown in Figure 9.7) lets you set your program's display. If you're running a graphical program, set it for full screen.

Most text-based programs run better in a window. Unlike Windows 3.1, Windows 95 handles windowed DOS programs extremely well, and there's no real gain to running them full screen unless you need the extra space for the program to look good.

Except for the full screen versus window option, the options on this page are best left alone unless you know why you're changing them. If you're sure you need to make a change, right-click an item and select What's This? If you understand what's in the box, you're hereby authorized to make the change.

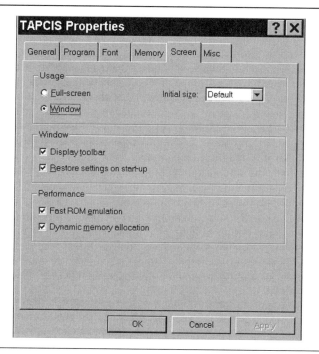

FIGURE 9.7: Display options for a DOS program

Switching from a Window to Full Screen (and Back Again)

To switch a DOS program window to full screen, just press Alt+Enter. Press Alt+Enter a second time to return to the window.

To switch from a DOS Program running full screen to the Windows 95 Desktop, press Alt+Tab.

Miscellaneous Properties

The Misc tab of the properties sheet (shown in Figure 9.8) lets you tweak several characteristics that don't fit in any of the other categories.

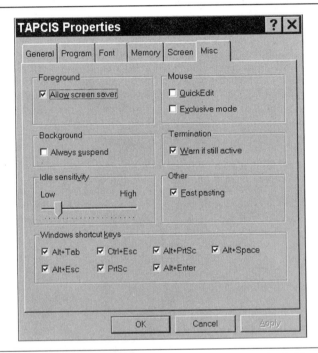

FIGURE 9.8: Setting other behavior characteristics of a DOS program

The properties you can set here include the following areas:

Allow Screen Saver   When this box is checked, the Windows screen saver is allowed to come on when this program is in the foreground. If this box isn't checked, an active DOS program will keep your screen saver from kicking in.

Quick Edit   Allows you to use your mouse to select text for cut-and-copy operations. If this box is cleared, you must use Mark on the Edit menu of the program to mark text.

Exclusive Mode   Lets the mouse work exclusively with this program. This means that when this program is open, the mouse won't be available outside this program's window.

Always Suspend When this box is checked, no system resources are allocated to this program while it's in the background (open but not the active window). If this is a communications or other type of program that you want churning away in the background while you do something else, don't check this box.

Warn If Still Active Some DOS programs are very fussy about being closed properly (like WordPerfect for DOS). When this box is checked, you'll get a warning message if you try to close the window without closing the program first.

Idle Sensitivity When this slider is set to high, the DOS program will release resources and processing time more quickly to other, foreground tasks. For communications programs, however, you will probably want to set this to the low side.

Fast Pasting This allows a faster method of pasting, but if you have troubles with pasting correctly in this application, clear the box.

Windows Shortcut Keys Generally you will want to leave these alone unless your DOS program absolutely needs to use one of these keystrokes. Clear the appropriate box or boxes if there are special keystrokes normally used by Windows 95 that you want passed on to your DOS program instead.

Making Stubborn DOS Programs Run

If your favorite DOS application is having trouble running in Windows 95, you can get it going in a variety of ways. They are presented here in approximately the order you should try them—from the relatively mild to the seriously serious.

 NOTE The default settings in Windows 95 are excellent for the vast majority of DOS-based programs and should only be messed with if you're having problems.

- Run the program full screen. You can do this by pressing Alt+Enter when the program is active, or from the program's properties sheet. Select Full-screen from the Screen page. This should be all that most graphical programs need, and with text-only programs this step can usually be skipped.

- Give the program only the kind of memory it absolutely needs. From the Memory page of the properties sheet, select None for any memory types that you know the program doesn't need. Most DOS programs will not use Extended (XMS) memory or DPMI memory, so those are good choices to try turning off first.

- Give the program the exact amount of memory it needs. If you know the program requires a minimum amount of memory, set the conventional memory setting of the Memory page to some figure slightly above that. This will ensure that the program will only attempt to run when sufficient memory is available.

- Protect the memory that the program uses. On the Memory sheet, check the Protected box in the conventional memory section.

- Turn off dynamic memory allocation on the Screen page. If the program uses both text mode and graphics mode (an example would be Symantec's TimeLine), this will prevent Windows 95 from trying to change the amount of memory allocated when there's a mode change.

- Turn off fast ROM emulation on the Screen page. This may make the program run a bit more slowly, especially in text mode, but if the program is having problems with writing text to the screen, this may help.

- Turn off the Windows 95 screen saver by clearing the Allow Screen Saver check box on the Misc page.

- Turn the idle sensitivity down to the minimum by moving the slider on the Misc page all the way to the left.

- If your program refuses to run from within Windows, try lying to it. Click the Advanced button on the Program page, and check the Prevent MS-DOS–based Programs from Detecting Windows box. Only do this as a last resort before trying DOS mode.

- OK, everything else failed, so it's time to get serious. Run the program in MS-DOS mode. If nothing else works, this will as a last resort. From the Advanced Program Settings dialog box of the Program page of the properties sheet, check the MS-DOS mode box. If the program needs special CONFIG.SYS and AUTOEXEC.BAT files, type them into the appropriate boxes, or use the current versions by checking the Use Current MS-DOS Configuration box.

TIP   This list of troubleshooting tips should help you get that recalcitrant DOS program to behave. But a word of warning: Never change more than one thing at a time!

If you try something and it doesn't work, return to the default settings and try the next one on the list. If you try to change too many things at once, you're likely to make the situation worse. And even if you do manage to improve the situation, you won't be able to tell which setting was the crucial one.

Placing an MS-DOS Prompt on the Desktop

As you've probably noticed by now, there's an MS-DOS Prompt listing on your Start ➢ Programs menu. Select it and you get a DOS window on your Desktop. You can use this window to run most DOS commands.

If you're the sort of person who frequently uses a DOS window, you can put a shortcut to the DOS prompt on your Desktop or in the Startup folder so it'll be ready and waiting on the Taskbar each time you start the computer. To make a shortcut to the DOS prompt window, follow these steps:

1. Right-click the Start button and select Open.

2. Double-click the Programs folder.

3. Scroll down until you see the MS-DOS icon (see Figure 9.9).

4. Right-click the icon and either select Create Shortcut to make a shortcut on the spot or drag and drop to another location and select Create Shortcut(s) Here when you get there.

Using DOS Commands

The DOS commands that come with Windows 95 are fairly few in number compared to DOS 6.22 or earlier. All the external DOS commands are in the Command folder inside your Windows folder.

Skill 9

FIGURE 9.9: Inside the Programs folder

Table 9.1 lists the commands and a brief description of what each one does.

TABLE 9.1: DOS Commands Available in Windows 95

Command Name	What It Does
attrib.exe	Displays or changes file attributes
chkdsk.exe	Reports on disk status and any errors found. Has been superseded by scandisk.exe
choice.com	Allows for user input in a batch file
debug.exe	Hexadecimal editor and viewer
diskcopy.com	Makes a full copy of a diskette. Same function available in Windows Explorer
doskey.com	Beloved of all DOS-geeks, edits command lines, makes macros
edit.com	New version of older file editor
extract.exe	Extracts files from a cabinet (.CAB) file

TABLE 9.1 (CONTINUED): DOS Commands Available in Windows 95

Command Name	What It Does
fc.exe	File compare
fdisk.exe	Makes and removes hard drive partitions
find.exe	Locates text in a file
format.com	Formats disks
label.exe	Adds, removes, or changes a disk label
mem.exe	Displays total memory, amount in use, and amount available
mode.com	Configures system devices
more.com	Displays output one screen at a time
move.exe	Moves one or more files
scandisk.exe	Checks a disk for errors and makes corrections
share.exe	Sets file locking. No longer needed in a DOS window, but can be used in MS-DOS mode
sort.exe	Sorts input
start.exe	Runs a program
subst.exe	Associates a drive letter with a particular path
sys.com	Copies system files to a disk, making the disk bootable
xcopy.exe	Copies whole directories including subdirectories
xcopy32.exe	A juiced-up version of xcopy with more functions plus the ability to copy long file names

There's not a whole lot of help available in Windows 95 for DOS commands, but you can get basic information if you go to a DOS prompt, type in the name of the command followed by / ?, and then press Enter.

Skill 9

Are You Experienced?

Now you can...

☑ **read and configure DOS properties sheets**

☑ **troubleshoot troublesome DOS programs**

☑ **put a DOS prompt on your Desktop**

S K I L L

10

Introducing the Applets

❑ Communicating with HyperTerminal

❑ Using the Phone Dialer

❑ Editing text with WordPad and Notepad

❑ Understanding the Clipboard

❑ Using the Character Map

❑ Calculating sums

❑ Packing the Briefcase

❑ Painting a picture

From the beginning, graphical operating systems have come with a comple-
ment of smallish programs such as calculators and text editors. Because of their
usually limited capabilities, these programs are called *applets* rather than applications. But for the most part, these programs are just as big as they need to be, so
they actually *are* full applications. But the name applet has stuck and generally
applies to programs that come as extras with an operating system.

In this chapter we'll discuss all the applets that aren't covered elsewhere. The
basic use of many of these programs is very simple, so we'll try to touch on some
of the not-so-obvious functions (when they exist).

Communicating with HyperTerminal

HyperTerminal provides the same functions as the Windows 3.1 applet called
Terminal. Along with your modem, you use it to connect with other computers,
bulletin boards, and online services. The difference HyperTerminal offers, when
compared to Terminal, is that it automates most of the process. It's still a very
stripped-down product compared to the stand-alone packages for modem connections, so if your needs go beyond an occasional connection to a bulletin board or
an infrequent FTP transfer, you'll probably want something with more functions.

Where to Find It

Here's how to find HyperTerminal:

1. Click the Start button on the Taskbar.

2. From the menu that appears, select Programs and then Accessories.

3. On the Accessories menu, select HyperTerminal. You'll see the
    HyperTerminal program group.

4. Double-click the HyperTerminal icon (marked Hypertrm). You will see
    something like the screen shown in Figure 10.1.

How to Use It

When you use HyperTerminal, each connection you make can be named and
provided with an icon that allows you to quickly identify connections so you can
make them again and again.

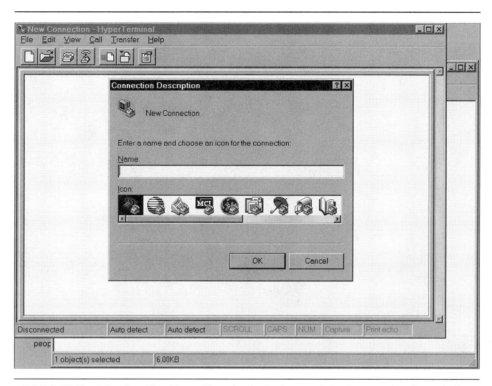

FIGURE 10.1: The HyperTerminal window and the Connection Description box are the starting points.

Let's create a fictional connection that will allow us to fill out the dialog box. Imagine you're a foreign correspondent working for a newspaper called the *Past Times*, and you need to log on to the paper's BBS to file your stories:

1. Type **Past Times** in the Name text box.

2. Scroll through the icons until you locate an icon that resembles a briefcase and umbrella—what better icon for a reporter?

3. Click the OK button. You'll see the Phone Number dialog box shown in Figure 10.2.

4. If the number you want to dial is located in a country other than the one listed in the Country Code list, click the downward-pointing arrow at the right end of the list box and select the correct country.

Skill 10

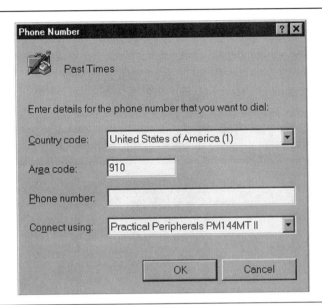

FIGURE 10.2: The Phone Number dialog box asks for information on where you want to dial.

5.   Enter the area code and phone number of the BBS in the appropriate text boxes and click OK.

6.   The Connect dialog box opens, but since this is the first time we've run this application, click the Dialing Properties button to check your settings. Look over the options in this dialog box and make sure that they're correctly set (see Figure 10.3).

7.   If you click the check box next to Dial Using Calling Card, a dialog box will open for you to enter your telephone credit card number.

8.   If you have to dial a number to get out of your business or hotel phone system (typically 9 or 7), enter this number in the text box next to the text that reads "To Access an Outside Line, First Dial" and enter the number (or numbers) you dial for long-distance access in the text box next to it.

9.   If you are dialing a number in the same area code but it's still necessary to dial an area code, check the box next to Dial as a Long-Distance Call.

10.   When you are through filling out this dialog box, click OK. You will see the dialog box shown in Figure 10.4.

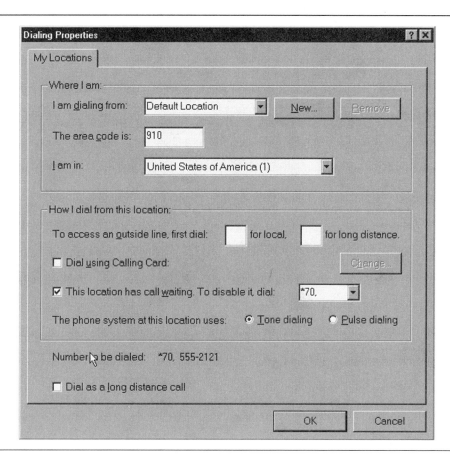

FIGURE 10.3: Check your dialing options.

 NOTE   If you're dialing a number that has a different area code, the Dial as a Long-Distance Call box will be grayed out.

11.   At this point, all you need to do is click Dial to make the connection. If all the settings you made in the previous dialog boxes are correct, the call will go through and you can use the BBS software to upload your story to the newspaper. We'll cover file transfers in a moment.

12. When you're through placing your call, pull down the Call menu and select Disconnect or click the icon that looks like a handset being hung up, and the connection will be broken.

13. When you close the window, you will be prompted to save the session.

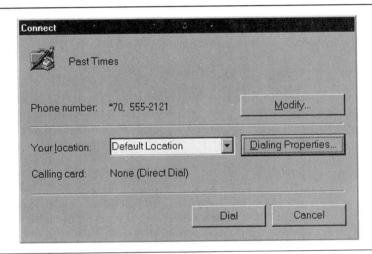

FIGURE 10.4: Click Dial to make your connection.

Sending Files

Once you have connected with a remote computer, you will probably want to upload or download files, which is the principal reason for making this sort of connection. The file-transfer protocols supported by HyperTerminal are:

- 1K Xmodem
- Xmodem
- Ymodem
- Ymodem-G
- Zmodem
- Kermit

Binary Files

To send a binary file, follow these steps:

1. After the connection is made, pull down the Transfer menu.

2. Select Send File. A dialog box will open.

3. Using the options in this dialog box (see Figure 10.5), specify the file to send. (Click the Browse button to locate and identify the file to be sent.)

4. Select the protocol for file transfer. Zmodem is the best choice because it combines speed and good error correction.

5. Click the Send button. The file will be transferred.

FIGURE 10.5: Here's where you select a file and the protocol to send it.

 TIP   Make sure the receiving computer can receive files in the protocol you choose. Zmodem and Xmodem are almost universal, but if you have a problem, this is one of the areas you should check.

Text Files

Text files are a little different from binary files. Most file-transfer software distinguishes between binary files and text files—sending one in Binary mode and the other in ASCII mode or Text mode. HyperTerminal is no different.

To send a text file, follow the steps for a binary file except choose Send Text from the Transfer menu. When you specify the file to send and click the Open button, the file will be sent as if you had typed it into the terminal program.

TIP Unless you're transferring files to a UNIX system, you're usually better off sending every file as a binary file. Even a little bit of formatting in the file can cause a text-file transfer to fail, while *any* file can be sent as a binary transfer.

And Receiving Them Too

To receive a file being sent from another computer, follow these steps:

1. Pull down the Transfer menu and select Receive File. That will open a dialog box that looks like the Send dialog box shown in Figure 10.5.

2. Click the Browse button to specify a file name and location for the received file.

3. Select a file-transfer protocol.

4. Click the Receive button to start receiving the file from the remote location.

NOTE Begin the previous steps when you hear the incoming call from the other computer. You have to do this yourself, because HyperTerminal is not smart enough to answer the phone.

Saving a Session

To help you remember how to navigate the complexities of a service you don't use very often, terminal programs provide *logging*—a way to save everything you do in a particular session to disk and/or print it on paper.

To save everything to disk:

1. Pull down the Transfer menu and select Capture Text.

2. By default, all the screen information in a session will be saved in a file called CAPTURE.TXT in the HyperTerminal folder inside the Accessories folder. Of course, you can use the Browse button to save the file in a different location. Click Start when you're ready.

3. Pull down the Transfer menu again. Now you will note that there is a tiny triangle next to the Capture Text option. Select it, and you will see a submenu with Stop, Pause, and Resume options to give you control over the capture.

4. If you prefer to send the session to the printer rather than to a file on your disk, pull down the Transfer menu and select Capture to Printer.

Using a Connection

As you recall, when we started using HyperTerminal, we created a connection with a name and an icon. This connection appears in the HyperTerminal program group. Any time you want to use this connection in the future, simply double-click its icon, and all the settings (telephone number and so forth) will be in place for you.

Any time you want to change the settings in a particular connection, open the connection, pull down the File menu, and select Properties.

Getting Your Phone Dialed

Do you frequently have to make a lot of telephone calls? Has your button-pressing finger ever felt as if it were going to fall off? If you have Windows 95 (and if you don't, why are you reading this?), you can turn over the grief of dialing to its capable, if virtual, hands. Phone Dialer is a handy little program that doesn't do a lot, but if you need it, it's terrific to have.

 NOTE   Essentially, Windows uses your installed modem to dial your telephone. In order for this scheme to work, you need to have a telephone on the same line you're using for your modem. If you have a separate phone line for data, you'll need an actual telephone on that line to use Phone Dialer.

Here's how to access Phone Dialer:

1. Click the Start button at the left end of the Taskbar.

2. Select Programs from the resulting menu.

3. Select Accessories from the Program menu and click Phone Dialer. You'll see the window shown in Figure 10.6.

Skill 10

FIGURE 10.6: Use Phone Dialer to prevent digit woe.

The Phone Dialer gives you two simple ways to make phone calls using your computer:

Speed Dialing   If you have a number you need in an emergency or one you call constantly, you can enter it in the Speed Dial list.

The Telephone Log   If you have a long list of numbers you call periodically, you can simply type those numbers into the Number to Dial text box and they will be added to a telephone log. You can access your log by clicking the downward-pointing arrow at the right end of the Number to Dial box.

Speed Dialing

To create a speed dial number, pull down the Edit menu and select Speed Dial. You will see the dialog box shown in Figure 10.7.

Here's how to set it up:

1.   Click the speed dial button you want to assign.

2.   In the Name text box, type the name of the person or place that you will dial with that button.

3.   Type the number to dial in the Number to Dial text box.

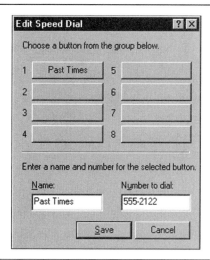

FIGURE 10.7: Speed Dial puts you on the telephone fast track.

4. Click Save. (You'll be returned to the Phone Dialer dialog box and the name you entered in the Edit Speed Dial dialog box will appear on the speed dial button you selected.)

5. To speed dial the number, just click the button and lift your telephone handset.

Using the Telephone Log

As mentioned at the top of this section, you can use the Phone Dialer in two ways. The quick and easy way is to use the speed dialer, but as you'll have noted, the speed dialer is limited to eight numbers. If you have more than eight numbers that you call on a regular basis, you'll have to use your log. Here's how:

1. Either type the number in the Number to Dial box or use the telephone keypad to punch in the number.

2. When the number's completely entered, click the Dial button and pick up your telephone. In a moment, you will be connected with the voice mail system at the number you are calling. (No one ever talks to real people anymore.)

3. To call the number again, pull down the Tools menu and select Show Log. This displays a list of all the numbers you have called.

4. To redial one of these numbers, double-click its entry in the log.

You can see how the Phone Dialer can be a terrific convenience if you spend a lot of time making calls.

Working with WordPad

WordPad is the successor to the Write program in Windows 3.1, and how you felt about Write may determine how you feel about WordPad. WordPad is an odd duck. It's more elaborate than Notepad but still falls way short of being a real word processing program. WordPad will read Write and Word for Windows 6 documents as well as Text and Rich Text formats.

To open WordPad, click the Start button and follow the cascading menus from Programs to Accessories. At the bottom of the Accessories menu you'll find WordPad.

 TIP   WordPad can be uninstalled using the Add/Remove Programs function in the Control Panel. However, if you use Microsoft Fax you'll need WordPad because it's the fax operation's text editor. If you use a different fax program such as WinFax or you don't fax from your computer at all, you can remove WordPad without worry.

Opening It Up

When you open WordPad (see Figure 10.8), it looks like most other editors and on the menus you'll find the usual things one associates with text editors. Pull down the menus to see the various options.

WordPad is different because it's completely integrated into Windows 95. You can write messages in color and post them to the Microsoft Network or send them via Windows Messaging, and recipients see your messages just as you wrote them—fonts, colors, embedded objects, and all. WordPad also has the distinct advantage of being able to load really big files.

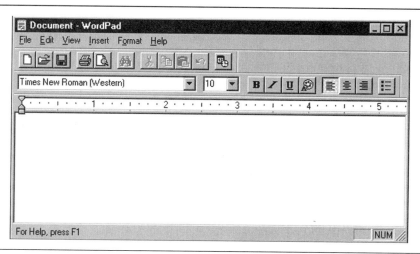

FIGURE 10.8: The opening screen for WordPad

 TIP   WordPad isn't a substitute for a full-featured word processing program like WordPerfect or Word for Windows. However, it may do quite well for you depending on your needs. Try it out and see.

Making and Formatting Documents

You can always click a document and drag it into WordPad. Documents made by Microsoft Word (.DOC) and Windows Write (.WRI), as well as text (.TXT) and Rich Text format (.RTF) documents, are all instantly recognized by WordPad. You can also just start typing.

Formatting Tools

The toolbar (Figure 10.9) and format bar (Figure 10.10) are displayed by default. You can turn either of them off by deselecting it from the list under the View menu.

Tabs are set using the ruler. Click the ruler at the spot where you want a tab. To remove a tab, just click it and drag it off the ruler.

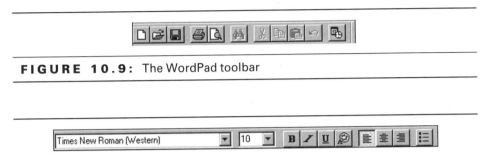

FIGURE 10.9: The WordPad toolbar

FIGURE 10.10: The WordPad format bar for manipulating text

Other Options

Other formatting tools are under Options on the View menu. This is where you can set measurement units as well as word wrap and toolbars for each of the different file types that WordPad recognizes.

Page Setup and Printing

The File menu has the usual Print command, but there's also a Page Setup item that you can use to set margins as well as paper size and orientation. Unlike its predecessor, WordPad can print envelopes as well as varying sizes of paper.

It may take some fooling around to get envelopes lined up correctly, but fortunately there's a Print Preview choice (also on the File menu). There you can see how the envelope or paper is lining up with your text. Adjust the margin in the Page Setup dialog box until you get it the way you want.

 TIP   To change printers, select Page Setup from the File menu. Click the Printer button and you can select any printer currently available to you.

Using Notepad

Notepad is a simple text editor with very few charms except speed. Double-click any text file and it will immediately load into Notepad (unless, of course, it's bigger than 64K, in which case you'll be asked if you want to load it into WordPad instead).

What It's Got

Notepad has the bare minimum of tools on its menus. You can:

- Search for characters or words
- Use Page Setup to set margins, paper orientation, customize the header and footer, and select a printer
- Copy, cut, and paste text
- Insert the time and date into a document

 NOTE   For some unfathomable reason, word wrap is not on by default in Notepad. You have to select it from the Edit menu. If you don't, the text you type in stays on one line forever and ever.

Learning What Clipboard Viewer Does

The Clipboard Viewer is not much different than the one shipped with Windows 3.1. When you copy or cut something, Windows needs to have a place to store it until you decide what to do with it. This storage place is called the Clipboard.

Sometimes you want to see what's on the Clipboard and maybe save its contents. Clipboard Viewer makes it possible for you to do this.

Taking a Look

To see the Viewer, click the Start button, and then select Programs ➢ Accessories ➢ Clipboard Viewer. You'll see a window like the one shown in Figure 10.11.

 NOTE   Immediately before snapping the screen shot of the Clipboard Viewer, we selected and copied the text you see in the figure. You can also press Alt+PrintScreen (which captures the active window to the Clipboard) or PrintScreen (which—on some computers—captures the entire screen to the Clipboard).

Skill 10

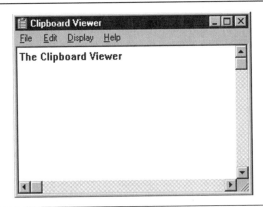

FIGURE 10.11: Clipboard Viewer

Saving the Clipboard's Contents

To save the current contents of the Clipboard, pull down the File menu and select Save. You can save files under a proprietary format identified by the .CLP extension. These files are (as far as I've been able to tell) only used by the Windows Clipboard Viewer.

Once you've saved the contents, you can use the Clipboard to copy and paste other material, and later, you can reload what you saved by pulling down the File menu and selecting Open. Pull down the Display menu and you'll be able to see all your options for viewing the data on the Clipboard.

Making the Most of Character Map

The fonts that show up in your word processor are very nice, but they often don't go beyond the characters found on your keyboard. What about when you need a copyright sign (©) or an "e" with an umlaut (ë)? With the Character Map you have access to all kinds of symbols including Greek letters and other special signs.

To start the Character Map, click the Start button in the Taskbar at the bottom of your Windows 95 screen. Select Programs ➢ Accessories ➢ Character Map to see the window in Figure 10.12.

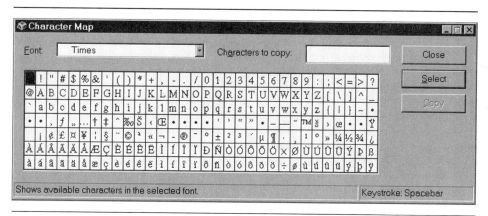

FIGURE 10.12: Unusual characters are available in the Character Map.

STORING AND REUSING DATA WITH THE CLIPBOOK

When you copy or cut something to the Clipboard, you lose the last thing that was there. The good news is that Windows 95 also has a ClipBook where you can save your clippings and reuse them. To install it, insert the Windows 95 CD-ROM in the drive and in the resulting window select Add/Remove Software.

Go to the Windows Setup tab, click Have Disk, click Browse, and find your way to *d*:\Other\Clipbook (where *d* is your CD-ROM drive letter). When you have the clipbook.inf file in the file name box, click OK twice.

Check ClipBook Viewer, then click Install. Clipbook will be added to the Start ➤ Programs ➤ Accessories menu.

Skill 10

Entering Characters

Select the font you want to use by clicking the downward-pointing arrow at the right end of the Font list box. To enter a character, double-click it in the window.

It will appear in the text box at the top right of the window. Continue double-clicking until you have the entire string of characters you want in the text box. When you have all the characters you want in the text box, click the Copy button halfway down the right side of the window. Then return to your application using the Taskbar or by pressing Alt+Tab until your application is selected.

Position the cursor on the spot where you want to place the character and select Paste from the Edit menu or just press Ctrl+V.

Using the Calculators

You actually have two calculators in Windows 95: a standard calculator, the likes of which you could buy for $2.95 at any drugstore counter, and a scientific calculator.

Just the Basics

To start the standard calculator, click the Start button in the Taskbar, and then select Programs ➤ Accessories ➤ Calculator to display the calculator shown in Figure 10.13.

Using the mouse, click the numbers and functions just as if you were pressing the keys on a hand-held calculator. Or if you have a numerical keypad on your keyboard, press NumLock and you can use the keypad keys to enter numbers and basic math functions.

FIGURE 10.13: The standard calculator is as basic as it gets.

Or One Step Beyond

To access the scientific calculator, pull down the View menu on the Calculator and select Scientific. This displays the item in Figure 10.14.

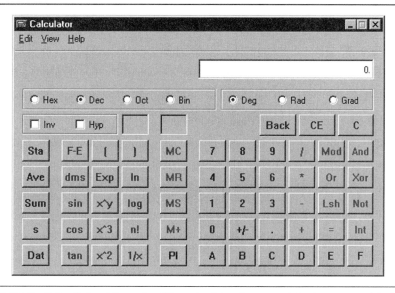

FIGURE 10.14: The scientific calculator is a good deal more sophisticated than the standard one.

 TIP   If you're not sure of the use for a function, right-click its button. You'll see a rectangle containing the words "What's This?" Click the text to see a short explanation of the function.

Getting Statistical

As a sample of what the scientific calculator can do, let's enter a list of data for deriving statistical results:

1.   Enter the first value in the series.

2.   Click the Sta button.

3. Click the Dat button.

4. Enter the second value in the series.

5. Click Dat.

6. Repeat steps 4 and 5 until you have entered the last value in the series.

7. Click Sta.

8. Click the function key that corresponds to the statistical command you want to enter.

Pasting in the Numbers

Both calculators can be used in conjunction with the Clipboard. Type a number in any application, and select it by dragging through it. Press Ctrl+C (for Copy). Press Alt+Tab until the calculator is selected (or click it in the Taskbar) and press Ctrl+V (for Paste). The number will appear in the number display of the calculator as if you had entered it from the calculator keypad.

Work your magic: adding, subtracting, multiplying, or deriving the inverse sine. You can pull down the Edit menu and select Copy, which places the contents of the display on the Clipboard—ready for you to paste into your document.

Packing a Briefcase

The Briefcase is not an applet in the usual sense. You won't find it listed under Accessories, for one thing. But you can always right-click the Desktop and select New ➤ Briefcase to create a new instance. Or a Briefcase may be on your Desktop from the original installation of Windows 95.

Briefcase is designed to help those with multiple computers keep a set of files synchronized. It may be your computer at work and your computer at home. Or maybe you have a desktop computer and a laptop where you work on the same files. When two computers are involved it's only a matter of time before things get confused as to which version of a memo or a speech is the *most current* version.

How It Works

When you open a Briefcase and copy a file into it, a link is made between the original and the copy in the Briefcase. This is called a *sync link*. After the link is made, you can work on the copy in the Briefcase or the original file and select Update (from inside Briefcase), and the latest version will be copied over the earlier version, keeping both in sync.

To move to the other computer, you copy the Briefcase to a floppy disk. At computer #2, open the Briefcase on the floppy. Copy the files from the Briefcase on the floppy (*not* the Briefcase itself) to the Desktop or another folder on computer #2. Work on the files and update the Briefcase when you're done. When you go back to computer #1, you can use the Briefcase on the floppy to update the files on computer #1.

Basic Steps

Here's how to make use of Briefcase:

1. Open the Briefcase on the Desktop of computer #1. (Rename it if you want.)

2. Copy the files to the Briefcase. Then copy the Briefcase to a floppy disk.

3. Take the floppy to computer #2. Open drive A: either in the Explorer or My Computer.

4. Open the Briefcase. Work on the files inside the Briefcase on computer #2.

5. When you're finished, save and close the files in the usual way.

6. Return the floppy to computer #1. Open the Briefcase on the floppy disk and select Update All from the Briefcase menu. This will open a window like the one in Figure 10.15.

7. Click the Update button.

What's Wrong About Briefcase

Briefcase has many weaknesses, as if it's just a test for a better version further down the road. Could be. Anyway, at this time, Briefcase has weaknesses along these lines:

- A Briefcase cannot be bigger than the size of the floppy disk you're copying to and since you have to use copies and not shortcuts, the floppy fills up real fast.

- The floppy can be synchronized with the files on only one computer, not both. That's why you have to work *inside* the Briefcase on the floppy drive of computer #2.

Skill 10

- Synchronization is not automatic. You must choose Update from the Briefcase menu.

- Briefcase is *not* easy to use. After a lot of practice, I still have problems getting it to work the first time.

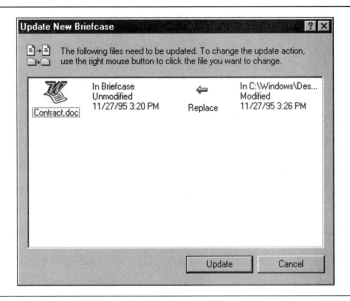

FIGURE 10.15: Briefcase finds differences between the Briefcase file and the original file on the hard disk.

Painting a Picture

As a drawing and painting program, Paint has its limitations, but it's nevertheless much improved over Paintbrush, included with Windows 3.1. To find Paint, look under the Accessories menu. It's not installed by default, so if you don't see it, use the Add/Remove Programs function in the Control Panel. (It's under Accessories on the Windows Setup page.)

What's New in Paint

If you've used the paint program in Windows 3.1, there are some improvements in this version:

> **Zooming**   Much better zooming capability, from 100 percent up to 800 percent.
>
> **Opaque As Well As Transparent Drawing**   With opaque drawing, your additions cover the existing picture; transparent drawing lets the existing object show through your additions.
>
> **More Options for Manipulation**   The new paint program has more choices for stretching, skewing, flipping, and rotating the object being drawn.

Committing Original Art

Open Paint and, using the tools down the left side of the window, make a drawing and/or painting. When you're done, you can:

- Select File ➤ Save and give the picture a name. You can save it as one of several different kinds of bitmaps (see the Save As Type list).

- Select File ➤ Send, which will open Exchange and let you select an e-mail recipient worthy of receiving your work.

- Select File ➤ Save As Wallpaper. This will let you tile or center your work of art as the wallpaper on your screen.

Modifying the Work of Others

Any file with the extension .BMP or .PCX or .DIB can be opened in Paint. Use the tools to make any modifications you want and then do any of the things listed in the section above.

Modified files are all saved as bitmaps (.BMP).

TIP   For a really good painting program at a very reasonable price, check out the excellent Paint Shop Pro. You can download a shareware version or buy the full version at the Web site: `http://www.jasc.com/psp4.html` or you can call Jasc at 612-930-9171.

Skill 10

Are You Experienced?

Now you can...

- ☑ use HyperTerminal and Phone Dialer
- ☑ create documents with WordPad and Notepad
- ☑ use the Clipboard Viewer
- ☑ find unusual characters and symbols with Character Map
- ☑ handle the calculators
- ☑ keep files synchronized with Briefcase
- ☑ manipulate graphics with Paint

and experience in direct-marketing based telefundraising. Minimum of 7 years experience in similar field. 4 year degree preferred. Proficient computer skills incl. Windows-based software applications required. Salary commensurate w/skills & exp. plus benefits. Send letter and resume to Well-Being Clinic, 543 Spring Ave., Daytonville, VA.

Executive Secretary
OfficePlus, an office supply & furniture company is looking for administrative support to VP. Requires 5 years min. of secretarial experience. proficiency with MS Word and Excel and excellent communication skills. Must be willing to learn database and desktop software. Fax: OfficePlus, Personnel 665-555-9122.

FACILITIES PLANNER Training Centers Inc. seeks individual to study & develop infrastructure requirements and capital improvement projects. Req's BA in Planning, Engineering, Architecture or rel. field w/ 7 years exp & knowl of Windows (Word, Excel) & graphics programs. 4 yrs' exp w PC's planning arch/eng or facilities mgmt & exp w/CAD. database mgmt & project scheduling pref'd. Fax: HR, 885-555-2398.

MANAGEMENT REPORTING ANALYST
Join the team that maintains the purchasing and logistics information systems that support order entry, provide product and contract information, track product utilization, and manage operating budget and inventory systems. Must be proficient in a high-level database system and Excel, Lotus 1-2-3, or similar applications. Fax resume to Data Systems Placement Services
444-555-9998.

MANAGER, ASSET MODELING
This worldwide logistics company is expanding it's transportation network. The successful candidate will have a Bachelor's degree in Economics, Finance or Business Mgmt, with a MBA degree preferred, a solid foundation in Mathematics, and excellent analytical skills. Knowledge of PC applications in Excel, Word, PowerPoint & Visio essential. Competitive benefits and compensation plan. Fax 966-555-2298/

Manager, Business Analysis
You will direct a team of Business Analysts and oversee timely completion of all projects in accordance with departmental policies & procedures. Requires BA/BS in Behavioral Health Sciences, Business Administration, MIS, or equivalent experience, system development/ analysis and software testing: strong project management and team building skills, and software development experience. Hart Corporate Services. Call J. Thornton 243-555-9583.

MARKET RESEARCH PROJECT MANAGER
SuperMouse Designs is creating a new research division. You will provide research consulting services to internal clients and manage external research providers. A BA/BS degree or equivalent with 4-5 years' experi-

have strong Word & Excel skills. Pls send cover letter, resume & salary req's to: Sommes Communications. Attn: HR/Job 85, 776 Bowser Lane, Bowtown, MA

MARKETING ASSISTANT
Supporting 2 Marketing Mgrs. you'll handle a variety of admin. responsibilities, direct mail coordination, desktop publishing, and ad space coordination. Require 1-2 years admin exper. and strong computer skills, esp. desktop pub., HTML, Office & Windows. Fax: R. Smith 365-555-8844.

OFFICE MANAGER
Join a growing firm that offers competitive salaries & benefits for a take-charge type. Responsible for all office purchases & operations, including a quarterly newsletter. Windows & MS Office experience req'd. Call 973-555-4545.

PC Support Specialist
High-end catalog company and specialty retailer has opening in MIS Dept. Support corporate associates with PC and network systems. Extensive PC hardware installation and configuration experience is required. Must be able to communicate effectively, and determine cause of problems, & develop solutions. Requires network admin. & multiple PC operating systems experience. (Windows, UNIX) Fax resume & salary reqs to High Profile Images 388-555-9634.

PROJECT ASST. Serve as a point person in HR office of fast growing biotech firm. Requires creative thinking and up-to-date office computer skills, esp. Word, PowerPoint & Excel. Fax resume to TruPoint Systems 689-555-1298.

PROJECT MANAGER
Public agency seeking environmental project manager to oversee 18-month marsh preservation project. Develop, analyze, organize & summarize planning data and financial info. Windows computer skills essential. Send resume to Public Planning Services, Attn: HR, 34 Marsh Lane, Willowdale, CA.

Sales/Computer
Expanding computer software & hardware store is looking for more qualified sales associates to staff our busy downtown location. Windows software experience required. Send resume and salary/commission requirements to General Manager, Computers For You, 433 Main St., Ontario, MN.

SALES SENIOR ASSOCIATE Work with customer service, account managers, marketing & brand management. You will handle distribution of sales materials and internal correspondence. You will need 1-2 years in sales admin. and basic office functions (mail, fax, phones etc.) plus PC skills. Computer troubleshooting skills a plus.

Sales: Sr. Account Coordinator
Looking Good, a national clothing chain is looking for seasoned sales pros to oversee sales operations. Qualified candidates must have 4-5 years sales mgmt exp. and strong

pros to oversee sales operations. Qualified candidates must have 4-5 years sales mgmt exp. and strong PC skills. A college degree, working knowledge of Excel, PowerPoint, Word and database software req'd. Fax resume and cover letter to: Looking Good, Attn: K. Ferkovich, 877 Goody Ave., Reno, NV.

SALES/COMPUTER
Expanding computer software & hardware store is looking for more qualified sales associates to staff our busy downtown location. Windows software experience required. Send resume and salary/commission requirements to General Manager, Computers For You, 433 Main St., Ontario, MN.

SALES SUPPORT ASSOCIATE
Work with customer service, account managers, marketing & brand management. You will handle distribution of sales materials and internal correspondence. You will need 1-2 years in sales admin. and basic office functions (mail, fax, ph)

Senior Calendar Clerk
Large international law firm is seeking qualified candidates with strong organizational and data entry skills, and extremely high level of service orientation and excellent oral and written communication skills. Applicants must possess a BA/BS degree, have knowledge of computer databases and Word or WordPerfect. Send resume and salary requirements to HR, Jackson Madison Madison Teller & Pewter, 1001 Main Street, Atlanta, GA

Sr. FINANCIAL ANALYST
JJO Enterprises seeking senior member of financial team. Requires a degree in Finance/Econ/ Acctg. minimum 3 yrs' public acct. exp. (CPA), Lotus/Excel, MS Word/WordPerfect proficiency. P&L/cashflow statement exp is preferred. Competitive salary/ benefits pkg. Fax: Mr. Rogers. JJO Enterprises 442-555-1267.

SENIOR LAW CLERK
Large international law firm is seeking qualified candidates with strong organizational and data entry skills, and extremely high level of service orientation and excellent oral and written communication skills. Applicants must possess a BA/BS degree, have knowledge of computer databases and Word or WordPerfect. Send resume and salary requirements to HR, Jackson Madison Madison Teller & Pewter, 1001 Main Street, Atlanta, GA

SENIOR SECRETARY
Bolan Lumber Co. looking for add'l office support staff. Type 60 wpm. Word/Excel/ Windows and some desktop publishing experience. Call Ron 336-555-9944.

TECHNICAL COMMUNICATOR
Biotech Systems is expanding and is seeking someone to develop & maintain user documentation/training materials and on-line help systems. Requires a BA/BS in Technical Communication or equiva-

support for our Corporate Planning Group. Req. a BA/BS with 4 years experience in financial analysis or system implementation or development. Attention to detail & time and resource mgmt. abilities are vital. Excel and PowerPoint req'd. Contact Financial Resources Executive Search at 443-555-2398.

Clerical Receptionist F/T position available in a fast-paced HR dept. You must be a self-starter, organized, and dependable. Excellent customer-service, written and verbal communication skills required. Computer experience a must. Norwell Medical Center, 100 Front St. Allentown, MO

Computer Operator/PC Technician
Large software retailer looking for someone with expert computer skills to assist in tech dept. as well as to give seminars for customers looking to upgrade. Successful candidate must have 3-5 years' technical experience and 2-3 years in customer service. Teaching experience a plus. Fax resume to Best Systems: 545-555-6677.

COMPUTERS
Immediate openings! Computer technicians with PC hardware and Windows experience. Send resume to: Delta Plus, 1200 Sutter St., San Francisco, CA.

Corporate Human Resources Mgr
Specialized background in Employment or Compensation & Benefits, and general knowledge of all other HR functions. PC skills essential. Fax resume to 334-555-9112.

Editorial Researcher Business publication seeking researcher responsible for weekly business lists, etc. Computer/Internet skills required. Must be fast, accurate & thorough. Salary DOE. Write: Researcher, 9106 Shasta Blvd. Pittsburgh, PA.

Editor/Reporter
National financial journal seeks experienced writer to cover the brokerage/financial services industry. Must have strong writing/editing skills and background in business reporting. Computer/word processor experience a must. Fax resume and clips to JIT 887-555-2256.

Engineering
Senior Industrial Engineer needed for large wholesale buyers club, to help reduce operating costs and increase revenues. A BS degree and at least 6 years in the distribution/transportation field are required. Strong business writing skills, PC proficiency using Microsoft Office and electronic communications is essential. Send cover letter and resume to HR/Job 445, AB Industries, 4498 Howard Blvd, Kansas City, MO

Executive Assistant
You'll need strong organizational, interpersonal, and analytical skills, coupled with good computer knowledge in applications such as Access, PowerPoint, Excel and Word. Send resume & salary history

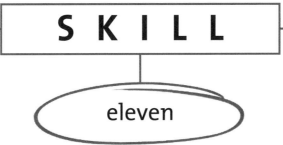

Using the Control Panel Tools

- ❏ Setting up accessibility options

- ❏ Adding and removing programs

- ❏ Adding and removing Windows 95 components

- ❏ Setting the date and time

- ❏ Installing and removing fonts

- ❏ Configuring keyboards and joysticks

- ❏ Using passwords

- ❏ Learning about system settings

If you've fooled around with the Control Panel at all, you can see that it acts as a sort of Mission Control for Windows 95. Some of the settings can be reached from other directions, but many can be reached only by way of the Control Panel. The tools in the Control Panel help you customize your Windows 95 even further. And if you share your computer with other people, the "Passwords" section will demonstrate how each user can have a unique Desktop.

You'll find a heading in this skill for the usual icons in the Control Panel (listed alphabetically). In some cases the settings behind a particular icon are complex and need more detail that a subsection can handle. In those cases, you'll be pointed to the correct skill.

NOTE   The Plus! for Windows 95 applications and many other programs put their own icons in the Control Panel. Consult the documentation that came with the programs for information on how to use these icons.

Accessibility Options

Accessibility
Options

The Accessibility Options are installed automatically when you install Windows 95. If you want them and they're not on your system, use Add/Remove Programs to add them. Double-click this icon and you'll find options for adding sound to the usual visual cues, adding visual cues to the sound signals, and making the keyboard and mouse easier to use for the millions of us with dexterity problems. Not all the settings are obvious, so when you come across one that's unclear, right-click the text and then click the What's This? button for more information.

After you've made your settings, don't leave until you click the General tab and check the Automatic Reset section. Put a check next to Turn Off Accessibility Features After Idle For if you want the options to be turned off if the computer isn't used for the period specified in the Minutes box. Clear the check box if you want to make the selection of options permanent.

TIP   The Toggle Keys option on the Keyboard page is of great help, especially if you often hit the Caps Lock key inadvertently and look up to find your text looking like: cALL lErOY jAMES IN cAPE vERDE. With Toggle Keys on, you'll hear a quiet but distinct warning beep when Caps Lock is switched on.

Add New Hardware

Add New
Hardware

The settings for this icon are covered in detail in Skill 13, "Adding Hardware."

Add/Remove Programs

Add/Remove
Programs

Windows 95 provides a good deal of aid and comfort when it comes to adding or removing programs from your system, especially adding and removing parts of Windows 95 itself. Click this icon in the Control Panel.

The Add/Remove function has three parts, one on each tab:

- Installing or uninstalling software applications

- Installing or removing portions of Windows 95

- Making a current Startup Disk to boot from if there's trouble

Install/Uninstall

A software producer who wants the license to put a Windows 95 logo on a product is required to make sure the program can uninstall itself. This proviso is intended to correct a problem in Windows 3.1. When using Windows 3.1, it was very difficult to completely get rid of some programs because their files could be spread all over the hard drive. The average person has no way of knowing whether a file called, let's say, FXSTL.DLL is disposable because it belonged to a long-gone program or whether deleting it will cause the system to fail.

Programs written for 3.1 (and most of us have some of those) don't have this uninstall capability. And a few programs that claim to have been written for Windows 95 can be uninstalled and still leave bits of themselves cluttering your hard disk. There are fortunately many fewer of these than there were two years ago.

How the major programs written for Windows 95 handle Add/Remove varies widely. Some will just uninstall themselves without a fuss; others give you the

Skill 11

option of removing all or just part of the program. You'll have to click the program and select Remove to see. *Nothing* will be uninstalled without your OK.

For now, this is an easy-to-use tool for installing new programs. Just put the program's first floppy disk in the drive (or if the program is on a compact disk, insert the CD in the proper drive) and click the Install/Uninstall tab. Click the Install button.

The program searches for an install routine first in drive A:, then drive B:, and finally in the CD drive. Figure 11.1 shows the result of one search. Click Finish to continue. After this, the install routine of the program being installed takes over.

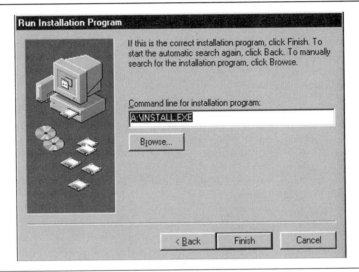

FIGURE 11.1: The Installation routine finds the Install or Setup file and proceeds to install the program.

Windows Setup

Click the Windows Setup tab to add or remove a component of Windows 95. The various parts are organized by groups (see Figure 11.2). You can highlight any group and click Details to see the individual components.

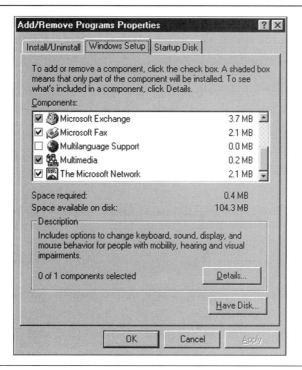

FIGURE 11.2: You can install or uninstall parts of Windows 95 from the Windows Setup tab.

As you click each item in a group, a description of the item's function displays at the bottom of the page. The rules are simple:

- If an item is checked, it's already installed. Don't remove the check mark unless you want it to be removed.

- If an item is not checked, it's not currently installed on your system. Put a check mark next to it, and it'll be installed.

- If the check box is gray, a part of the component is already installed. Click the Details button to specify which parts you want to add or remove.

Click OK once or twice until the window closes. If your Windows installation came on floppies, you'll be asked for one or more disks. If you installed from a CD, you'll have to return the Windows 95 CD to the CD drive.

TIP   To reinstall some part of Windows 95, you'll need to first uninstall it (remove the check mark before its name) and then click OK and close the Add/Remove Programs dialog box. After that step, you can reopen Add/Remove Programs and select the component to be installed.

Startup Disk

If your computer came with Windows 95 already installed, you probably don't have a startup disk. You may have made a startup disk if you installed Windows 95 yourself. Of course, you may have since lost the disk or made major changes to your system, in which case it's wise to make a new one. Simply click the Startup Disk tab and select Create Disk. You'll be prompted for a floppy and the new Startup disk will be made.

A current startup disk can be helpful (even invaluable) to a technician if one day your system fails to boot on its own. So it's best to make a new startup disk either monthly or whenever you make a major change in software or any change at all in hardware.

Date/Time

Date/Time

To reset the day and time shown on your computer, double-click this icon. The date and time function comes in handy when you're traveling and using a laptop. It works to change the time zone or to set the correct time on your computer's clock.

Without any outside help, Windows 95 will reset your clock for daylight saving time in the time zone you've selected. It even knows that Arizona and eastern Indiana don't use daylight time, but you have to be sure the operating system knows where *you* are. Use the drop-down box to select the correct time zone.

TIP   The Windows 95 sold in the box (as opposed to later versions that come pre-installed on computers) has a light bar on the Time Zone map. You can click this bar and drag it to your location on the map—that way you don't have to know the name of your time zone much less how many hours plus or minus it is from Greenwich Mean Time. This very cool feature was dropped apparently for international geopolitical reasons having to do with boundary disputes. Or something. Anyway, it's gone.

Other time and date information:

- Position the mouse pointer over the time display at the end of the Taskbar to see the current month, day, and year.

- For a shortcut to the Date/Time windows, right-click the time display on the Taskbar and select Adjust Date/Time.

- To remove the time from the Taskbar, click the Start button and select Settings ➤ Taskbar. Clear the check mark next to Show Clock.

Display

Behind the Display icon in the Control Panel are all the settings that affect your screen display including colors, screen savers, resolutions, and type faces in windows and dialog boxes. Skill 3, "Customizing the Desktop," covers the necessary information on these settings.

Fonts

TrueType fonts are managed in Windows 95 in a clear and understandable way. To see the list of fonts on your computer, click this icon in the Control Panel.

Selecting and Viewing Fonts

The Fonts folder is a little different from the usual run of folders in that the menus show some new items. In the View menu shown in Figure 11.3, you'll find, in addition to the choices for viewing icons and lists, an option called List Fonts by Similarity.

 TIP   If your font list is very long and unwieldy, select View ➤ Hide Variations. That will conceal font variations such as italic and bold and make the list easier to look through.

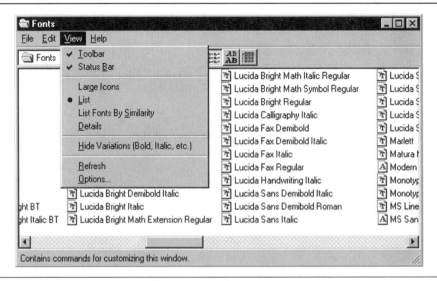

FIGURE 11.3: The Fonts folder has a different View menu.

Select a font in the drop-down box at the top and the other fonts will line up in terms of their degree of similarity (see Figure 11.4). Before you make a commitment, you can right-click any of the font names and select Open (or just double-click). A window will open with a complete view of the font in question.

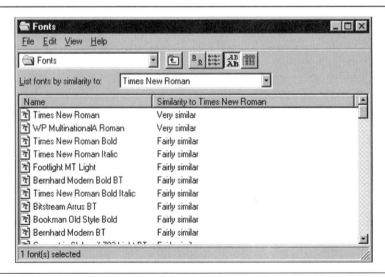

FIGURE 11.4: You can view fonts in terms of their similarities to one another.

TrueType fonts that you may have located elsewhere can be moved into this folder. Figure 11.5 shows a newly acquired font being dragged into the folder.

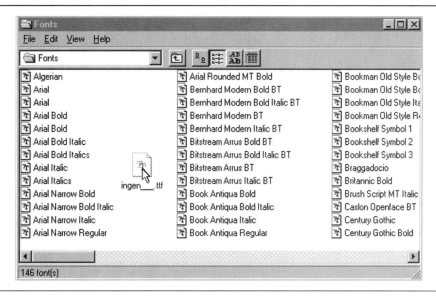

FIGURE 11.5: Move fonts into the Fonts folder just as you'd move any object—drag and drop or cut and paste

Fonts don't have to be physically located in the Windows/Fonts folder to be recognized by Windows 95. You can make a shortcut to a font in another folder and put the shortcut in the Fonts folder. The shortcut is all you need for the font to be installed. Fonts that are identified with an icon like the one shown here are not TrueType fonts.

They're not scaleable, which means that at large point sizes they tend to look quite crummy (see Figure 11.6). Many of these fonts can be used only in certain, limited point sizes.

Installing New Fonts

Installing new fonts is a pretty easy project. Just open the Fonts icon in the Control Panel and select Install New Font from the File menu. In the Add Fonts window (Figure 11.7) you can tell the system the drive and directory where the font(s) reside. If there's one or more TrueType fonts at the location you specify, they'll show up in the List of Fonts window.

Skill 11

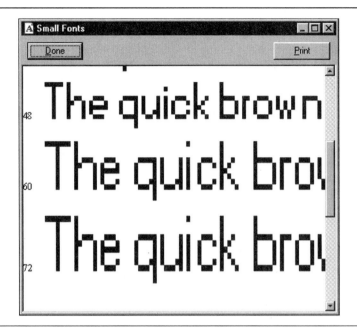

FIGURE 11.6: Fonts that aren't TrueType do not scale up well.

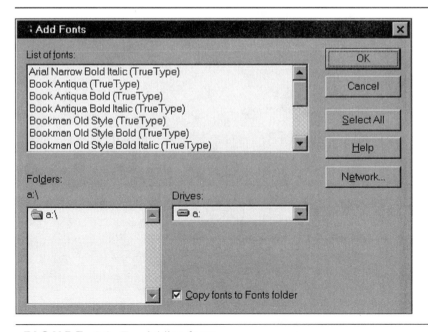

FIGURE 11.7: Adding fonts

Highlight the font or fonts you want installed and click the OK button. Packages like Microsoft's TrueType Fonts for Windows (designed for Windows 3.1) may need to be installed like other programs. Use Add/Remove Programs, described earlier in this skill.

NOTE   Other types of fonts, such as those installed by the Adobe Type Manager, will reside elsewhere on your hard drive, depending on the location you selected. You can't put them in the Fonts folder or view them by double-clicking. However, numerous applications can display fonts and most font installing programs have their own viewers.

Joystick

If you have a joystick attached to your computer when Windows 95 is installed, this icon will appear in the Control Panel.

Double-click it to open a properties sheet for calibrating your existing joystick or adding a second (or third or fourth) joystick to the setup.

TIP   To add a joystick at a later time, turn off your computer and plug in the joystick. Restart your computer. If the joystick icon doesn't appear in the Control Panel, then Windows 95 was unable to detect it. Use Add New Hardware to install it.

You can use a troubleshooting button in case your joystick stops working in a particular game. As you can see in Figure 11.8, there's a joystick type for all occasions.

Keyboard

The installation routine of Windows 95 finds the keyboard plugged into your computer and recognizes it, so you normally don't have to fuss with these settings. But if you need to change keyboards, adjust the keyboard's speed, or install a keyboard designed for another language, click this icon in the Control Panel.

Skill 11

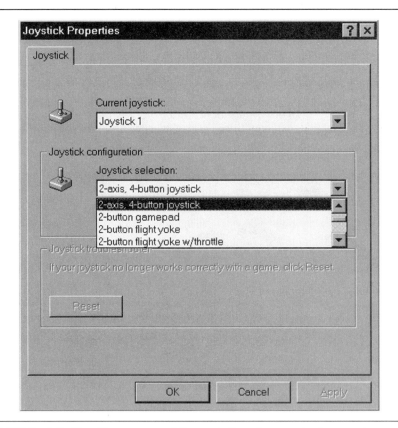

FIGURE 11.8: Choose one of the varieties of game devices or choose Custom and configure your own.

The three tabs on the Keyboard properties sheet cover these different types of settings—explained in the following sections.

Changing Your Keyboard

If you're changing keyboards or Windows 95 recognizes one type of keyboard when in fact you have a different kind, go directly to the General tab. The Keyboard Type window shows what Windows 95 thinks is your keyboard. If that's wrong, click the Change button and follow these steps:

1. On the Select Device page, click Show All Devices.

2. Select the correct keyboard from the list shown. If you have some special installation software, click Have Disk.

3. Click OK and Windows 95 will install the correct keyboard either from your disk or from its own set.

You *may* have to shut down and restart your computer for the keyboard to be completely recognized.

Keyboard Speed

Click the Speed tab to adjust keyboard rates. Here are the available settings:

Repeat Delay   Determines how long a key has to be held down before it starts repeating. The difference between the Long and Short setting is only about a second.

Repeat Rate   Determines how fast a key repeats. Fast means if you hold down a key you almost instantly get vvvvvvvvvvvvery long streams of letters. (Click the practice area to test this setting.)

Cursor Blink Rate   Makes the cursor blink faster or slower. The blinking cursor on the left demonstrates the setting.

Keyboard Languages

If you need multiple language support for your keyboard, click the Language tab. Click the Add button to select languages from Afrikaans to Swedish—including 15 varieties of Spanish. If you have more than one language selected, the settings on the Language tab let you choose a keyboard combination to switch between languages (see Figure 11.9).

Highlight the language you want to be the default (the one that's enabled when you start your computer) and click the Set As Default button.

Check Enable Indicator on Taskbar and an icon will appear on your Taskbar. Right-click it and you can instantly switch between languages.

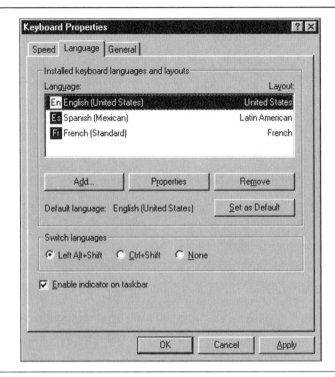

FIGURE 11.9: Setting up your keyboard for more than one language

Mail and Fax

Mail and fax services are pretty big subjects so we've devoted entire skills to them. Mail—confusingly also called messaging, Internet mail, and Exchange—is covered in Skill 15. Sending and receiving faxes using the built-in Windows Fax program is described in Skill 16.

Modems

The settings behind this icon are covered in Skill 13.

Mouse

 Everything you ever wanted to know (and more) about mouse settings—including the use of settings connected to this icon—can be found in Skill 2, devoted entirely to mouses and their uses.

Multimedia

 Read Skill 12 for information on the multimedia applications that come with Windows 95 and how to set them up. The settings behind this icon are covered there as well.

Network

 In the past, anything to do with networks would be way beyond the scope of this sort of book. Networking was strictly for gurus and masochists. But Windows 95 has networking tools that allow almost anyone to make a simple network so that a few computers can connect and share files and printers.

How to set up the absolutely basic network and even some not-so-basic options are all covered in Skill 18.

32bit ODBC

 ODBC (Open Database Connection) is a Microsoft standard for providing a uniform access method to local databases such as Access or dBASE for Windows, network server databases such as Paradox for Windows, and relational databases like Oracle, Sybase, or InterBase. Since many vendors provide ODBC drivers, both for their own databases and often for others, keeping track of which ODBC driver is being used for which database can be a pain.

In Windows 95, you control which data sources are accessed with which driver using the ODBC application on the Control Panel.

When you double-click the ODBC icon, it brings up the Data Sources dialog box shown in Figure 11.10. From here you can add, delete, and configure the drivers for the supported databases on your system. Which databases you have drivers for will depend on which applications you have installed.

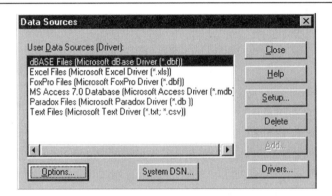

FIGURE 11.10: Configure ODBC drivers here.

PC Card

PC Card
(PCMCIA)

On a laptop you may be using one or more PC cards (the new name for the PCMCIA card). If you don't have a built-in modem, a PC Card modem will do the job. Or you may use a network PC Card so you can plug your laptop into the network at your job.

In general Windows 95 recognizes PC Cards "on the fly." In other words, you don't need to reboot the machine. Just plug the card in and in a few seconds, Windows 95 will pop up a dialog box announcing it has detected the device and asking if you want to configure it now.

Rarely do you have to do anything out of the ordinary, but if you need to, come to the Control Panel and double-click the PC Card (PCMCIA) icon. The dialog box shown in Figure 11.11 will open.

In this dialog box you can stop and remove a PC Card and allow for the PC Card icon to display on the Taskbar. On the Global Settings tab, you can even manually set the addresses for the shared memory space. (Leave the Automatic setting ON unless you truly feel you don't have enough hassles in your life.)

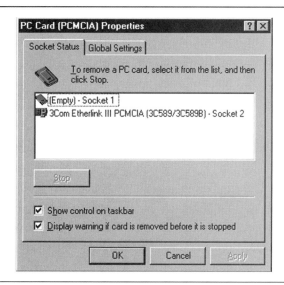

FIGURE 11.11: PC Card settings

Passwords

Passwords

When you sign onto Windows 95 for the first time, you're asked to provide a name and password. If you're the only one using a computer and you don't want to deal with a password every time you turn on the machine, leave the password blank. Then double-click the Network icon in the Control Panel, and under Primary Network Logon (on the Configuration page) make sure Windows Logon is selected. You won't be troubled with a request for a password again.

On the other hand, if you later want to start using a password or change the one you have, double-click this icon in the Control Panel.

Click the Change Windows Password button and enter the information requested. (If you had no previous password, leave the Old Password field empty.)

One Computer, Many Users

Everyone who sets up Windows 95 does the Desktop in a unique way. This is great—until you have to share your computer with another person (or even persons). Fortunately, Windows 95 allows you to set up a profile for each user. You'll each have to log on with your name and particular password, but once you do, the Desktop that appears will be the one you set up—programs, shortcuts, colors, and so forth, all just as you arranged.

Setting Up a User Profile

To allow user profiles, you'll need to follow these steps:

1. Double-click the Passwords icon in the Control Panel.

2. Select the User Profiles tab. Click the button for the second choice: Users can customize their preferences.

3. Select the kinds of settings you want individual users to be able to change and save:

   - Desktop icons and Network Neighborhood
   - Start menu and Program groups

   You can allow either, both, or none of these. Any changes you allow other users to make will affect their profiles only.

4. Click OK when you're finished.

After enabling user profiles, every time you restart Windows 95, you (and everyone else who uses the computer) will need to sign on with a name and password. The first time a new user signs on, the Desktop will look like it did at the time user profiles were enabled. But all changes, subject to the restrictions you set in step 3 above, will be saved for that user.

Removing a User Profile

To get rid of a user profile, sign on under a different name and password. Use the Find function to search for the user's name. For example, if the user signed on as "Alfie," you should find ALFIE.PWL in the Windows folder and a folder named Alfie in the Profiles folder. Delete both the file and the folder to get rid of the profile and all things associated with it. (Don't be put off by the alarming message about deleting USER.DAT; it's just a copy and the original is still in the Windows directory.)

To eliminate all user profiles, log on and go back to the Passwords properties sheet and change the User Profile setting.

You can also bypass all user profiles at startup by clicking Cancel in the dialog box that asks for name and password; so don't be misled into thinking these are *security* devices, they're strictly for convenience.

Security Issues

Windows 95 was not designed to be a high-security system, even though there are some security provisions. User profiles and passwords provide some security though they can be bypassed. All someone has to do is boot in Safe Mode by pressing F8 at bootup and selecting Safe Mode from the menu.

You can prevent this by opening the file MSDOS.SYS in a text editor such as Notepad. Under Options, add the line

```
BootKeys=0
```

and then save the file. Shut down and restart your computer.

On a network, you can improve the security for your computer through using some or all of these:

- Share resources selectively.

- Don't enable remote administration (in Password properties).

- Always use a password.

- Prevent others from having physical access to your computer.

This last is probably the most important because that's how most security breaches occur. It's all very much like the old saying that "locks are for honest people." The security measures in Windows 95 will not discourage a knowledge-able person determined to make mischief, but they can help protect against inadvertent misuse.

 TIP   If you're in a situation where you absolutely, positively need maximum security, you should investigate running Microsoft Windows NT—a system that can be made very secure.

Skill 11

Power

Click this icon to set the power management tools for your laptop. Only a couple of settings are here. You can set whether to turn PC Cards off when not in use and how long then laptop should wait (during a period of inactivity) before switching to low power.

 NOTE   The Power and the PC Card icons are available on laptop (notebook) computers only. You won't see them on a desktop computer.

Printers

This icon in the Control Panel is a shortcut to your Printers folder (also seen in My Computer and Windows Explorer).
Details on how to install, remove, or change the settings of printers are all in Skill 13, "Adding Hardware."

Regional Settings

Use the Regional Settings icon in the Control Panel to set the variations in how numbers, time, and dates are formatted in different parts of the world. For example, if you're using a program that supports international symbols, changing the Regional Settings can affect how the program displays currency, time, and numbers. To change these settings, double-click the icon shown here.

First select the geographic area you want to use, then confirm or change the individual settings. Your system will have to be rebooted for the settings to take effect system-wide.

Sounds

What with Windows 95's emphasis on multimedia, it's no surprise that playing sound on your computer is easier than ever. All the settings for sound are covered in Skill 12, "Working with Multimedia."

System

As long as your computer is running properly, you won't need to be changing the settings controlled through this icon. But when odd behaviors are plaguing your computer, this is a good place to look for possible solutions.

 NOTE Right-clicking My Computer and choosing Properties can also access the properties sheet that opens when you double-click the System icon in the Control Panel.

General

The General page only tells you the version of Windows 95, the registered owner, and a little bit about the type of computer being used. The most important information starts on the next page.

Device Manager

The Device Manager page shows what your system thinks is going on. Usually this is a reflection of reality, but when something is wrong with your computer, this is often the place you'll see it first.

The plus sign to the left of an item indicates there's more to see under that entry. To get the details of the setup for each item, highlight it, and click Properties.

Skill 11

TIP   A list of hardware interrupts, DMA addresses, and memory addresses can be found by highlighting Computer and selecting Properties.

Hardware Profiles

Hardware profiles are something you may need if you're using a portable computer with a docking station. In a limited number of circumstances, you may need to configure alternate setups when the hardware on your system changes.

If you think this might be your situation, consult the Windows 95 help files for instructions.

Performance

The Performance tab is used almost exclusively for troubleshooting. For example, Windows 95 is pretty good at figuring out what will work best on your system, but it's not always perfect. Because of the mixture of older (16-bit) applications in a newer (32-bit) system, there may come a time when you want to check that your system is running optimally (see Figure 11.12).

Troubleshooting

Behind the File System button on the Performance page is a Troubleshooting page with options for changing some fundamental operations (see Figure 11.13). For example, let's say you have a piece of hardware that refuses to run properly under Windows 95. Sometimes, you can isolate the problem by disabling one or more of the options in Troubleshooting. In any case, the Performance entries are for solving problems. If you don't have problems, leave them alone. Even then, proceed carefully.

 NOTE   There's much more on hardware troubleshooting in Skill 13.

Hard Disk

Also in the File System properties is a page called Hard Disk (see Figure 11.14). On this page make sure the Typical role of your machine is set correctly. Read-ahead optimization should be on full—though it will not be of much help in improving performance unless you keep your hard disk defragmented. (More on using Defrag in Skill 14.)

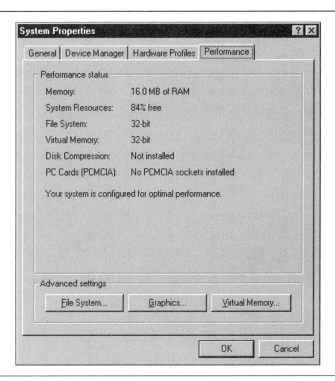

FIGURE 11.12: Information on your system's performance

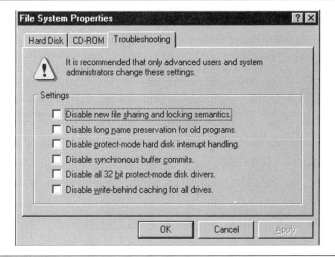

FIGURE 11.13: Troubleshooting options for performance problems

Skill 11

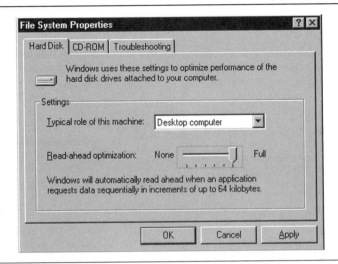

FIGURE 11.14: Hard disk performance settings

CD-ROM

The CD-ROM page of the File System properties has settings for optimizing the performance of your CD-ROM drive. Set the Optimize access pattern to match the type of CD-ROM drive you have. An incorrect setting may have noticeable performance effects.

 TIP
In Windows 95 when you insert a CD in the drive, it automatically opens on your Desktop. Want to change that action? Double-click the System icon, click the plus sign next to CD-ROM, highlight the CD-ROM name, and click the Properties button. Click the Settings tab. Remove the check from Auto Insert Notification to stop the automatic opening of every CD.

Are You Experienced?

Now you can...

- ☑ set up the accessibility options
- ☑ add and remove programs
- ☑ organize your fonts
- ☑ configure joysticks, keyboards, and passwords
- ☑ check out your system settings
- ☑ use the other Control Panel options

Skill 11

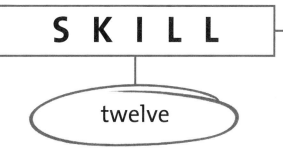

SKILL

twelve

Working with Multimedia

- ❏ Setting up multimedia

- ❏ Playing and programming CDs

- ❏ Playing video

- ❏ Recording and playing sound

- ❏ Turning the volume up (and down)

- ❏ Associating sounds with computer events

The multimedia capabilities built into the most recent computers and now implemented by Windows 95 may strike you more as toys than as anything useful. People who use computers intensely as writers, accountants, and computer consultants do aren't looking for more ways to get distracted, but for ways to remove distractions. Who needs moving pictures or music to get a book written?

But publishing is different in the age of the computer, and so are accounting and data crunching. Books can be published online with animation, pictures, or music. Spreadsheets can include pictures of products or factories to make data more concrete. Databases can include pictures of clients and employees to make information more personal.

This skill covers the CD Player, Media Player, and Sound Recorder built into Windows 95. The first can be used for your private enjoyment or to accompany a presentation with a soundtrack. The second and third can be used to display and enhance multimedia presentations.

Later in this skill, we'll talk about how you connect sound files to different actions on the computer—for example, a program opens and a particular sound plays.

Finding the Multimedia

Ordinarily, you find all the multimedia applications by clicking the Start button and proceeding through Programs ➤ Accessories ➤ Multimedia. But you won't have a Multimedia menu in your Accessories menu if the multimedia applications weren't installed at the time Windows 95 was installed. If this is the case, it's easily remedied:

1. Go to the Control Panel and click Add/Remove Programs.

2. Click the Windows Setup tab at the top of the Add/Remove Programs Properties dialog box.

3. Scroll through the list of options in the dialog box until you locate Multimedia.

4. Double-click Multimedia to see a list of multimedia programs available.

5. Click the check boxes next to as many programs as you want to install. (For the purposes of this skill, make sure CD Player, Media Player, Sound Recorder, and Volume Control are all selected.)

6. OK your way out and insert your Windows 95 disk(s) as requested to complete the installation.

Playing and Programming the CD Player

The CD Player enables audio CDs using your CD-ROM drive, sound card, and speakers. If you want to listen through external speakers, a sound card is required. But even without a sound card, you can listen through headphones plugged into the CD-ROM drive itself.

To open the CD Player, follow these steps:

1.   Click the Start button on the Taskbar.

2.   Select Programs.

3.   Select Accessories in the Program menu.

4.   Select Multimedia in the Accessories menu to open the Multimedia menu.

Depending on the programs you selected when you installed Windows 95, you'll probably have several applications on this menu.

Starting It Up

To start the CD Player, follow these steps:

1.   Locate CD Player among the programs in the Multimedia menu.

2.   Click the CD Player option. That will start the program. You will see the window shown in Figure 12.1.

All you have to do is supply a music CD. The player will play it through your sound card and speakers (plugged into the audio jacks on the back of the CD-ROM controller) or through the headphone jack in the front of your CD-ROM drive.

FIGURE 12.1: You can change the CD Player's look through the View menu.

Skill 12

TIP   By default, the CD Player will start playing the minute you put a music CD in the drive. To overrule the automatic play for a particular CD, hold down the Shift key while you insert the CD. To turn this automatic play feature off completely (or back on), right-click the My Computer icon and select Properties. On the Device Manager page, double-click CD-ROM, highlight your CD-ROM drive's name, and click Properties. On the Settings page, click Auto Insert Notification. With a check in the box, music CDs will play automatically. Without the check, you need to open the CD Player applet yourself.

How It Works

Just as a demonstration, I popped a music CD in the drive and clicked the large triangle next to the digital read-out (the Play button). The CD Player (with Disk/Track info enabled from the View menu) can be seen in Figure 12.2.

FIGURE 12.2: The CD Player at work

Notice that several of the buttons that were gray and unavailable in Figure 12.1 (when there was no CD in the drive) are now black and available in Figure 12.2.

Play   At the top, the large triangle is gray because the CD is playing. (There's no reason to click the Play button when the CD is playing; but if you do, no harm is done.)

Pause   Next to the Play button is a button with two vertical bars. This is the Pause button. Click it to hold your playback while you run to answer the door or the phone.

Stop   The last button at the right end of the top tier is the Stop button. Click it when you're tired of listening to the music or when the boss walks into your office. It will stop playback dead.

Previous Cut   The first button at the left end of the second tier of buttons looks like a double arrowhead pointing left toward a vertical line. Click once to move to the beginning of the current piece, click twice to move to the previous cut on the CD.

Skip Back   The second button on the second tier looks like a double arrowhead pointing left. This is the Skip Back button. Each time you click it, you will move back one second in the music.

Skip Forward   The third button on the second tier is the Skip Forward button. It looks like a double arrowhead pointing to the right. Each time you click it, you will move one second forward in the music.

Next Track   The fourth button on the second tier is the Next Track button. It looks like a double arrowhead pointing right toward a vertical bar. It will take you instantly to the next song.

Eject   The final button at the right end of the second tier of buttons looks like an arrow pointing upward. It is the Eject button. It will cause your CD-ROM drive to stick its tongue out at you—which is what it looks like when your CD is ejected from most drives.

Setting Time and Play Options

Is that all there is? Certainly not. Want even more information? Click the digital readout. Before you click, the readout will tell you the current track number and the elapsed time for that track. The first time you click, you'll see the track number and the time remaining on the track. The second click will display the time remaining for the entire CD (as shown in Figure 12.3).

FIGURES 12.3: Showing the amount of play remaining on the entire CD

If you want to set these without clicking on the digital display, pull down the View menu and select from:

- Track time elapsed

- Track time remaining

- Disc time remaining

The Options menu lets you opt for continuous play, random play, or intro play. Select the Preferences option. It allows you to set the font size for the digital read-out as well as the length of intro play (10 seconds is the default).

 TIP   Want a shortcut to CD Player or Media Player on your Desktop? Open the Windows folder and look for the file CDPLAYER.EXE or MPLAYER.EXE, then right-click and drag the file to the Desktop. Release the right mouse button and select Create Shortcut(s) Here.

Editing the Play List

And if that's not enough, there's an entire layer of the CD Player we haven't even touched yet. Here's how to access it:

1. Pull down the Disc menu.

2. Select Edit Play List. You will see the dialog box shown in Figure 12.4.

Using this dialog box, you can do something that owners of CD players often never get the hang of—programming your player to play specific songs in a specific order.

By Track Number

As an example, let's set up the CD Player to play Tracks 5, 12, and 3 on this particular CD. Here's how:

1. Click the Clear All button to clear all the entries on the Play List.

2. Double-click Track 5 in the Available Tracks list box. It will appear in the Play List.

3. Double-click Track 12, and then double-click Track 3 in the Available Tracks list box.

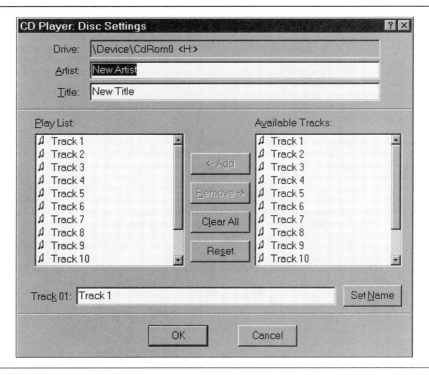

FIGURE 12.4: Programming a play list

By Track Name

If you'd rather deal with track names than track numbers, you can insert names for each of the tracks (or just the ones you care about) as follows:

1. Click a track—for this example, we'll click Track 3 in the Available Tracks list.

2. Click the text box next to the Set Name button.

3. Refer to your CD packaging to get the name of the third song on the CD.

4. Type the name in the text box. (You can type it next to Track 3, or delete the track and type the name instead.)

5. Click the Set Name button. In the Available Tracks list and in the Play List, Track 3 will be replaced with the name you just typed.

6. Just for the sake of completeness, click the text box marked Artist and type the performer(s) name.

7. Highlight the text box marked Title and type the CD's title.

8. Click the OK button.

Once you've supplied your CD Player with this information, the program will remember it, recognize the CD, and follow your programmed instructions every time you play it.

TIP   If you have a CD-ROM player capable of playing multiple disks, Multidisc Play will be an option on the Options menu. Select it, and when you click the downward-pointing arrow at the right end of the Artist box, you will see each of the CDs available to you. Select the CD you want to play.

Playing Files with the Media Player

These days the word "media" conjures up more talk show blather about how the media is to blame for everything. Not this media. The media in this section are fun—never trouble.

Let's begin, as always, by first opening the program:

1. Click the Start button on the Taskbar.

2. Select Programs.

3. Select Accessories from the Programs menu.

4. Select Multimedia from the Accessories menu.

5. Select Media Player from the Multimedia menu.

You should see something similar to the window shown in Figure 12.5.

FIGURE 12.5: The Media Player

The Media Player will play Video for Windows animated files (.AVI), sound files (.WAV), MIDI files (.MID and .RMI), or your audio CD. Yes, that's right. You can use Media Player to play your music CDs just like CD Player except that Media Player offers fewer customization options.

Playing Files

Windows 95 comes with a variety of multimedia files—especially on the CD-ROM version. To play a file, follow these steps:

1. Pull down the Media Player Device menu and select the type of file you want to play.

2. Locate the file you want to play, double-click or highlight it, and select Open.

3. Click the right-pointing arrow (the Play button).

You can select sections of animation or movies just like you select recorded music tracks (see the "Playing and Programming the CD Player" section earlier in this skill). Although the buttons are in different places than the ones on the CD Player, you should be able to identify them by their icons.

Copying and Pasting Files

You can copy and paste sound, animation, or movie files using the Select buttons, which look like tiny arrows pointing down (begin selection) and up (end selection) above a horizontal bar.

Selecting a Section

To select a section of either an audio or video file:

1. Listen (or watch) until you reach the point where the section begins.

2. Click the begin selection button.

3. Continue listening or watching until you reach the end of the section.

4. Click the end selection button.

5. Pull down the Edit menu and select Copy Object. (The piece you have selected will be placed on the Clipboard for pasting into any document that supports sound or video files.)

Getting Looped

If you want a piece of music, film, or animation to repeat continuously, pull down the Edit menu and select Options. Click the option marked Auto Repeat. Your media file will play over and over until:

- The end of time

- You turn off the media player

- Or you lose your mind and destroy your computer with a fire ax

Recording and Playing with the Sound Recorder

If you have an audio input device on your computer (either a microphone or a CD-ROM player), you can use the Sound Recorder to make a .WAV file you can associate with a Windows event or send in a message.

Making .WAV Files

Here's how to make a .WAV file with the Sound Recorder:

1. Open Sound Recorder in the Multimedia menu under Accessories.

2. Select New from the File menu.

3. To begin recording, click the button with the dark red dot.

4. Start the CD or start speaking into the microphone.

5. Click the button with the black square to stop recording.

6. Select Save from the File menu to save the sound clip.

Figure 12.6 shows the Sound Recorder recording from a CD being played in the Media Player.

The Sound Recorder also lets you play other types of sound clips in the Media Player and record them as .WAV files. The .WAV files you make can be played back with the Sound Recorder or the Media Player.

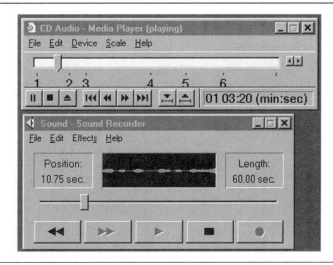

FIGURE 12.6: Use the Sound Recorder to make your own .WAV files.

 TIP   To easily associate a .WAV file with an event in Windows 95, move the file to the Media folder (inside the Windows folder).

Setting Special Effects and Editing

Use the Effects menu to change some of the sound's qualities—to add an echo or decrease the speed. The sound can also be edited, using the menu controls.

Adjusting the Volume Control

The Volume Control panel not only lets you adjust the sound level but also individually tune different types of files. The easiest way to reach the Volume Control panel is to right-click the small speaker icon at the end of the Taskbar and select Volume Controls. You can also open it from the Multimedia menu under Accessories (see Figure 12.7).

Skill 12

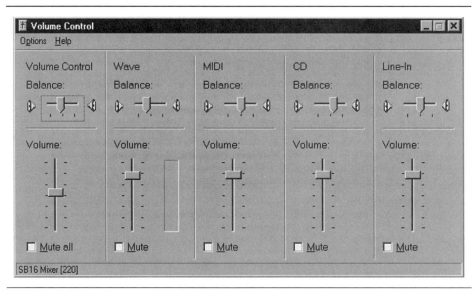

FIGURE 12.7: The Volume Control panel

Setting Tone Controls

For tone controls (bass and treble), select Advanced Controls from the Options menu. This will put an Advanced button at the bottom of the Volume Control window. Click this button to open the page shown in Figure 12.8.

Use the slider controls to increase or decrease the treble and bass tones. These settings will affect all the sound files you play.

NOTE If Advanced Controls is dimmed on your screen, it just means that your hardware doesn't support these functions.

Setting Volume Control Display

Figure 12.7 shows the default settings for Volume Control, but you can decide which devices you want to show on the Volume Control panel. Open Volume Control and select Properties from the Options menu. This will open the window shown in Figure 12.9.

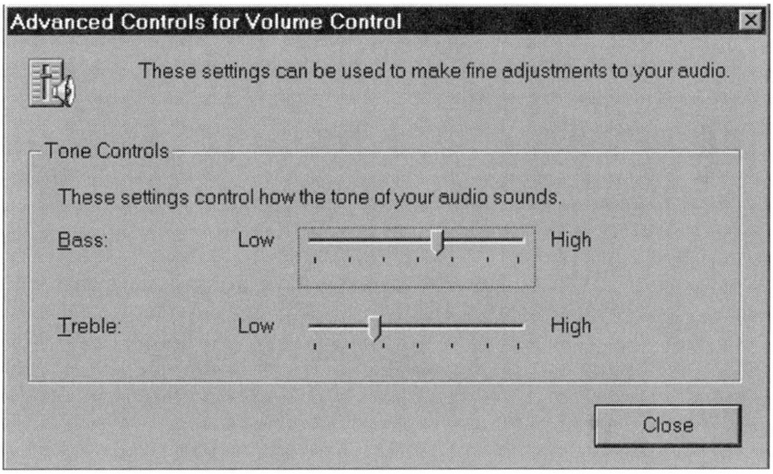

FIGURE 12.8: The slider controls that adjust tone

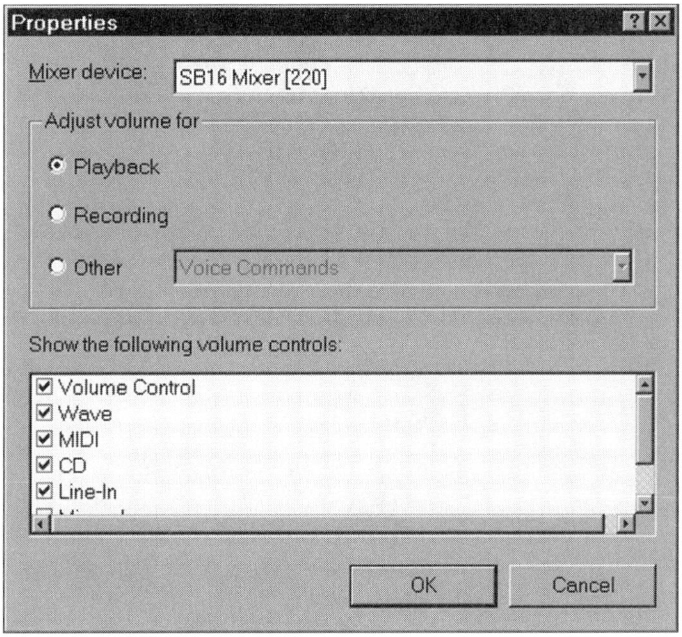

FIGURE 12.9: Selecting the controls you want shown on the Volume Control panel

Select Playback and check the devices you want shown on Volume Control. Likewise you can display recording levels. The choices will probably differ based on your specific computer hardware.

Learning More Multimedia Settings

A Multimedia icon in the Control Panel contains mostly advanced settings but some basic ones too.

Double-click this icon and poke around, right-clicking anything you don't understand to get a box of explanation. The terms here will be unfamiliar to anyone who's a novice at computer-based sound and video. Experiment but also take care not to remove a device unintentionally. If you do, you may have to run the Add New Hardware icon in the Control Panel to get the device back.

Setting Sound Controls

What with Windows 95's emphasis on multimedia, it's no surprise that you can have a sound play at almost any time. Double-click the Sounds icon in the Control Panel to set and change sound schemes.

NOTE   To hear the sounds that come with Windows 95, you'll need a sound card and speakers (or you can wear headphones).

A Sheet Full of Sounds

The Sounds properties sheet is shown in Figure 12.10. The Events window lists everything on your system that can be associated with a sound. Most are Windows events. For example, opening a program can cause a sound, as can maximizing or minimizing a window, and many other actions.

Many of the new programs coming out now also include sound capabilities. Their sounds may not end up in the list shown on this sheet because they're configured for the specific program.

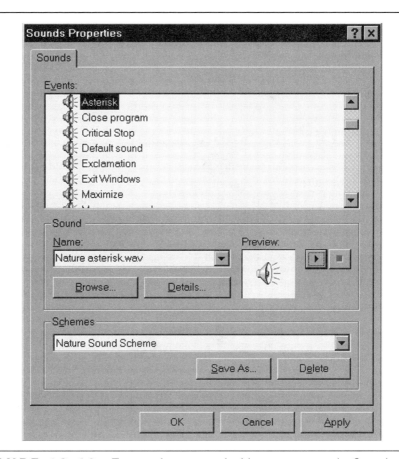

FIGURE 12.10: To associate a sound with an event, use the Sounds Properties dialog box.

If there's a Speaker icon next to the event, a sound is associated with it. Highlight the event—the name of the sound file will appear in the Name window—and click the button next to the Preview window to hear its sound.

Sound schemes are included with Windows 95 (many more if you have the Plus! for Windows 95 package installed) and you can choose one of them from the drop-down list.

Skill 12

NOTE   If sound schemes don't appear in the Schemes drop-down list, you'll need to install them. Go to the Add/Remove Programs icon in the Control Panel. Under the Windows Setup, click on Multimedia and select the sound schemes you want. Select OK, and then follow the instructions.

Customizing a Sound Scheme

All the sound schemes that come with Windows are nice enough but none of them are perfect. There are either too many sounds, not enough, the wrong sounds attached to various events, or whatever. Fortunately, there's a way to make as many customized sound schemes as you like. Here's how:

1. Double-click the Sounds icon in the Control Panel.

2. If there's a sound scheme that's close to the one you want, select it from the Schemes drop-down list. Otherwise, select Windows Default.

3. Starting at the top of the Events list, select an item with which you want to associate a sound.

4. Select a file from the Name drop-down list. To make sure it's the one you want, click the Preview button to hear it.

5. Select (none) in the Name list for events that you want to keep silent.

6. Repeat steps 3–5 until you've completed the list.

7. Select Save As to save this particular assortment of sounds under a specific name. (The new scheme will appear in the Schemes drop-down list.)

TIP   Windows 95 stores all its sound files in the Windows\Media folder. You'll probably want to move any additional sound files you acquire to that folder because using a single location makes setting up and changing sound schemes much easier.

Are You Experienced?

Now you can...

- ☑ use the CD Player
- ☑ play audio and video files
- ☑ record .WAV files and play them back
- ☑ attach sounds to different computer events

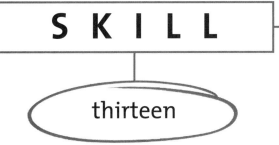

S K I L L

thirteen

Adding Hardware

❏ Adding new hardware

❏ Making a modem work

❏ Adding or removing a printer

❏ Adding a joystick

❏ Configuring a keyboard

❏ Troubleshooting hardware

Changing hardware on a PC has always been a challenge, to say the least, because most PCs are made up of, perhaps, a hard drive from one manufacturer, a video card from another, a sound card built somewhere in Asia, and a modem manufactured by someone you never heard of. Before Windows 95, getting all these disparate parts to work together was a real chore. And once everything was functioning, changing your system by installing a new hard drive or a different modem was more grief than most could bear.

This has begun to change with the wide adoption of what's called the *Plug-and-Play* standard. Any hardware built to this standard will be recognized and installed by Windows 95 without fuss or muss. But even older hardware—like that modem handed down to you by your annoyingly techie brother-in-law—can be installed in just a few steps. In this skill you'll see how easy it is to get Windows 95 to recognize your new hardware, as well as how to troubleshoot any hardware that gets flaky.

Adding New Hardware

With hardware built to the Plug-and-Play specification, you can shut down the computer, install the new hardware and, when you turn the computer on again, Windows 95 will detect the new hardware and do whatever's necessary to make the device work.

This is, of course, the ideal situation. You do nothing. Windows 95 does everything. Always try this approach first.

 WARNING Be cautious of phrases such as "works with Plug and Play" or "works with Windows 95." Neither phrase is very meaningful because practically everything works with both Plug and Play and Windows 95. What you're looking for when you buy new hardware is a device that's built to the Plug-and-Play standard. Also watch out for anything that's a too-good-to-be-true bargain. It may well be from a company dumping the last of their non–Plug-and-Play stock. You don't want to buy old technology.

Other devices (most notably modems) have to be pointed out to Windows 95, which is where the Add New Hardware Wizard comes in.

Add New Hardware

Double-click this icon in the Control Panel and the first page of the Wizard opens (see Figure 13.1).

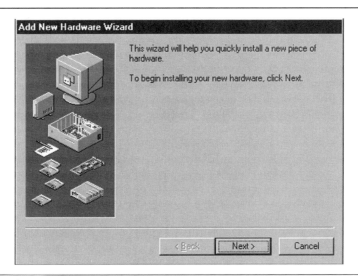

FIGURE 13.1: The first page of the Add New Hardware Wizard

 NOTE Wizards are scattered throughout Windows 95. Think of them as small programs that guide you through multistep procedures.

On the second page of the Wizard, you'll be asked if you want Windows 95 to detect the hardware or if you want to supply the information yourself. Let Windows 95 do the detecting. That usually works very well. Carefully read every page of the Wizard as you go so you know what's going on.

You'll see the page (shown in Figure 13.2) with a bar across the bottom showing how near you are to finishing. The bar will sometimes look as if it's stalled and nothing's happening, but be patient. Unless the computer is completely silent for at least five minutes, there's still activity going on.

After the search, the Wizard will tell you what it found and ask you to confirm its findings. If it's all correct, click Finish and the installation process will be completed.

 NOTE If the Wizard finds some hardware but it's *not* the hardware you just installed, cancel the installation and start the Wizard again, only this time select No when you reach the question, "Do you want Windows to search for your new hardware?" Then follow the instructions in the next section.

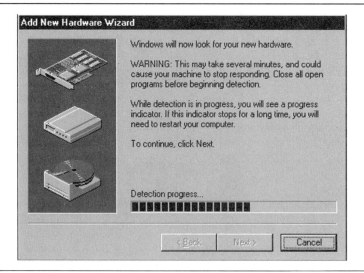

FIGURE 13.2: The hardware detecting process

When You Have to Help the Wizard

But what if, at the end of the search, Windows 95 comes up empty (as shown in Figure 13.3)?

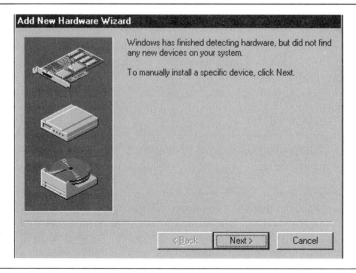

FIGURE 13.3: Windows 95 has made an attempt but can't see your new hardware.

Don't worry, this just means that you have to provide some help. Click the Next button and you'll see a list of hardware types (see Figure 13.4). Let's say you're adding a sound card to your system. Scroll down until you see Sound, Video, and Game Controllers and click it once. Click the Next button again.

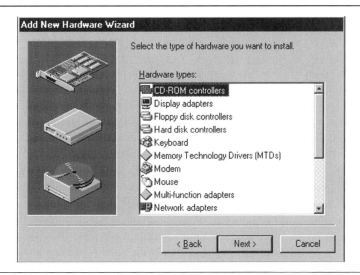

FIGURE 13.4: Now you get to tell Windows 95 what hardware has been added to your system.

The Wizard now shows a box with two panes. The left one is a list of manufacturers. Find the name of the company that made your new piece of hardware and highlight it by clicking the name once. That will open a list of models on the right (as shown in Figure 13.5).

NOTE   The name or number of your model may be on the hardware itself; it will certainly be in the documentation. Don't have the documentation? Then guess. Seriously—if you guess wrong, no harm done. You'll just have to run the Add New Hardware Wizard and try again.

TIP   The Have Disk button is used only when you know that the hardware in question requires some files (called *drivers*) that Windows 95 doesn't provide. These files would be on a disk that came with the hardware. This doesn't happen very often. Most of the time the Windows 95 drivers will work best.

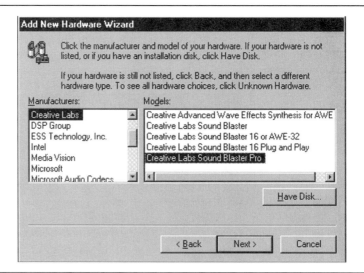

FIGURE 13.5: Selecting the manufacturer and model

Highlight the model and click the Next button. What happens next depends on the hardware being installed. Just be sure to read all the instructions you receive. For example, installing a sound card may produce something like the screen shown in Figure 13.6. It's wise to print out such settings on the off-chance these settings are in conflict with some other piece of hardware.

 TIP   Modems and printers can be installed from the Add New Hardware Wizard but installation is easier using other methods, as described later in this skill.

Continue following the Wizard's instructions until the installation is complete.

Still Not Working?

If you've tried the previous steps and your system still can't see the hardware in question, there's plenty more you can do before calling in an expert. Of course, you can go for the expert now and forget the rest of this if you're too uncomfortable messing around with your computer. But you're unlikely to do any harm trying these steps and you might actually fix the problem yourself!

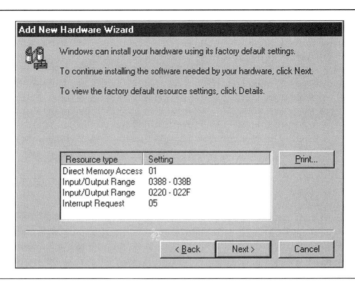

FIGURE 13.6: Some installations will produce a window like this one. Print out and save this information. If everything works fine, you can throw the printout away.

Open the System Properties dialog box (Properties of My Computer or System from the Control Panel), and click the Device Manager tab. Click the + beside the type of device you are having trouble with, then choose the particular device. Click Properties, then the Resources page, and see if there are any conflicts shown. If there are, then you'll probably want to run one of the Troubleshooting Wizards from the Windows 95 Help system.

If the thing that isn't working is attached to your computer, as opposed to something inside the box, here are a few things to check:

Power   Check that the power to the device is on. Even if it is, try turning the power off and back on. This single step will clear an amazing percentage of all hardware problems.

Cable Connections   Make sure the cable that connects it is solidly attached at both ends, with all the screws that lock the connectors screwed in.

Cable Integrity   Check the cable and make sure that your cat hasn't decided that it looked like a tasty supplement to her kibble.

If the problem is with something inside the computer box, it gets trickier. First, shut down Windows 95 completely and turn the power off. Then carefully remove the screws that hold your computer's box together and put them somewhere safe and remove the cover. Here are a few things to check:

Cables   Check that all the cables are firmly attached and that there is no obvious physical evidence of problems (a worn spot or burn mark).

Cards   Make sure that all the cards are firmly placed in their slots. It's easy to install a card in such a way that it's sort of loose. This will cause the device to work intermittently or not at all.

Dirt   Over time, the amount of dust and dirt that builds up inside your computer's box is astounding. This can actually degrade performance or cause a device to stop working since the dirt can provide a conductive path. Remove dirt either by using a small amount of compressed air or one of those tiny computer vacuums. Or you can just do what everybody else does, huff and puff and blow the dirt loose.

When you have checked everything you can inside the computer box, before you put the cover back on, power the computer back up and see if you have corrected the problem.

Most video problems can be traced to a driver problem and are out of your scope of control. But here are a few things to look at:

Distortion   If your picture is highly distorted, especially along one edge, you may be suffering from interference with other equipment or monitors in the area. Check where your cable is running, and try moving it to see if that helps. If not, you may need to figure out which piece of equipment is causing the interference and move either it or the computer.

Setting Defaults   Your video card needs to have its options set from DOS and won't let you just run the utilities in a DOS window from inside Windows 95? Well, in the first place, shame on the manufacturer! But to get around this problem, shut down Windows 95, selecting Restart the Computer in MS-DOS mode. Once you've run the utility that the video card requires, you can exit and reboot into Windows 95 again.

With video problems it's usually fruitful to get in touch with the manufacturer of the card and ask about "new drivers." Don't be shy, this is one inquiry they're *very* used to getting.

Adding a Modem

In the past, modems (along with printers, discussed in later sections) have been the worst possible pains-in-the-neck to get installed. There's been steady improvement over the years, and Windows 95 moves the process forward by miles. Modems are still quirky animals, but Windows 95 gives you a lot of help in solving whatever problems might arise.

All the steps for getting a modem up and running are included with (what else?) the Modem Wizard. To get started, double-click the Modems icon in the Control Panel.

In the window that opens, you'll see which modem (or modems) are set up on the computer.

If you have no modem on the computer and want to install one, follow these steps:

1. Shut down Windows 95 (click the Start button and select Shut Down). Then turn the computer off. Connect the modem to the computer:

    - If it's an external modem, you need to plug it into a serial port on the back of the computer box. You'll also need to plug the modem's electrical cord into an outlet, connect a phone line from the modem to a phone jack, then make sure to turn the modem *on* before proceeding.

    - For an internal modem, you'll need to open the computer box. The instructions that came with the modem should help.

2. Turn your computer back on and let Windows 95 start. Double-click the Modems icon in the Control Panel.

3. In the Modems Properties window, click the Add button.

4. Windows 95 will volunteer to find the modem for you and install it. Take advantage of this offer and click Next.

5. The system will search the communications ports and report its findings. Figure 13.7 shows what was found on my computer.

6. If the finding is correct, click the Next button. If Windows 95 came up with wrong information, click the Change button and select the right manufacturer and type from the list provided and *then* click Next.

The process will continue and you'll be notified of a successful installation.

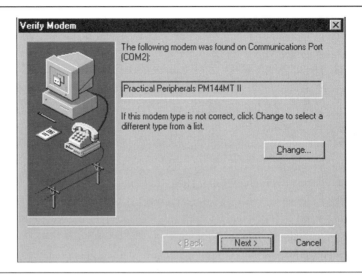

FIGURE 13.7: Windows 95 reports on the modem it found.

 NOTE   For information on selecting the right modem, see Skill 15.

Removing a Modem

If you change modems (or install the wrong one), it's easy to correct the situation:

1. Open the Modems icon in the Control Panel.

2. On the General page, highlight the modem name.

3. Click the Remove button, and it's gone!

 TIP   Some modem problems in Windows 95 arise when pre-Windows 95 communications software intervenes and changes a modem setting without your knowledge. If you repeatedly get a "Modem Will Not Initialize" message, try removing the modem from Windows 95 and then installing it again. Sometimes, just shutting down the computer and starting it up again will do the trick. You may even need to switch software or upgrade your existing software to a Windows 95 version.

Setting Modem Properties

To find the hardware-type settings for your modem, double-click the Modems icon in the Control Panel. Highlight your modem (if it isn't already) and select Properties, which opens the properties sheet for this particular modem (see Figure 13.8).

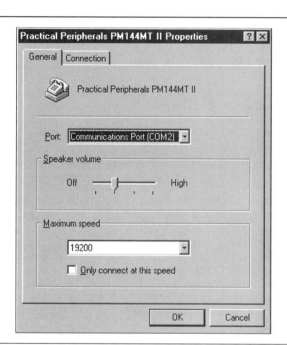

FIGURE 13.8: Check here for the modem settings.

The General Page

On the General page are:

- The full name of the modem
- The port it's connected to
- A slider for setting the volume of the modem speaker
- A drop-down box for setting the maximum speed

You rarely need to fool with these settings (except for volume, which is strictly a matter of preference). That's because they come from what Windows 95 knows about your specific modem. Only change the settings when you've had some difficulty with your modem being recognized or you're sure a particular setting is wrong.

The Connection Page

On the Connection page are more of the hardware settings. Again, unless you have a good reason for changing the Connection preferences, leave them alone. The Call Preferences can be changed if you find the default ones unsuitable.

Advanced Settings

If you click the Advanced button, you'll see the window in Figure 13.9. These settings are rarely anything to be concerned about. They're just here for those odd and infrequent times when it might be necessary to force error correction or use software for error control. The one thing on this page that might be used more often is the log file. If you're troubleshooting a bad connection, check Record a Log File before you try to connect, and Windows 95 will produce a text file of exactly what happened. The file will be called MODEMLOG.TXT and will be placed in the Windows folder. Some communications software will not produce a MODEMLOG.TXT.

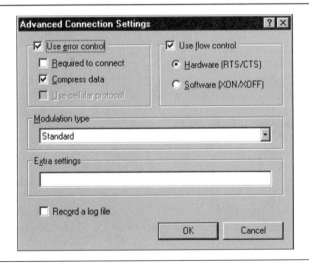

FIGURE 13.9: The Advanced settings can sometimes help with a difficult connection.

Dialing Properties

In addition to centralizing the modem's hardware and software settings, you also want to enter information about how you're dialing and from where you're dialing. Windows 95 allows for the configuring of multiple dialing locations, so if you travel with your computer, you can make calls from your branch office (or the ski resort in Gstaad where you take your vacations) without making complex changes.

Double-click the Modems icon in the Control Panel, then click Dialing Properties on the General page and fill out the information for your location. Click the New button to supply additional locations. When you change physical locations, you need only tell Windows 95 where you are (see Figure 13.10) and all your necessary dialing information will be loaded.

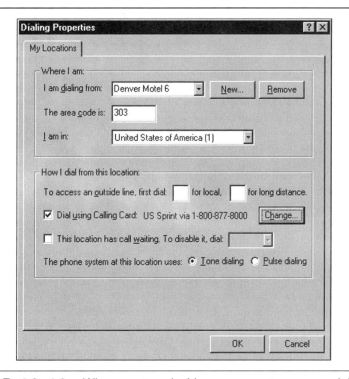

FIGURE 13.10: When you travel with your computer, you won't have to redo your communications settings when you change locations.

Troubleshooting Modems

As a rule, when your modem is uncooperative, it's for obvious reasons:

- It's not plugged into a phone line.

- The modem's turned off or it's not plugged into an active electrical socket (external modems).

- One or more programs have confused the settings.

This last item happens more often in Windows 95 because of the new TAPI (Telephony Applications Programming Interface) standard. Like most technology designed to make things better in the future, it has a way of making life somewhat worse here in the present.

 NOTE   For more on TAPI and what it means, see Skill 15.

There's no question that communications programs written for Windows 3.1 and not updated for Windows 95 can change your modem's settings. Not *all* older programs—just some. If this happens, you'll then try to use another communications program and get an error message that says something like "Initialization Failure" or "Modem Not Recognized."

The problem can usually be fixed by removing your modem (as described earlier in this skill) and then reinstalling it. This isn't really difficult but it is an annoyance and a delay. Permanent solutions are to:

- Upgrade to the Windows 95 version of the software.

- Change to a communications program that doesn't cause other programs to fail.

Another problem in Windows 95 is that most programs can't share a communications port. You become aware of this when you have fax software loaded and ready to receive a fax and then try to connect to America Online or CompuServe or your Internet provider. In this case you'll get a message like "The Modem Can't Be Found" or "The Modem Is Not Responding." The immediate solution is to close the fax software before starting another communications program. The long-term fixes are to:

- Upgrade all your communications programs to ones that are TAPI-aware.

- Use programs that combine fax and communications in one package.

Printing is generally a lot easier in Windows 95 than in any previous system. As in Windows 3.1, printers are set up to use a common set of drivers so you don't have to configure each program independently for printing. Adding or removing a printer is as easy as point and click, and sharing printers over a network is painless.

Printers are accessible through the Printers folder inside My Computer, off the Start menu under Settings, or in the Printers folder in the Control Panel. And, of course, you can drag a shortcut to the Printers folder (or any of the printers in it) to your Desktop. Open the Printers folder to see what printers are installed for your system.

Adding a Printer

Setting up a printer is part of the installation routine. But if your printer isn't installed or you want to add another printer or a network printer, it's easy to do.

For a printer that's connected directly to your computer, double-click the Printers folder and follow these steps (clicking the Next button after each entry):

1. Select Add Printer.

2. When the Add Printer Wizard starts, click Next, and check the Local printer entry. (This step will be skipped if you're not on a network.)

3. Highlight the name of the printer's manufacturer and the model name.

4. Select the port you want to use. Unless you know of some special circumstances, choose LPT1.

5. Type in the name you want the printer to be known by and indicate whether this is to be the default printer for all your Windows programs. If this is the printer you plan to use most of the time, select Yes. Otherwise, say No—you'll still be able to select the printer when you want to use it.

6. Print a test page to verify all is well. Then click Finish.

Adding a Network Printer

HP LaserJet 4

A network printer (indicated by this icon) is plugged into someone else's computer—a computer you have access to via a network.

To install a network printer so you can use it, double-click the Printers folder and follow these steps (clicking Next after each entry):

1. Double-click Add Printer. When the Add Printer Wizard starts, click Next, and then select Network printer.

2. You'll need to tell the system the address of the printer, so click the Browse button to look for available printers. Highlight the printer (as shown in Figure 13.11) and click OK.

3. If you expect to print from DOS programs, click Yes so the system can add the necessary information to the printer setup.

4. Enter the name you want to call the printer and check whether you want this printer to be the default printer. Only check Yes if you expect to be using the network printer for the majority of your printing.

5. Print a test page to make sure everything's running properly and click Finish.

FIGURE 13.11: Selecting a printer on the network

 TIP To be able to use a printer set up this way, both the printer and the computer it's connected to must be switched on.

Removing a Printer

Sometimes you may need to uninstall a printer, which is quite easily done. Just right-click the printer's icon in the Printers folder and select Delete. You'll be asked to confirm the deletion. You may also be asked if you want to delete files associated with this printer that won't be necessary if the printer is gone. If you're getting rid of the printer permanently, select Yes. If you're planning on reinstalling the same printer soon, select No.

Setting Printer Properties

To get at the settings for a printer, you need to right-click the printer's icon and select Properties. On the properties sheet that opens, you can set details as to fonts, paper, how the printer treats graphics, and so on.

The printer driver that Windows 95 installed to run the printer makes the most of these settings. Change ones you need to change but avoid changing settings if you're not clear what the setting does. You can inadvertently disable your printer. If this happens, you can usually cure it by removing the printer (see the previous section) and then installing it again.

Troubleshooting Printers

Besides the usual paper jam problems that we all hate, you can easily run into subtle conflicts between your application program and the printer drivers, as well as downright bugs in either. Here are some things to try, in roughly the order to try them:

Printer Online   This happens all the time, especially if the printer's not right next to you where you can see it. Make sure the Online light is on.

Power   Turn the power off and back on. This does two things. It forces you to check that the power is actually on, and, more to the point, it causes the printer to do a complete reset getting back to the known starting point that Windows 95 expects to find it in.

Cable   Check the cable connections on both ends.

Switch Boxes, "Buffalo Boxes," Spoolers   There are all sorts of ways to share a printer that are left over from the bad old DOS days. With networking built into Windows 95 these probably won't last long, but if you have one of these boxes, temporarily connect the printer directly to your computer, with nothing in between except the actual cable (and that one, a nice short one). Now try printing. If you can print now, you know the problem isn't the printer itself. It's the device between your computer and the printer.

Network Print Servers   Same approach as for switch boxes. Try connecting directly to the printer without the intervening network connection.

Test File   Print a simple test file from Notepad—a few words are enough to know if Windows 95 is recognizing the printer. If the test file prints, but you have a problem with more complicated printing from your application, chances are you have a problem with the application or possibly the printer driver. Check with the company that makes the application for a newer version or check with the manufacturer of your printer to see if there's a newer driver.

If none of these help, try the print troubleshooter that comes with Windows 95. Select Help from the Start menu. On the Contents page, double-click Troubleshooting and select If You Have Trouble Printing. The guide is interactive in that you select the problem you're having, and then you're stepped through the process of finding a solution.

No matter how much Windows 95 does to let you simply plug in your new hardware and play with it immediately, sooner or later you're going to have problems with either a new piece of hardware or an existing one. Sometimes the source of the problem is a subtle conflict between two (or more) pieces of hardware but much more often the root cause is something fairly simple and straightforward.

Open the System Properties dialog box (Properties of My Computer or System from the Control Panel) and click the Device Manager tab. Click the type of device you are having trouble with and see if there are any conflicts shown. If there are, then you'll probably want to run one of the Troubleshooting Wizards from the Windows 95 Help system.

Windows 95 provides an outstanding tool for resolving conflicts and getting stuff working called the Hardware Conflict Troubleshooter (shown in Figure 13.12). This little gem, reached off the Help menu, will resolve the vast majority of any hardware problems you might have. Just follow the directions, and click the buttons as required. We're not going to trace through every step of using this tool because there are just too many directions it could branch in, depending on what it finds, and how you respond to its questions.

If your problem is a sort of general "it doesn't work" where "it" is some device, there are a few things to look for or think about. If none of these seem to fit the bill, start the Windows 95 Help system and see if there's a Wizard for it in the Troubleshooting section, as shown in Figure 13.13.

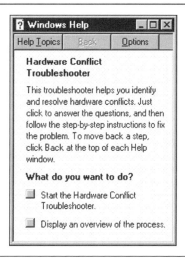

FIGURE 13.12: The Hardware Conflict Troubleshooter is an excellent tool for resolving hardware problems.

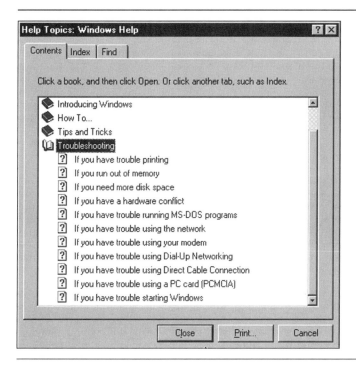

FIGURE 13.13: The Windows Help system has excellent troubleshooting Wizards to help you locate and resolve problems.

Adding a Joystick

If you have a joystick attached to your computer when Windows 95 is installed, this icon will appear in the Control Panel.
Double-click it to open a properties sheet for calibrating your existing joystick or adding a second (or third or fourth) joystick to the setup.

TIP To add a joystick later, turn off your computer and plug in the joystick. Restart your computer. If the joystick icon doesn't appear in the Control Panel, then Windows 95 was unable to detect it. Use Add New Hardware to install it.

There's a troubleshooting button in case your joystick stops working in a particular game. As you can see in Figure 13.14, a joystick type exists for all occasions.

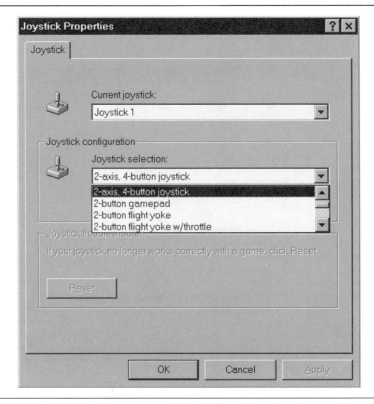

FIGURE 13.14: Choose one of the devices listed or choose Custom and configure your own.

Configuring a Keyboard

Keyboard

The installation routine of Windows 95 finds the keyboard plugged into your computer and recognizes it, so you normally don't have to fuss with these settings. But if you need to change keyboards, adjust the keyboard's speed, or install a keyboard designed for another language, click this icon in the Control Panel.

The three tabs on the Keyboard properties sheet cover these different types of settings; they're explained in the following sections.

Changing Your Keyboard

If you're changing keyboards or Windows 95 recognizes one type of keyboard when in fact you have a different kind, go directly to the General tab. The Keyboard Type window shows what Windows 95 thinks is your keyboard. If that's wrong, click the Change button and follow these steps:

1. On the Select Device page, click Show All Devices.

2. Select the correct keyboard from the list shown. If you have some special installation software, click Have Disk.

3. Click OK and Windows 95 will install the correct keyboard either from your disk or from its own set.

You *may* have to shut down and restart your computer for the keyboard to be completely recognized.

Adjusting the Keyboard Speed

Click the Speed tab to adjust keyboard rates. Here are the available settings:

Repeat Delay   Determines how long a key has to be held down before it starts repeating. The difference between the Long and Short setting is only about a second.

Repeat Rate   Determines how fast a key repeats. Fast means if you hold down a key you almost instantly get vvvvvvvvvvvvery long streams of letters. (Click the practice area to test this setting.)

Cursor Blink rate   Makes the cursor blink faster or slower. The blinking cursor on the left demonstrates the setting.

Setting Keyboard Languages

If you need multiple language support for your keyboard, click the Language tab. Click the Add button to select languages from Afrikaans to Swedish—including 15 varieties of Spanish. If you have more than one language selected, the settings on the Language tab let you choose a keyboard combination to switch between languages (see Figure 13.15).

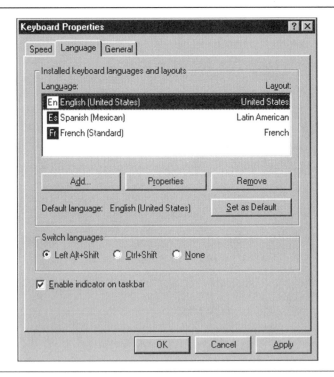

FIGURE 13.15: Set your keyboard for a different language or for multiple languages.

Highlight the language you want as the default (the one that's enabled when you start your computer) and click the Set As Default button.

Check the Enable Indicator on the Taskbar box and an icon will appear on your Taskbar. Right-click it and you can instantly switch between languages.

Are You Experienced?

Now you can...

- ☑ add new hardware
- ☑ add or remove a modem or printer
- ☑ add a joystick
- ☑ configure a keyboard
- ☑ troubleshoot hardware

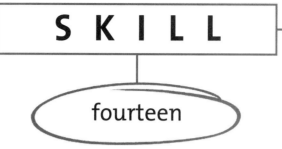

Keeping Your Work Safe

- ❏ Maintaining your hard drive with ScanDisk

- ❏ Getting faster hard drives with Disk Defragmenter

- ❏ Saving files using Backup

- ❏ Compressing drives to gain more space

- ❏ Using the Resource Meter

The basic disk tools needed to safeguard your system are included with Windows 95, so the packages of utilities needed in the past are no longer needed. Of course, if you want special things, such as Norton Utilities or a particular backup program, feel free to buy what you like. Just make sure any utility programs you use are Windows 95–compatible so you don't damage any of your data.

In this skill, we'll talk about the various disk tools, what they do, and how best to use them. You'll find your list of installed tools by clicking the Start button and then selecting Programs ➤ Accessories ➤ System Tools.

Taking Care of Your Drive with ScanDisk

A computer is a very complex system. Lots of stuff goes on behind the scenes that you never know about. Like most complex systems, errors are made by the system itself, and if not corrected, can pile up into serious problems.

ScanDisk is protection against the accumulation of serious problems on your hard drive. It's a direct descendant of the CHKDSK utility in DOS with added features like those in the justly famous Norton Disk Doctor.

 NOTE   If your computer is running a version of Windows that came pre-installed, you will notice that ScanDisk runs automatically when you turn off the computer without properly shutting down, and then reboot.

Running ScanDisk

To run ScanDisk, follow these steps:

1. Select ScanDisk from the System Tools menu under Accessories. This will open the window shown in Figure 14.1.

2. Highlight the drive you want tested.

3. Select the type of test and whether you want ScanDisk to automatically fix all errors or prompt you.

4. Click Start to run.

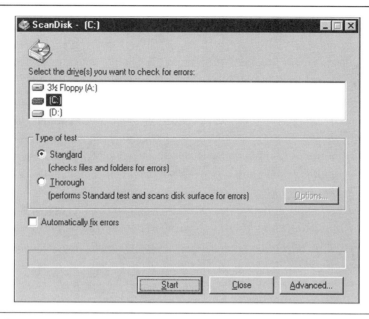

FIGURE 14.1: The ScanDisk dialog box

 NOTE   If you check the Automatically Fix Errors box, ScanDisk will repair most errors without consulting you again. Such corrections are made based on settings you can review by clicking the Advanced button.

Changing ScanDisk Settings

Click the Advanced button to see (and change) the settings that ScanDisk uses:

Display Summary   This setting controls when you see the summary of ScanDisk's findings after a check (see Figure 14.2).

Log File   By default, ScanDisk creates a new log detailing its activities every time it's run. If you want one long continuous log or no log at all, change the setting.

Cross-Linked Files   A cross-link occurs when more than one file tries to use the same area (cluster) on the hard drive. Whatever information is in the cluster is probably correct only for one file (though it might not be correct for either of them). The default setting attempts to salvage order out of the mess by copying the information in the cluster to both files contending for the space. This is the best of the three settings—it may not save any of your data but the other two options definitely won't.

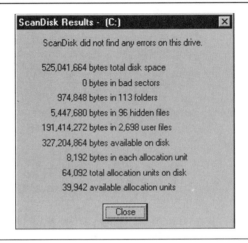

FIGURE 14.2: ScanDisk's summary report on a scanned drive

Lost File Fragments File fragments are a fact of computer life. You can leave the default setting to convert them to files. They'll be given names like FILE0001 and FILE0002 and deposited in your root folder (that's the C: folder that contains a lot of folders but some files too). The odds are very high that these fragments aren't anything useful, and they do take up valuable disk space. We've changed our default setting to Free but you can be extra cautious and leave it at Convert to Files. (Just remember to look at these files periodically and delete the junk.)

Check Files For The default is to look just for invalid names, though you can add dates and times if you want. It will slow down ScanDisk's progress but not dramatically.

Check Host Drive First If you have a compressed drive, errors are sometimes caused by errors on the host drive. Leave this box checked so the host drive will be examined first.

TIP You should run ScanDisk frequently. Once a week is a good idea. And at least once a month you should run its Thorough testing procedure, so the hard disk surface is checked for problems in addition to the standard checking of files and folders.

Defragmenting Your Disk

Windows 95 is much like the operating systems that preceded it, in that when it writes a file to your disk it puts the file anywhere it finds room. As you delete and create files over time, they begin to be distributed on the hard disk as a piece here, a piece there, another piece somewhere else.

This isn't a problem for Windows 95—it always knows where the pieces are. But it will tend to slow file access time because the system has to go to several locations to pick up one file. When a file is spread over multiple places, it's said to be *fragmented*. The more fragmented files you have the slower your hard drive will run.

As a matter of good housekeeping then, Disk Defragmenter should probably be run about once a month. Here's how it's done:

1. Select Disk Defragmenter from the System Tools menu.

2. Use the drop-down list shown in Figure 14.3 to choose the drive you want to defragment. Click OK.

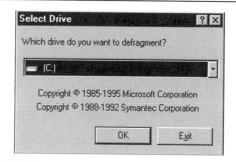

FIGURE 14.3: Select the drive you want to defragment from the drop-down list.

3. Disk Defragmenter will provide you with a report on the degree of defragmentation. Click the Advanced button to see the options box shown in Figure 14.4. Here's what the options mean:

- By default, Full Defragmentation is selected. This is the best option because although it's a little slower than the other two options, both files and free space are consolidated. If you just defragment files, the free space is still in clumps and future files you create are bound to be even more fragmented. If you consolidate free space only, the files you already have will probably become even more fragmented.

- If the Check Drive for Errors box is selected, Disk Defragmenter checks the drive for errors before defragging. If it finds errors, you'll be advised of this fact and Defragmenter won't continue.

- Select whether these options are for this session only or should be saved for future sessions.

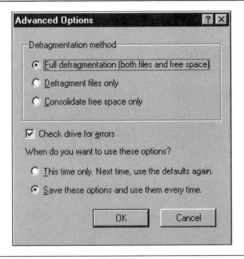

FIGURE 14.4: Choosing Disk Defragmenter options

 NOTE   When Disk Defragmenter has found an error on your disk, run ScanDisk (described earlier in this skill) to repair the problem, and then run Defragmenter again.

4. Click Start. You can click Show Details to get a cluster-by-cluster view of the program's progress. Or you can just minimize Disk Defragmenter and do something else. If what you do writes to the hard drive, Disk Defragmenter will start over—but in the background and without bothering you.

TIP   A useful tool in the Plus! for Windows 95 package is a program called System Agent that lets you automate regular runs of both ScanDisk and Disk Defragmenter, so you don't forget to do these chores.

Backing Up Your Hard Disk

Your hard disk has (or will soon have) a lot of material on it that's valuable to you. Even if it's not your doctoral dissertation or this year's most important sales presentation, you'll have software (including Windows 95) that you've set up and configured *just so*.

Hard disk crashes are really quite rare these days, but if you are unlucky enough to have a crash, not having a recent backup can change your whole perspective on life. So don't lose your sunny disposition—resolve now to do frequent backups of your important files. If you are lucky and/or cautious enough to have a tape drive or other high-capacity backup system, you should also make less-frequent backups of your entire system.

Getting Started

To start the Backup program, click the Start button, then select Programs ➤ Accessories ➤ System Tools and finally Backup.

NOTE   If the Backup program isn't on the menu, you'll need to install it. Go to Add/Remove Programs in the Control Panel and use Windows Setup to add Backup.

Figure 14.5 shows the opening window you'll see when you open Backup the first time.

Once you have read this dialog box, if you don't want to see it again click the box next to "Don't Show This Again" and click the OK button.

FIGURE 14.5: Read the information in Backup's opening dialog box.

Tape Drive or Floppies

If you have a tape drive and it's been installed properly, Backup will find it and prepare to back up to it.

 NOTE   Not all tape drives are supported. To find the list of ones that are, click the Help menu and select Help topics. Click Using Tapes for Backup to see what's compatible with Backup. If your tape drive isn't among those listed, don't give up. Call the manufacturer of the tape drive and see if they have a driver—a program that will enable Windows 95 to use your tape drive. These programs are almost always free.

If Windows 95 doesn't find a tape drive, it'll present you with a message telling you that if you really do have a tape drive, it isn't working and what to do about it. If you really don't have a tape drive, just click OK. You'll be backing up to floppies (which you already know).

 NOTE   If you have two hard drives, backing up from one to the other is as safe as any other method. But you must use two physically separate hard drives, not just different partitions on a single hard drive.

Full System Backups

Next, Backup will create a file set designed to back up everything. This will automatically be called Full System Backup, and, if you use it, it will back up everything, including system files.

 TIP   If your hard disk suddenly sounds like it's full of little pebbles, there's nothing more comforting than having a Full System Backup on your shelf. You should make a Full System Backup when you first install Windows 95, after you install new applications, and occasionally thereafter.

Defining a File Set

What is a file set? Backup is based on the idea that you have a large hard disk with perhaps thousands of individual files and perhaps hundreds of different folders. You don't usually want to back up everything on the disk. Usually you'll be backing up a few folders—the folders containing your Corel drawings, your Excel spreadsheets, your WordPerfect documents, your appointment book, your customer database, and so on.

Therefore, you need to tell Backup which folders need to be backed up every day or every week. Once you have a solid backup of your entire hard disk, you'll want to back up only certain folders on a regular basis (that'll be covered a little later). You probably don't need to back up your whole Corel package every week, because if worst comes to worst, you could reinstall it. Backing up a program that large takes forever and these days almost all the major programs are huge. The file set tells Backup which files and folders to back up.

Regular Backups

Regular backups involve less than the entire disk and will probably depend on how valuable certain files are, how difficult they would be to re-create, and how often they change.

 TIP   You might want to make several file sets for backups of different depths. Back up really important folders at the end of every work day (or at lunch) and less important ones at the end of major projects. How to create a backup file set is covered in the following section.

Creating a Backup

In this section we'll create a backup to demonstrate how it's done. If Backup isn't running, start it now. (See the instructions earlier in this skill.) Once you get through the initial dialog boxes, you should see the window shown in Figure 14.6.

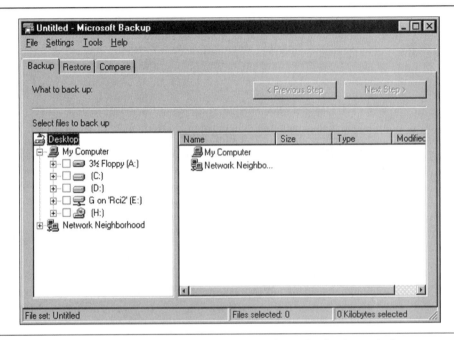

FIGURE 14.6: Choosing what to back up from the Backup window

Clicking the objects in the section on the left tells Backup which device, folders, or individual files you want to back up.

NOTE   Each of the drives shown in the Backup window has a tiny check box next to it. If you want to back up the entire device—every file and folder from the root to the farthest branch—click this box to automatically select everything. This in itself may take several minutes.

Backing Up Particular Files or Folders

Here's how you can back up particular files or folders. For the sake of this example, we'll back up a single file, but the principle is the same for a larger selection:

1. Click your hard disk's name in the list. That will make all of the folders in the root folder of your hard disk appear in the list at the right.

 NOTE
When you look at the Backup window, it simply looks like a list of folders. Where are the files? The folders appear at the top of the list, so they may be the only things visible to you. If you use the scroll bar at the right edge of the list to move to the bottom of the list, you will see the files in the root folder of the selected device. We'll get down to the file level shortly.

2. Search through the list of folders to find your Windows 95 folder. If you want to back up every file and folder in Windows, you should click the box to the left of the Windows folder name. Instead, we are going to select a single file to back up.

3. Double-click the Windows folder. You'll see even more folders; scroll down until you start seeing individual files like those in Figure 14.7.

4. Scroll through the files in the folder until you locate the file called WIN. In the Type column, it will say Configuration Settings.

 NOTE
If you have file extensions turned on, the file will be listed as WIN.INI.

5. If the files are not in alphabetical order, you can click the Name block at the top of the list to list them alphabetically. Or you might want to click the Type block and search through the configuration files for WIN.

6. When you have located the file, click the tiny box to the left of the file name in the list.

7. Click the Next Step button at the top-right corner of the Backup window. This will give you a list of devices to use for the backup.

8. Select a device for the backup from the list at the left in the window by double-clicking it. For our example, we will pick our A: drive.

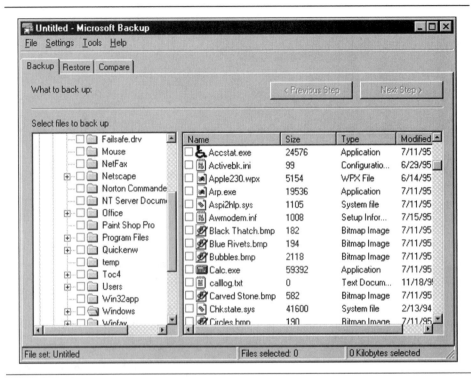

FIGURE 14.7: Looking at files in the Windows folder

9. To save the file set, pull down the File menu and select Save.

10. In the resulting dialog box, we'll use the name WIN as the name of the file set.

11. Click OK. The file set will be saved.

12. Click the Start Backup button at the upper-right corner of the Backup window.

13. Backup will display a dialog box asking for a name for your backup file. Make sure you have inserted the proper medium in the proper backup device (in this case a 3.5-inch floppy in the A: drive). Type in WIN as the backup file name and click OK. The backup will begin immediately. As the backup proceeds, you will see the dialog box shown in Figure 14.8.

14. The final step is to click the OK button.

FIGURE 14.8: Watching the progress of the backup

 TIP   If you want to keep this file set for future use, after you choose a destination for the backup, select Save from the File menu. Specify a name for your file set. When you next want to use it, start Backup and select Open File Set from the File menu.

Backing Up an Existing File Set

Let's do a backup of an existing file set. Since we just created it, let's use the WIN file set. Here's what to do:

1. Begin by shutting down Backup. Click the X icon at the extreme upper-right corner of the Backup window.

2. Start Backup by following the instructions earlier in this skill.

3. When you get to the Backup window, pull down the File menu and select Open File Set.

4. In the Open dialog box, double-click the icon WIN (or whatever you used as the name of the file set we just created). The file set will open.

5. Click the Next Step button at the top-right corner of the Backup window.

6. Select a device to which you want to save the backup (from the list in the left part of the window) by double-clicking the device icon. For this example, select drive A: as the destination.

7. Click the button at the top right marked Start Backup.

8. You will be prompted for the name of the backup.

9. Make sure your backup medium (floppy disk or tape) is in the device selected, and then click OK to begin the backup process.

 TIP   Windows 95 has already made a Full System Backup file set. Open and use this file set when you want to back up everything on your computer.

Choosing Backup Options

To use Backup's other options, pull down the Settings menu and select Options. This will display a dialog box showing four tabs: General, Backup, Restore, and Compare. When you click the Backup tab, you'll see the following options:

- Quit Backup after operation is finished

- Full backup of all selected files or backup of selected files that have changed since the last backup

- Verify files (make sure they were backed up properly)

 NOTE   Naturally, verifying your backup will be safer than not, but the backup is much slower with verify on.

- Use data compression

- Format tape, if needed

- Erase on tape backup

- Erase on floppy disk backup (erases contents of disk before making backup)

Making Comparisons

The purpose of Compare is to make sure a backup is current. Since we've already completed a backup of a single file, let's compare that file we backed up to the original:

1. Start Backup (see the steps earlier in this skill).

2. When you get to the Backup window, click the Compare tab to check the backup against the original.

3. Although it's not at all clear, you are being asked to identify the location of the backup file, so click the icon for drive A:. A list of all of the backups on drive A: will appear. Select the one you want to compare.

4. Click the Next Step button. At the top of the left list box you should see WIN (the name of the backup set), From Drive C: (the origin of the files in the set), and then WINDOWS (the name of the folder from which the file was backed up—all these will differ if you're using a different backup set). Click the check box to the left of the Windows folder.

5. In the right list box you will see the files from the Windows folder that are part of this backup set. If you are using the backup set you created earlier, this will be the single configuration settings file called WIN. The check in the box to its left indicates it will be included in the compare operation.

6. Click the button marked Start Compare in the upper-right corner of the Backup window, and the comparison will proceed.

Error Messages

If there are differences between the backup file and the file on your disk, you will be notified. In this case, after doing the backup of WIN.INI to the floppy, I loaded the WIN.INI file on the hard drive into a word processor and added an extra carriage return to the file so it would be different from the file backed up. I ran Compare and was notified there was a difference and then was asked if I wanted to see the report shown in Figure 14.9.

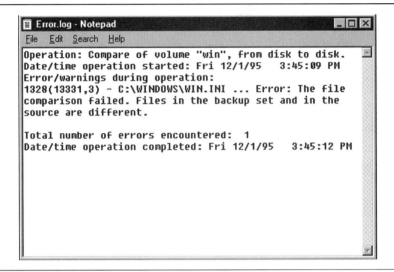

FIGURE 14.9: Reviewing an error report

Compare Options

Pull down the Settings menu, select Options, click the Compare tab, and a dialog box shows you the following options:

- Quit Backup after operation is completed.

- Compare to file in original location, in an unspecified location, or in a specific alternate location—a single folder.

Restoring Files Later

Restore is useful for more than recovering from disaster. It's a good way to move large files off your hard disk when they aren't immediately needed, and then restore them at a later date.

How to Do It

We'll use Restore to restore the WIN configuration file we backed up earlier. (On the disk, it's called WIN.INI.) Follow these steps:

1. Start Backup.

2. When you get through all the introductory dialog boxes, click the tab at the top of the Backup window marked Restore.

3. In the list at the left side of the window, click the device from which the restore is to be made—floppy drive A:. A list of the backup files on drive A: will appear in the right side of the Backup window.

4. Select the backup file from which you want to restore.

5. Click Next Step. As with compare, use the left pane to select the folder whose files you want to restore. In the right pane, select the specific files you want to restore if you don't want to restore all the files in the selected folder.

6. Click the Start Restore button, and the restoration will proceed.

Dealing with Problems

If there are problems with the restore, you'll see a dialog box giving you the option of seeing a report something like the one in Figure 14.10.

The insertion and then deletion of a single carriage return caused the error here. After changing the file on the hard disk, I saved the file. This made the time/date stamp on the file on the hard disk more recent than the stamp on the backed up file. So there's an error when attempting to restore the backed up file because it's now older than the one on the hard drive. Allowing the restoration of an older file over a newer one is not usually a good idea.

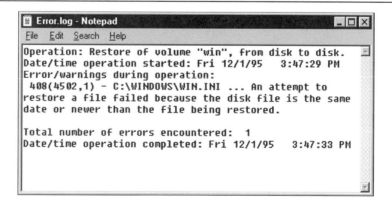

FIGURE 14.10: A report on why a restore operation went wrong

Options for Restoring

Pull down the Settings menu, select Options, and in the Options dialog box, click the tab marked Restore. These are the options you're given:

- Quit Backup after operation is completed

- Restore to the original location, an alternate location, or to a specified folder in an alternate location

- Verify restore (which exacts a price—it adds to the length of time of the restore, but also makes it more reliable)

- Never overwrite files

- Overwrite older files only (this option is set on my system, in order to generate the error shown in Figure 14.10)

- Overwrite files (if this is selected, you have the additional option of being prompted before the files are overwritten)

Some Additional Backup Options

The Tools menu in Backup contains three options: Format Tape, Erase Tape, and Redetect Tape Drive. If you have a tape drive, you will need to format your tapes before using them. If you have an old tape, you may want to erase it before using it again to prevent problems with Backup overwriting existing files on the tape. If you install a tape drive after you have run Backup the first time (or if Backup failed to recognize an existing tape drive), you will want to run Redetect Tape Drive.

Drag-and-Drop Backup

On the Settings menu there is also an option called Drag and Drop, which lets you place Backup on your Desktop as an icon. You can then back up a file set by dragging it to the Backup icon and dropping it. If you want to use this option, select it from the Settings menu and confirm the settings in the dialog box: Run Backup Minimized, Confirm Operation before Beginning, and Quit Backup after Operation Is Finished. By default these are set On.

Here's how to place Backup on your Desktop as an icon:

1. Right-click the Start button and select Open.

2. In the window that opens, double-click in turn on Programs ➢ Accessories ➢ System Tools.

3. Right-click the Backup icon and drag it to the Desktop.

4. Release the mouse button and select Create Shortcut(s) Here from the pop-up menu.

When you're ready to back up a particular file set, you can find it in the Program Files ➤ Accessories folder and then drag and drop it on the Backup icon on the Desktop. An easier way is to make a folder called Backup. Put shortcuts to your file sets and to Backup inside. If you want, put a shortcut to the folder on your Desktop. Then all you have to do is open the folder and drag the appropriate file set to the Backup icon to start a backup.

Making More Room on Your Hard Disk

The first disk compression programs were born six or seven years ago when hard drives cost up to $5 for each megabyte of storage space. These programs were slow and not all that reliable. Now that hard drives cost as little as 20 cents per megabyte and compression is no longer a big issue, compression is very fast and very reliable. Compression just means that all or a portion of your hard drive can be made to appear much larger than it actually is.

Windows 95 supports two varieties of disk compression: DoubleSpace and DriveSpace. DriveSpace is the program supplied with Windows 95. DoubleSpace is a slightly different, older version that had its first incarnation with MS-DOS 6. Windows 95 creates only DriveSpace compressed drives.

 NOTE   Windows 95 works with drives that are compressed with Stacker, SuperStor, and AddStor, in addition to DriveSpace and DoubleSpace.

How Compression Works

Let's say you have one hard drive labeled C: and use DriveSpace to create a compressed drive D:. The compressed drive is not a separate partition of your hard drive. It's actually a file referred to as the CVF (compressed volume file) in the root folder of the C: drive. C: drive is called the *host* drive for this CVF.

If you make it using Windows 95, it'll be called DRVSPACE.000. Not that you'll *see* this file when in Windows. To Windows 95 and all your programs, it'll appear just as drive D:.

If you want to see the file, you'll have to turn off its setting as a hidden file. Don't bother. There is nothing useful you can do with a CVF. Don't delete it, attempt to change it, or anything else. *Only* approach a compressed drive through DriveSpace. If you want to remove compression, use DriveSpace to do it.

Compressing a Drive

You'll need at least 2MB of free space on your C: drive if that's the one being compressed. If it's another drive or floppy disk, you'll need 768K of free space before compression. Follow these steps:

1. Click on the Start button, then select Programs ➤ Accessories ➤ System Tools and then DriveSpace.

2. DriveSpace will check your system and report on what it finds (shown in Figure 14.11).

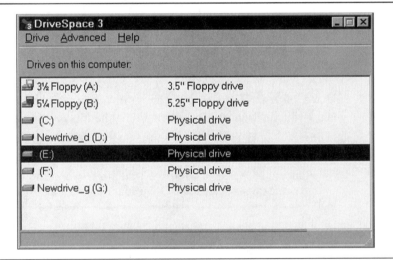

FIGURE 14.11: Viewing drives in the DriveSpace 3 window

3. Highlight the drive you want to compress and select Compress from the Drive menu.

4. The next window (Figure 14.12) shows the status of the drive and what the status will be after compression.

5. Click the Start button to compress files and free space on the drive.

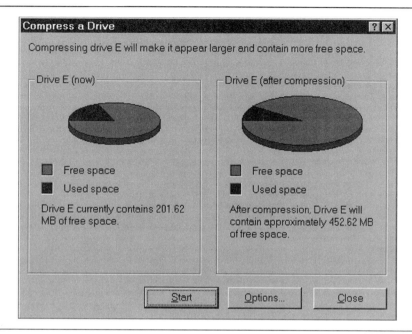

FIGURE 14.12: Seeing what will be gained if you use compression.

 NOTE   Compressed drives can't be larger than 512MB, unless you're using DriveSpace 3 from Plus! for Windows 95.

At the end of the compression process, you'll see a window like the one in Figure 14.13 showing the amount of space you've gained by compressing.

Behind the Options Button

Figure 14.12 shows an Options button. Click it and you can see how Windows is planning to proceed. In the above example, I told Windows 95 that I wanted to compress drive E:—free space and files included. Figure 14.14 shows that the new host drive will be J: and it will be hidden.

There will still be a drive E: (what I'll see as drive E: will be the new CVF) and the 2MB left on the host drive won't be visible since it'll now be the hidden drive J:.

You can change these options, leaving more free space on J: and making it visible or changing the drive letter designation for the host drive.

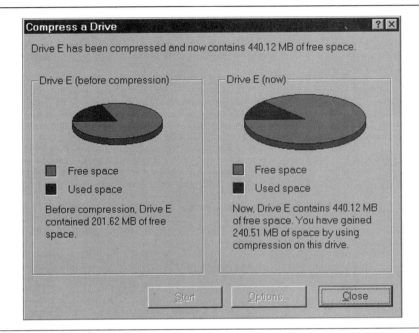

FIGURE 14.13: After you compress a drive, this window opens to show you the before and after.

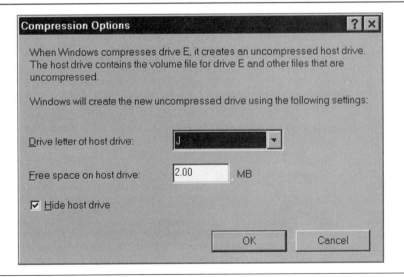

FIGURE 14.14: Viewing the compression options

TIP   You can change the designated drive letter for the drive that contains the Windows 95 folder.

Compressing Free Space

To make a compressed volume from the free space on a drive, open DriveSpace and follow these steps:

1. Highlight an existing drive.

2. Select Create Empty from the Advanced menu.

3. Read the text surrounding the boxes (see Figure 14.15) and you'll see what's proposed. You can change the content of the text boxes with drop-down arrows next to them.

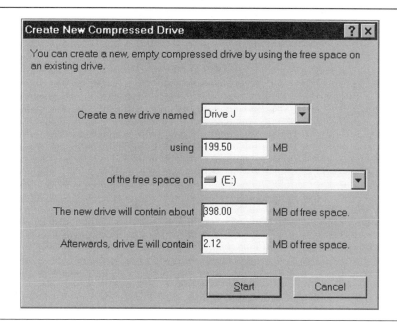

FIGURE 14.15: Creating a new compressed drive

Changing the Size of a Compressed Drive

If there's free space on your compressed drive, you can add free space to the host drive by making the compressed portion smaller. Likewise, if you have free space on the host drive, you can make the compressed portion larger—as long as you keep within the 512MB maximum size for compressed drives.

To change the size of a compressed file, follow these steps:

1. Start DriveSpace, then highlight an existing drive. Select Adjust Free Space from the Drive menu.

2. Move the slider bar to adjust the free space.

Removing a Compressed Drive

A compressed drive can be removed (that is, the drive returned to its pre-compression state) quite easily as long as there's enough space on the host drive for all the files once they're decompressed.

To remove a compressed drive, follow these steps:

1. Open DriveSpace and highlight the drive you want to uncompress.

2. Select Uncompress from the Drive menu.

3. The window shown in Figure 14.16 will open and show you the current state of the drive and what it will look like after being uncompressed.

4. You'll see a warning notice advising that your computer will be unusable during the uncompress cycle and advising you to back up important files first. Click Uncompress Now if you're ready to proceed.

A window with a progress bar will open so you can see how far along the process has gone. At the end you'll also get a window much like the one in Figure 14.16, except this one will show the results.

 NOTE   Feel free to experiment with compressing and uncompressing drives and looking at other options on the DriveSpace menus. Microsoft has made DriveSpace very sturdy. You can even turn off the machine in the middle of a compress operation and when you turn the machine back on, DriveSpace will pick up right where it left off.

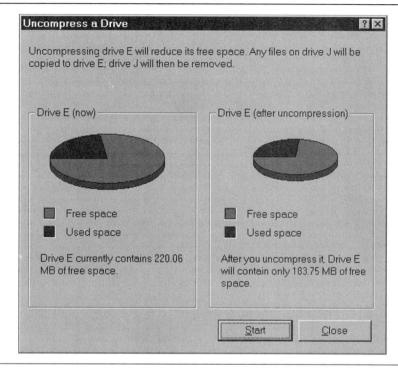

FIGURE 14.16: The before and after views of a drive you've elected to uncompress

Using the Resource Meter

The Resource Meter is a handy little device if you're keeping track of resources on your computer. It's pretty hard to run out of resources in Windows 95 but you can get awfully low if you have enough windows open.

To put Resource Meter on the end of your Taskbar, take these steps:

1. Right-click the Start button and select Open.

2. In the window that opens, double-click Programs, then Accessories, and finally System Tools.

3. Right-click Resource Meter and select Create Shortcut.

4. Right-click the new shortcut and select Cut.

5. Next go to the Windows Startup folder. This can be done by using this icon on the toolbar at the top of the window. Click it twice to move up two levels to Programs.

6. Double-click Startup. When the Startup window opens, right-click in an empty area and select Paste from the pop-up menu.

The next time you start up your computer, a small icon will be placed on your Taskbar. Place your pointer on the icon and a flyover box will open showing available resources. Or right-click the icon and select Details. A window like the one in Figure 14.17 will open.

There's no point in trying to describe what the different resources mean because the explanation would involve terms like *memory heaps* and *device contexts*. Suffice it to say that if any of these numbers starts approaching zero, it's time to close some open programs to give yourself more maneuvering room.

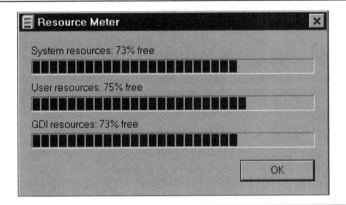

FIGURE 14.17: The Resource Meter window

Are You Experienced?

Now you can...

- ☑ run ScanDisk to check the health of your hard drive
- ☑ back up and restore files
- ☑ compress your hard drive to get more space
- ☑ install the Resource Meter

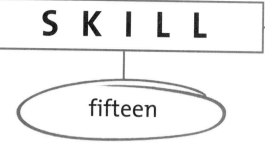

S K I L L

fifteen

Sending and Receiving E-mail

- ❏ Choosing a connection

- ❏ Selecting an Internet service provider

- ❏ Connecting through America Online, CompuServe, Microsoft Network, and AT&T WorldNet

- ❏ Setting up Dial-Up Networking

- ❏ Sending and receiving e-mail

For the first decade or so of the PC's existence, most people who had computers—whether at work or at home—used them as independent, stand-alone machines. But in the last few years, the focus has shifted to what's called *connectivity*. This can mean everything from e-mail and Internet connections to networks of varying degrees of complexity.

Windows 95 incorporates more ways of connecting to the outside world than any other operating system. It has built-in fax capability (covered in Skill 16), the Microsoft Network, software to connect to several online services, and an Internet browser (we'll get to that in a bit) that also lets you send mail and read Internet news.

Starting Simple

The whole question of connecting to the Internet can appear very bewildering—mainly because there are several ways to get to the same place. You should choose whatever is most convenient for you. In this skill, we talk about e-mail—Skills 19 through 25 are about Internet Explorer and how to use it to investigate the phenomenon of the World Wide Web.

E-mail that travels outside your house or business goes by way of the Internet. You must have some connection to the Internet to send and receive mail. The software you use to send and receive mail can be Windows Messaging, Internet Explorer, or some third-party program such as Eudora or Netscape Navigator.

 NOTE Internet Explorer and Netscape Navigator are browsers that include a mail component—so you can combine the functions in one piece of software.

The connection can be through a simple Internet service provider (ISP) that provides a "pass-through" connection. You call their computers over the phone line, and their computers are connected to the Internet backbone. The other kind of connection is through a commercial online service such as America Online, the Microsoft Network, or CompuServe. The online services also provide a pass-through connection but add a great deal of their own content, such as discussion groups, reference material, and special interest areas devoted to hobbies, health, sports, travel, games, and many, many more subjects.

Any Internet connection is suitable for sending and receiving e-mail.

What Kind of Connection?

Choosing a way to connect your computer to the Internet is a trade-off between performance and cost; more money gets you a faster link between your own system and the backbone. While the difference between file transfers through a modem and a high-speed link can be dramatic, the cost of improved performance may not always be justified. For most home users and many small businesses, a dial-up telephone line and a 28.8 kbps modem is still the most cost-effective choice.

NOTE   The Internet backbone is composed of the very high-speed lines that link the major nodes on the Internet. Communications giants like AT&T, MCI, and Sprint own these lines.

If it's available in your area, you might want to consider ISDN (Integrated Services Digital Network) as an alternative to conventional POTS (Plain Old Telephone Service) lines. ISDN is more expensive and complicated to install and configure, but once it's in place, it offers substantially faster network connections. Your Internet service provider can tell you if ISDN service is available and explain how to order the lines and obtain the necessary interface equipment.

In a larger business, where many users can share the same link to the Internet, a connection with more bandwidth is probably a better approach. Many users can share a single high-speed connection through a LAN, so the cost per user may not be significantly greater than that of a second telephone line.

If your PC is already connected to a LAN, you should ask your network administrator or help desk about setting up an Internet account; it's likely there's already some kind of connection in place.

As with most decisions related to data communications, when you ask, "What kind of connection should I use?" the simple answer is, "The fastest and most reliable you can afford."

Choosing a Modem

For most individuals and small businesses, the most practical way to connect is through a dial-up telephone line and a modem. *Modem* is a made-up word constructed out of *modulator-demodulator*. A modem converts digital data from a computer into sounds that can travel through telephone lines designed for voice communication (that's the *modulator* part), and it also converts sounds it receives from a telephone line to digital data (that's the *demodulator* part).

For reasons of economy, convenience, or simplicity, let's say you've decided to go with an inexpensive connection to the Internet through a modem and a telephone line. What now? If you don't already have a modem, go find one. There are three things to consider when you choose a modem: speed, form, and compatibility.

Modem Speed

The speed of a modem is the maximum number of data bits that can pass through the modem in one second. You might find some extremely inexpensive 9600 bps (bits per second) modems, but that's really too slow for programs like Internet Explorer. Don't waste your time and money. Anything slower than 9600 bps is useful only as a paper weight. New modems have maximum speeds of either 33.6K bps or 56K bps. As a rule, buy the fastest modem you can afford.

Modem Form

Modems come in three forms: internal, external, and on a credit-card size PCMCIA card (also known as a PC Card). Each type has specific advantages and disadvantages:

- Internal modems are expansion cards that fit inside your PC. They're the least expensive type of modem, and they don't require special data cables or power supplies. However, they're a nuisance to install, and they don't include the status lights that show the progress of your calls.

- External modems are separate, self-contained units that are easy to install and move between computers. They cost more than internal modems, and they need a separate AC power outlet. In order to use an external modem, your computer must have an unused serial (COM) connector.

- PC Cards are small, lightweight devices that fit into the PCMCIA slots on many laptop computers. They're the most convenient modems for people who travel with their PCs, but they're also the most expensive.

Modem Compatibility

The other thing to consider when you choose a modem is compatibility with standards. In order to connect your computer to a distant system, the modems at both ends of the link must use the same methods for encoding and compressing data.

Therefore, you should use a modem that follows the international standards for data communication. The standard for 33.6K modems is V.34bis, although it's referred to more commonly as just 33.6K. The important standard for 28,800 bps modems is called V.34; the standard for slower modems is V.32bis. Don't even consider a modem that doesn't follow one of these standards.

Using a National ISP

The greatest advantage of using a national or international ISP is that you can probably find a local dial-in telephone number in most major cities. If you want to send and receive e-mail or use other Internet services while you travel, this can be extremely important.

The disadvantage of working with a large company is that it may not be able to provide the same kind of personal service that you can get from a smaller, local business. If technical support requires a long-distance call plus 20 minutes on hold, you should look for a different service provider.

Many large ISPs can give you free software that automatically configures your computer and sets up a new account. Even if they don't include Internet Explorer in their packages, you should be able to use some version of the program along with the application programs they do supply.

 TIP

Most of these proprietary Winsock programs are designed to work with both Windows 3.1 and Windows 95, so you won't be able to use the 32-bit version of Internet Explorer unless you use Microsoft's Dial-Up Networking program instead of the ISP's proprietary Winsock.

You can obtain information about Internet access accounts from these national service providers:

AT&T WorldNet	1-800-WORLDNET (1-800-967-5363)
internetMCI	1-800-955-6505 (Business)
	1-800-550-0927 (Home)
SPRYnet	1-800-SPRYNET (1-800-777-9638)
GNNnet	1-800-819-6112
IBM Global Network	1-800-455-5056
PSInet	1-800-774-0852
Netcom	1-800-353-6600

Many local telephone companies and more than a few cable TV companies are also planning to offer Internet access to their subscribers. If it's available in your area, you should be able to obtain information about these services from the business office that handles your telephone or television service.

Using a Local ISP

The big national and regional services aren't your only choice. In most metropolitan areas and in a growing number of other places, smaller local service providers also offer access to the Internet.

If you can find a good local ISP, it might be your best choice. A local company may be more responsive to your particular needs and more willing to help you get through the inevitable configuration problems than a larger national operation. Equally important, reaching the tech support center is more likely to be a local telephone call.

But unfortunately, the Internet access business has attracted a tremendous number of entrepreneurs who are in it for the quick dollar—some local ISPs are really terrible. The most terrible:

- Don't have enough modems to handle the demand

- Don't have a high-capacity connection to an Internet backbone

- Don't know how to keep their equipment and servers working properly

- Have unhelpful technical support people

- Make you spend long waits on hold

If a deal seems too good to be true, it probably is.

To learn about the reputations of local ISPs, ask friends and colleagues who have been using the Internet for a while. If there's a local computer user magazine, look for schedules of user group meetings where you can find people with experience using the local service providers. If you can't get a recommendation from any of those sources, look in the list of ISPs at http://thelist.com.

 TIP No matter which service you choose, wait a month or two before you print your e-mail address on business cards and letterhead. If the first ISP you try doesn't give you the service you expect, take your business someplace else.

Using an Online Service

Windows 95 includes the software to subscribe to America Online, CompuServe, and AT&T WorldNet. You can pick one or more of these or get online with another provider altogether. Both CompuServe and America Online offer free trials of their service. But be advised that you have to provide a credit card or bank information to get that free trial, and you must remember to cancel if you decide the service isn't for you; otherwise you'll keep being charged whether you're using the service or not.

AT&T WorldNet actually offers completely free access to the Internet. The catch is that you need to be an AT&T long-distance customer and the free access is for five hours per month for a year. If you use the Internet just to send and receive e-mail, that may well be plenty of time. However, if you're going to be using your connection for searching the Web or playing games, you're better off with unlimited access for a flat rate. As of this writing, America Online, AT&T WorldNet, and the Microsoft Network all offer flat-rate programs.

 TIP   Because of the way Internet mail works, your address will be different at each provider. Maybe you like the idea of having multiple e-mail addresses, but most people will probably be happier with only one e-mail address to give out and only one location from which they have to retrieve mail.

America Online

To set up the free trial version of America Online, double-click the AOL and Internet icon in the Online Services folder (on your Desktop). Follow the directions on the screen. AOL will first connect you to an 800 number and download a list of local access numbers. Pick one near you (and a backup number for those busy signals) and the sign up will continue.

Your modem will dial the modem at the local access number. That modem is connected to a computer that's part of the AOL network and from there you can jump to the Internet (though AOL has lots of its own features).

AOL made its reputation primarily through its chat groups or what they call their "People Connection." If you like the idea of chatting online, there are always lots of people talking live in the many, many chat rooms on AOL.

TIP   Don't forget that just about everything online is done while you're connected through your phone line. That means the phone line will be tied up for long periods of time, and if your connection is a toll call, you'll very quickly run up phone bills of ferocious dimensions. Check the access numbers you're using to be sure they are indeed the closest and cheapest for you to use.

America Online's Internet connection software is easy to use. Moving from page to page on the World Wide Web is fast—though connecting to the Internet through AOL in the evenings can be frustrating. Lots of busy signals. (AOL swears they're adding new hardware and connection points to solve the problem this very moment!)

AT&T WorldNet

AT&T WorldNet will give you five hours of free access every month for a year—*if* you're an AT&T long-distance customer on the phone line you're using. Otherwise, you pay $4.95 per month for three free hours (additional hours are $2.50 each) or $19.95 per month for unlimited access.

To install the software for AT&T WorldNet, double-click the WorldNet icon in the Online Services folder. Follow the directions on the screen. Early in the process, you'll need to restart your computer. After you reboot the computer, you'll a screen like the one in Figure 15.1. Most of what's there is advertising fluff, but it's helpful to read, to get a feeling for what the service has to offer. Take your time—at this point all the activity is taking place on your computer; you're not paying for any phone calls or connection time.

If you decide to go ahead, click the How to Sign Up button, then the next Sign Me Up! field. The software will connect you through an 800 toll-free call to AT&T WorldNet for the enrollment procedure.

The first page you'll see has the AT&T WorldNet Service Agreement and Operating Policies. Scroll down to read it. You should read it all, but critical sections are (4) Operating Policies; (5) Copyright, Licenses, and Idea Submissions; (6) Use of the Service; and (7) Member Identifiable Information. Then all you need to do is keeping reading pages, supplying the needed information, and then clicking the Next button to move on.

Once the enrollment is completed, you'll be using Internet Explorer as your Internet interface.

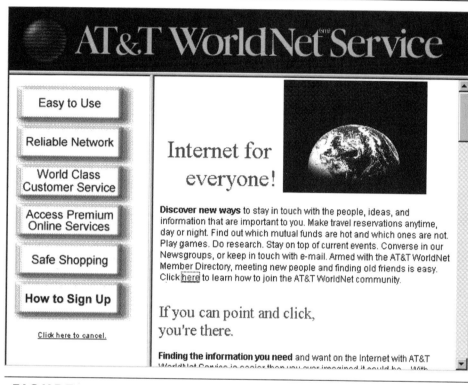

FIGURE 15.1: The introductory material for AT&T WorldNet

YOU *CAN* BE TOO CUTE

Avoid too much creativity when selecting an e-mail address. You may start off sending mail to just your friends and old college roommates, but it's very likely that your field of vision will expand. And once you start visiting newsgroups concerned with your profession or start corresponding with fellow accountants or Zoroastrians, an e-mail address like Fuzzbunny or DogLips can put you at a distinct disadvantage.

NOTE   See Skills 19 through 25 for much more on Internet Explorer.

CompuServe

CompuServe is the oldest of these online services, though based on their flashy new software, they certainly don't look it (see Figure 15. 2). CompuServe's strong points are to be found in its forums. There are special interest forums on every-thing from horses to genealogy and the Civil War to women in aviation. These forums are organized into *threads*, so a discussion can be followed easily.

FIGURE 15.2: CompuServe's opening screen

In addition, CompuServe has the best selection of technical support forums under one roof, so to speak. Got a problem with WordPerfect for Windows? Drop in to the WPWIN forum and post a message. Many hardware and software makers have Web sites as well, but nothing beats CompuServe for a direct line to company representatives or experienced users.

To install CompuServe 3, double-click the Csi icon and follow the steps on the screen. With the software included with Windows 95, you get your first 10 hours on CompuServe free (as long as you use them in the first month; unused hours don't carry over). After that, you get five free hours for $9.95 per month with extra hours at $2.95 each.

 NOTE Also included is software for CompuServe's WOW! service, born in 1996 and deceased in early 1997. You might as well delete the WOW! icon because it won't connect you to anything anymore.

The Microsoft Network

Of all the online software, the Microsoft Network is the most closely integrated with the Windows 95 operating system (not surprisingly). It also has the easiest e-mail software, Windows Messaging (that's the Inbox) on your Desktop.

MSN's introductory offer is 10 free hours followed by a rate of $6.95 for five hours each month with additional hours billed at $2.50 each. There's also an unlimited access rate of $19.95 per month.

 NOTE If you have no Microsoft Network icon on your Desktop, go to Add/Remove Programs in the Control Panel. On the Windows Setup page, scroll down to Microsoft Network and install.

After you go through the usual sign-up procedures—supplying your name and address and credit card information—you'll be connected. The interface is that of Internet Explorer. Microsoft Network has many of its own features, but it's primarily a gateway to the Internet. The browser is speedy and the visual effects are splendid.

After you join, you'll see a screen advising you of a "new look" for MSN. What this means is that soon you'll be receiving a CD in the mail that will have an update to the Microsoft Network software. A very nice upgrade it is, too. It adds new features and speeds up your navigation. And all you need to do is put the CD in your CD-ROM drive and follow the on-screen directions.

TIP   If you have trouble connecting, try the MSN Signup and Access Troubleshooter. To get at it, right-click the Microsoft Network icon on your Desktop, select Connection Settings from the pop-up menu, and then click the Help button.

Member IDs and Passwords

The Microsoft Network is somewhere between CompuServe and America Online when it comes to how you're identified online. With CompuServe you use your full name in most places—though there are provisions for using nicknames in the CB area and in some forums. AOL members sometimes use their full names (if they're short enough), but they're greatly outnumbered by people using whimsical handles like STUDMUFIN or KUTESTUF.

Passwords are another matter—you can be as silly as you want as long as the password is one you'll remember (but would be hard for someone else to guess). Passwords must be from eight to 16 characters long, and using combinations of letters and numbers is best.

The opening screen for the Microsoft Network has an option to have the software remember your password. This is handy if you're in a situation where security isn't a big concern.

What's There Now

It's difficult to get too specific about what's on the Microsoft Network because there's a lot of stuff and MSN is constantly changing and adding more. Currently however, the services are divided into five main categories (see Figure 15.3):

MSN Today   The screen that greets you when you first sign on. News of interest to all members and announcements of special events are shown here. Look for hypertext links to further information.

E-mail   Click here to see any incoming electronic mail. (Windows Messaging will be opened automatically.)

Favorite Places   As you navigate the network, you'll undoubtedly find spots you'd like to visit again. To make this easy, you can put a link in Favorite Places to any place you've found. Next time you want to go back, you'll just open this folder and click the icon for the spot you want to visit.

Member Assistance   Problems with connections, questions about billing, account changes, and stuff like that are all addressed here.

Categories   This is a visual table of contents for the entire Microsoft Network, and it's a good place to start your exploring.

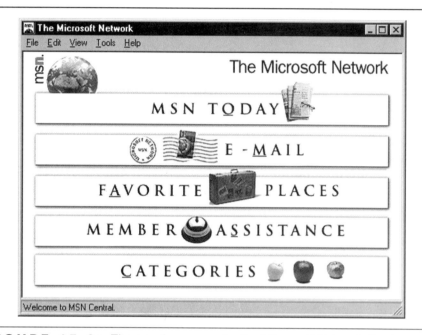

FIGURE 15.3: The opening screen for the Microsoft Network. Don't get too used to it because the CD you'll get in the mail will change this look.

Right-click the MSN icon at the end of the Taskbar to get the menu shown here.

This is the quickest way to sign out as well as to jump to other functions, including MSN Central (the page shown in Figure 15.3).

Skill 15

Things You'll See

As you move around the Microsoft Network, you'll encounter objects both familiar and unfamiliar. Here are some definitions for things you may see:

Folders   When you click Categories, for example, you're opening a top-level folder. Click a topic, and you enter the subfolder. It's just like navigating through a series of folders in the Explorer.

Kiosks   Click here to get the subject matter of a forum, identify who's managing the forum, and view the latest updates on forum activities.

 NOTE   Forums are special-interest areas covering particular subjects. A forum usually includes a bulletin board where you can read and post messages, perhaps a chat room, and some files or other information relevant to the subject matter.

Chat Rooms   Places for real-time discussions. The appeal of these areas is the immediacy—you're actually talking live to others who are online in the same moment. The disadvantage is that discussions can be slow and hard to follow when there are multiple participants.

Newsgroups   These are special interest discussion groups on the Internet. These groups are used by everything from the Human Genome Project to comic book collectors all over the world. Thousands of these groups exist. All of them can be read through MSN but some are read-only, which means you can't post your own message.

BBS   Special interest areas on MSN where you can post and read messages.

Not every folder will have a clear labeling as to what's inside, so you'll have to do a bit of poking around.

For those really special places, right-click the file or folder in the MSN, drag it to your Desktop, and select Create Shortcut(s) Here. The shortcut contains all the information needed to reconnect later and take you right back to that spot. You can also copy shortcuts into messages you send by e-mail to point your friends to your favorite MSN resources.

JUST WHO'S IN CHARGE HERE?

A question that comes up often is: Who runs the Internet?

Well...nobody.

Some international bodies such as the ISO (International Standards Organization), CCITT (Comité Consultatif International de Télégraphique et Téléphonique), and few others set standards for how information is transmitted around the Internet and how modems talk to one another.

In terms of content, your Internet Service Provider (ISP), whether it's America Online or a local company, can control only what's public on its machines. In other words, CompuServe will remove an abusive or obscene posting in one of its forums. But only the sender and the receiver read private e-mail.

Some ISPs don't care what people transmit over their machines. Other ISPs are set up for the sole purpose of providing a home for pornography or fascist rants. This is the nature of the Internet.

My solution, and I recommend it, is to avoid newsgroups with names that are a direct tip-off. If you stumble across a Web page that you find offensive, leave and don't go back. Don't hang around.

Each of the big online companies has some device for parental filtering of Internet content. If you're getting to the Internet through a gateway other than the big companies mentioned in this skill, you'll need to get and install an Internet filter such as Specs, SafeSurf, or Net Nanny if you have children you want to keep away from the raunchier areas. You can set up your own criteria for Internet places that are off-limits to the tots.

Skill 15

Setting Up Windows 95 Dial-Up Networking

If you've chosen an ISP other than Microsoft Network, you must set up a Dial-Up Networking profile that will dial your ISP's closest telephone number whenever you start Internet Explorer or some other Winsock-compliant application program.

Creating a new profile is not difficult, but it's a little more complicated than simply clicking an option in the Setup Wizard. To configure a Dial-Up Networking connection profile, you must complete two separate procedures: load the software and create a connection profile.

Loading the Software

If you didn't load Dial-Up Networking when you installed Windows 95, you must add it before you can connect to the Internet. Follow these steps to add the software:

1. Open the Control Panel.

2. Double-click the Add/Remove Programs icon.

3. Click the Windows Setup tab to display the Windows Setup dialog box.

4. Select the Communications item from the Components list and click the Details button.

5. Make sure there's a check mark next to the Dial-Up Networking component and click the OK button.

6. When you see a message instructing you to insert software disks, follow the instructions as they appear.

7. When the software has been loaded, restart the computer.

8. The Control Panel should still be open. Double-click the Network icon.

9. Click the Add button to display the Select Network Component Type dialog box, shown in Figure 15.4.

10. Select Protocol in the list of component types and click the Add button.

11. Select Microsoft from the list of manufacturers and TCP/IP in the list of network protocols. Click the OK button.

12. You should see TCP/IP in the list of network components. Click the OK button to close the dialog box.

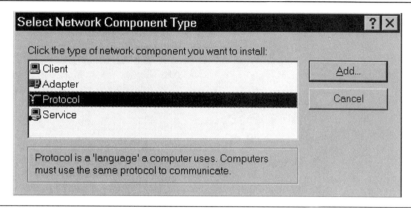

FIGURE 15.4: Use the Select Network Component Type dialog box to set up Dial-Up Networking.

Creating a Connection Profile

Once you've added support for TCP/IP networking, you're ready to set up one or more connection profiles. Follow these steps to create a profile:

1. Start Dial-Up Networking from either the My Computer window on the Desktop or the Programs ➤ Accessories menu.

2. Double-click the Make New Connection icon.

3. The Make New Connection Wizard will start. The name of the computer you will dial is also the name that will identify the icon for this connection profile in the Dial-Up Networking folder. Therefore, you should use the name of your service provider as the name for this profile. If you have separate profiles for telephone numbers in different cities, include the city name as well. For example, if you use SPRYnet as your access provider, you might want to create profiles called SPRYnet Chicago and SPRYnet Boston.

4. Click the Next button to move to the next screen, and type the telephone number for your ISP's PPP access.

5. Click the Finish button to complete your work with the Wizard.

6. You will see a new icon in the Dial-Up Networking window. Right-click this icon and select the Properties command.

7. Click the Server Type button in the dialog box that appears (see Figure 15.5).

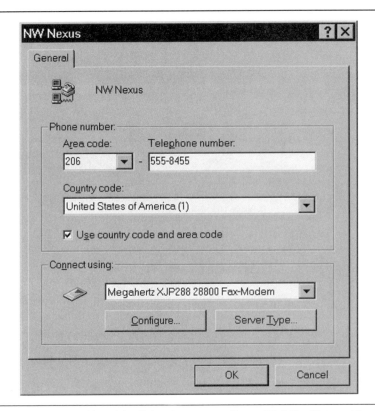

FIGURE 15.5: Use this dialog box to configure Dial-Up Networking.

8. When the Server Types dialog box, shown in Figure 15.6, appears, choose the PPP option in the drop-down list of dial-up server types.

9. Make sure there are check marks next to these options:

   Log on to Network

   Enable Software Compression

   TCP/IP

10. Click the TCP/IP Settings button.

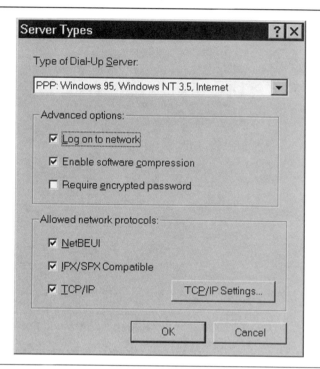

FIGURE 15.6: Use the Server Types dialog box to set up a PPP connection.

11. Ask your ISP how to fill in this dialog box. You will probably use a Server Assigned IP Address and specific DNS addresses, but your ISP can give you the exact information you need.

12. Click the OK buttons to close all the open dialog boxes.

To confirm you have set up the connection profile properly, turn on your modem and double-click the new icon. When the Connect To dialog box appears, as shown in Figure 15.7, type your user ID and password and click the Connect button. Your computer should place a call to the ISP and connect your system to the Internet.

If you have accounts with more than one ISP, or if you carry the same computer to different cities, you can create separate connection profiles for each ISP or each telephone number. By choosing a connection profile before you start any Winsock application, you can make your connection through a profile other than the default.

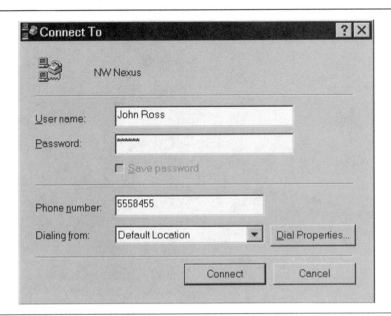

FIGURE 15.7: The Connect To dialog box shows the name and telephone number of your ISP.

Changing the Default Connection

When setup is complete, you will have a Dial-Up Networking connection profile for each of your ISPs. Internet Explorer and other Winsock-compliant programs will use the current default to connect your computer to the Internet whenever you start the programs.

To change the default, follow these steps:

1. Right-click the Internet icon on your Desktop and select the Properties command from the menu.

2. When the Internet Properties dialog box appears, click the Connection tab to display the dialog box shown in Figure 15.8.

3. Choose the name of the Dial-Up Networking connection profile you want to use from the drop-down list.

4. Click the OK button to close the dialog box.

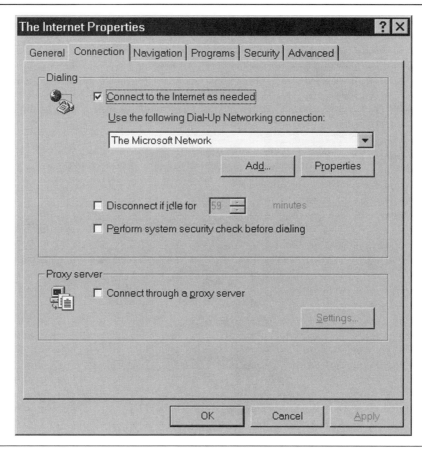

FIGURE 15.8: Use the Connection tab to change the default connection profile.

Easy E-mail

You can send and receive e-mail through CompuServe, America Online, and AT&T WorldNet. Connect to the service and follow the directions for e-mail. However, for all three of those services, you'll need some additional software to read and write your mail when you're not connected "live" to the service. Without that software, you have to do everything while connected. That can drastically increase the time you're keeping the phone line tied up and—if you pay for Internet access by the hour—it can also cost you plenty. With Windows Messaging you can send and receive mail very quickly and then read your mail and compose your messages at your leisure.

To install Windows Messaging, double-click the Inbox icon on your Desktop.

Deselect the check box in front of Microsoft Fax to just install the e-mail for Microsoft Network Online Service (as shown in Figure 15.9) then click Next.

TIP   Fax services can be made much more reliable by placing them in a separate profile. See Skill 16 for how to install and use Windows Fax.

FIGURE 15.9: Setting up the Inbox

Next you just have to follow these steps:

1. The system will create a location for your Address Book. This is where you'll enter the e-mail addresses you use. Accept the default location.

2. Next you'll see the path to your personal folder file. This is the storage spot for incoming and outgoing messages. More than one personal file (as well as Address Books) can be created if you have need for them.

3. The next dialog box will announce that you're done and the Windows Messaging Inbox will open.

TIP   If you find the default view of Messaging unhelpful, try selecting Folders from the View menu so it's easy to see if you're looking at messages you've received, sent, deleted, or planning to send (the Outbox).

Adding Addresses

To add someone's address to the Personal Address Book, follow these steps:

1.   Click on the Inbox icon on your Desktop.

2.   Select Address Book from the Tools menu.

3.   Select New Entry from the File menu. This will open the New Entry box shown in Figure 15.10. The entry types listed will depend on the types of services you have installed.

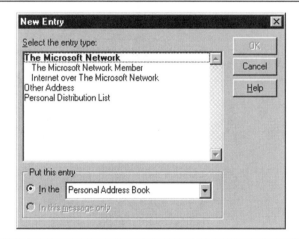

FIGURE 15.10: Making an entry to the Address Book

4.   Select one of the services based on whether the address is an Internet address or a Microsoft Network member (Microsoft Network members have e-mail addresses that end with msn.com). Then click OK.

5.   Provide the information requested, and click OK when you're done.

Now, whenever you select New Message from the Compose menu, you can click the To button. This takes you to your Personal Address Book where you can select a recipient.

Writing Messages

To send a message, click the Inbox on your Desktop to open the Windows Messaging. Select New Message from the Compose menu. Address and type your message, and then select Send from the File menu.

TIP   If you have Remote Mail enabled, you'll have to select Deliver Now Using from the Windows Messaging Tools menu to send mail.

Attaching Files to Your Messages

To attach a file to a message, click the file and drag it into the body of the message as shown in Figure 15.11.

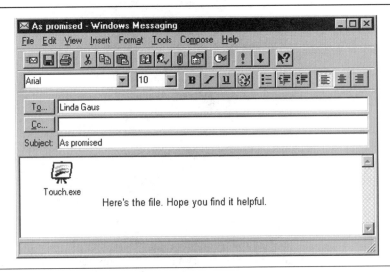

FIGURE 15.11: Drag and drop a file into an e-mail message.

Or if the file isn't where you can see it easily, select the paper clip icon from the toolbar and an Insert File dialog box will open (see Figure 15.12). Use the tool in this box to locate the file you want. Double-click on the file and select whether it's to be sent as text (in the message itself) or as a mail attachment.

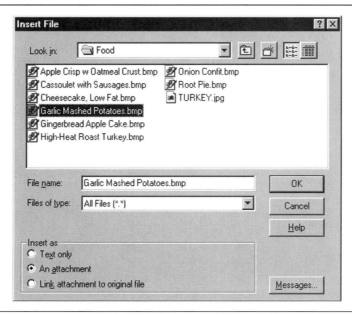

FIGURE 15.12: Finding a file to be sent with an e-mail message

Sending and Receiving Mail with Windows Messaging

How (and whether) Internet mail is delivered to your Inbox depends on whether your Internet connection is a so-called dial-up connection (you use a modem and a phone line) or a LAN connection (the modem is somewhere on your network and the connection is made there). Either way, you can go get your mail when you want it or you can have it done automatically.

With an automatic connection, your Internet mail server is queried as soon as you open Windows Messaging and then as often thereafter as you specify. For a dial-up connection, that means Windows Messaging will open the phone line, dial your Internet service provider, and connect to your mailbox. To set up an automatic connection, follow these steps:

1. Open Windows Messaging and select Services from the Tools menu.

2. Highlight Internet Mail and click Properties.

3. Click the Connection tab, make sure you have Automatic showing in the lower drop-down box, and then click Transfer Options.

4. Select how often you want the network to check for mail messages. Select OK three times.

 TIP Windows Messaging is a little easier to understand if you select View ➢ Folders. It makes it easier to see what you've sent, what's been received, and so forth.

Two Kinds of Internet Mail

Windows Messaging is the way to go if you're any of the following:

- A member of the Microsoft Network
- Using Microsoft Mail
- Writing and reading mail offline
- Want to use an e-mail client to get mail from other locations

Internet mail in Internet Explorer is for:

- On-the-fly sending and receiving of Internet mail
- Mail sent and received through your Internet provider whether it's Microsoft Network or an independent provider

---

Setting Up Remote Mail Preview

With remote mail preview, Windows Messaging will call your mail server and show you the headers for any messages waiting there. You can then select the ones you want to read and transfer them to the Windows Messaging Inbox.

To set up remote preview:

1. Open Windows Messaging, select Services from the Tools menu, highlight Internet Mail, and click Properties.

2. Click the Connection tab. Make sure you have Selective showing in the drop-down windows.

3. Click OK twice. Close and then restart Windows Messaging.

4 When you want to check for mail, select Remote Mail from the Tools menu.

5. From the Tools menu for Remote Mail, choose To Connect, Connect and Update Headers, or Connect and Transfer Mail.

6. If you connect to select particular mail, highlight the messages you want to transfer to your Inbox and select Transfer Mail from the Tools menu.

Reading Messages

To read a message in your Inbox, just double-click it. If you want to know what any of the buttons mean, just position your pointer over one and a descriptive box will pop open.

 TIP　　If you're used to getting Internet mail using other software, you'll notice that the Windows Messaging window shows only the name of the person sending you the mail with no clue as to the origins. Most of the time this doesn't matter, but if you need to see the entire Internet header, select Properties from the File menu, and then look at the Internet tab.

Are You Experienced?

Now you can...

☑ understand and choose an Internet connection

☑ choose a modem

☑ select an Internet service provider

☑ use an online service

☑ set up Windows 95 Dial-Up Networking

☑ master e-mail

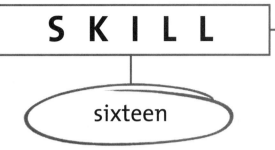

S K I L L

sixteen

Sending and Receiving Faxes

❏ Setting up Microsoft Fax service

❏ Sending and receiving faxes

❏ Dealing with a failed fax

❏ Forwarding a fax

The fax program that comes with Windows 95 is quite serviceable if your needs are relatively modest. But if you need to send and receive dozens of faxes a week, you may want to stick with your existing fax software. (See the "It's TAPI Standard Time" sidebar first.)

It's important that the fax service be in its very own profile as described next. Installing e-mail and fax in the same profile will greatly increase the chances of the fax service working only intermittently, if at all.

Installing the Fax Service

If you've already installed Windows Messaging, you add the fax service separately. If you haven't installed Messaging, you can still make a fax profile. Here are the steps:

1. Click the Start button and select Settings ➤ Control Panel. Click the Mail icon.

2. In the next dialog box, click the Show Profiles button.

3. Next will be a dialog headed Mail. In this box, click the Add button. This will open the Inbox Setup Wizard.

4. Check the Microsoft Fax box and remove the checks in front of any other services. Click Next.

5. In the next dialog box, you'll be asked to provide a name for the fax profile. Use Fax or Microsoft Fax or any other name that distinguishes this profile from any others—particularly the profile you use to send and receive e-mail. Click Next.

6. Select a fax modem. Your modem should be highlighted in the window. Click Properties to set the Answer mode, speaker volume, and other settings.

7. Do you want Microsoft Fax to answer every incoming call? Usually, the answer is No, unless the modem is connected to a dedicated line. With a No setting here, a fax icon will still appear on your Taskbar. You can right-click it when a fax call comes in, and then select Answer Now.

8. Enter your name and fax number. This is needed for your fax headers as well as for determining local versus long-distance calls.

9. If you don't mind having your mail and faxes mixed in the same folders, you can accept the default Personal Address Book and Personal Folders (on the next dialog box). Or you can supply new addresses such as fax.pab and fax.pst.

10. Next you'll be asked if you want to automatically run the profile when Windows starts. Make your choice and click Next. The last dialog box reports the successful installation.

If you do decide to use the same folders for both fax and mail, confusion can arise. Suppose your old pal Eduardo has a fax number, plus an Internet mail address, *and* an MSN address, you'll have to make a separate entry for each one. And when you click the To button on a new message, you'll see your friend's name three times with no indication of which address is which.

Admittedly, this is the dumbest idea anywhere in Windows 95, but you can bypass it somewhat. When you add a new name to the Address Book, include a notation to help you later (as shown in Figure 16.1).

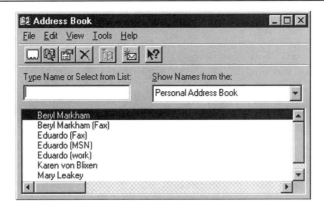

FIGURE 16.1: If you plan ahead, you can differentiate among multiple listings for the same person in the Address Book.

Some of the settings you make during this installation are done without any real knowledge of how the choices will work out in actual practice. Fortunately, all of them can be changed; in fact, the whole next part of this chapter is about how to make those fine-tuning adjustments.

IT'S TAPI STANDARD TIME

TAPI is yet another in the continuing series of cryptic computer acronyms. It stands for Telephony Applications Programming Interface. What that means (short version) is that new communications programs will be able to adopt the settings you've already made on your system: modem type, port, and that sort of stuff. Up until now, you've had to tell each communications program what kind of modem you have, where it is on your computer, and sometimes even the dreaded initialization string. And if you buy a new modem, you have to do all that stuff all over again for every program.

TAPI puts a stop to that nonsense. All programs written to the TAPI standard will be able to detect the settings of your modem. If you change modems, you just go to the Modem icon in the Control Panel, delete the old modem, and install your new one. Another aspect of TAPI is that you can set up various locations you're calling from and when you select one, any TAPI application can use that information to properly dial the number—whether it's a local call, a long-distance call, or charged to a particular credit card.

TAPI-compliant software can also share a single phone line. You can have fax software on auto-receive all the time. Want to check your e-mail? The fax software will politely step aside and, after the call is finished, reinstate itself on auto-receive.

The communications capabilities built into Windows 95—such as the fax software, HyperTerminal, and Phone Dialer—are all TAPI-compliant. The bad news is that pre-Windows 95 software is not, though many programs released in the past year or so have adopted the TAPI standard.

Working with Faxes

There are at least two ways to send a fax: double-click the Inbox icon on your Desktop and select New Fax from the Compose menu, or prepare the fax in your word processor or other application, and then select Microsoft Fax as your printer. You can receive a fax either by having the Microsoft Fax system set to Auto-Receive or by receiving manually.

Sending Faxes

The first time you send a fax, a Compose New Fax Wizard opens and guides you through the process. The first window lets you change the location you're dialing from—if you're not using a portable machine, put a check in the box to tell the system you don't need to see this window again.

Follow these steps:

1. In the Compose New Fax window, type in the name of the addressee and fax number or click Address Book to get a listing from there.

2. If you typed in the name and fax number, click Add to List. (Add additional names if you want this fax sent to multiple recipients.)

3. Click Next.

4. Indicate whether you want a cover page sent with this fax and if so, what kind.

5. Click Options to change when the fax should be sent, the message format, and other properties for this message.

6. Type in a subject header, and then the contents of the fax message. If you're faxing from a word processor, leave this page blank.

7. Next you'll be given the opportunity to include a file with this fax. The file you choose will be opened in the application that created it and then "printed" to the fax. Use the Add File button to locate the file.

8. When you're done, the fax will be sent immediately unless you've made a change under Options to schedule a different time for sending.

Skill 16

Sending Multi-Page Faxes

A weakness of Microsoft Fax is that unless you're faxing directly from a word processing program, you have no way of sending more than one page per fax call. This can be a great deal of trouble—imagine scanning in a contract and faxing it to your lawyer one page at a time!

With a scanner and the Imaging program (Start ➤ Programs ➤ Accessories ➤ Imaging) you can append pages to one another and send them all in a bunch.

You can use your regular scanning software to scan in the pages and save them as TIF or another graphic file format:

1. Open Imaging and select Open from the File Menu. Open the first page of the fax.

2. Select Page ➤ Append ➤ Existing Page and then select the second scanned page.

3. Keep selecting until you have all of the pages then select File ➤ Print ➤ Microsoft Fax (or whatever you named your fax profile).

4. The Fax Wizard will start, asking for the recipient's name and phone number and whether to send a cover sheet and so on. Make your selections and the fax will be sent.

You can also use Imaging as the software for the scanning. Select Scan New from the File menu. Scan in the first page of the fax. Then select Page ➤ Append ➤ Scan Page for each subsequent page.

 NOTE   If your Windows 95 came preinstalled on a computer after November 1996, you'll have the Imaging program. Otherwise you'll have a thing called Fax Viewer that is a good deal less helpful.

 TIP   Imaging can also put together multipage faxes from pages that have been saved in any of several graphic formats including BMP, PCX, JPG, as well as TIF.

Dealing with a Fax That Fails

Occasionally, you'll have a fax that fails to go where it's supposed to. Maybe you had to cancel in mid-stream, maybe the connection was broken, or the fax at the other end dumped you before the transfer was complete.

The transfer will appear to have taken place and the fax will end up in the Sent folder of Windows Messaging. Within a few seconds, though, a new message from the "System Administrator" will appear in your Inbox. Double-click the message and you'll see a report on why the fax failed (see Figure 16.2).

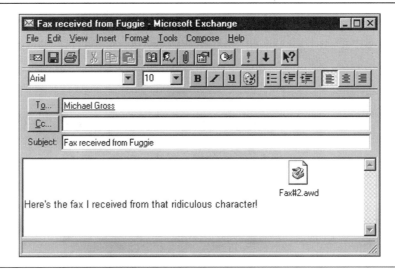

FIGURE 16.2: The report on a failed fax transmission

Click the Send Again button and then the Send icon at the left of the toolbar in the next dialog box.

 TIP Failed messages are returned with a message reporting why the message did not go through.

Receiving Faxes

To reset the fax answer mode after installation, open Windows Messaging by double-clicking the Inbox. If the fax service is installed, a miniature fax machine will appear at the end of the Taskbar. Right-click this icon and select Modem Properties. Figure 16.3 shows the same Fax Modem Properties window. Here you can select one of the three options:

- Answer After (select the number of rings)
- Manual
- Don't Answer

If you select Manual, you'll hear the phone ring when a fax is coming in and it will be up to you to right-click the Fax Modem icon on the Taskbar and select Answer Now from the pop-up menu.

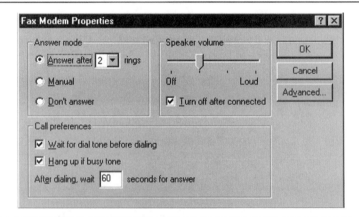

FIGURE 16.3: Setting some fax properties

 NOTE   While you have automatic answer or manual enabled, you won't be able to use other communications programs to dial out unless the programs are TAPI-aware. It's a mixed bag, too. AT&T WorldNet has no trouble dialing out and when you disconnect, your fax software is still in place. On the other hand, AOL flat refuses to dial out unless you close the fax services. You'll have to experiment to find out what works for you.

Using a Fax-Back Service

Many companies provide fax-back service wherein you can make a phone call and documents you need are faxed back to you. To use a fax-back service, just select Start ➢ Programs ➢ Accessories ➢ Fax ➢ Request a Fax.

The Wizard will guide you, though the steps are very simple. First you have to specify what particular document you're seeking or if you want everything at the site. Then you're asked for the fax number and to specify when the call should be placed. That's all there is to it.

Reading Faxes

When you receive a fax, it will appear in the Windows Messaging window. You can double-click it to open the Fax Viewer and see the fax displayed. From this window, you can zoom in or print the fax. Or manipulate it in different ways. If you want to forward the fax to someone else, highlight the fax in the Inbox and select Forward from the Compose menu.

Forwarding a Fax (or Message)

When you receive a message or a fax, the Inbox window will have a button for forwarding the message on to another recipient. But what if it's a fax you want to send by e-mail or an e-mail that you'd like to fax to someone? Click the item's icon on the Inbox window and drag the item to a Message window (see Figure 16.4) or to your Desktop (so you can put it in a message later). You can then send the message using Microsoft Fax, containing the icon in any way you choose. If you're faxing a document made in another application such as Word or Word-Perfect, the embedding of e-mail messages won't work. Yet. (Someday it will—in Windows 2000 or WordPerfect 10—but not today.)

 TIP   Those unfortunates who are not yet using Windows 95 won't be able to open and read a fax file in the .AWD format sent in an e-mail message. For those backward souls, you'll need to forward the fax as a fax (highlight the name in the Inbox and click on the Forward button). The fax system will deliver the fax to the recipient as a printed document.

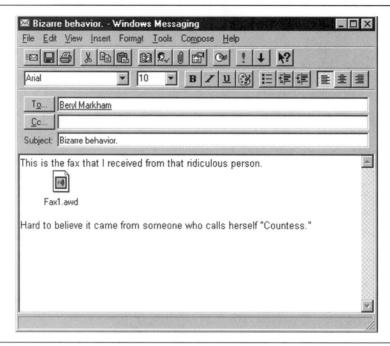

FIGURE 16.4: Sending a fax embedded in an e-mail message

Are You Experienced?

Now you can...

- ☑ install Microsoft Fax services
- ☑ send and receive faxes
- ☑ scan and send multi-page faxes
- ☑ cope with a failed fax
- ☑ read and forward faxes

based telefundraising. Minimum of 7 years experience in similar field. 4 year degree preferred. Proficient computer skills incl. Windows-based software applications required. Salary commensurate w/skills & exp. plus benefits. Send letter and resume to Well-Being Clinic, 543 Spring Ave., Daytonville, VA.

Executive Secretary
OfficePlus, an office supply & furniture company is looking for administrative support to VP. Requires 5 years min. of secretarial experience. Proficiency with MS Word and Excel and excellent communication skills. Must be willing to learn database & desktop software. Fax: OfficePlus, Personnel 665-555-9122.

FACILITIES PLANNER Training Centers Inc. seeks individual to study & develop infrastructure requirements and capital improvement projects. Req's BA in Planning, Engineering, Architecture or rel. field w/ 7 years exp & knowl of Windows (Word, Excel) & graphics programs, 4 yrs exp w PC's planning arch/eng or facilities mgmt & exp w/CAD, database mgmt & project scheduling pref'd. Fax: HR. 885-555-2398.

MANAGEMENT REPORTING ANALYST
Join the team that maintains the purchasing and logistics information systems that support order entry, provide product and contract information, track product utilization, and manage operating budget and inventory systems. Must be proficient in a high-level database system and Excel, Lotus 1-2-3, or similar applications. Fax resume to Data Systems Placement Services 444-555-9998.

MANAGER, ASSET MODELING
This worldwide logistics company is expanding it's transportation network. The successful candidate will have a Bachelor's degree in Economics, Finance or Business Mgmt, with a MBA degree preferred, a solid foundation in Mathematics; and excellent analytical skills. Knowledge of PC applications in Excel, Word, PowerPoint & Visio essential. Competitive benefits and compensation plan. Fax: 966-555-2290/

Manager, Business Analysis
You will direct a team of Business Analysts and oversee timely completion of all projects in accordance with departmental policies & procedures. Requires BA/BS in Behavioral Health Sciences, Business Administration, MIS, or equivalent experience, system development/analysis and software testing; strong project management and team building skills, and software development experience. Hart Corporate Services. Call J. Thornton 243-555-9583.

MARKET RESEARCH PROJECT MANAGER
SuperMouse Designs is creating a new research division. You will provide research consulting services to internal clients and manage external research providers. A BA/BS degree or equivalent with 4-6 years' experi... proces...

send cover letter, resume & salary req's to: Sommes Communications, Attn: HR/Job 85, 776 Bowser Lane, Bowtown, MA.

MARKETING ASSISTANT
Supporting 2 Marketing Mgrs, you'll handle a variety of admin. responsibilities, direct mail coordination, desktop publishing, and ad space coordination. Require 1-2 years admin. exper, and strong computer skills, esp. desktop pub. HTML, Office & Windows. Fax. R. Smith 365-555-8844.

OFFICE MANAGER
Join a growing firm that offers competitive salaries & benefits for a take-charge type. Responsible for all office purchases & operations, including a quarterly newsletter. Windows & MS Office experience req'd. Call 973-555-4545.

PC Support Specialist
High-end catalog company and specialty retailer has opening in MIS Dept. Support corporate associates with PC and network systems. Extensive PC hardware installation and configuration experience is required. Must be able to communicate effectively, and determine cause of problems, & develop solutions. Requires network admin, & multiple PC operating systems experience (Windows, UNIX) Fax resume & salary reqs to High Profile Images 388-555-9634.

PROJECT ASST. Serve as a point person in HR office of fast growing biotech firm. Requires creative thinking and up-to-date office computer skills, esp. Word, PowerPoint & Excel. Fax resume to TruPoint Systems 689-555-1298.

PROJECT MANAGER
Public agency seeking environmental project manager to oversee 18-month marsh preservation project. Develop, analyze, organize & summarize planning data and financial info. Windows computer skills essential. Send resume to Public Planning Services, Attn: HR., 34 Marsh Lane, Willowdale, CA.

Sales/Computer
Expanding computer software & hardware store is looking for more qualified sales associates to staff our busy downtown location. Windows software experience required. Send resume and salary/commission requirements to General Manager, Computers For You, 433 Main St., Ontario, MN.

SALES SUPPORT ASSOCIATE Work with customer service, account managers, marketing & brand management. You will handle distribution of sales materials and internal correspondence. You will need 1-2 years in sales admin, and basic office functions (mail, fax, phones etc.), plus PC skills. Computer troubleshooting skills a plus.

Sales: Sr. Account Coordinator
Looking Good, a national clothing chain is looking for seasoned sales pros to oversee sales operations. Qualified candidates must have 4-5 years sales mgmt exp. and strong PC skills. A college degree, working knowledge of Excel, PowerPoint, Word and database software req'd. Fax resume and cover letter to: Looking Good, Attn: K. Ferkovich, 877 Goody Ave., Reno, NV.

SALES/COMPUTER
Expanding computer software & hardware store is looking for more qualified sales associates to staff our busy downtown location. Windows software experience required. Send resume and salary/commission requirements to General Manager, Computers for You, 433 Main St., Ontario, MN.

SALES SUPPORT ASSOCIATE
Work with customer service, account managers, marketing & brand management. You will handle distribution of sales materials and internal correspondence. You will need 1-2 years in sales admin. and basic office functions (mail, fax, ph)

Senior Calendar Clerk
Large international law firm is seeking qualified candidates with strong organizational and data entry skills, and extremely high level of service orientation and excellent oral and written communication skills. Applicants must possess a BA/BS degree, have knowledge of computer databases and Word or WordPerfect. Send resume and salary requirements to HR, Jackson Madison Madison Teller & Pewter, 1001 Main Street, Atlanta, GA.

Sr. FINANCIAL ANALYST
JJO Enterprises seeking senior member of financial team. Requires a degree in Finance/Econ/Actg; minimum 3 yrs' public acct. exp. (CPA), Lotus/Excel, MS Word/WordPerfect proficiency. P&L/cashflow statement exp is preferred. Competitive salary/benefits pkg. Fax: Mr. Rogers, JJO Enterprises 442-555-1267.

SENIOR LAW CLERK
Large international law firm is seeking qualified candidates with strong organizational and data entry skills, and extremely high level of service orientation and excellent oral and written communication skills. Applicants must possess a BA/BS degree, have knowledge of computer databases and Word or WordPerfect. Send resume and salary requirements to HR, Jackson Madison Madison Teller & Pewter, 1001 Main Street, Atlanta, GA.

Senior Secretary
Bolan Lumber Co. looking for add'l office support staff. Type 60 wpm. Word/Excel/ Windows and some desktop publishing experience. Call Ron 336-555-9944.

TECHNICAL COMMUNICATOR
Biotech Systems is expanding and is seeking someone to develop & maintain user documentation/training materials and on-line help systems. Requires a BA/BS in Technical Communication or equiva...

Group. Req. a BA/BS with 4 years' experience in financial analysis or system implementation or development. Attention to detail & time and resource mgmt. abilities are vital. Excel and PowerPoint req'd. Contact Financial Resources Executive Search at 443-555-2398.

Clerical Receptionist F/T position available in a fast-paced HR dept. You must be a self-starter, organized, and dependable. Excellent customer-service, written and verbal communication skills required. Computer experience a must! Norwell Medical Center, 100 Front St, Allentown, MD

Computer Operator/PC Technician
Large software retailer looking for someone with expert computer skills to assist in tech dept. as well as to give seminars for customers looking to upgrade. Successful candidate must have 3-5 years' technical experience and 2-3 years in customer service. Teaching experience a plus. Fax resume to Best Systems: 545-555-6677.

COMPUTERS
Immediate openings! Computer technicians with PC hardware and Windows experience. Send resume to Delta Plus, 1200 Sutter St, San Francisco, CA.

Corporate Human Resources Mgr
Specialized background in Employment or Compensation & Benefits, and general knowledge of all other HR functions. PC skills essential. Fax resume to 334-555-9112.

Editorial Researcher Business publication seeking researcher responsible for weekly business lists, etc. Computer/Internet skills required. Must be fast, accurate & thorough. Salary DOE. Write: Researcher 9106 Shasta Blvd., Pittsburgh, PA.

Editor/Reporter
National financial journal seeks experienced writer to cover the brokerage/financial services industry. Must have strong writing/editing skills and background in business reporting. Computer/word processor experience a must!, fax resume and clips to JIT 887-555-2256.

Engineering
Senior Industrial Engineer needed for large wholesale buyers club, to help reduce operating costs and increase revenues. A BS degree and at least 6 years in the distribution/transportation field are required. Strong business writing skills, PC proficiency using Microsoft Office and electronic communications is essential. Send cover letter and resume to HR/Job 445, AB Industries, 4498 Howard Blvd., Kansas City, MO

Executive Assistant
You'll need strong organizational, interpersonal, and analytical skills, coupled with good computer knowledge in applications such as Access, PowerPoint, Excel and Word. Send resume & salary history to MaxProducts at 553 Edgewater...

based telefundraising. Minimum... years experience in similar fiel... year degree preferred. Profi... computer skills incl. Windows-b... software applications requ... salary commensurate w/skills &... plus benefits. Send letter... resume to Well-Being Clinic,... Spring Ave., Daytonville, VA.

FACILITIES PLANNER
Training Centers Inc. seeks individ... to study & develop infrastru... requirements and capital impr... ment projects. Req's BA in Plan... Engineering, Architecture or rel.... w/ 7 years exp & knowl of Win... (Word, Excel) & graphics progr... 4 yrs exp w PC's planning arch... or facilities mgmt & exp w/... database mgmt & project sched... pref'd. Fax: HR. 885-555-2398.

Management Reporting Analyst
Join the team that maintains... purchasing and logistics inform... systems that support order... provide product and contract... mation, track product utilization... manage operating budget... inventory systems. Must be p... cient in a high-level database sy... and Excel, Lotus 1-2-3, or si... applications. Fax resume to... Systems Placement Services... 555-9998.

MANAGER, ASSET MODELING
This worldwide logistics compan... expanding it's transportation... work. The successful candidate... have a Bachelor's degree... Economics, Finance or Busi... Mgmt, with a MBA degree... ferred; a solid foundation... Mathematics; and excellent an... cal skills. Knowledge of PC app... tions in Excel, Word, PowerPoi... Visio essential. Competitive ben... and compensation plan. Fax... 555-2298/

Manager, Business Analysis... You will direct a team of Busi... Analysts and oversee timely com... tion of all projects in accord... with departmental policies & p... dures. Requires BA/BS... Behavioral Health Sciences, Busi... Administration, MIS, or equiv... experience, system developm... analysis and software testing: st... project management and te... building skills, and software d... opment experience. Hart Corpo... Services. Call J. Thornton 243-5... 9583.

MARKETING ASSISTANT
Supporting 2 Marketing Mgrs, y... handle a variety of admin. resp... bilities, direct mail coordina... desktop publishing, and ad s... coordination. Require 1-2 y... admin. exper and strong comp... skills, esp. desktop pub. H... Office & Windows. Fax. R. S... 365-555-8844.

MARKET RESEARCH PROJECT MANA...
SuperMouse Designs is crea... new research division. You wi... vide research consulting servi... internal clients and manage... research providers. A BA/BS... or equivalent with 4-6 years'... ence with full servi...

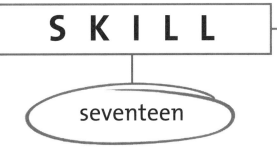

S K I L L

seventeen

Getting Remote Access

❑ Dialing another computer

❑ Dialing your home computer from outside

❑ Using Briefcase to keep your files in sync

In this skill, we're going to configure Dial-Up Networking (DUN) so you can connect to your company's network via Windows 95. You may want to use DUN to connect to other places either from your regular Desktop or from a laptop you take on the road with you. We'll also show you how to set up a Briefcase to keep your mobile files and your base system files synchronized.

 NOTE   If you haven't already installed a modem, do so now. See the section on modems in Skill 14.

Configuring Dial-Up Networking

Dial-Up Networking (DUN) simply means you use a modem and a phone line to connect one computer to another computer. The other computer may be at work, at an Internet service provider, or even at home when you're traveling. To make a link of this sort you'll first have to create the dial-up connection.

 TIP   Some dial-up connections are automated. For example, if you're using America Online software to connect to America Online, the dial-up connection is made automatically and doesn't involve "dial-up networking" as described in this skill.

Creating a New Connection

Creating a new connection to another system, whether it's your Internet service provider or your computer at work, is simply a matter of following the Wizard and answering a few questions. This next set of steps shows how it's done:

1. Select Start ➤ Programs ➤ Accessories ➤ Dial-Up Networking as shown in Figure 17.1. This will open up the Dial-Up Networking folder.

 NOTE   If Dial-Up Networking isn't on the Accessories menu, it just means that it hasn't been installed yet. Use the Windows Setup tab of the Add/Remove Programs icon in the Control Panel.

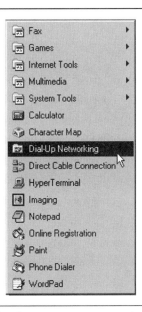

FIGURE 17.1: Use the Start menu to get to the Dial-Up Networking folder.

2. The first time you open the Dial-Up Networking folder, you'll see only the Make New Connection icon.

NOTE   Depending on how Windows 95 is already configured, you may go right past the Make New Connection icon to the Make New Connection Wizard. You may have to double-click this icon to open up the Wizard that walks you through the process of creating your Dial-Up Networking connection.

3. Type in a name for the connection, and click the Next button. The default is My Connection. Unless you're sure of never having another DUN connection, give this one a descriptive name such as **Home** or **Office Mail**.

4. Type in the phone number for the new connection, as shown in Figure 17.2, and click the Next button.

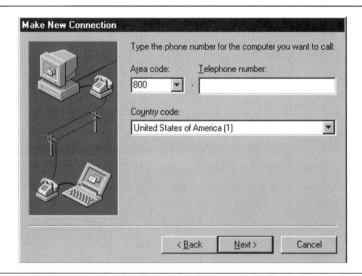

FIGURE 17.2: Each connection, even if it's a local number, gets full information about area and country codes.

5. Click the Finish button, and you'll have a new icon for the connection in the Dial-Up Networking folder.

Using Your Connection

If you want to connect to a Windows NT Remote Access Server, or an Internet service provider that supports PPP or, in fact, most systems you will be connecting to, using your new DUN connection is easy. Just follow these steps:

1. Double-click the new icon in your Dial-Up Networking folder, and the Connect To dialog box shown in Figure 17.3 will open.

2. If your user name on the remote system is different from your current user name, you will need to change the User Name box to whatever your name is on the remote system.

3. Enter your password. If you want to have Windows 95 remember your password for this remote system, check the box.

 **WARNING**   It's probably not a good idea to ask Windows 95 to remember your password unless you're confident no one else has access to the computer you're using.

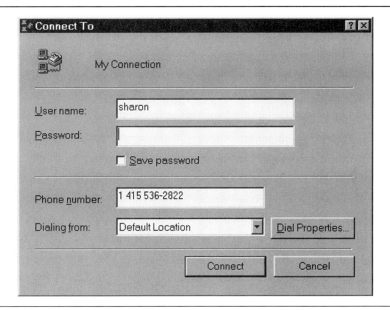

FIGURE 17.3:   The connection to a remote system is started in the Connect To dialog box.

4. If you're dialing from the same location as when you set up the connection, click the Connect button and you'll see the Connecting To status box.

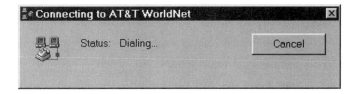

5. Once you're connected, you can use the files, printers, and other resources of the other computer just as if you were right next to it on a network—except a bit slower because the phone line is much "narrower" in terms of data transmission than a regular network cable.

NOTE   A Dial-Up Networking connection differs from a full network connection in one significant way. Browsing the Network Neighborhood you will not always see the other computer when you're connected remotely. But if you don't see it, open Windows Explorer and select Tools ➤ Find ➤ Computer.

TROUBLESHOOTING THE CONNECTION

While Windows 95 will correctly set up your Dial-Up connection most of the time, every once in a while it'll mess up—or you'll want to do something just a bit irregular. Here are some quick tips on what to look out for and settings you might need to change:

- Check all your modem settings.
- Check that the server type is set correctly.
- If you're in a location different from your usual one, add a new location description and settings.
- Turn on the modem's speaker to listen for the connection tone when you dial.
- Set your modem's properties to open a terminal window after dialing to see if your server is asking a question you didn't expect.
- Choose a different network protocol to do the connection.

See the section in this skill called "Setting the Server Type" for more information on setting up your server and modem.

Setting the Server Type

The default server type for Windows 95 is PPP:Windows 95, Windows NT 3.5, Internet. If you're not connecting to one of these, right-click the icon for the connection in the Dial-Up Networking folder (not a shortcut to it) and select Properties. This will open the property sheet for the connection shown in Figure 17.4.

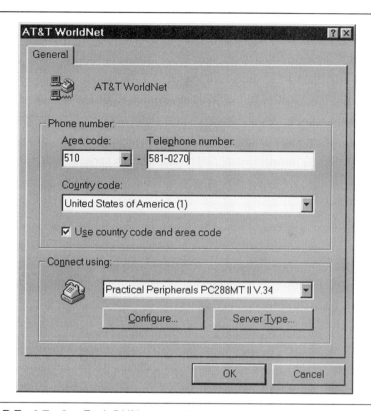

FIGURE 17.4: Each DUN connection has its own properties sheet.

Click the Server Type button to open up the Server Types dialog box shown in Figure 17.5.

From here you can set a variety of options including the network protocols to use, the server type, and logon options:

- **Type of Dial-Up Server** Lets you choose the default: a standard PPP connection, NRN for connecting to a NetWare Network, or the Windows for Workgroups type for connecting to older Windows for Workgroups or Windows NT 3.*x* networks. (If you have installed SLIP networking you will have a choice for it as well.)

- **Log on to Network** Automatically logs you onto the network you are connecting to using your current Windows user name and password. This logon and password may well be different from the dial-up password you entered in the Connect To dialog box.

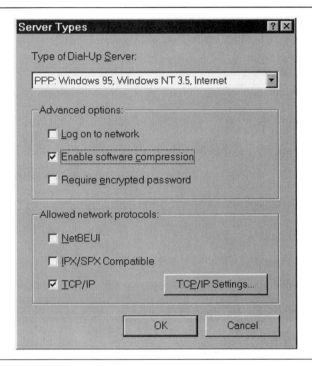

FIGURE 17.5: Use this dialog box to choose your remote server type and connection options.

- **Enable Software Compression** If available on the remote system in a compatible form, will compress data sent over the link automatically, increasing the speed of the connection.

- **Allowed Network Protocols** Lets you choose the networking protocols to use with this connection. The default is to select all three, but if you know what your remote server is using you can deselect the ones you don't need.

- **TCP/IP Settings** Opens the dialog box shown in Figure 17.6. If you're not using a TCP/IP connection, the button will be grayed out. Specify your IP address for this connection, or let the server automatically assign one, whichever is appropriate. Leave the rest of the settings alone unless you know what they mean and why you need to change them. They should be correct for the vast majority of connections.

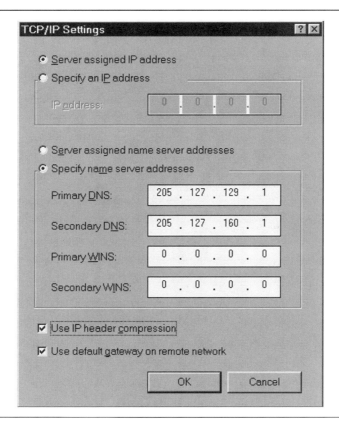

FIGURE 17.6: Here's where you set the TCP/IP properties for your Dial-Up connection.

Adding New Locations

When you use your portable computer to log onto a remote network—whether it's the Internet by way of your Internet service provider or your company network—you're likely to have to do it from different locations at different times. Here's how to add these additional locations:

1. Double-click a connection icon to open the Connect To dialog box.

2. Click the Dial Properties button and you'll get the Dialing Properties dialog shown in Figure 17.7.

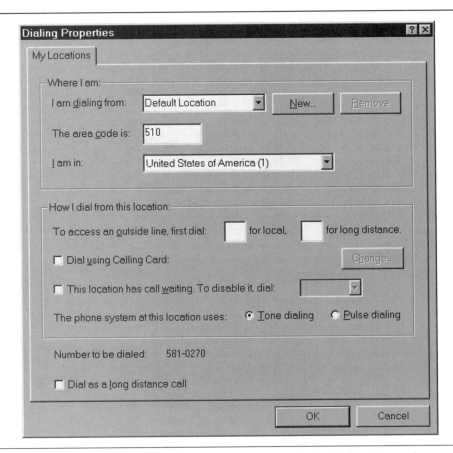

FIGURE 17.7: Adding a new location is done in the Dialing Properties dialog box.

3. To add a location, click New and type in a name for the location.

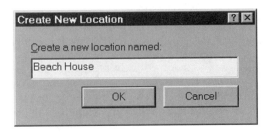

4. Enter the area code and other details about how you access the telephone system from this location. Now, whenever you need to call from a particular place, select the location and all the settings will still be in place.

 NOTE   For more details on the Dialing Properties dialog box, see the HyperTerminal section of Skill 10.

MAKING A REMOTE ACCESS SERVER

Perhaps you want to be able to call your own computer at home when you're traveling. You'll use Dial-Up Networking on your portable computer, but you also need to be able to set up the home machine so it can be called—and will answer!

Windows 95 alone doesn't allow your home computer to be a Remote Access Server (RAS), but if you have the Plus! for Windows 95 package, you'll find that this feature is included. This is a much more limited server than the one included in Windows NT. The Plus! version allows only a single connection to access your machine at any one time. To enable the service, open up the Dial-Up Networking folder and select Dial-Up Server from the Connections menu.

Click the Allow caller access radio button, and set a password for access to your computer. I know passwords are a nuisance, but it's sensible to have a password when you are opening up your home machine in this way. After all, this limited server neither knows nor cares who is calling or where they are calling from. It also provides access to everything available on your machine without regard to the sharing properties you may have set up if you are on a LAN—so a password is essential.

Skill 17

Coordinating Your Files with the Briefcase

The Briefcase is a tool for keeping files on two different computers in sync. If you travel with a laptop, you probably have a set of files that relate in some way to another set of files on your home or office computer. The Briefcase will keep copies of the files coordinated, so you're always working with the latest version.

 NOTE If you don't have Briefcase installed, use Add/Remove Programs in the Control Panel to add it. It's under Accessories.

Setting It Up

Open the Briefcase icon on your portable computer. Drag files from shared folders on your main computer to the Briefcase.

 NOTE To share a folder, right-click it, select Properties, and then the Sharing tab. If the connection is made by direct cable, the files/folders don't have to be shared.

That's all that's necessary to get things started. After you've worked on the files and want to coordinate the versions on both computers, reconnect the computers and follow these steps:

1. Click the Briefcase icon to open it.

2. Select Update All from the Briefcase menu. You'll see a window that looks like the one in Figure 17.8. (On the left is a list of files on the machine you're using, and on the right are the corresponding files on the other computer. The middle shows the suggested action.)

3. You can change the action for any pair of files by right-clicking the action. You'll get a menu of choices as shown in Figure 17.9.

4. Click Update when you're finished and all the files will be updated as you specified.

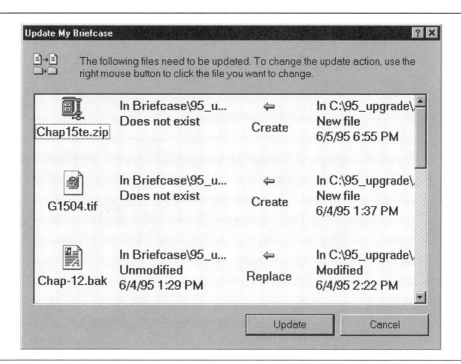

FIGURE 17.8: This Briefcase contains files that need to be updated.

Using Briefcase on a Floppy Disk

If a cable or a network doesn't connect your portable and your main computer, you can use Briefcase on a floppy disk to keep files synchronized. Follow the next set of steps to see how it's done:

1. Open the Briefcase on your Desktop and drag in the files or folders you want to keep synchronized.

2. Move the Briefcase to a disk in your floppy drive.

3. Take the floppy and put it in the disk drive on your portable machine. You can now work with the files in the Briefcase.

4. When you're ready to synchronize the files between your two machines, take the floppy from the portable and put it into the disk drive on the main machine.

5. Double-click the disk drive to open it. Right-click My Briefcase and choose Update All. You'll be presented with the same dialog box shown in Figure 17.9.

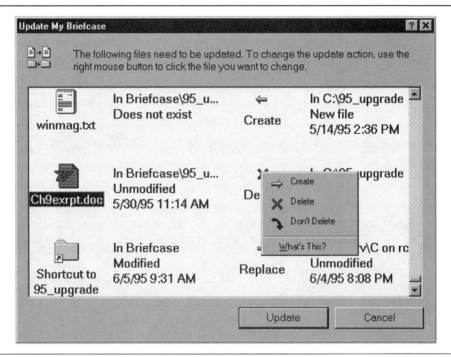

FIGURE 17.9: You don't have to accept Briefcase's suggestions.

NOTE   It's important not to edit (or update) both copies of a file because all Briefcase can do is show you the most recent copy and suggest it as the one you want to copy over the older one. If the older copy contains changes that were never carried over to the newer one (because files weren't synchronized before the newer file was created), then the changes in the older file will be lost.

Working with Multiple Briefcases

You can make a Briefcase anywhere. Just right-click in a folder and select New and then Briefcase. You can use this new Briefcase folder to keep any files on your computer or on a network synchronized. Just make sure that the folders in question are Shared (right-click and select Properties and then Sharing).

Are You Experienced?

Now you can...

☑ **dial another computer from your own machine**

☑ **add dial-up locations**

☑ **dial your home computer from another location**

☑ **use Briefcase to update files on separate computers**

scheduli...
yrs admin.
Perfect or
nalytical a
e a must.

ARY
is looking
vidual with
nizational
/Excel, MS
ficiency in
of 60-65
erstanding
ent. Send
ncial Corp.
Lubbock.

NAGER Will
or creative
s, schedule
us projects.
nderstand
and print
fax 555-

ANALYST
s company
to provide
and end
Corporate
BA/BS with
n financial
rentation
n to detail
nt. abilities
PowerPoint
Resources
555-2398.

TIONIST
in a fast-
t be a self
depend
er-service.
munication
er experi-
Medical
ntown, MD

TECHNICIAN
looking for
computer
ept. as well
customers
cessful can-
ears' tech-
3 years in
ing experi-
e to Best
6672.

urces Mgr
ound in
nsation &
nowledge of
PC skills
o 334-555-

Business
researcher
y business
ernet skills
accurate &
OE. Write:
ssta Blvd.

RTER
rnal seeks
ver the bro-
s industry.
ing/editing
n business

---

based teleindraising. Minimum of 7
years experience in similar field. 4
year degree preferred. Proficient
computer skills incl. Windows-based
software applications required.
Salary commensurate w/skills & exp.
plus benefits. Send letter and
resume to Well-Being Clinic, 543
Spring Ave., Daytonville, VA.

Executive Secretary
OfficePlus, an office supply & furniture company is looking for administrative support to VP. Requires 5
years min. of secretarial experience,
proficiency with MS Word and Excel
and excellent communication skills.
Must be willing to learn database &
desktop software. Fax: OfficePlus,
Personnel 665-555-9122.

FACILITIES PLANNER Training
Centers Inc. seeks individual to study
& develop infrastructure requirements and capital improvement projects. Req's BA in Planning,
Engineering, Architecture or rel. field
w/7 years exp & knowl of Windows
(Word, Excel) & graphics programs.
4 yrs' exp w PC's planning arch/eng
or facilities mgmt & exp w/CAD.
database mgmt & project scheduling
pref'd. Fax: HR, 885-555-2398.

**MANAGEMENT REPORTING
ANALYST**
Join the team that maintains the
purchasing and logistics information
systems that support order entry,
provide product and contract information, track product utilization,
and manage operating budget and
inventory systems. Must be proficient in a high-level database system and Excel, Lotus 1-2-3, or similar applications. Fax resume to Data
Systems Placement Services
444-555-9998.

MANAGER, ASSET MODELING
This worldwide logistics company is
expanding it's transportation network. The successful candidate will
have a Bachelor's degree in
Economics, Finance or Business
Mgmt, with a MBA degree preferred, a solid foundation in
Mathematics; and excellent analytical skills. Knowledge of PC applications in Excel, Word, PowerPoint &
Visio essential. Competitive benefits
and compensation plan. Fax: 966-
555-2298/

Manager, Business Analysis
You will direct a team of Business
Analysts and oversee timely completion of all projects in accordance
with departmental policies & procedures. Requires BA/BS in
Behavioral Health Sciences, Business
Administration, MIS or equivalent
experience, system development,
analysis and software testing; strong
project management and team
building skills, and software development experience. Hart Corporate
Services, Call J. Thornton 243-555-
9583.

Market Research Project Manager
SuperHouse Designs is creating a
new research division. You will provide research consulting services to
internal clients and manage external
research providers. A BA/BS degree
or equivalent with 4-6 years' experi-

---

send cover letter, resume & salary
req'a to: Sommes Communications,
Attn: HR/Job 85, 776 Bowser Lane,
Bowtown, MA.

MARKETING ASSISTANT
Supporting 2 Marketing Mgrs,
you'll handle a variety of admin.
responsibilities, direct mail coordination, desktop publishing, and ad
space coordination. Require 1-2
years admin. exper. and strong
computer skills, esp. desktop pub,
HTML, Office & Windows. Fax. R.
Smith 365-555-8844.

OFFICE MANAGER
Join a growing firm that offers competitive salaries & benefits for a
take-charge type. Responsible for
all office purchases & operations,
including a quarterly newsletter.
Windows & MS Office experience
req'd. Call 973-555-4545.

PC Support Specialist
High-end catalog company and
specialty retailer has opening in
MIS Dept. Support corporate associates with PC and network systems. Extensive PC hardware installation and configuration experience
is required. Must be able to communicate effectively, and determine
cause of problems, & develop solutions. Requires network admin. &
multiple PC operating systems
experience. (Windows, UNIX) Fax
resume & salary reqs to High
Profile Images 388-555-9634.

PROJECT ASST. Serve as a point
person in HR office of fast growing
biotech firm. Requires creative
thinking and up-to-date office computer skills, esp. Word, PowerPoint
& Excel. Fax resume to TruPoint
Systems 689-555-1298.

PROJECT MANAGER
Public agency seeking environmental project manager to oversee 18-
month marsh preservation project.
Develop, analyze, organize & summarize planning data and financial
info. Windows computer skills
essential. Send resume to Public
Planning Services, Attn: HR., 34
Marsh Lane, Willowdale, CA.

Sales/Computer
Expanding computer software &
hardware store is looking for more
qualified sales associates to staff
our busy downtown location.
Windows software experience
required. Send resume and
salary/commission requirements to
General Manager, Computers For
You, 433 Main St., Ontario, MN.

SALES SUPPORT ASSOCIATE Work with
customer service, account managers, marketing & brand management. You will handle distribution of
sales materials and internal correspondence. You will need 1-2 years
in sales admin, and basic office
functions (mail, fax, phones etc.),
plus PC skills. Computer troubleshooting skills a plus.

Sales: Sr. Account Coordinator
Looking Good, a national clothing
chain is looking for seasoned sales
pros to oversee sales operations.
Qualified candidates must have 4-5
years sales mgmt exp. and strong

---

pros to oversee sales operations.
Qualified candidates must have 4-5
years sales mgmt exp. and strong
PC skills. A college degree, working
knowledge of Excel, PowerPoint,
Word and database software req'd.
Fax resume and cover letter to:
Looking Good, Attn: K. Ferkovich,
877 Goody Ave. Reno, NV.

SALES/COMPUTER
Expanding computer software &
hardware store is looking for more
qualified sales associates to staff our
busy downtown location. Windows
software experience required. Send
resume and salary/commission
requirements to General Manager,
Computers For You, 433 Main St.,
Ontario, MN.

**SALES SUPPORT
ASSOCIATE**
Work with customer service, account
managers, marketing & brand
management. You will handle
distribution of sales materials and
internal correspondence. You will
need 1-2 years in sales admin
and basic office functions
(mail, fax, ph)

Senior Calendar Clerk
Large international law firm is seeking qualified candidates with strong
organizational and data entry skills,
and extremely high level of service
orientation and excellent oral and
written communication skills.
Applicants must possess a BA/BS
degree, have knowledge of computer databases and Word or
WordPerfect. Send resume, and
salary requirements to HR, Jackson
Madison Madison Teller & Pewter,
1001 Main Street, Atlanta, GA

Sr. Financial Analyst
JJO Enterprises seeking senior
member of financial team. Requires
a degree in Finance/Econ/
Acctg, minimum 3 yrs' public acct.
exp. (CPA), Lotus/Excel, MS
Word/WordPerfect proficiency.
P&L/cashflow statement exp is
preferred. Competitive salary/
benefits pkg. Fax: Mr. Rogers,
JJO Enterprises 442-555-1267.

SENIOR LAW CLERK
Large international law firm is seeking qualified candidates with strong
organizational and data entry skills,
and extremely high level of service
orientation and excellent oral and
written communication skills.
Applicants must possess a BA/BS
degree, have knowledge of computer databases and Word or
WordPerfect. Send resume and
salary requirements to HR, Jackson
Madison Madison Teller & Pewter,
1001 Main Street, Atlanta, GA

Senior Secretary
Bolan Lumber Co. looking for add'l
office support staff. Type 60 wpm.
Word/Excel/ Windows and some
desktop publishing experience. Call
Ron 336-555-9944.

TECHNICAL COMMUNICATOR
Biotech Systems is expanding and
is seeking someone to develop &
maintain user documentation/train-
ing materials and on-line help systems. Requires a BA/BS in
Technical Communication or equiva-

Group. Req. a BA/BS with 4 years'
experience in financial analysis or
system implementation or development. Attention to detail & time and
resource mgmt. abilities are vital.
Excel and PowerPoint req'd.
Contact Financial Resources
Executive Search at 443-555-2398.

Clerical Receptionist F/T position
available in a fast paced HR dept.
You must be a self-starter, organized, and dependable. Excellent
customer-service, written and verbal communication skills required.
Computer experience a must!
Norwel Medical Center, 500 Front
St. Allentown, MD

Computer Operator/PC Technician
Large software retailer looking for
someone with expert computer
skills to assist in tech dept. as well
as to give seminars for customers
looking to upgrade. Successful candidate must have 3-5 years' technical experience and 2-3 years in customer service. Teaching experience
a plus. Fax resume to Best Systems:
545-555-6672.

COMPUTERS
Immediate openings! Computer
technicians with PC hardware and
Windows experience. Send resume
to: Delta Plus, 1200 Sutter St. San
Francisco, CA.

Corporate Human Resources Mgr
Specialized background in
Employment or Compensation &
Benefits, and general knowledge of
all other HR functions. PC skills
essential. Fax resume to 334-555-
9112.

Editorial Researcher Business
publication seeking researcher
responsible for weekly business
lists, etc. Computer/Internet skills
required. Must be fast, accurate &
thorough. Salary DOE. Write:
Researcher, 9106 Shasta Blvd.,
Pittsburgh, PA.

Editor/Reporter
National financial journal seeks
experienced writer to cover the bro-
kerage/financial services industry.
Must have strong writing/editing
skills and background in business
reporting. Computer/word processor experience a must!, fax resume
and clips to JIT 887-555-2256.

Engineering
Senior Industrial Engineer needed
for large wholesale buyers club, to
help reduce operating costs, and
increase revenues. A BS degree and
at least 6 years in the
distribution/transportation field are
required. Strong business writing
skills, PC proficiency using Microsoft
Office and electronic communications
is essential. Send cover letter and
resume to HR/Job 445, AB
Industries, 4498 Howard Blvd.,
Kansas City, MO

Executive Assistant
You'll need strong organizational,
interpersonal, and analytical skills,
coupled with good computer
knowledge in applications such as
Access, PowerPoint, Excel and
Word. Send resume & salary history

---

based teleindraising. Minim
years experience in similar
year degree preferred. P
computer skills incl. Window
software applications
Salary commensurate w/skil
plus benefits. Send lett
resume to Well-Being Clin
Spring Ave. Daytonville, VA.

FACILITIES PLANNER
Training Centers Inc. seeks in
to study & develop intra
requirements and capital i
ment projects. Req's BA in P
Engineering, Architecture or
w/7 years exp & knowl of W
(Word, Excel) & graphics p
4 yrs exp w PC's planning
or facilities mgmt & exp
database mgmt & project sc
pref'd. Fax: HR, 885-555-2

Management Reporting Ana
Join the team that maint
purchasing and logistics info
systems that support orde
provide product and contra
mation, track product utilizat
manage operating budg
inventory systems. Must b
cient in a high-level database
and Excel, Lotus 1-2-3, or
applications. Fax resume
Systems Placement Service
555-9998.

MANAGER, ASSET MODELI
This worldwide logistics co
expanding it's transportal
work. The successful candi
have a Bachelor's dep
Economics, Finance or B
Mgmt, with a MBA degr
ferred; a solid founda
Mathematics; and excellent
cal skills. Knowledge of PC
tions in Excel, Word, Powe
Visio essential. Competitive
and compensation plan. Fa
555-2298/

Manager, Business Ana
You will direct a team of
Analysts and oversee timely
tion of all projects in ac
with departmental policies
dures. Requires BA/
Behavioral Health Sciences,
Administration, MIS or e
experience, system devel
analysis and software testin
project management an
building skills, and softwa
opment experience. Hart C
Services, Call J. Thornton 2
9583.

MARKETING ASSISTA
Supporting 2 Marketing Mg
handle a variety of admin,
bilities, direct mail coor
desktop publishing and
coordination. Require 1-
admin. exper. and strong
skills, esp. desktop pub.
Office & Windows, Fax.
365-555-8844.

Market Research Project M
SuperHouse Designs is
new research division. You
vide research consulting se
internal clients and man
research providers. A BA/
or equivalent with 4-6 yea
ence with full exp

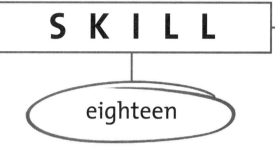

S K I L L

eighteen

Making a Network

- ❏ Selecting the best network type
- ❏ Getting the necessary hardware
- ❏ Doing the construction
- ❏ Making a quick-and-dirty network

One of the best things about Windows 95 is that it comes with networking included. The first part of this skill describes the basic types of networks you might consider, how they work, and the choices available for hardware. If you want to make a network and you'd like to understand what you're doing, this is necessary information.

On the other hand, if you want to make a network and you don't *care* whether you understand what you're doing, skip ahead to the section called "Networking for *Anyone*" toward the end of this skill. You'll find instructions on how to make a very simple but fully functional network (called a *peer-to-peer network*)—which is all that's ever needed for a home or small business setup.

 NOTE   A few words of advice: If you've never used a network, you'll come across some terms you haven't seen before, but don't worry. All the terms are explained and defined as necessary. The point of this skill is not to turn you into a networking guru (that's many books' worth of information), but to make it possible for you to build a network to do what you need to do.

Picking among Networks

There are essentially two types of networks—client/server and peer-to-peer (the latter is the type discussed in this skill):

- **Client/Server:** This type of network, the most typical being ones that use Microsoft Windows NT Server or Novell NetWare, has one or more computers that are servers. A server can't be used for anything other than taking care of the network's needs, and it runs a special operating system. While these kinds of networks have definite advantages, they really don't become compelling until your network gets to be a lot bigger than the two to five computers we're talking about here. The costs in hardware, software, and general complexity are additional reasons that client/server networks are uninviting for someone trying to connect just a few computers.

- **Peer-to-Peer:** This second network type is the topic of this skill. In a peer-to-peer network, each computer has just as much importance as any other computer in the network. If you only need to connect a couple of computers together to share some files and a printer, this is the way to go. It's easy to set up, requires almost no network administration to maintain, and the cost is minimal. You don't need to buy any additional hardware except for the actual networking boards themselves and the cable. You don't need any special software either since the networking is built right into Windows 95.

Learning the Hardware Basics

To set up your network, all you really need is one network card per computer, enough pieces of network cable to connect them all, and the actual connectors, terminators, and so on for the cable.

Before you jump in and start buying network cards and cabling, you have to decide what kind of cabling to get, and how you are going to arrange your network. There are at least four different options for cabling, but as you'll learn in the following sections, only two of them make any sense in a small network situation.

Understanding Thin Ethernet

Up until the last couple of years, the most common way to connect personal computers in a network was to run a thin piece of coaxial cable from computer to computer. The cable looks a lot like cable-TV wire (although it isn't the same stuff), with a single, often solid, copper wire down the center with a braided shield, like that shown in Figure 18.1. This is easily the simplest (and cheapest) way to connect two or three computers in reasonably close proximity to one another.

 NOTE   The cable for this connection method can be called: Thinnet, 10Base-2, Thin Ethernet, or co-ax (short for coaxial)—you may hear any of these variations. All Thin Ethernet is Ethernet but not all Ethernet is Thin Ethernet.

The total cost to connect two computers, including all cabling, cards, terminators, and connectors can easily be cheaper than $200; and if you are really scrimping, you could manage it for cheaper than $100—not that I'd recommend going for the absolute cheapest. (Remember that it's the cheap person who ends up paying the most!)

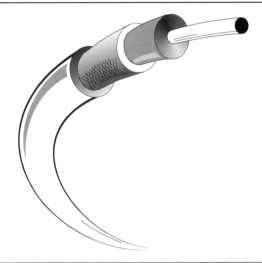

FIGURE 18.1: Thin Ethernet uses a coaxial RG-58 cable with a conductor and a braided shield.

The Thin Ethernet Advantage

Thin Ethernet has some definite advantages besides its simplicity. Because the cabling is shielded, it's fairly resistant to electrical noise, and the maximum, practical total distance your network can span is higher than with its primary competitor: unshielded twisted pair. Of course, distance isn't likely to be a major concern with a small network of the type we're talking about, but if you need to connect computers on different floors or even different buildings, Thin Ethernet is definitely the way to go.

Hooking It Up

The most common method of hooking up a Thin Ethernet network is to hook each computer to the next one with a piece of cable between them as shown in Figure 18.2.

Hooking one computer to the next is called daisy chaining. It has the advantage of being simple and easy to understand, and it does not require any extra hardware. Once you get everything set up (assuming good quality cable and connectors), you pretty much don't need to worry about it or think about it again. At least until you decide to start moving furniture around.

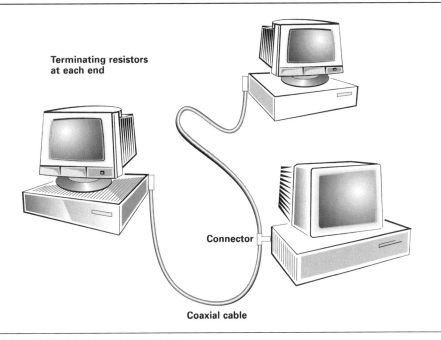

Terminating resistors
at each end

Connector

Coaxial cable

FIGURE 18.2: A daisy chain connection

One Shortcoming

Daisy chaining has one major disadvantage. If you have one bad piece of cable or a single bad connector in the network, the entire network is down. Finding the bad connector or bad piece of cabling can be an extremely frustrating task if you don't have specialized (read expensive) tools. But if you buy good quality cable, connectors, and terminators, this problem should not arise.

Understanding Twisted Pair

In recent years, wiring based on twisted pair (or more properly, unshielded twisted pair cable) has started to replace Thin Ethernet cable as the network cabling of choice. It's easy to install, requiring essentially the same skills as installing phone cable, and since it's smaller and flatter, it's easier to hide and more wires fit through a given space.

The cable, called variously 10Base-T, twisted pair, unshielded twisted pair, and UTP, looks a lot like standard phone cable and uses four pair of wires twisted together as shown in Figure 18.3. It has no shielding other than the inherent shielding effect of the twisted wires themselves, and while it looks a lot like standard phone cable, the two types are not interchangeable.

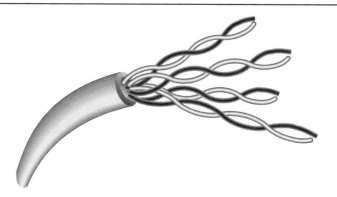

FIGURE 18.3: Twisted pair wiring resembles a standard phone cable.

The Star Connection

Unlike Thin Ethernet, twisted-pair cables are not connected in a daisy chain but are connected in a star configuration as shown in Figure 18.4. The cabling to each individual workstation radiates out from a central hub. This has the distinct advantage of keeping a single bad cable or connector from bringing the whole network down—making it much easier to find the source of the trouble.

Some Disadvantages

A small disadvantage of twisted pair is that you need to buy a hub for the center of your star. A hub for a small four-person-or-fewer network can be as little as $75, though you can pay double that for the best hubs of the same capacity.

The other disadvantages of twisted pair are not particularly important. The effective maximum cable length of a cable from the hub to an individual workstation is substantially less than the maximum length between workstations with

Thin Ethernet. In addition, the cabling itself is less resistant to physical abuse and electrical noise. Neither of these, however, is likely to be a major factor for most small setups.

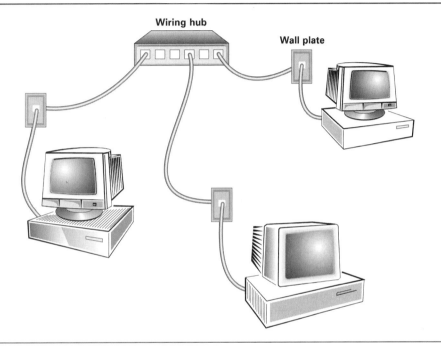

FIGURE 18.4: In a star configuration, a single bad connector or a bad piece of cable won't cause the whole network to fail.

Choosing the Network Card

You can't have a network without some way for your computers to connect to the cable. This takes a network card of some sort.

 NOTE   For the purposes of this skill, I'll treat laptop PC Cards for networks no differently than a card that plugs into your PC. The network itself doesn't much care, after all, so why should we?

First Choose Your Cable

Before you buy a network card you must decide what kind of cable you want to use. Network cards come with one or more connectors on them, and you need to make sure your card supports the connection you'll need. If you aren't sure, you can always get a combo card that supports multiple types of cabling, but they cost a bit more than single interface types.

 TIP   Combo cards let you easily change your mind about cabling without having to buy all new network cards. Because permanent cable installation is such a major undertaking, however, you're unlikely to change it very often. You're probably better off just buying the card you need for the cabling you're buying *now*.

And Then Pick a Card

Should you get a 16-bit card, or a 32-bit card? Should it be a standard ISA bus card, or a VLB or PCI card? The answers to these questions depend on how you intend to use your network, but here are some general rules:

- **16-Bit ISA Bus Card**: This is more than adequate. On a small network you are unlikely to need anything more than this card can handle, and they're generally pretty cheap.

- **PCI Network Card**: If your machine has a PCI bus with an available expansion slot, you might want to consider getting one of these. They're just becoming available and they're fast and relatively cheap. Plus, Windows 95 will support them as full Plug-and-Play devices.

- **EISA Bus Card**: If you have an EISA bus computer, excellent and very fast network cards are available. If you expect to use your network a lot or have more than a couple of machines on it, you will probably want to consider this option. Like all EISA cards, however, an EISA network card is going to cost you substantially more than a simple ISA card from the same manufacturer.

- **VLB Card**: Don't spend the extra money for a VLB card. The VL bus, while perfectly adequate for video, its original purpose, is just not up to the electrical demands of a network card.

TIP   It's absolutely necessary that you have the documentation for your computer to know what kinds of devices your machine will or will not work with. Otherwise, you'll have to call in one of those expensive consultants—and that would defeat the whole purpose of this skill.

Choosing Connectors and Terminators

To the later regret of both users and administrators, two types of hardware that frequently get ignored (both in planning and implementation) are connectors and terminators. The most common point of failure on a network isn't the cable or the network cards but the hardware that connects the cables to the cards and marks the start and end of the network.

NOTE   Connectors are T-shaped with the middle leg connecting to the network card. Another leg is connected to the network cable coming *to* the computer. On a machine that's in the middle of the network chain, the third leg is for cable going onto the next computer. On the first and last machine in the chain, the third leg takes a terminator.

For a typical small network, these little pieces will run as much as a quarter of the cable's cost, and they are the first place people tend to get cheap. After all, a $2 generic T-connector at the local Computers 'R' Us looks just as good as an $8 AMP brand one from the Black Box catalog.

Wrong! This is one place it doesn't pay to get frugal. Get the best ones you can. It will save you time, aggravation, and grief. In the long run, it will save you money.

Adding Cards and Protocols

Before you can actually use Windows 95 as a network, you need to install the network card into your computer and bind one or more network protocols to use the card.

NOTE   A *protocol* is just a fancy word for the method that your software (Windows 95 in this case) uses to talk to your hardware—and through cabling, to other computers.

IRQs, Addresses, Memory, and Such

Old-fashioned network cards required you to manually configure their IRQs, addresses, and other depressingly obscure stuff. Every time you acquired a new piece of hardware, you ran the risk of it interfering with your network card and having to go through the whole process again. If you got it wrong, you were out of business—usually your computer wouldn't even boot, much less work properly, if it did manage to struggle into life. You had no choice but to open the box, pull the card out, take another guess about what jumper to change to what position, and try the whole process again.

Well, those days are gone, thank heavens. The modern network card, even a simple 16-bit ISA card, uses an EEPROM (Electrically Erasable Read Only Memory) or Flash ROM to control its settings, and they can be configured by a simple software program included with the card. (There are still some of the old cards around, so make sure you don't get one.)

If you do end up with a conflict, just use Windows 95's Hardware Conflict Troubleshooter Wizard to figure out where the problem is and resolve it. For more on this amazing Wizard and further help in resolving hardware conflicts, see Skill 13.

Using the Add New Hardware Wizard

Add New Hardware

When you physically install the card, Windows 95 will notice the change the next time it boots up and will run the Add New Hardware Wizard to configure it. This process should happen automatically, but you can always run it manually if for some reason it doesn't happen by itself. Just click the Add New Hardware icon in the Control Panel.

The Add New Hardware Wizard shown in Figure 18.5 will walk you through the process of adding your new network card to your system. In addition, it will automatically install the minimal level of network support—adding the Microsoft client layer, so you can use files on someone else's Windows 95 computer and both the NetBEUI protocol and the IPX/SPX-compatible protocol. (For more instruction on using the Add New Hardware Wizard, see Skill 13.)

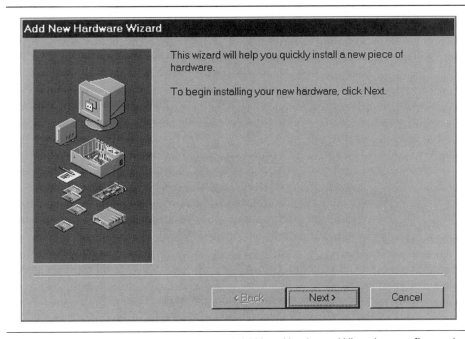

FIGURE 18.5: You can use the Add New Hardware Wizard to configure the network card.

 NOTE   You can use either protocol. Until recently, most Microsoft networking products used NetBEUI. IPX/SPX is the protocol used on Novell NetWare networks and is now being used in Microsoft's newer networking products as the default. On a Windows 95 network, you're marginally better off using IPX/SPX.

Using the Network Wizard

The Add New Hardware Wizard usually produces the Network properties sheets for you (shown in Figure 18.6), but if it doesn't, you can run it yourself. Just open the Control Panel and double-click the Network icon.

The Network icon opens up the Network dialog box where you can add all sorts of neat stuff. Some or all of it may have been added already when you installed the new network card into your computer. If it isn't there, or if you didn't get all you need or want, this is where you can add in the rest.

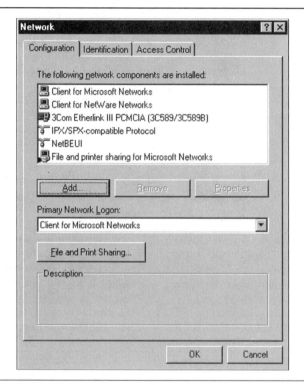

FIGURE 18.6: Add, remove, or configure network elements from the Network properties sheet.

The Network dialog box lets you add client protocols, hardware adapters, networking "stacks" or protocols, and networking services to your Windows 95 configuration.

 NOTE In the following sections, we'll just cover how to add the most basic of protocols and the minimum services for your small network.

Selecting a Network Client

You select a network client so you can use services on another machine (like their locally attached printer or their hard disk). The default configuration includes clients for both Microsoft Networks and Novell NetWare Networks. If you're using Windows 95 as a peer-to-peer network, you can pass on the Client for NetWare choice because you will only be using the built-in Microsoft networking.

NOTE   To remove the NetWare client, just highlight it, and then click the Remove button. You can always add it later if you need to.

TIP   Unless you have an unlimited amount of memory and a Pentium-120 (or better) processor, save both memory and resources by installing only the network protocols you really need. While the memory hit is well hidden by Windows 95, there's still, sadly, no free lunch.

If you don't see the Client for Microsoft Networks listed in the Network dialog box under the heading: "The following network components are installed," click the Add button, and then double-click the Client icon in the Select Network Component Type box as shown in Figure 18.7.

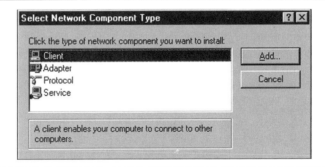

FIGURE 18.7: Selecting a network component type

Clicking the Client icon opens the Select Network Client box shown in Figure 18.8. Highlight Microsoft, select Client for Microsoft Networks, and then click OK.

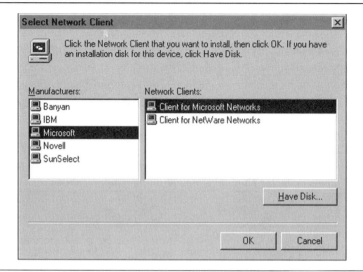

FIGURE 18.8: Adding the client for a Microsoft network

Installing Service Choices

The default installation doesn't install services, which is OK if you don't want anyone else to use the resources of your computer. If you're setting up your local network to have one main machine—the one with the fax modem, the big hard drive, the printer, and such—that everyone else will share, then you install the File and Printer Sharing (described in the next paragraph) on that machine alone. But if you're going to have computers sharing with each other, you'll need to add File and Printer Sharing to all the computers that will share their resources with others.

Select the Service choice from the Select Network Component Type box shown in Figure 18.7. Again, highlight Microsoft in the resulting Select Network Service dialog box shown in Figure 18.9, select File and Printer Sharing for Microsoft Networks, and click OK. This will add the necessary network services to allow you to let others on the network use your documents and folders as well as any printers or fax modems attached to your computer.

NOTE File and Printer Sharing is necessary only on machines that will share their resources with others.

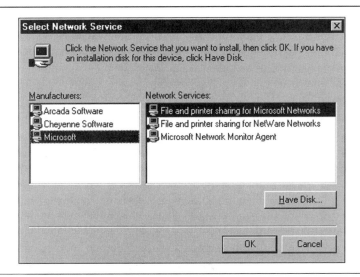

FIGURE 18.9: Adding file and print sharing allows others to use the resources on your computer.

These actions should be enough to get our network configured and ready to go. You will need to reboot each machine to add the necessary hardware and software components, because these changes are more than Windows 95 can do on the fly.

 TIP   If you have a notebook computer with PC Card (PCMCIA) support, once you have done the initial installation of the network components, you can insert or remove the network PC Card and Windows 95 will detect the change without rebooting.

Using Your Network

OK, you got all the hardware up and configured, the cables are in, the whole thing is connected, and now you actually want to do something with your network like sharing files or documents, as they're called in Windows 95.

Sharing and Mapping Drives

The simplest way to share files on your new network is to first share the drive or drives they reside on. Others on the network can map your drive to look like a local drive on their own computer.

To share a drive with others on your network, follow these steps:

1. Right-click the drive letter in Explorer or in My Computer, and you get the familiar menu.

2. When you select Sharing from the menu, you get the properties page for the drive, with the Sharing tab in front, as shown in Figure 18.10.

3. Just click the Share As button and the rest of the options on the tab become available, as shown in Figure 18.11.

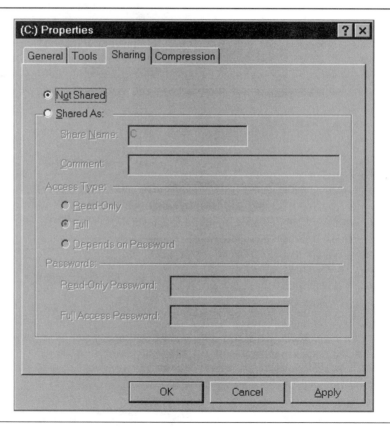

FIGURE 18.10: You control whether the drives are shared.

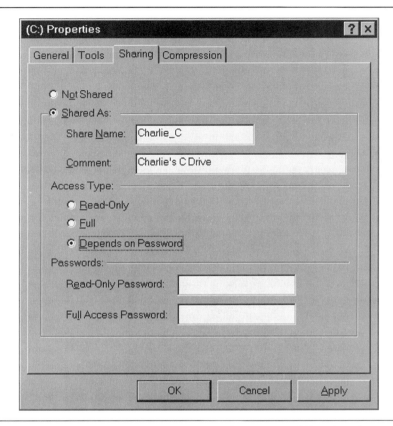

FIGURE 18.11: Some users can have full access while others have read-only access.

4. By specifying different passwords for the different access levels, you can let some users have full access to your drives, while others can read files on the drives but can't change anything.

5. Once you've got things set up the way you want them, someone can use one of your drives as if it were on his or her own computer by double-clicking the icon that represents your computer in Network Neighborhood. This brings up a window (like the one in Figure 18.12) showing the drives or folders you are sharing with others.

6. The user completes the process by right-clicking the drive to be used and selecting Map Network Drive from the menu to get the dialog box shown in Figure 18.13.

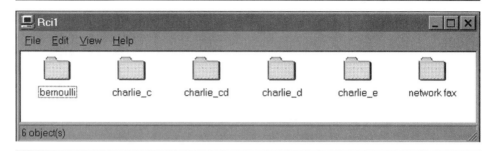

FIGURE 18.12: Using Network Neighborhood to see what drives are available on other computers

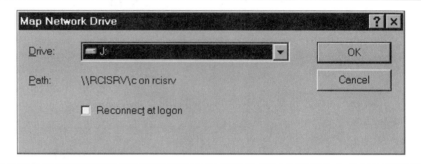

FIGURE 18.13: Mapping a drive on another computer so it looks just like another drive on *your* computer

Sharing Printers

Sharing printers is another important reason for a network. You can give everyone access to a printer without having to shell out the money to put a laser printer next to everyone's desk. Windows 95 makes this easy and painless. The person who has the printer attached to a PC simply shares it the same way they would share a drive or folder.

From the remote user's standpoint, using someone else's printer is no different from using one attached to your computer. The following steps show how to set it up.

Add Printer

1. First you add it as a new printer. (Like most things in Windows 95, you can do this from several different places.) One easy way is off the Start button. Select Settings ➢ Printers to open the Printers folder, and then double-click the Add Printer icon.

2. This opens the Add Printer Wizard. You'll end up with something like Figure 18.14 after you select Network Printer. Type in the location for the printer if you know it or just use the Browse button to find the printer on the network.

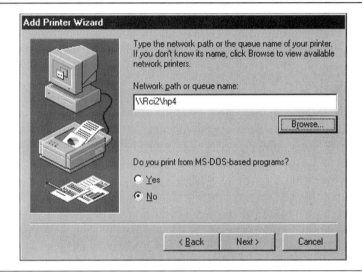

FIGURE 18.14: Adding a network printer requires only a few easy steps.

3. If you think there's any chance you'll ever need to print something produced by a DOS program, make sure you click the Yes button for "Do you print from MS-DOS programs?" Click the Next button again and select a printer port to capture for your DOS programs, since most of them are going to need to think they are printing to a specific port.

4. Give the printer a name, and you're done.

Now you can use this printer exactly as if it were directly connected to your computer, as long as the computer with the printer attached is up and running.

THE UNIVERSAL NAMING CONVENTION

Drive letter mapping provides complete compatibility with applications written before Windows 95, but it goes against the concept of documents and folders as being the central things we work with—not drives and files. After all, I don't really care where the document representing the outline for this book is stored. What I care about is getting at it when necessary, even if it's stored on someone else's machine. Double-clicking on it starts the application that created the outline and then opens the outline so I can update it.

This method doesn't require any drive mappings at all, thanks to something called the Universal Naming Convention (UNC). Under this convention, the outline is known as: \\Rcisrv\No Experience\OUTLINE.DOC. The UNC will be used more and more in the future. It will enable any machine added to the network to find \\Rcisrv\No Experience\OUTLINE.DOC on the network without having to know anything else about it.

Learning All About Passwords

An important network topic not yet discussed is passwords. Everyone hates passwords. They're a pain. We know that. And if you don't want a password on your PC, that's your decision.

But you really need a password if:

- There are ever more than two people on the network.

- You ever intend to make a direct connection to the outside world.

- You ever have business-critical data stored on any of the machines on your network.

If your needs are minimal, you can make the password easy to remember; but the best password is one that can't be easily guessed. If you will be directly connecting your computer to the Internet, we strongly urge you to adopt strict password guidelines and stick to them.

NOTE   For more on passwords in general, see Skill 11.

Here are some *bad* ideas for passwords:

- Your name, nickname, or logon name
- Your spouse's, child's, or parent's name
- Your pet's name
- Your license plate or Social Security number
- Common swear words or combinations of them
- Any of the above, spelled in reverse

Ideal passwords are a mixture of uppercase and lowercase letters and numbers or other non-alphabetic characters that don't spell anything, yet are easy to read, pronounce, type, and are at least six characters in length. Something like "SoAfa4!"

TIP   If you don't use a password and you're endlessly annoyed by the network password logon each time you boot your machine, you can get rid of it. Open the Network applet in the Control Panel. On the Configuration page, look for Primary Network Logon. Open the drop-down list and select Windows Logon. Now you can boot your machine without having to enter a password.

Connecting via Direct Cable

You may not need a network if all you need is to occasionally connect two computers. For example, if you use a laptop at home or on the road and you need to transfer files back and forth. For the cost of a simple cable, maybe $10–20, you can easily connect two computers for this purpose.

Skill 18

Choosing a Cable

The cable you want is like a parallel printer cable—except that a printer cable has one end made to attach to the computer and the other end to attach to the printer. The cable you need has the computer end on *both* ends. The cable can be described variously as a File Transfer Cable, a LapLink Cable, a DOS6 Interlink Cable, or, to be absolutely correct, a Parallel DB25 Male/Male cable.

A serial cable can also be used, if necessary (though they're not as fast as parallel cables). Look for one of the special four-headed cables that have both 25-pin and 9-pin connections at each end. That way you'll be sure to have the right connector no matter what your serial ports look like. These serial cables will have similar names to the parallel port version, but will have "serial" in the name and will have female connectors at each end.

Using the Direct Cable Connection Wizard

Once you have the cable, all it takes to connect your two computers is to open up the Direct Cable Connection Wizard shown in Figure 18.15. This is located on the Accessories menu of the Start menu.

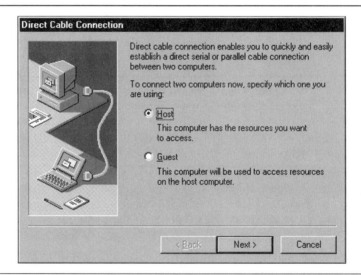

FIGURE 18.15: Use the Direct Cable Connection Wizard to attach computers over a simple cable.

NOTE   No Direct Cable Connection on the menu? You'll have to install it from Add/
Remove Programs ➤ Windows Setup ➤ Communications, then come back.

Once started, the Wizard prompts you through the steps to connect the two computers. One side will be the host—sharing its resources with the guest computer:

1. Start the Wizard on both computers, and select one as the host and the other
    as the guest.

2. Click Next and choose the port to connect the two computers, as shown in
    Figure 18.16. Choose the same type of connection on both the host and guest
    computer.

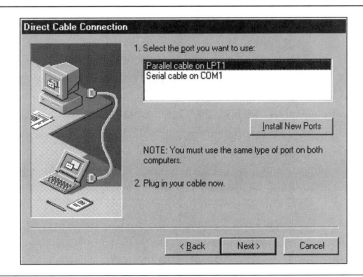

FIGURE 18.16: Use either a serial or a parallel connection between
computers.

 NOTE   If some critical parts aren't installed, you'll get a message when you click Next
that tells you to first install the Dial-Up Adapter and then rerun the Direct Cable
Connection Wizard. Follow the instructions on the screen and come back to this
point.

3. Plug in the cables if you haven't already, and click Next again.

4. On the host computer, as shown in Figure 18.17, you choose if you want to require a password for this access.

FIGURE 18.17: You can even require a password for the connection.

5. Click Next again on both computers and Windows 95 will try to hook up the two computers. And, assuming you have the right cable, it shouldn't have any problem at all.

6. On the host side, you'll see a confirmation that the two computers are connected. On the guest side, you'll see a typical Network Neighborhood window like that in Figure 18.18 showing all the shared and accessible folders on the host computer.

WARNING   If the guest computer, which should generally be the laptop, is connected on a network at the same time you're connecting over a direct cable connection, you may lose the network connection. Close down any network applications you are running on the guest machine before firing up the direct cable connection.

FIGURE 18.18: The guest computer can use any of the shared drives on the host computer.

Networking for *Anyone*

Even a year or two back, building the simplest network called for an expert to be imported, because only a few (very expensive) people knew the magic incantations to construct a network—and more importantly, to *keep* it running. This expert cost the earth, and you were totally at his or her mercy. When the network failed, you had no choice but to call in this human money-drain.

Complex networks still call for complex solutions, but most people don't need a complex setup. Most people just need to share files and programs and maybe a printer. If this is what you want to do, here's how you can, in a few easy steps, set up a fully functional network.

Buying the Hardware

You need a minimum amount of hardware. Go to a store that sells computer equipment and buy:

1. Two network cards. Make sure they're Plug-and-Play compatible. Cards are circuit boards that fit into slots inside your computer.

2. Cable to connect the computers. You'll need RG58 Thin Ethernet (Ethernet) cable with BNC connectors at either end. (This cable looks a lot like the wire used to run cable TV into your house, but it's not interchangeable.)

3. Two 50-ohm terminators. One for each machine.

You can get the cards, terminators, and cable for under $100 total. However, if you can afford to pay more, you'll get better quality. But even really good cards and cable should add up to less than $300. Shop around for the best prices on the more expensive cards and cable.

 NOTE Make sure you get enough cable to connect the two computers without the cable itself becoming a tripping hazard. You don't need to worry about length limitations—Thin Ethernet can be run up to several hundred yards!

Installing the Hardware

To install the pieces, you'll need a small Phillips screwdriver and possibly a slotted screwdriver as well. Also have a cup or other container for the screws you'll remove and otherwise immediately lose. Follow these steps:

1. With the computers turned off, install a network card in an available slot in each computer.

2. T-shaped connectors (called, not surprisingly, T-connectors) come with the cards. You attach one point to the cable, the second point to the network card, and the third gets a terminator. Check the instructions that come with the card to see which goes where.

Configuring the Network

Now you need to follow several (uncomplicated) steps on each computer:

1. Restart the computer and let Windows 95 detect the new card. (If it's not detected, try Add New Hardware, and specify the card you have.)

2. Double-click the Network icon in the Control Panel.

3. Highlight your network card in the list of network components and then click the Properties button. Select the Bindings tab.

4. Select either NetBEUI or IPX/SPX. The one you "bind" with will act as your networking protocol. Choose the same protocol on each machine. (You can even choose both, but there will be a cost in memory and you don't *need* both.) Click OK.

NOTE TCP/IP may be one of the choices, but you don't want to include it for this kind of network because it's much more complex to set up.

5. On the Configuration page, click the File and Print Sharing button and enable sharing.

6. Click the Identification tab. Each computer should have a different name but the same workgroup name. Click OK.

7. Shut down and restart both computers.

Sharing the Resources

To make drives or individual folders on one computer available to the other computer, open Explorer and right-click the drive or folders and select Sharing from the pop-up menu. Configure the sharing properties.

To share a printer, open the Printers folder (in My Computer or the Control Panel) and do the same.

You can also have one or more of the drives on the other computer show up in your computer's Explorer, so you can access files and folders easily. To *map* another computer's drive to your computer, follow these steps:

1. Double-click the Network Neighborhood icon, then on the Workgroup name, and finally on the name of the other computer. All the drives that have been shared by the other computer will appear in the window.

2. Right-click the first drive you want to appear on your computer and select Map Network Drive. A window will open. In this case, the drive called C: on the other computer will be mapped as E: because the computer doing the mapping already has a drive C: and drive D:.

3. Click Reconnect at Logon only if you'll be accessing this drive a lot. If you leave it unchecked, your computer will connect only when you request access to drive E: by selecting it in Windows Explorer (or My Computer).

4. Click OK when you're finished.

HP LaserJet 4

You can map any or all of the drives on the other computer. Resources you've shared with the other computer will have an icon with a hand like the one shown here.

Skill 18

HP LaserJet 4

The same resource from your computer will appear on the *other* computer with an icon like the one shown here.

This kind of network will work quite well. If you need a more complicated setup, one with many computers or one that requires a server, you'll need the advice of an expert or you can study and become an expert yourself.

Are You Experienced?

Now you can...

- ☑ decide on a network type
- ☑ purchase the hardware and configure it yourself
- ☑ make a direct cable connection
- ☑ build the simplest type of network

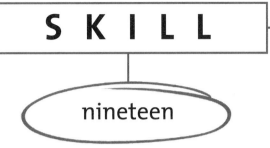

S K I L L

nineteen

Introducing the Internet

- ❏ Understanding how the Internet connects computers

- ❏ Connecting to other computers with Telnet and FTP

- ❏ Participating in Internet newsgroups

- ❏ Exchanging e-mail through the Internet

- ❏ Finding information with gopher

- ❏ Accessing the World Wide Web

To get the most out of Microsoft Internet Explorer, you should begin with a general understanding of the Internet itself. This skill contains an explanation of the Internet's basic structure and descriptions of the major Internet services that you can reach through Internet Explorer.

Learning the Structure of the Internet

When you connect a pair of computers together through a communications link, the two machines can exchange commands, messages, data files, and programs. If you connect a third computer, you have the beginnings of a network. Using a computer connected to a network, you can run programs and read files on other computers connected to the same network.

In the simplest possible terms, the Internet is a worldwide "network of networks" that connects computers around the world together. All of these computers use the same timing and data formats, known as *networking protocols*. Since 1969, the Internet has expanded from its origins as an experimental network that included computers operated by a handful of American universities and government contractors. By 1973, the network reached Europe, and now extends to millions of computers in just about every country of the world.

Strictly speaking, you don't connect your computer directly to the Internet, but to a network that connects to other networks through a network *backbone*. Interconnections (called *gateways*) between these backbones make it possible for a computer on one network to exchange messages and data with another computer connected to any other network. Figure 19.1 is a simplified diagram of the Internet's interconnected backbones.

 NOTE   In the United States and Canada, the Internet's backbones are a series of very high-speed communications lines owned primarily by communications giants such as AT&T, Sprint, and MCI. A few of the large Internet service providers (ISPs) own portions of the backbones, others lease their portions. In other countries, government authorities or a few private companies own the backbones.

The set of networking protocols that controls the Internet is known as TCP/IP (Transmission Control Protocol/Internet Protocol). The specifications for TCP/IP include the addressing schemes that identify each computer on the Internet and rules for several kinds of programs, such as file transfer and remote command entry.

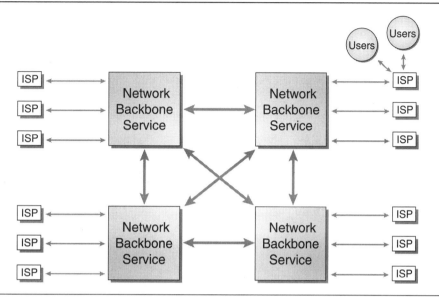

FIGURE 19.1: The Internet is a worldwide network of networks.

One of the most important features of the Internet is that it isn't limited to a specific type of computer or operating system. Versions of TCP/IP can run on just about any kind of computer built in the last 20 years. Therefore, you can connect your desktop PC through the Internet to a room-filling mainframe computer just as easily as you can connect it to another PC. TCP/IP programs always present the same appearance to the network, regardless of the type of computer on which they're operating.

It might be helpful to think about the Internet as a system similar to the utility that provides the electric power you use in your house and your office. On one side, there are a variety of devices that generate electric power—hydroelectric dams, coal-fired generators, nuclear reactors, windmills, and others. All of these sources provide electricity to the same distribution grid in a form that meets a commonly accepted specification (alternating current at 50 or 60 cycles per second). At the receiving end, toasters, refrigerators, computers, and vacuum cleaners all can use power that comes from the grid.

As Figure 19.2 shows, the Internet is a huge distribution grid for data. Connecting one computer to the Internet doesn't accomplish anything useful; but when you connect it *through* the Internet to another computer, you can reasonably expect that each machine will recognize and understand the commands and data that it receives from the other.

Skill 19

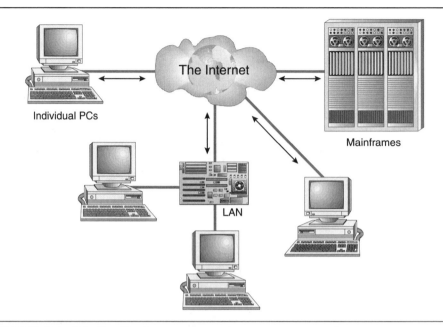

Individual PCs

Mainframes

LAN

FIGURE 19.2: The Internet connects computers together.

Understanding Clients and Servers

Before we start to talk about specific features and functions you can use through the Internet, you should understand one more general concept. With very few exceptions, the programs and services that operate through the Internet use a *client/server* design in which a client program on the user's computer sends commands or information requests to a server, which may respond by creating a live connection or by sending data back to the client.

For example, to download a copy of a file located on another computer, you must use a program called an FTP (File Transfer Protocol) client, which sends a file request to an FTP server program on a computer that contains a file archive. When the server program receives the request, it locates the file and sends a copy back to the client.

Electronic mail (e-mail) is more complicated, because there's more than one server in the path between origin and destination, but it still uses a client/server model. Here are the steps involved in delivering an e-mail message:

1. The person who sends the message uses an e-mail client program to send the message to a post office server.

2. The post office server examines the header of the message and identifies the address of each recipient.

3. The post office server sends the message through the Internet to the mail server that handles mail for each recipient's address.

4. The mail server stores the message in the recipient's mailbox.

5. The recipient uses an e-mail client program to request new messages from the mail server.

6. The mail server sends the messages in the recipient's mailbox back to the client.

In all cases, a client sends a request to a server and the server responds by sending a file or other data back to the client. This is even true in a Telnet connection, where it appears that you have a live connection to the server. In fact, the client sends commands to the server, which interprets and processes each command and sends the result back to the client.

Microsoft Internet Explorer is a particularly flexible type of client program called a *Web browser*, which can obtain files and other data from several different kinds of servers. In the rest of this skill, we'll explain how each of these servers works.

Connecting with Telnet

Before the days of desktop personal computers, people exchanged commands with computers through terminals that sent commands to the computer and received and displayed the computer's responses on a printer or a video monitor screen. Telnet is the Internet tool that connects one computer to a second computer as a distant terminal. In other words, the Telnet server (also called a *host*) treats incoming commands from the Internet as if they came from a terminal

Skill 19

connected directly to the host. Entering commands through a Telnet client program produces exactly the same results as typing them on a local terminal.

Telnet has several common uses. If you have an account on a distant computer (the "distant" machine might be across the hall or halfway around the world), you can use any other computer with an Internet connection to send commands and retrieve data from the first machine. For example, Figure 19.3 shows a Telnet connection to The Well, an online conference service based in California.

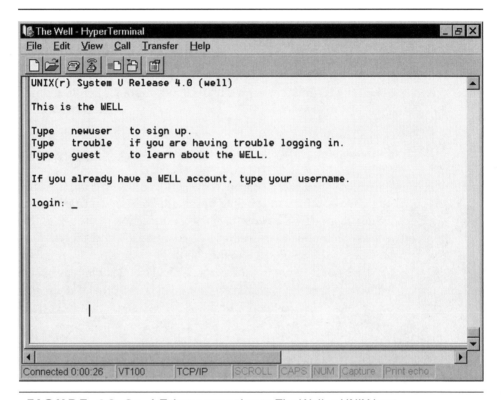

FIGURE 19.3: A Telnet connection to The Well, a UNIX host.

Other computers are configured as public Telnet hosts. Even if you don't have an account on one of these systems, you can still use some of the host's programs. Many libraries make their catalogs accessible through the Internet on public Telnet hosts.

Internet Explorer is not a Telnet client, but there's a separate Telnet program included in Windows 95. Internet Explorer can use this Telnet program to establish links to Telnet hosts.

Transferring Files with FTP

FTP (File Transfer Protocol) is an Internet tool for uploading and downloading files between computers. A file transfer must take place between a client and a server, but the files can move in either direction (either from the server to the client or from the client to the server).

FTP servers are fairly straightforward; when a server receives a file request from an FTP client, it sends a copy of that file back to the client. Other commands instruct the server to send the client a directory of files or to accept an upload from the client.

FINDING A GOOD FTP TOOL

There's a separate FTP client program included with Windows 95, but it's a text-based utility that runs in a DOS window. If you don't already know how to use FTP, don't waste your time with it. For an FTP tool separate from the one in Internet Explorer, you can find several in FTP archives (use Explorer to download them). One of the best is WSFTP32. To download WSFTP32, open Internet Explorer and follow these steps:

1. In the Internet Explorer's address line, type in the following exactly and press the Enter key:

   ```
   ftp://ftp.usma.edu/msdos/winsock.files/
   ```

2. Scroll down the page and double-click wsftp32a.zip and the file will be downloaded.

You can find more information about using Internet Explorer to download files from FTP archives in Skill 24, along with a description of Archie, a tool for searching through many archives to locate specific files.

Most often, you will use FTP to download files from public file archives on FTP servers. There are thousands of these archives, with hundreds of thousands of files, located all over the Internet. For example, many software companies maintain FTP archives that contain upgrades, drivers, and patches for their products. Other archives contain huge collections of shareware and freeware programs. If you can establish a connection to one of these servers through the Internet, the owners are happy to let you download copies of these files at no charge. Other FTP archives contain copies of scholarly papers and reports, graphic images, and recipes, among many other things.

These archives are sometimes known as "anonymous FTP" archives, because they accept the word "anonymous" as a logon name, with the user's e-mail address as a password. When Internet Explorer connects to an FTP server, it automatically handles the anonymous logon unless you instruct it to send a different name and password.

Not all FTP servers accept anonymous logons, and those that do frequently limit access to files in specific directories. If you have your own account on an FTP server, you may be able to download programs and data files that are not available to members of the public, and to upload files to the server.

Communicating via Newsgroups

Many Internet users participate in ongoing conversations in *newsgroups* devoted to almost every imaginable topic, from cellular biology and general semantics to making wine at home and restoring antique phonographs. There are many thousands of these groups on the Internet, with new ones added all the time. In each newsgroup, participants post individual *articles* that may either be replies to earlier articles or completely new postings.

Some newsgroups are not much more than question-and-answer sessions for technical or hobby topics ("Can anybody tell me how to align my 1937 Whoopee-Flow diathermy machine?"), but many others have evolved into online communities with their own traditions and personalities. The relationships that develop in some newsgroups have been described as an alternative reality based on typing.

 **WARNING**

Anyone with an Internet connection can post an article to a newsgroup, whether they know anything about the subject. Except for replies to the original message, there's no quality control over the information that appears in Net news. There's no assurance that the person posting an authoritative description of the latest weapons systems didn't get the information out of a Tom Clancy novel. Nor is there any assurance that the person claiming to be Tom Clancy is in fact that person.

The set of standards for distributing news through the Internet is called Network News Transfer Protocol, so you might also see news servers called NNTP servers.

A news client program (also called a *newsreader*) performs several tasks:

- It downloads and displays a list of newsgroups currently available on the news server.

- It allows a user to "subscribe" to individual newsgroups.

- It downloads and displays a list of articles in the currently selected newsgroup, sorted by subject, originator, time, or sorted into threads, with replies and other comments following questions.

- It allows users to select and read individual articles.

- It provides a method for posting new articles and replies to existing articles.

When you post an article to a newsgroup, your news client program transfers the article to your Internet access provider's news server, which distributes copies to all the other news servers that support the newsgroup in which you posted the article (some news servers don't include every newsgroup).

Communicating via Electronic Mail

Electronic mail (also known as e-mail) is the process of sending and receiving messages and files between individual addresses. Unlike news, in which the same messages are accessible to anybody who wants to read them, the Internet's e-mail system delivers messages (and files) to specific recipients.

E-mail is not a substitute for either telephone calls or postal mail. It's a new communications medium that has its own set of advantages and disadvantages. It's faster and less expensive than writing letters, and it's not as intrusive as a ringing telephone. And because you're not on a live connection to the recipient of your message, you can take all the time you need to reflect on what you have to say before you send it. But it doesn't permit the kind of live interaction that takes place during a telephone call, and it may not be as secure or private as a written letter.

The rules for Internet e-mail are defined in a specification called Simple Mail Transfer Protocol, or SMTP. An e-mail message passes through these steps on its way from originator to recipient:

1. The person originating the message uses a mail client program to compose the text and, if necessary, to attach a file to the message.

2. The mail client program sends the message to the post office server where the user has an account.

3. The post office server connects to the mail server where the recipient's mail-box is located, and transfers a copy of the message.

4. The recipient's mail client program connects to the mail server to check for new mail, either on a regular schedule or on in response to a command.

5. If there are messages in the recipient's mailbox, the mail server downloads them to the client.

Internet Explorer is not an e-mail client program, but it has links to external programs, such as the Microsoft Exchange client e-mail program that's included in Windows 95 or with the Internet Mail program that's available with the newsreader.

Introducing Gopher

The amount of information available through the Internet can be mind-boggling. There are literally millions of separate files, databases, and other online resources ready and waiting for you to download. But they won't do you much good unless you know how to find them.

The Internet Gopher was the first large-scale attempt to organize the Internet's resources into logical menus. It was created at the University of Minnesota (home of the Golden Gophers) in 1991 as a guide to information services on the university campus, but it quickly spread to the Internet.

A gopher server contains one or more menus with pointers to items that may be located anywhere on the Internet. Some menus are lists of items related to a specific topic or of items supplied by the owner of the server. Others are arranged by location; still others are more-or-less random links to items that the person who created the menu considered interesting or amusing. For example, Figure 19.4 shows part of a list of gopher resources located in the state of Oregon.

Most gopher menus also include pointers to other menus, so the overall effect is a vast, interconnected list of lists. The top-level menu, on a server at the University of Minnesota (the "Mother Gopher") has links to every gopher server in the world. Most menus have links to higher-level menus, so it's usually possible to move from one menu to any other menu with a small number of jumps.

Reduced to basics, just about everything that moves through the Internet is a downloadable file, a live Telnet connection, a public news article, or a private e-mail message. When you select an item from a gopher menu, your gopher client identifies the resource type and connects your computer to the server that contains that item. If the resource is a file, the client program downloads a copy to your own computer and uses a local file viewer to display its contents. If it's a Telnet server, the client displays instructions for logging on to the host. If the server is a database, the gopher client asks for the specific information for which you're looking.

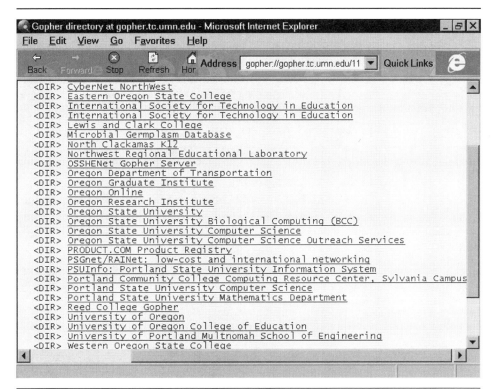

FIGURE 19.4: A top-level gopher menu

As an Internet browsing tool, the World Wide Web has overshadowed gopher, but it's still an efficient and effective way to locate files and services online. It's also an excellent way to discover unexpected goodies in servers that you didn't know about before you started wandering around in gopherspace. Either as part of a Web browser like Internet Explorer or as a separate client program, gopher should be part of your Internet toolkit.

Discovering the World Wide Web

The World Wide Web blends text, images, and access to files and other Internet resources into a seamless display. Unlike gopher menus, which have a formal hierarchical structure, Web pages can have *hot links* anywhere within their design. Clicking on a link may take a user to another location within the same page, to another Web page, or to any other type of Internet resource, including gopher menus, FTP archives or individual files, Telnet hosts, and newsgroups. The destination of a link may be on the same server as the current Web page or anywhere else on the Internet. It's also possible to jump to an e-mail editor that automatically addresses a message to a specific recipient.

The rules that define the World Wide Web are called Hypertext Transfer Protocol (HTTP). HTTP was originally designed at the European Particle Physics Laboratory in Geneva as a way to move technical information across the Internet; footnotes and cross-references in reports and other documents could be formatted as links, so readers could easily obtain additional data without losing their place in the original document.

HTTP identifies every file on every computer connected to the Internet with a unique Uniform Resource Locator (URL) code, which specifies the type of file and its exact location. All URLs use this format:

```
type://address/path/file.ext
```

The *type* portion of the address shows the type of server that contains the file. The most common types are:

Web pages	`http://`
FTP servers	`file://` or `ftp://`
Gopher	`gopher://`
Telnet	`Telnet://`

If you don't include a *path* and *file.ext* in a URL, your HTTP client program will jump to the page or directory that the server's owner has chosen as the default, or *home page*.

It's not universally observed, but many commercial Web sites have named their servers `www.`*name*`.com`. Therefore, if you're looking for a company's Web site, you can try a link to `http://www.`*name*`.com`. For example, the URL for the top-level Microsoft home page is `http://www.microsoft.com`, and the URL for British Airways is `http://www.british-airways.com`.

Today, HTTP and Web browser programs like Internet Explorer have become much more complex and sophisticated than they were two or three years ago. They can combine graphic elements, audio and video, along with text, still pictures, and interactive access to databases and other services to create an almost unlimited variety of interesting variations. And since a Web page can contain links to just about anything, anywhere on the Internet, a Web browser combines the functions of many different kinds of client programs. A program like Internet Explorer can be all you need to take advantage of most of the things the Internet has to offer.

Figure 19.5 shows a typical Web page. This page contains information about Andorra, a tiny country in Europe. The underlined words on this page are links to other parts of the same page and to other pages with related information. The variety of typefaces, the flag and other images, and the decorative background make a Web page like this one a great deal more interesting than a simple gopher menu.

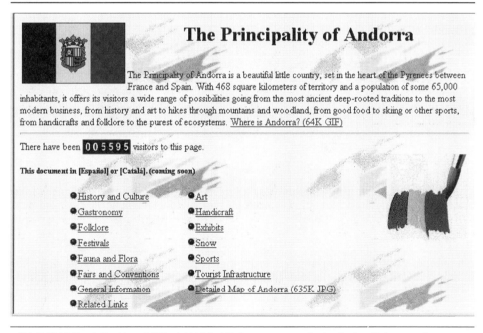

FIGURE 19.5: A World Wide Web page usually includes links to other Internet resources.

Browsing the Web looks more complicated than using one of the other Internet tools, but the underlying structure is about the same: A client program (the browser) sends commands to a server, which sends files, messages, and other data back to the client. The Web is more flexible than other Internet services because it can move text, images, and different kinds of files and other data through the same client program. It's more attractive than many other tools because it can integrate text, pictures, and other images into a single screen.

Are You Experienced?

Now you can...

- ☑ know how the Internet connects computers
- ☑ understand Telnet, FTP, and gopher
- ☑ grasp the workings of Internet newsgroups
- ☑ know the basics of e-mail through the Internet
- ☑ understand the World Wide Web

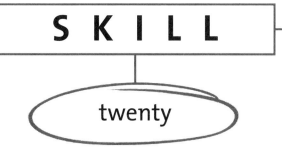

Connecting to the Internet

❏ Choosing an Internet service provider

❏ Using winsock.dll files

❏ Making connections with more than one online service

❏ Adding Internet access to an MSN account

Before you can use Internet Explorer (or any other Internet application program), you must connect your computer to the Internet. In this skill, you will find information about choosing an Internet service provider; making the connection through a modem, a LAN, or other link; and installing and configuring your system for a TCP/IP connection.

If you already have an Internet connection that supports other TCP/IP Internet client programs, you may be able to use it with Internet Explorer. If that's the case, you can skip this skill.

Choosing a Service Provider

As you know, the Internet is the result of connecting many networks to one another. Therefore, you can connect your own computer to the Internet by obtaining an account on one of those interconnected networks.

Several different kinds of businesses offer Internet connections, including large companies with access points in many cities, smaller local or regional Internet service providers, and online information services that provide TCP/IP connections to the Internet along with their own proprietary information sources. You can use Internet Explorer with a connection through any of these services.

When you order your account, you should request a PPP connection to the Internet. PPP—which stands for Point-to-Point Protocol—is a standard type of TCP/IP connection that any Internet service provider (ISP) should be able to supply.

Connecting through an Online Service

If you already have an account with an online information service, you can use the same account for access to the Internet. Three of the four major services—America Online (AOL), CompuServe, and Prodigy—have built-in Web browsers, but it's also possible to use Internet Explorer as an external add-on program though AOL and CompuServe. The fourth major service, Microsoft Network, uses Internet Explorer as its default browser. In most cases, Internet Explorer (or Netscape Navigator, for that matter) is faster and easier to use than the browsers supplied by the online services.

Like the software supplied by nationwide Internet-only services, the programs provided by AOL, CompuServe, and Prodigy are all 16-bit packages designed to work with both Windows 3.1 and Windows 95. Therefore, you must use them with Internet Explorer for Windows 3.1, even if you are running Windows 95.

Using America Online

To use Internet Explorer through AOL, you must either upgrade to AOL's Version 3 software or download a winsock.dll file from AOL's Winsock Central area (keyword: **Winsock**). Because the AOL Winsock is a 16-bit program, you'll need the Windows 3.1 version of Internet Explorer, even if you have installed Windows 95. When AOL introduces software for Windows 95, it will be compatible with the 32-bit version of Internet Explorer.

Installing AOL's Winsock   Follow these steps to install AOL's Winsock:

1. Download the winsock.dll file from AOL.

2. Look in your \windows directory for a winsock.dll file. If you find one, rename it to winsock.old.

3. Copy winsock.dll from c:\aol25\download to your \windows directory.

Using Internet Explorer with AOL   To use Internet Explorer (or any other Winsock-compliant client program) through AOL, follow these steps:

1. Start AOL and connect as you would to use AOL's own services.

2. Minimize the AOL window.

3. Double-click the Internet Explorer icon.

Using CompuServe

CompuServe's Winsock is very much like AOL's, but it's included in the WinCIM 2.01 package, so you don't need to download it separately.

Copying the CompuServe Winsock   In order to use the CompuServe Winsock with Internet Explorer, you must have a copy of the winsock.dll program in your \windows directory or some other directory in your DOS path. Follow these steps to copy the program:

1. Look in your \windows directory for a winsock.dll file. If you find one, rename it to winsock.old.

2. Copy the winsock.dll file from your c:\cserve\mosaic directory to the \windows directory.

Using Internet Explorer with CompuServe   To use Internet Explorer (or any other Winsock-compliant client program) through CompuServe, follow these steps:

1. Start WinCIM and connect as you would to use CompuServe's own services.

2. Minimize the WinCIM window.

3. Double-click the Internet Explorer icon.

Using More Than One Online Service

If you want to use Internet Explorer and other TCP/IP programs through more than one online service, or if you have accounts with both an online service and a separate ISP, things will be more difficult. You will have conflicts between the winsock.dll files that connect you to each service. Although the files have the same name, they are not cross-compatible.

When you start a client program, it looks for winsock.dll in this order:

1. In the same directory as the client program

2. In your \windows directory

3. In the directories in your DOS path

The application tries to use the first Winsock file it finds, even if some other Winsock is currently connected. Therefore, you must make sure that the one you want to use is the same one the application finds.

There are several ways to work around this problem, but none are particularly attractive:

• Copy a new winsock.dll file into the \windows directory each time you want to connect through a different service.

• Maintain multiple copies of Internet Explorer and other programs in separate directories, with a different Winsock file in each directory.

• Use Internet Explorer with just one ISP or online service.

• Use an ISP to connect to the Internet, and then use the TCP/IP option to reach the online services.

These are all more or less unsatisfactory solutions to the problem. If you have the space on your hard drive, the best choice is probably to create several directories and place a Winsock file and a copy of Internet Explorer in each one. Create separate shortcuts on the Windows 95 Desktop or Start menu called *Internet Explorer via AOL* and *Internet Explorer via SPRYnet* (or whatever Internet access providers you're actually using).

If you use Windows 95 and you have accounts with more than one ISP (rather than online information services), you don't need to worry about this problem; you can find instructions for creating and using multiple Dial-Up Networking connection profiles in Skill 15.

NOTE   Skill 15 has more on the major online providers in terms of what they offer (besides Internet access) and what they cost.

Connecting to the Internet through Microsoft Network

Along with all those other service providers, Microsoft has an Internet access product of their own. The Microsoft Network (MSN) was established as an online information service that would compete with AOL and CompuServe. But a few months after it was launched, Microsoft announced that MSN would be converted to an Internet-based service with content areas that would be available to any Internet user.

Microsoft wants you to use their Internet access service, so they've made it extremely easy to load and configure a Windows 95 Dial-Up Networking connection to MSN. If you already have an account with MSN, or if there's an MSN telephone number that supports Internet access within local calling range of your office or home, the Microsoft service may be the easiest (but probably not the least expensive) way to set up a Windows 95 Internet connection.

When you install Internet Explorer, the Setup Wizard will ask if you want to connect through Microsoft Network or through some other service provider. If you choose MSN and don't already have an MSN account, the Wizard will step you through the process of finding a local telephone number and establishing a new account. If you already have an MSN account, you can easily add Internet access:

1.   Double-click the MSN icon.

2.   When the Sign In window appears, click the Settings button.

3. Click the Access Numbers button.

4. In the Microsoft Network dialog box, choose Internet and the Microsoft Network as your service type.

5. Click the Change buttons to select the closest Primary and Backup telephone numbers.

6. Click the OK buttons to close all the dialog boxes and save your selections.

When setup is complete, you will have a Dial-Up Networking connection profile for Microsoft Network, and if you specified a backup telephone number, a separate backup connection profile.

Changing the Default Connection

When setup is complete, you will have a Dial-Up Networking connection profile for each of your ISPs. Internet Explorer and other Winsock-compliant programs will use the current default to connect your computer to the Internet whenever you start the programs.

To change the default, follow these steps:

1. Right-click the Internet icon on your Desktop and select the Properties command from the menu.

2. When the Internet Properties dialog box appears, click the Connection tab to display the dialog box shown in Figure 20.1.

3. Choose the name of the Dial-Up Networking connection profile you want to use from the drop-down list.

4. Click the OK button to close the dialog box.

Using Alternative Connection Methods

A telephone connection is the most common and least expensive way for individuals to reach the Internet, but it's not your only option. If they're not available now, high-speed data services will probably become available from your telephone company, cable TV service, and other new information utilities within the next few years. You can also use Internet Explorer with high-speed network connections through a corporate LAN or a campus-wide network.

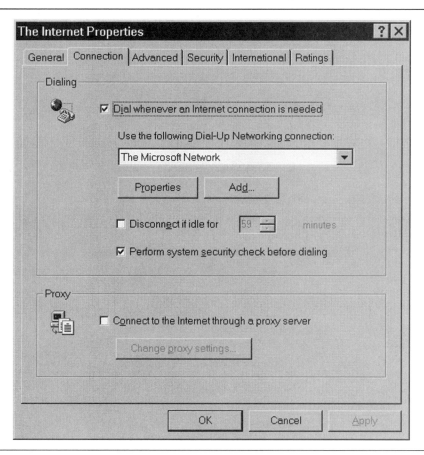

The Internet Properties ? X

General | Connection | Advanced | Security | International | Ratings |

Dialing

☑ Dial whenever an Internet connection is needed

Use the following Dial-Up Networking connection:

The Microsoft Network ▼

Properties   Add...

☐ Disconnect if idle for   59 ➕   minutes

☑ Perform system security check before dialing

Proxy

☐ Connect to the Internet through a proxy server

Change proxy settings...

OK   Cancel   Apply

FIGURE 20.1: Use the Connection tab to change the default connection profile.

Each of these services requires a special network interface device that allows your computer to send and receive data more quickly than the COM port can handle it. The specific hardware and software requirements are different for each type of connection; your network service provider will tell you exactly what you need.

As far as Internet Explorer is concerned, the only difference between a dial-in connection to the Internet and a faster network link is the amount of time it will take to download and display Web pages and other files. All of the features and functions of Internet Explorer will work with any kind of Internet connection.

NOTE   A discussion of the different kinds of connections can be found in Skill 15.

Are You Experienced?

Now you can...

- ☑ choose an Internet service provider
- ☑ use winsock.dll files
- ☑ make connections with more than one online service
- ☑ add Internet access to an MSN account

schedul-
s admin.
rfect or
lytical &
a must.

RY
looking
dual with
izational
Excel, MS
ciency in
f 60-65
rstanding
nt. Send
ial Corp.
Lubbock.

GER Will
creative
schedule
projects.
derstand-
and print-
ax 555-

ANALYST
company
y provide
and end-
orporate
/BS with
financial
entation
to detail
abilities
werPoint
esources
55-2398.

ONIST
n a fast-
be a self-
depend-
-ser vice.
unication
experi-
Medical
own, MD

commn
oking for
mputer
t. as well
ustomers
ssful can-
ars' tech-
years in
s experi-
to Best
672.

rces Mgr
ng in
isation &
wledge of
PC skills
334-555-

Business
searcher
business
net skills
ccurate &
: Write:
a Blvd.

TER
al seeks
r the bro-
industry,
g/editing
business

based telefundraising. Minimum of 7 years experience in similar field. 4 year degree preferred. Proficient computer skills incl. Windows-based software applications required. Salary commensurate w/skills & exp. plus benefits. Send letter and resume to Well-Being Clinic, 543 Spring Ave., Daytonville, VA.

Executive Secretary
OfficePlus, an office supply & furniture company is looking for administrative support to VP. Requires 5 years min. of secretarial experience, proficiency with MS Word and Excel and excellent communication skills. Must be willing to learn database & desktop software. Fax: OfficePlus, Personnel 665-555-9122.

FACILITIES PLANNER Training Centers Inc. seeks individual to study & develop infrastructure requirements and capital improvement projects. Req's BA in Planning, Engineering, Architecture or rel. field w/7 years exp & knowl of Windows (Word, Excel) & graphics programs. 4 yrs exp w PC's planning arch/eng or facilities mgmt & exp w/CAD, database mgmt & project scheduling pref'd. Fax: HR, 885-555-2398.

MANAGEMENT REPORTING ANALYST
Join the team that maintains the purchasing and logistics information systems that support order entry, provide product and contract information, track product utilization, and manage operating budget and inventory systems. Must be proficient in a high-level database system and Excel, Lotus 1-2-3, or similar applications. Fax resume to Data Systems Placement Services 444-555-9998.

MANAGER, ASSET MODELING
This worldwide logistics company is expanding it's transportation network. The successful candidate will have a Bachelor's degree in Economics, Finance or Business Mgmt, with a MBA degree preferred, a solid foundation in Mathematics, and excellent analytical skills. Knowledge of PC applications in Excel, Word, PowerPoint and Visio essential. Competitive benefits and compensation plan. Fax: 966-555-2298/

Manager, Business Analysis
You will direct a team of Business Analysts and oversee timely completion of all projects in accordance with departmental policies and procedures. Requires BA/BS in Behavioral Health Sciences, Business Administration, MIS, or equivalent experience, system development/analysis and software testing, strong project management and team building skills, and software development experience. Hart Corporate Services. Call J. Thornton 243-555-9583.

Market Research Project Manager
SuperHouse Designs is creating a new research division. You will provide research consulting services to internal clients and manage external research providers. A BA/BS degree or equivalent with 4-6 years' experi-

send cover letter, resume & salary req's to: Sommes Communications, Attn: HR/Job 85, 776 Bowser Lane, Bowtown, MA.

MARKETING ASSISTANT
Supporting 2 Marketing Mgrs., you'll handle a variety of admin. responsibilities, direct mail coordination, desktop publishing, and ad space coordination. Require 1-2 years admin. exper. and strong computer skills, esp. desktop pub., HTML, Office & Windows. Fax: R. Smith 365-555-8844.

OFFICE MANAGER
Join a growing firm that offers competitive salaries & benefits for a take-charge type. Responsible for all office purchases & operations, including a quarterly newsletter. Windows & MS Office experience req'd. Call 973-555-4545.

PC Support Specialist
High-end catalog company and specialty retailer has opening in MIS Dept. Support corporate associates with PC and network systems. Extensive PC hardware installation and configuration experience is required. Must be able to communicate effectively, and determine cause of problems, & develop solutions. Requires network admin. & multiple PC operating systems experience. (Windows, UNIX) Fax resume & salary reqs to High Profile Images 388-555-9634.

PROJECT ASST. Serve as a point person in HR office of fast growing biotech firm. Requires creative thinking and up-to-date office computer skills, esp. Word, PowerPoint & Excel. Fax resume to TruPoint Systems 689-555-1298.

PROJECT MANAGER
Public agency seeking environmental project manager to oversee 18-month marsh preservation project. Develop, analyze, organize & summarize planning data and financial info. Windows computer skills essential. Send resume to Public Planning Services, Attn: HR, 34 Marsh Lane, Willowdale, CA.

Sales/Computer
Expanding computer software & hardware store is looking for more qualified sales associates to staff our busy downtown location. Windows software experience required. Send resume and salary/commission requirements to General Manager, Computers for You, 433 Main St., Ontario, MN.

Sales Support Associate Work with customer service, account managers, marketing & brand management. You will handle distribution of sales materials and internal correspondence. You will need 1-2 years in sales admin. and basic office functions (mail, fax, phones etc.), plus PC skills. Computer troubleshooting skills a plus.

Sales: Sr. Account Coordinator
Looking Good, a national clothing chain is looking for seasoned sales pros to oversee sales operations. Qualified candidates must have 4-5 years sales mgmt exp. and strong

PC skills. A college degree, working knowledge of Excel, PowerPoint, Word and database software req'd. Fax resume and cover letter to: Looking Good, Attn: K. Perkovich, 877 Goody Ave., Reno, NV.

SALES/COMPUTER
Expanding computer software & hardware store is looking for more qualified sales associates to staff our busy downtown location. Windows software experience required. Send resume and salary/commission requirements to General Manager, Computers for You, 433 Main St., Ontario, MN.

SALES SUPPORT ASSOCIATE
Work with customer service, account managers, marketing & brand management. You will handle distribution of sales materials and internal correspondence. You will need 1-2 years in sales admin. and basic office functions (mail, fax, ph)

Senior Calendar Clerk
Large international law firm is seeking qualified candidates with strong organizational and data entry skills, and extremely high level of service orientation and excellent oral and written communication skills. Applicants must possess a BA/BS degree, have knowledge of computer databases and Word or WordPerfect. Send resume and salary requirements to HR, Jackson Madison Madison Teller & Pewter, 1001 Main Street, Atlanta, GA

Sr. Financial Analyst
JJO Enterprises seeking senior member of financial team. Requires a degree in Finance/Econ/Accts, minimum 3 yrs' public acct. exp. (CPA), Lotus/Excel, MS Word/WordPerfect proficiency P&L/cashflow statement exp is preferred. Competitive salary/benefits pkg. Fax: Mr. Rogers, JJO Enterprises 442-555-1267.

SENIOR LAW CLERK
Large international law firm is seeking qualified candidates with strong organizational and data entry skills, and extremely high level of service orientation and excellent oral and written communication skills. Applicants must possess a BA/BS degree, have knowledge of computer databases and Word or WordPerfect. Send resume and salary requirements to HR, Jackson Madison Madison Teller & Pewter, 1001 Main Street, Atlanta, GA

Senior Secretary
Bolan Lumber Co. looking for add'l office support staff. Type 60 wpm. Word/Excel/Windows and some desktop publishing experience. Call Ron 335-555-9944.

TECHNICAL COMMUNICATOR
Biotech Systems is expanding and is seeking someone to develop & maintain user documentation/training materials and on-line help systems. Requires a BA/BS in Technical Communication or equiva-

Group. Req. a BA/BS with 4 years' experience in financial analysis or system implementation or development. Attention to detail & time and resource mgmt. abilities are vital. Excel and PowerPoint req'd. Contact Financial Resources Executive Search at 443-555-2398.

Clerical Receptionist F/T position available in a fast paced HR dept. You must be a self-starter, organized, and dependable. Excellent customer-service, written and verbal communication skills required. Computer experience a must! Norwell Medical Center, 100 Front St. Allentown, MD

Computer Operator/PC Technician
Large software retailer looking for someone with expert computer skills to assist in tech dept. as well as to give seminars for customers looking to upgrade. Successful candidate must have 3-5 years' technical experience and 2-3 years in customer service. Teaching experience a plus. Fax resume to Best Systems: 545-555-6677.

COMPUTERS
Immediate openings! Computer technicians with PC hardware and Windows experience. Send resume to: Delta Plus, 1200 Sutter St. San Francisco, CA.

Corporate Human Resources Mgr
Specialized background in Employment or Compensation & Benefits, and general knowledge of all other HR functions. PC skills essential. Fax resume to 334-555-9112.

Editorial Researcher Business publication seeking researcher responsible for weekly business lists, etc. Computer/Internet skills required. Must be fast, accurate & thorough. Salary DOE. Write: Researcher, 9106 Shasta Blvd., Pittsburgh, PA.

Editor/Reporter
National financial journal seeks experienced writer to cover the brokerage/financial services industry. Must have strong writing/editing skills and background in business reporting. Computer/word processor experience a must! Fax resume and clips to JIT 887-555-2256.

Engineering
Senior Industrial Engineer needed for large wholesale buyers club, to help reduce operating costs and increase revenues. A BS degree and at least 6 years in the distribution/transportation field are required. Strong business writing skills, PC proficiency using Microsoft Office and electronic communications is essential. Send cover letter and resume to HR/Job 445, AB Industries, 4498 Howard Blvd. Kansas City, MO

Executive Assistant
You'll need strong organizational, interpersonal, and analytical skills, coupled with good computer knowledge in applications such as Access, PowerPoint, Excel and Word. Send resume & salary history

based telefundraising. Minimum... years experience in similar f... year degree preferred. Pr... computer skills incl. Windows... software applications... re... Salary commensurate w/skills... plus benefits. Send letter... resume to Well-Being Clinic... Spring Ave., Daytonville, VA.

FACILITIES PLANNER
Training Centers Inc. seeks ind... to study & develop infrast... requirements and capital im... ment projects. Req's BA in Pl... Engineering, Architecture or re... w/7 years exp & knowl of W... (Word, Excel) & graphics pro... 4 yrs exp w PC's planning a... or facilities mgmt & exp w... database mgmt & project sch... pref'd. Fax: HR, 885-555-239...

Management Reporting Analy... Join the team that maintai... purchasing and logistics infor... systems that support order... provide product and contract... mation, track product utilizatio... manage operating budge... inventory systems. Must be... dent in a high-level database... and Excel, Lotus 1-2-3, or... applications. Fax resume to... Systems Placement Services... 555-9998.

MANAGER, ASSET MODELIN...
This worldwide logistics com... expanding it's transportation... work. The successful candida... have a Bachelor's degr... Economics, Finance or B... Mgmt, with a MBA degre... ferred, a solid foundatio... Mathematics, and excellent a... al skills. Knowledge of PC a... tions in Excel, Word, PowerP... Visio essential. Competitive b... and compensation plan. Fax... 555-2298/

Manager, Business Analy... You will direct a team of B... Analysts and oversee timely c... tion of all projects in acc... with departmental policies &... dures. Requires BA/B... Behavioral Health Sciences, B... Administration, MIS, or eq... experience, system develo... analysis and software testing... project management and... building skills, and softwar... opment experience. Hart Co... Services. Call J. Thornton 24... 9583.

MARKETING ASSISTAN...
Supporting 2 Marketing Mgrs... handle a variety of admin. re... bilities, direct mail coord... desktop publishing, and ad... coordination. Require 1-2... admin. exper. and strong co... skills, esp. desktop pub... Office & Windows. Fax: R... 365-555-8844.

Market Research Project Ma...
SuperHouse Designs is... new research division. You w... vide research consulting ser... internal clients and manage... research providers. A BA/BS... or equivalent with 4-6 years'...

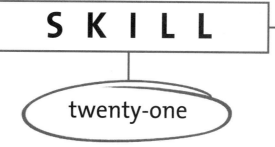

Browsing the World Wide Web

❏ Using the features of the Internet Explorer screen

❏ Jumping to Web pages

❏ Choosing, changing, and customizing Start Pages

❏ Working with Internet search tools

Installing and configuring Internet Explorer and connecting your computer to the Internet are essential steps that you must complete before you can explore the World Wide Web. Once you make your connection, you're ready to start looking around.

In this skill, you'll find the information you need to use Internet Explorer to display Web pages and other Internet resources. After you spend a little time working with the program, you will stop noticing the details of Internet Explorer and devote your attention to the Web pages themselves.

Starting Internet Explorer

In Windows 95, you can start Internet Explorer by double-clicking the Internet icon on your Desktop, or by selecting the Internet Explorer command in the Start menu's Programs submenu. When Internet Explorer starts, it will look for an active connection to the Internet through your Winsock stack. If you use a modem and telephone line to make your connection, and there isn't an active connection, the Winsock will automatically use Dial-Up Networking to dial your ISP and set up a new TCP/IP link.

One of the benefits of a Winsock connection is that you can use it with more than one application program at the same time. If you have other Internet tools, such as a Telnet client or IBM's News Ticker program, you can run them along with Internet Explorer through the same network connection. This can be especially convenient when you're using one program to download a large file and another to read your e-mail or participate in an online conference.

GETTING A NEW VERSION

Changes to Internet Explorer—both minor and major—are being made regularly. When a new version is available, it's posted for free download at http://www.microsoft.com/ie/default.asp. To download the latest version, open the IE Help menu and select About Internet Explorer. The box that opens shows which version of Internet Explorer you're running. Don't download a version with a lower number because it will be older than the one you already have.

The Internet Explorer Screen

Figure 21.1 shows the main Internet Explorer screen. If you have used Windows 95 for more than a couple of hours, you will probably recognize many parts of the Internet Explorer layout.

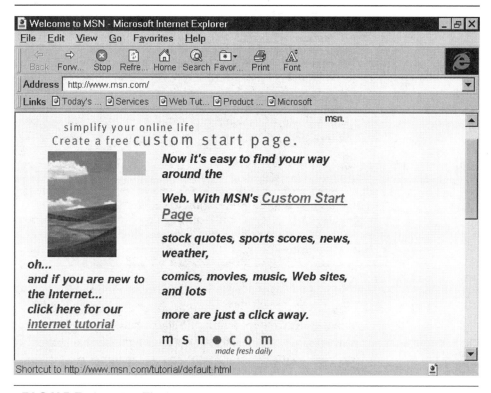

FIGURE 21.1: The Internet Explorer screen uses many standard Windows 95 conventions.

The Internet Explorer screen includes these features and functions:

- **Title Bar** The title bar contains the name of the current Web page or other file on display in the Internet Explorer window, along with the familiar sizing buttons and Close button.

- **Menu Bar** The menu bar contains a set of menus that each of which includes individual commands that you can use to control the way Internet Explorer works. You can find a complete command summary in Skill 25.

Skill 21

- **Toolbar**   The Internet Explorer toolbar has three parts: a set of command buttons that duplicate many of the most frequently used menu commands, an address field, and a group of Quick Links that you can assign to your most frequently used Web sites. Move your cursor over a button or a Quick Link and the icon changes from black and white to color. To enter a command from the toolbar or jump to a Quick Link site click a button. Using the Address field and Quick Links to go to Web pages is explained later in this skill.

- **Activity Indicator**   The Internet Explorer symbol to the right of the toolbar is animated when Internet Explorer sends and receives data from the network.

- **Main Window**   The main portion of the Internet Explorer screen displays the text, images, and other graphic elements of the most recent Web page or other file.

 NOTE   The Web pages and other data you see in Internet Explorer are on your own computer or LAN. Internet Explorer downloads copies of files from distant servers, but it doesn't maintain a live connection to the server after the download is complete.

- **Status Bar**   At the bottom of the Internet Explorer window, the status bar supplies additional information about the current Web site. When you move your cursor to a link, the status bar shows the destination of that link. During a file transfer, the status bar displays a bar graph that shows the progress of the transfer. If a Web page includes multiple pictures, graphic elements, audio clips, or other files, the status bar will display the name of the file that is being transferred. Some Web pages also include a special script that places a scrolling message that moves across the status bar.

- **International Globe**   If you have more than one installed language, a globe is visible in the status bar. To change character sets, click the globe.

Changing the Toolbars' Appearance

You can use the General Options dialog box to hide one or more of the three toolbars (the Standard toolbar, the Address bar, and the Quick Links toolbar). It's also possible to combine two or more of the toolbars on a single line by dragging and dropping. When more than one toolbar occupies the same line, you can view the hidden toolbar by dragging left or right.

To move the toolbar, follow these steps:

1. Place your cursor over the name of the section you want to move. Notice that the cursor changes to a pointing finger.

2. Hold down your right mouse button and drag the portion of the toolbar up or down.

To move a toolbar within the same line, place your cursor over the double bar at the left side of the toolbar you want to move, and drag left or right.

Creating Your Own Quick Links

The Links toolbar contains five Quick Links to specific Web sites. When you install Internet Explorer, all five Quick Links are assigned to Microsoft sites, but you can assign each link to any other URL that you visit frequently.

The default Quick Links are:

- **Today's Links**   Click Today's Links to jump to MSN's Link Central page, which contains links to a selection of new and timely Web sites, including pages devoted to current sports and news events, interesting new Web services and recent movies and television shows.

- **Services**   Click Services to jump to a page with links to a variety of online information sources, including financial services, telephone and address directories, home and garden information, and online reference books.

- **Web Tutorial**   Click Web Tutorial to jump to a series of Web pages that provide an introduction and guide to using and understanding the Internet.

- **Product Updates**   Click Product Updates to jump to a Microsoft page that contains information about the latest versions of Internet Explorer and links to file downloads.

Skill 21

- **Microsoft** Click Microsoft to jump to a page with links to information about Windows and other Microsoft products and free downloads of programs, patches, and add-on software for Microsoft programs.

Follow these steps to change your Quick Links:

1. Jump to the Web page or other site that you want to define as the destination of a Quick Link.

2. Open the View menu and select the Options command.

3. Click the Navigation tab to display the dialog box shown in Figure 21.2.

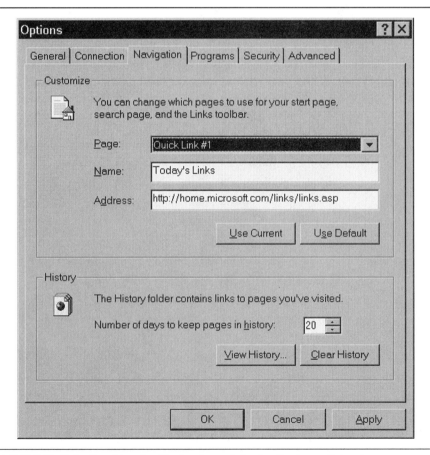

FIGURE 21.2: Use the Navigation tab in the Options dialog box to create new Quick Links.

4. Click the arrowhead at the right side of the Page field to open the drop-down menu.

5. Click the Quick Link number that you want to change.

6. Click the Use Current button to assign a Quick Link to the current Web page.

7. In the Name field, type the name for the site that you want to appear in the Links toolbar. Try to limit the name to about nine characters, so the entire name can fit on the link button.

Moving around the Web

The whole World Wide Web is built around seamless links from one place on the Internet to another. Any Web page can include links to other files that may be physically stored on the same computer or on any other computer connected to the Internet. At its center, Internet Explorer is a tool for retrieving Web pages and following those links.

There are several ways to tell Internet Explorer which Web page or file you want to see next:

- Click a link in the currently visible page.

- Type the URL of a new site in the Address field.

- Choose a URL from a list of favorites.

- Choose a URL from a list of sites you've visited before.

- Use the Back and Forward buttons in the toolbar to return to a site you've recently seen.

- Click one of the Quick Links.

- Double-click a shortcut to a Web site from the Windows Desktop or Start menu.

Typing an Address

When you discover a Web site address in a magazine article, on a TV show, in an online mention in e-mail or a newsgroup, or from some other source, you can visit that site by typing its URL into Internet Explorer. Simply type the URL of the

Skill 21

Web site, or other Internet file or service you want to see into the Address bar, and then press the Enter key.

Address	http://www.unitedmedia.com/comics/alleyoop/index.html	▼

If you don't include the URL type, Internet Explorer assumes that you're trying to reach a Web page or other HTML document, and it will automatically add `http://` to the beginning of the URL. Therefore, you'll reach exactly the same Web site whether you type `www.well.com` or `http://www.well.com`.

To reach some other type of server, such as an FTP archive, a Telnet host, or a gopher server, you must type the full address, including the type designator. For example, the URL for an FTP site might be `ftp://ftp.archive.edu`. If you leave out the type (`ftp://`), Internet Explorer will try to reach the wrong kind of server.

TIP   If you don't know the address for a company's home page, try `http://www`
`.name-of-company.com`. It doesn't always work, but it's the most common URL
for a business home page.

You can also use the Address field to open up a file located on your own computer's hard drive, a floppy disk, a CD-ROM, or another computer connected to yours through a LAN. For example, to see a file called schedule.txt in your `c:\calendar` folder, type `c:\calendar\schedule.txt` in the Address field. You don't need to worry about a URL type identifier when you load a local file into Internet Explorer, but you should remember that DOS and Windows use the backslash (\) to separate folders in a path, instead of the forward slash (/) used by most Internet servers.

Using Hot Links

Except for Web sites like `www.incrediblelink.com` and `www.sausagevendor.com`, the usual hot links on the Internet are places on a Web page that contain jumps to other Web pages, files, and online services. A link may be a word or phrase in a block of text, a graphic image such as a picture of a push-button, or an image map that contains links to several different URLs, depending on the exact location within the image map. Figure 21.3 shows a Web page with several links.

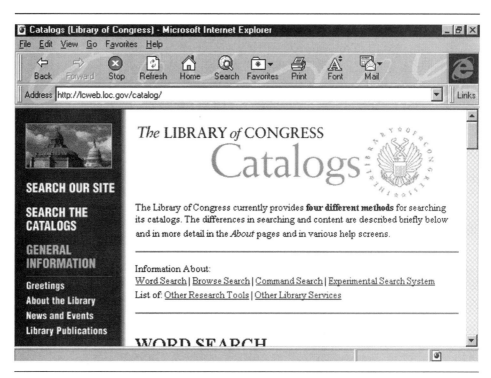

FIGURE 21.3: Click a link to jump to another Web page.

When you move your cursor over a link, the cursor changes to a pointing finger, and the destination of the link appears in the status bar at the bottom of the Internet Explorer window, as shown in Figure 21.4. To move to the page described, click the link.

FIGURE 21.4: When you move the cursor over a link, the destination appears in the status bar.

Skill 21

TIP   Internet Explorer displays text links in a different color from other text. If an entire picture or other image is a link to another Web site, you may see a colored border around the image.

Returning to Sites You've Recently Visited

After you've viewed a Web page, Internet Explorer stores a copy in a temporary folder, so you can return to that page without needing to wait for another download. This is very convenient because Internet Explorer can load and display a file from your hard drive a lot more quickly than it can transfer it from a distant server. However, there are two possible drawbacks to this technique: If the original Web page has changed since the original download, you won't see the changes, and your hard drive will rapidly fill up with Web pages.

Fortunately, there are ways to work around both problems. Select Options from Internet Explorer's View Menu, then click the Advanced tab. The Advanced Options dialog box includes a Temporary Internet Files settings button that opens the dialog box shown in Figure 21.5.

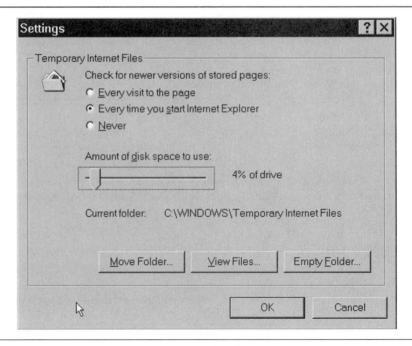

FIGURE 21.5: Use the Settings dialog box to control the way Internet Explorer uses temporary Internet files.

The Settings dialog box includes these options:

- **Check for Newer Versions of Stored Pages**   When the Once per Session option is active, Internet Explorer will retrieve a new (and possibly updated) copy of a Web page the first time you request it during an operating session—even if the page is already in the Temporary folder. When the Never option is active, Internet Explorer always uses the file in the Temporary folder. To check for a new version of a Web page you've already seen, click the Refresh button in the Command toolbar or the View menu.

- **Amount of Disk Space to Use**   Move the slider to the left to reduce the maximum size of the Temporary Internet Files folder, or to the right to increase the maximum size of the folder.

- **Move Folder**   Click the Move Folder button to change the path of the folder that contains your temporary files.

- **View Files**   Click the View Files button to open your Temporary Internet Files folder. To view a file in a new Internet Explorer window, double-click the name of that file.

- **Empty Folder**   Click the Empty Folder button to delete all the files in your Temporary Internet Files folder.

Using the History Folder

Whenever you view a Web site, Internet Explorer adds a shortcut to that site to the History folder. You can use these shortcuts to return to Web sites you've recently visited. There are two ways to display the contents of the History folder:

- Click the down-arrow at the right side of the Address field in the toolbar. Select the URL you want to revisit to jump to that site.

- Open the Go menu and select the Open History Folder command. Select a shortcut to jump to that site.

Moving Forward and Backward

Internet Explorer uses the History list to identify backward and forward links. Use the Back Command in the toolbar or in the Go menu to return to the Web page from which you jumped to the current page. Use the Forward command in the toolbar or the Go menu to repeat the last jump you made from the current site.

Skill 21

TIP   The Back command is particularly useful when you try to follow a series of links, but you discover that you've reached a dead end—either a link to a site that's no longer available or a site that doesn't have any links that you want to follow. You can retrace your steps to return to a page with other links that you want to follow.

Using More Than One Window at a Time

Normally, when you click a link or enter a URL in the Address field, Internet Explorer loads the new page into the same window. But sometimes it's convenient to keep the current page visible while you open a new page in a separate Internet Explorer window. For example, you might want to read the text in one window while you wait for the next one to load, or you might want to keep one eye on a page that automatically updates the World Cup score, while you conduct other business in a second window.

To open another copy of the current Web page in a new window, select the New Window command in the File menu.

To jump to a new Web page and load it into a new window, follow these steps:

1. Move your cursor over the link to the Web site you want to visit.

2. Press your right mouse button to display the right-click menu.

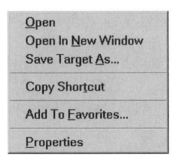

3. Select the Open in New Window command.

The new window works the same as the existing one. Once it's open, you can use the Address field, the Favorites list, the History list, and other navigation tools to move around the Web, while keeping an earlier page visible in the other window.

NOTE   If you have more than one Web browser program installed on your computer, the Open in New Window command will start your default browser, even if it's not Internet Explorer.

Using Start Pages and Home Pages

Every time you start Internet Explorer, the program will automatically load and display the page that you have specified as your Start Page. Almost every other Web browser calls this the home page, and that's probably what you'll see it called online. The icon on the Open Start Page command button in the Internet Explorer toolbar is a little house marked "Home," so it would appear that Microsoft's designers also think of the Start Page that way.

Unfortunately, "home page" also has another meaning: It's a page that an individual or organization uses to provide pointers to other related pages or files. For example, many people have created home pages that contain links to information about their hobbies, favorite entertainers, and other interests. Businesses have home pages with links to separate pages about each of their products or divisions.

Choosing a Start Page

Your Start Page is the first Web site you will see every time you start Internet Explorer, so it's a good idea to choose a page that contains information you can actually use. Replace the Internet Explorer default Start Page with one of these options or another you like:

- Microsoft's Custom MSN Start Page option.

- A home page from another online information provider, such as the GNN Whole Internet Catalog (http:www.gnn.com/wic/index.html) or PC Computing's Web Map (http:www.zdnet.com/pccomp/java/webmap/).

- One of the online search tools described later in this skill, such as Yahoo, Lycos, AltaVista, or search.com.

- Your own home page with links to your favorite sites, using an HTML editor, such as the free Internet Assistant add-ons, Excel, and other application programs to Microsoft Word. You can download Internet Assistant from the Microsoft Office Web site at http://www.microsoft.com/msword/fs_wd.htm.

Skill 21

Changing Your Start Page

To change the Start Page, follow these steps:

1. Jump to the page you want to use as your Start Page.

2. Open the View menu and select the Options command.

3. Click the Navigation tab to display the dialog box shown in Figure 21.6.

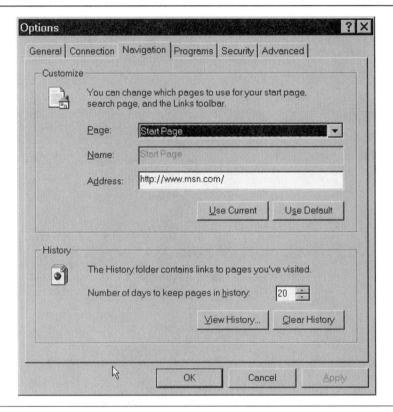

FIGURE 21.6: Use the Navigation tab of the Options dialog box to change your Start Page.

4. Choose the Start Page option in the Page field.

5. Click the Use Current button in the Change Address box to define the current page as your Start Page.

Creating a Custom MSN Start Page

Internet Explorer's default Start Page is http://www.msn.com, as shown in Figure 21.7.

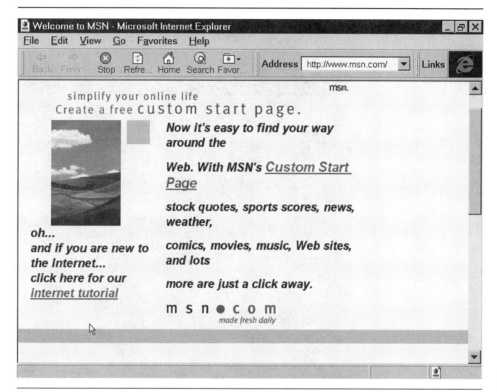

FIGURE 21.7: The default Internet Explorer Start Page is www.msn.com.

Microsoft offers a free service on the default page that can add links to up to a half dozen Web sites. In addition, you can make links to news, weather, sports, ski conditions, a daily cartoon, and other useful or entertaining information.

To customize your Start Page, follow these steps:

1. Start Internet Explorer.

2. If it's not your home page, jump to http://www.msn.com. The MSN home page will appear.

3. Click the Start Page link. The Custom Options page will appear.

4. You can use the Custom Options page to add the features and functions listed in the following table to your version of the MSN Start Page.

5. When you have selected all of the items you want to see in your Start Page, click the Set Up Page button at the bottom of the Custom Options page. Figure 21.8 shows part of a customized Start Page.

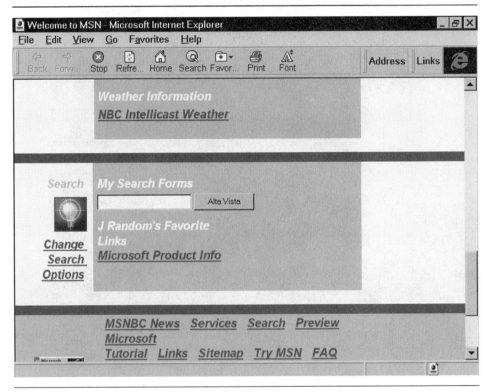

FIGURE 21.8: Customized Start Pages contain links to Web sites chosen by each user.

Feature or Function	Description
Favorite Links	Use the Favorite Links fields to add jumps to up to half a dozen URLs that you expect to visit frequently. For each entry, choose the type of URL (`http`, `ftp`, or whatever) from the drop-down list in the left-hand column. Type the site's address in the middle column, and a brief description in the right column. Your Start Page will use the text of the description in the list of links.
Search Forms	Search Forms are online databases you can use to find Web sites and other Internet resources. It's a good idea to include search fields for one or two of these services in your Start Page. You can find more detailed information about search tools later in this skill.
Stock Quotes	If you want to use the Internet to keep track of your stocks or other investments, type the ticker symbols of the stocks you want to follow in one or more of the Stock Quotes fields. Your Start Page will include links to a page that contains recent prices for these stocks.
Sports Scores	Click the box next to the name of a league to add links to recent scores to your Start Page.
News	Choose one or more categories of news to include links to the latest stories from Reuters or Ziff-Davis.
TV	Click your time zone to add a link that contains a schedule of television programs to your Start Page.
Comic Strips	Click the name of one or more comic strips to include links to recent episodes on your Start Page.
Weather Information	Place a link to a weather map on your Start Page or display the map itself. Or you can choose a local forecast.

Skill 21

Feature or Function	Description
Ski Reports	If you select one or more states, provinces, or countries from the drop-down lists, your Start Page will include links to reports of current ski conditions within that locale. Along with well-known ski resorts in Vermont, Utah, and Colorado, you can include some unlikely places like North Dakota, Kansas, Indiana, and Rhode Island. Apparently, there really are ski resorts in all those places.
Web Picks	Web Picks are links to Web sites that are interesting or unusual, or Web sites whose owners have paid to be listed. The Web Picks change every few days.
MSN Today	Click the MSN Today box to include links to special events on Microsoft's online information service.
Movie Link	Select Movie Link to include a link to a list of movies that are playing in theaters near you.
Music Clip	If you have a sound card and speakers in your PC, you can play a musical selection when you open your Start Page.
Graphics	If you have a high-speed connection to the Internet, choose High Graphics to display your Start Page with complex graphics and animated images. If you're using a modem and dial-up telephone line, Medium or Low graphics are better choices.
Background Color	Choose the color you want as a background for the customized links in your Start Page. As a rule, light background colors are your best choice.
Text Color	Choose a contrasting color for the text on your Start Page. Dark letters on a light background are easiest to read.

Feature or Function	Description
Viewed Link Color	A viewed link is a link to a site that you have recently visited. Choose the color you want your Start Page to use for viewed links.
Unviewed Links Color	An unviewed link is a link to a site that you haven't recently visited. Choose the color you want your Start Page to use for unviewed links.
Welcome	Select the Welcome option to include a message in your Start Page that greets you by name. (This seems like a complete waste of space, but if it amuses you, go ahead and use it).
Personal Info	The Start Page uses the name and address that you type in the Personal Info fields to retrieve your local weather forecasts, movie information, and so forth. If you want Microsoft to send you announcements of new services, fill in your e-mail address and place a check mark in the Add Me to Your Mailing List box.

Tips on Customizing Your Start Page

There's no particular reason to create a list of Favorite Links in your Start Page rather than using the Favorites menu. Since you can open the Favorites menu at any time, even if your Start Page is not visible, it might be faster and easier to choose an item from the menu instead of returning to your Start Page.

If you're really serious about tracking your investments, you might want to try a program that updates and displays stock quotations in a separate window rather than adding a stock quotes link to your Start Page. You can find pointers to about half a dozen stock quote programs through TUCOWS (`www.tucows.com`).

If your computer has a sound card and speakers, you might be tempted to include a short piece of music that will play whenever you open your Start Page. This may seem like a clever idea at first, but you will probably want to turn it off after about the third or fourth time you've heard the same tune. If you're using the program in an office, you probably won't want to broadcast to everybody within earshot every time you start browsing the Word Wide Web (and it's a safe bet that they won't want you to do so).

Using Internet Search Tools

The World Wide Web resembles a huge library where all the books are arranged by size and color. You may stumble across a lot of interesting things by accident, but without a catalog to tell you exactly where to look for a particular item, specific information is extremely difficult to find. In the library, you can search for a book by looking up the title or subject in a catalog or by asking a librarian for help. Internet search tools serve a similar purpose.

When you look for, say, Hebrew dictionaries in a library catalog, you will discover that the Dewey Decimal number is 492.43. Since the librarian places books on the shelves in numerical order, you'll find Hebrew books (492.4) between books about Balto-Slavic languages (491.8) and those about the Arabic language (492.7). Once you know where to look, a dictionary is easy to locate.

On the Internet, URLs serve the same purpose as the library's shelf numbers. And like the library catalog, the Internet's search tools can point you to the item you want to find.

Most Web search tools work in a similar manner: You type the words you want to search for and click a Search button. The search engine looks for those words in a database and displays a list of URLs that match your request, with links to each one. To examine a possible match, click the link. If that's not what you want, click the Back button to return to the list and try another item.

There are about two dozen major general-purpose Internet search tools, and a couple hundred more specialized ones. Each uses a somewhat different set of rules to conduct its search, and each will give you a different list of URLs in response to a request. Some tools search for individual pages, others will take you to entire sites, and still others search through the text of each page rather than limiting their searches to titles or keywords. Some include subjective reviews or ratings of individual sites, while others list everything they find.

Therefore, the same search through several different services can produce radically different results. For example, a search for the keywords **"Joseph Conrad"** produced 244 hits with Yahoo, 4351 with Lycos, and about 30,000 with AltaVista. A search for "**Andrew Jackson**" produced 55 hits using Lycos, 231 with Open Text, and about 2,000 matches with AltaVista.

If you're looking for a popular Web site, you can probably find it with almost any search engine. But if you want everything related to a specific subject, perform the same search through several different services.

WARNING   The links that a search tool identifies are not always useful, especially when you enter more than one keyword, because some search engines include partial matches that include just one word in the search phrase. For example, a search for "**Andrew Jackson**" using the Magellan search engine produced 85 matching links. However, only one of the first 10 had anything to do with the seventh president; the other nine were pointers to a Web page about the Jackson State University Computer Science Department, Steve Jackson Games, and singers named Alan Jackson, Michael Jackson, and Joe Jackson.

Jumping to a Search Tool

Internet Explorer makes it easy to jump to the search tool of your choice, or to a Web page that contains links to several different search tools. When you select the Search the Internet command in the Go menu, or click the Search button in the toolbar, the program opens the URL specified as your Search Page in the Start and Search Pages Options dialog box.

The default Internet Explorer Search Page is located at Microsoft's msn.com Web site. As Figure 21.9 shows, this page contains links to nearly a dozen Internet-wide search engines, and another search engine that searches only Microsoft Web pages.

The default page is about as good a starting point as any, although it doesn't include one of the largest and best of the current batch of search tools, Digital's AltaVista (www.altavista.digital.com), which conducts full-text searches in more than 21 million pages.

TIP   One excellent alternative to the MSN page is c|net's search.com (http://www.search.com), which contains links to more than 250 separate search engines.

Skill 21

Changing Your Search Page

To change your designated Search Page, follow these steps:

1.   Jump to the page you want to use as your Search Page.

2.   Open the View menu and select the Options command.

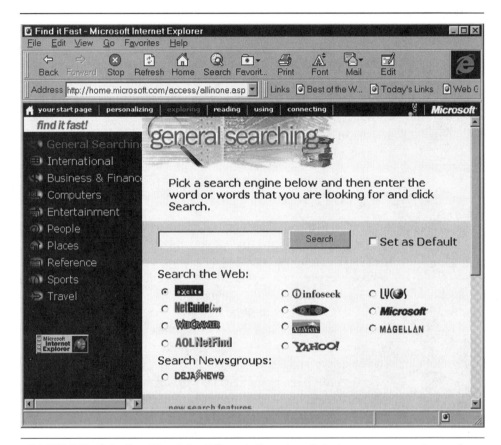

FIGURE 21.9: The default Search Page has links to many separate services.

3. Click the Navigation tab.

4. Open the drop-down menu shown in Figure 21.10.

5. Click Search Page.

6. Click the Use Current button.

FIGURE 21.10: Select Search Page from the drop-down list.

Jumping to Favorite Pages

Favorite pages are Web sites that you have included in your own list of URLs that you want to visit again. Netscape and most other Web browsers call these lists "bookmarks." To return to a page, open the Favorites menu and select the listing for the page you want to see.

You can also create shortcuts to Web sites on your Windows Desktop or Start menu. When you click a shortcut, Internet Explorer opens and automatically loads the page you requested. You can find information about working with favorite pages and shortcuts in Skill 23.

After you learn how to use the navigation tools in this skill, you should be able to find just about anything on the Internet. But there's more to the World Wide Web than just jumping between URLs. In the next skill, you will find out how to use more complex Web pages with interactive elements, and how to send information back to a Web server.

Are You Experienced?

Now you can...

- ☑ configure Internet Explorer
- ☑ jump to Web pages
- ☑ choose and customize your Start Page
- ☑ work with Internet search tools

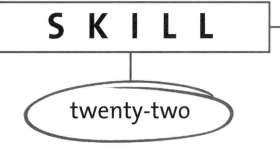

S K I L L

twenty-two

Working with Interactive Web Pages

- ❏ Filling in text fields

- ❏ Choosing check boxes

- ❏ Selecting from radio button options

- ❏ Choosing from drop-down menus and scroll bar lists

- ❏ Using Submit and Reset buttons

The simplest Web pages contain text, maybe a picture or two, and links to other Internet sites. But many Web designers have built additional features into their designs that allow you, as a visitor to their site, to send information back to the Web server. Some Web sites use these features to obtain information from visitors, such as their names and e-mail addresses; others provide remote access to other programs that run on the same computer as the server, or on other computers connected to the server through a LAN. As a category, these interactive Web tools are called *forms*.

Forms make it possible to do a lot more than just reading text, looking at pictures, and jumping to other pages through hot links. Among other things, you can search for other Internet files and services; obtain airline schedules and make flight reservations; order books, flowers, and computer equipment from online retailers; and play games with a computer or with other human players. One of the most common uses of fill-in-the-blank forms in Web pages is a space where you can send the server your credit card number or password, so the people who run the Web site can charge you for the information or services they supply.

In Internet Explorer, most forms on Web pages look like the options and commands you see in Windows dialog boxes. In this skill, you will learn how to work with the most common types of forms that appear in Web pages.

Filling In Text Fields

A text field is a space where a user can type a string of characters that the browser will send back to the server. You'll see many Web pages that instruct you to enter your name or password, or the keywords for a database search, into a short text field to obtain access to additional information. Other pages have larger text fields where you can type a brief message to the people who maintain the Web site.

For example, Figure 22.1 shows part of the Sybex Web site. You can use this Web page to send in suggestions regarding Sybex's products.

World Wide Web search tools are another place where Web designers use text fields. In the search page, shown in Figure 22.2, each of the text fields is a link to a different destination. When you type a keyword into one of the text fields and click a Search button. Internet Explorer sends your request to the specific search engine you requested; the destination doesn't have to be on the same server that sent you the Web page that contains the form.

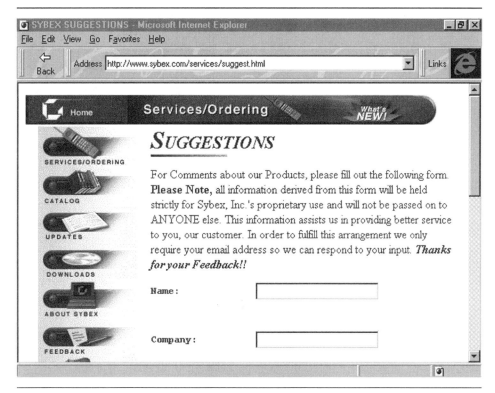

FIGURE 22.1: To send data back to a Web server, type it into a text-entry field.

Choosing Check Boxes

Check boxes are multiple-choice options; you can select as many as you want. When you click a check box, Internet Explorer will place a check mark in the box. Click again to remove the check mark.

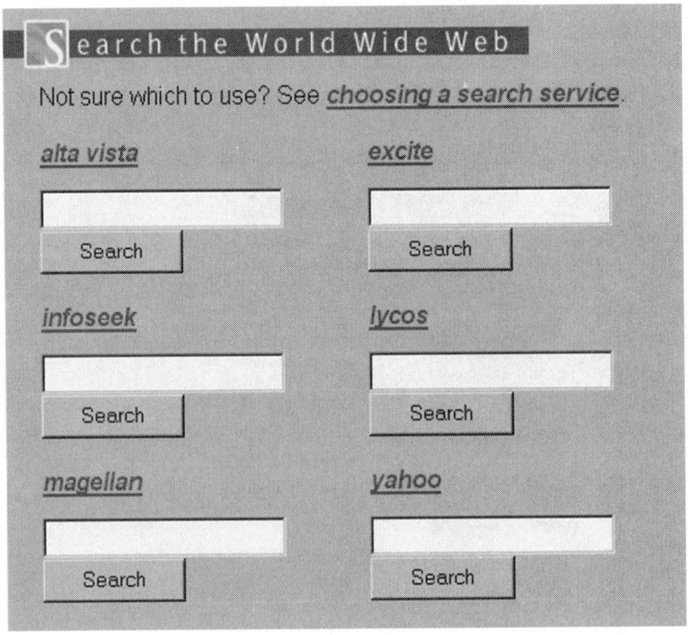

FIGURE 22.2: Each search text field sends a search request to a different destination.

Using Radio Buttons

Radio buttons are like the buttons on your car radio: You can select only one option at a time. In any group of radio buttons, there's always one, and only one, active option. When you click a radio button, you automatically turn off the previously selected option.

Unlike check boxes, which are square, Internet Explorer shows radio buttons as circles. The currently active button has a dot inside the circle.

For example, Figure 22.3 is part of MSN's Custom Options configuration page. Because you can select only one item from each group of options, the radio buttons limit your choice to just one selection in each group.

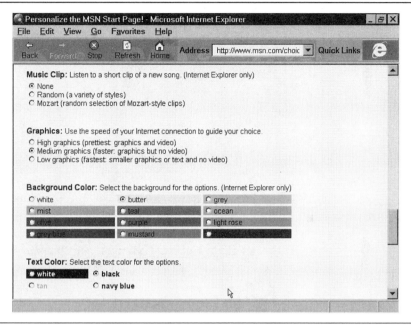

FIGURE 22.3: Only one radio button in a group of buttons can be active.

Recognizing Drop-Down Menus and Scroll Bar Lists

Sometimes a Web page designer may want to offer a long list of options without taking up the space on the page that a radio button for each option would fill. There are two list forms that squeeze many choices into a tight space: drop-down menus and scrollbar lists.

A drop-down list displays the currently selected option in a box, like the example in Figure 22.4, which is taken from an online airline reservation service. When you click the arrow button next to the box, a menu of other options appears. To change the active option, click the one you want.

Scroll bar lists display only a few options on the Web page but allow you to move up or down the list to see additional choices. To make a selection, highlight the item you want; if it's not visible, click the up-arrow and down-arrow buttons, or drag the scroll bar up or down.

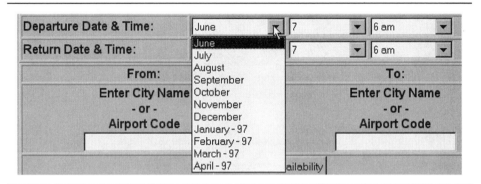

FIGURE 22.4: To open a drop-down menu, click the button at the right of the menu field.

The scroll bar menu in Figure 22.5 is a list of airlines from the same reservation service. Only three airlines are visible, but the entire list contains more than 200 choices.

FIGURE 22.5: Use the arrow buttons or the scroll bar to move up and down a scroll bar list.

Clicking Submit and Reset Buttons

When you click an option or choose an item in a menu, you're working with a copy of the current Web page downloaded from a server to your computer. In other words, the server doesn't receive any of your input until you instruct your computer to transmit the data. Therefore, every Web page that uses interactive forms includes at least one Submit button (it doesn't always say "Submit" on the button, but that's the default name). Until you click that button, the information in the forms doesn't go anywhere. Figure 22.6 shows the Submit buttons in several interactive Web pages.

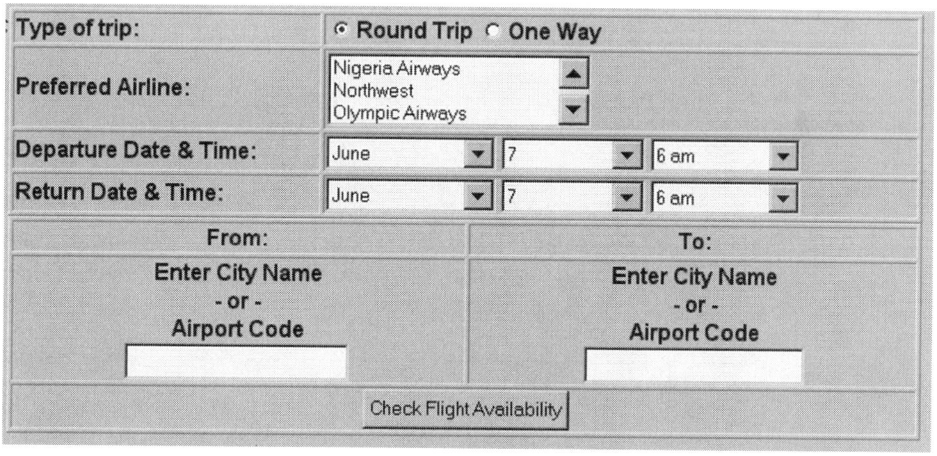

Type of trip:	⊙ Round Trip ○ One Way						
Preferred Airline:	Nigeria Airways ▲ Northwest Olympic Airways ▼						
Departure Date & Time:	June ▼	7 ▼	6 am ▼
Return Date & Time:	June ▼	7 ▼	6 am ▼

From:	To:
Enter City Name - or - Airport Code	Enter City Name - or - Airport Code

Check Flight Availability

FIGURE 22.6: Click the Submit button to send your filled-in form back to the server.

Some Web pages have more than one Submit button, especially if they contain forms that send information to different servers. That's how a Web site like search.com is able to let users send requests to several search engines from the same page. Assuming the page is reasonably well organized, it should be obvious which button is associated with a particular set of forms.

Until you click the Submit button, you can edit text fields and mess around with other types of form fields to your heart's content. But sometimes, especially in a long and complicated questionnaire, you might want to cancel everything and start over again. That's what the Reset button is for. Most considerate Web page designers include a Reset button (which, like the Submit button, may have a label other than "Reset") in all their forms. When you click a Reset button, Internet Explorer deletes everything in the form that contains the button, so you've got a clean slate to start over again. It does not send anything back to the server.

You might also want to use the Reset button when you use the Back command to return to a Web page after you have sent a request for information to the server. For example, if your first search for information from a database doesn't give you the information you want, you can return to the search page to try another set of keywords.

Playing Interactive Games

Many Web site developers have created interactive games that you can play through the Internet. Most of these games don't use forms, but they're "interactive" because the server responds to your actions by uploading a new screen when you "move" by clicking the game board, or entering characters into a blank field.

For example, the collection of interactive Web games at Boston University (www.bu.edu/games/games.html) includes the Minesweeper game shown in Figure 22.7. When you click a square, the server shows you if there's an explosive mine under it. If you guess wrong, the mine blows up, and you lose the game.

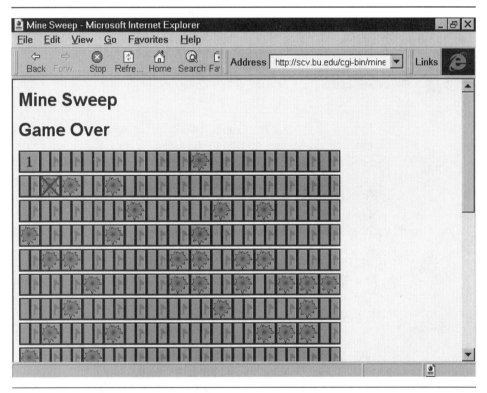

FIGURE 22.7: The World Wide Web version of Minesweeper

There's not much difference between this Minesweeper game and the version on the Windows 95 CD-ROM, except that the online Minesweeper sends your moves hundreds or thousands of miles (unless you're playing from Boston where the game is based), and it takes longer to respond. Even so, it's a good demonstration of an interactive game. Over time, more complicated and sophisticated games and other interactive services are certain to appear on Web sites. As ActiveX extensions and Java programs become more common, Web site developers will create animated action games and interactive application programs that allow you to run programs across the Web as if they were located on a local computer.

Moving between Web sites and returning data to a server through forms and other interactive pages, using the techniques described in this and the previous skill, are the two most basic functions you need to understand in order to navigate the World Wide Web with Internet Explorer. In the next skill, you can learn how to create a list of your favorite Web sites and set up shortcuts from the Windows Desktop directly to Web pages.

Are You Experienced?

Now you can...

- ☑ fill in text fields
- ☑ choose check boxes and radio buttons
- ☑ recognize drop-down menus and scroll bar lists
- ☑ use Submit and Reset buttons

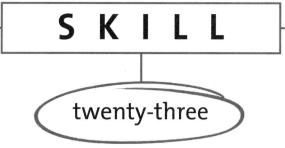
Returning to Favorite Web Pages

❑ Adding Web pages to the Favorites list

❑ Managing your Favorites list

❑ Creating your own hot list page

❑ Creating shortcuts to Web pages

As you wander around the World Wide Web and Internet, you'll stumble onto sites that you may want to revisit—and yet you have no idea how you got to the site in the first place. You could write down the URL of each site on a notepad, and then retype it into Internet Explorer's address field when you want to return, but that approach is both tedious and seriously prone to error. There's a much easier way—you can use shortcuts to interesting Web sites.

In fact, there are two easier ways. Create a list of links to your favorite pages that you can open from within Internet Explorer, or place shortcuts to Web sites on your Desktop or Start menu, just like shortcuts to programs and files located on your own hard drive. In this skill, we'll talk about using both of these techniques.

Working with the Favorites List

When you come across an interesting Web page, you can save a link to that page by adding it to your list of favorites. Later, you can return to that page by opening the list and clicking the name of the page.

For example, the Web page at http://www.irs.ustreas.gov/prod contains a daily installment of *The Digital Daily*, as shown in Figure 23.1. The Internal Revenue Service put together this snazzy site to give the taxpayers access to tax forms, instructions, and publications. You can even file your taxes online. The site is updated daily, so it's a good candidate for your Favorites list.

 NOTE   In Netscape and other Web browsers, this list of sites that you want to revisit is called a *bookmark list*. A Web page that suggests that you "bookmark this site" is encouraging you to add it to your Favorites list.

Adding Items to the Favorites List

To add the current Web page to your Favorites list, follow these steps:

1. Open the Favorites menu.

2. Select the Add to Favorites command.

FIGURE 23.1: *The Digital Daily* Web site contains new information every day.

If you prefer, you can use the menu that appears when you click with your right mouse button. When you use the right-click menu to add an item to your Favorites list, the exact location determines whether you'll add the current page or a link to the Favorites list:

- If your cursor is over a link when you right-click, you'll add the destination of that link to your list, rather than the current page.

- If you right-click a picture or other graphic, you'll add that image to the list without the rest of the current Web page.

- If the cursor is over any other part of a page, you'll add the current page to your list.

Opening the List

Now that you have added some Web sites to your Favorites list, how do you return to those sites? You can open the list from the menu bar or the toolbar. Either way, you'll see a menu like the one in Figure 23.2. To return to one of the sites on your list, click the name of that site.

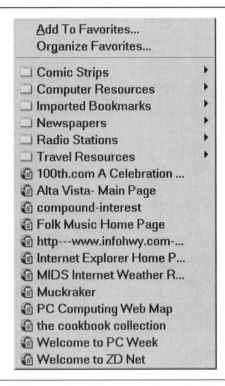

FIGURE 23.2: Select an item from your Favorites list to go to that site.

If your list has too many entries, the bottom of the list might run off the screen. When that happens, you can display the whole list by clicking on the Organize Favorites command at the top of the menu. Rather than keeping everything in one list, you should break it into smaller groups, organized by category. The next section explains how to do that.

Organizing Items in Your Favorites List

Internet Explorer stores shortcuts to each item on your list of favorite Web sites in a Windows 95 folder called Favorites. Like other Windows 95 folders, the Favorites folder can contain an unlimited number of items, which you can display in the Organize Favorites dialog box as either a list of titles or a detailed list.

 TIP   Internet Explorer can open and display local files (including Windows 95 folders) just as easily as it downloads files from the Internet. In fact, all the pages you see in Internet Explorer are really copies that you've downloaded to your computer. Therefore, the program treats the Favorites folder (which is a subfolder located within the top-level Windows folder) just like any other Web page. You can open this folder—or any other folder on your hard drive or LAN—by typing the path in the Internet Explorer address field.

After you use the Organize Favorites command to display the contents of this folder, you can do most of the same things that you can do from any other Windows 95 folder:

- Open files (which may be shortcuts to Web pages)
- Change the way the program displays the files in the folder
- Add and delete files and subfolders
- Import files or shortcuts to files
- Move files to subfolders
- Change the names of files
- Change the icon assigned to a file

Changing the Appearance of the List

The Organize Favorites dialog box, shown in Figure 23.3, offers two view options: List and Details. To change views, use the buttons at the top of the dialog box.

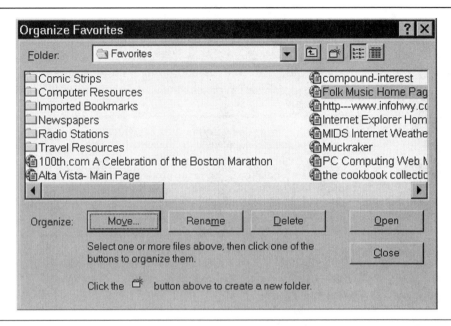

FIGURE 23.3: The Favorites list can appear as either a list or a set of icons.

 TIP   If you use List view or if you just like messing around with your screen layout, you can assign a distinctive icon to each item on the list. See the section "Changing a Web Shortcut Icon" later in this skill for more information.

Adding Other Items to Your Favorites List

The Favorites list is not limited to Web sites. It can also include shortcuts to any other program, data file, or folder on your own computer or on a computer connected to yours through a LAN. This feature can make Internet Explorer even more flexible.

Here are some of the things you might want to add to your Favorites list:

- Copies of HTML documents or text files stored on your hard drive.

- A shortcut to the Notepad program. When you want to extract text from a Web page, you can select and copy the text, open Notepad, paste the selected text, and save it as a text file.

- A shortcut to the Windows Desktop folder (`c:\windows\desktop`). If you keep shortcuts to frequently used files and programs on your Desktop, you can use the Favorites list to open them from within Internet Explorer. If you do create a shortcut to your Desktop, you should also use the Shortcut tab in the Properties dialog box to change the shortcut icon to the one shown here.

- A shortcut to your e-mail program or some other Internet client program.

Creating New Subfolders

Once your list of favorite Web pages reaches about a dozen entries, you should think about moving some of them into subfolders. If there are a few Web sites that you expect to revisit more often than others, you can leave shortcuts to those pages in the main Favorites list (or you could create Quick Links to those sites), and move less frequently used items to subfolders. You can organize your short- cuts to suit yourself. For example, sort methods include:

- By topic

- In alphabetical groups (A through D, E through H, and so forth)

- In separate folders for particular types of Web sites, such as FTP archives or news summaries

The Favorites list places folders at the top, with an arrow at the right side of the list window. When you move your cursor over the name of a folder, the submenu appears, as shown in Figure 23.4.

To create a new folder, follow these steps:

1. Open the Favorites list from the Internet Explorer menu bar.

2. Click the Organize Favorites command.

3. When the Organize Favorites dialog box appears, click the Create New Folder button.

4. A new folder will appear at the bottom of the list, as shown in Figure 23.5.

5. Type the name you want to assign to this folder, and press the Enter key.

Skill 23

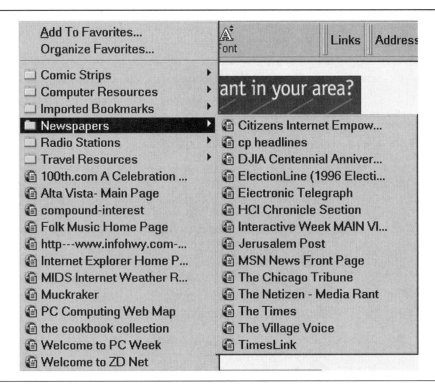

FIGURE 23.4: A submenu appears when you move your cursor over a folder.

The next time you open the Favorites list, the name of the new folder will move to the top of the list, in alphabetical order relative to other folder names. To move an item from the main list to a subfolder, follow these steps:

1. Select the name of the Web page or folder you want to move.

2. Click the Move button.

3. When the Browse for Folder dialog box appears, select the destination folder and click the OK button.

When your list gets even larger and more complicated, you might consider placing subsubfolders within subfolders. For example, create a subfolder called Travel, with separate subsubfolders called Airlines, Trains, and Hotels. Or you may want separate subsubfolders for each letter within an alphabetical list.

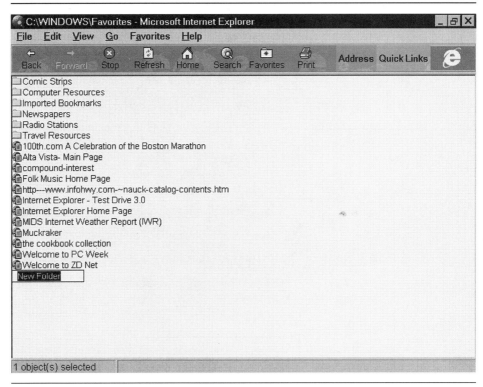

FIGURE 23.5: The new folder appears at the bottom of the list of Favorite pages.

Cleaning Out the List

So there you are, surfing your way around the World Wide Web, finding all kinds of amusing and interesting Web sites. "Add to Favorites." Click. "Add to Favorites." Click. Click. Click.

The next time you open your list of Favorites, it has dozens of items, most of whose names you don't recognize. And when you select a site, you cannot imagine why you thought it was worth saving in the first place. What made you think you'd ever want to return to the History of Corn Flakes home page?

It's time to do some serious weeding. If you're not going to use a link, there's no reason to keep it on your list. On the other hand, it's entirely reasonable to maintain a "not-so-hot list" separate from the main folder. You might want to keep this list in a subfolder or in a separate folder with a shortcut from the Favorites list. This secondary list will be just a couple of mouse-clicks away, but its contents will be out of the way when you're looking for your daily news updates.

To clean up your list, follow these steps:

1. Open your Favorites folder from the Favorites menu or toolbar.

2. Look through the list for links to Web pages that you don't recognize.

3. Double-click the entry or icon for the first doubtful item to take one more look at this Web page.

4. Decide if you think this page is important enough to save on your list of Favorites. Then click the Back button to return to the list.

5. To remove an item from your Favorites list, use the Organize Favorites command to open the Organize Favorites dialog box.

6. Select the item you want to remove and click the Delete button.

7. If you want to keep this item on your list, consider changing the name to something that identifies it more clearly. Click the Rename button to change the description of the currently selected item.

TIP   As a rule of thumb, your top-level Favorites list should have no more than 16 to 18 items in it—maybe a few more if you have a larger screen. When the list gets bigger than that, it's time to start moving things to submenus.

Importing a Netscape Bookmark List

In Netscape Navigator, bookmarks serve the same purpose as favorites in Internet Explorer. If you're using Netscape Navigator as well as Internet Explorer, or if you've decided to replace Navigator with the Microsoft program, there's an easy way to transfer your Netscape bookmarks to Internet Explorer. Microsoft has a free utility that will find your Netscape bookmark file and copy its contents to your Internet Explorer Favorites folder.

To find this conversion program, use Internet Explorer to jump to `http://www.microsoft.com/ie/download/winbm2fv.exe`. After the program downloads, it will start automatically. When conversion is complete, your Favorites list will include your Netscape bookmarks, along with the items that were already in your Favorites folder.

Making Your Own Hot List

The Favorites list is easy to use, but it doesn't tell you much about the Web sites that are listed. If you want to give yourself more information about each link, you might want to create a local Web page with a one- or two-sentence description of your favorite sites. If you place a link to your hot list page in the top level of your Favorites list, you can jump to the hot list with two mouse-clicks.

Creating a Hot List Page

The easiest way to create a quick-and-dirty HTML page (and quick and dirty is all you'll need for your own hot list because you're the only person who will see it) is to use one of the freeware or shareware HTML editor programs that you can download through the Web. You can find a guide to currently available HTML editors at TUCOWS (The Ultimate Collection of Winsock Software) at `http://www.tucows.com` and mirror sites around the world. Look for collections of HTML editors for Windows 3.1 and Windows 95 in the Utilities sections.

When you save your HTML hot list, name the file `hotlist.htm`. Figure 23.6 shows a sample hot list set up as a Web page. Each item on the list includes a link to another site and a description of the information or service that's offered at that site. To jump to a site, click the link, just as you would on any other Web page.

Adding the Hot Link Page to Your Favorites List

When the page is ready to use, follow these steps to add it to your Favorites list:

1. Open the folder that contains the `hotlist.htm` HTML document.

2. Double-click the `hotlist.htm` icon. Internet Explorer will open and load `hotlist.htm`.

3. Open the Favorites menu and select the Add to Favorites command.

4. When the Add to Favorites dialog box appears, change the name to **A Better Hot List**.

The next time you open your Favorites list, you should see a link to this page at or near the top of the alphabetical list of Web sites, but after all the folders. Click the link to open the page.

Skill 23

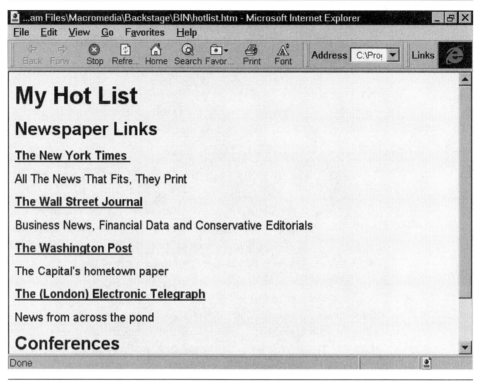

FIGURE 23.6: Use a local HTML document as a hot list containing more information than the Favorites folder.

Creating and Using Web Shortcuts

Internet Explorer extends Windows 95's file-management features to files that it downloads through the Internet. Therefore, you can set up shortcuts to Web pages in exactly the same way that you use shortcuts to programs, documents, and data files located on your own hard drive. In fact, the Favorites list and the History list in Internet Explorer are really just Windows 95 folders full of shortcuts to Web sites.

Like other shortcuts, a Web shortcut may be located on your Desktop, in any folder, or on your Start menu. When you click a shortcut to a Web site, three things happen:

- Internet Explorer starts.

- Dial-Up Networking connects your computer to the Internet.

- Internet Explorer downloads a copy of the Web page specified in the shortcut.

The benefit of using a shortcut is obvious: You can go directly to a Web page with just a couple of mouse-clicks.

You can create a shortcut to the current Web page, to a graphic file embedded in the current Web page, or to a link on the current page.

Creating a Shortcut to the Current Web Page

To create a shortcut to the current Web page, load the target page in Internet Explorer. Either select the Create Shortcut command on the File menu or move your cursor to a place on the page that is not a link or an image, and select the Create Shortcut command from the right-click menu.

When you create a shortcut, Internet Explorer places the shortcut icon on your Windows Desktop, as shown in Figure 23.7. You can drag-and-drop the icon from the Desktop to any folder or to a diskette, network drive, or other destination, just as with any other shortcut.

Changing a Web Shortcut Icon

Internet Explorer uses the same icon for all Web shortcuts, but it's easy to change the icon to something that's related to the contents of the target Web site.

TIP   You can download more icons than any rational person could ever want from the file archives at http://www.sct.gu.edu.au/~anthony/icons/ or http://www.download.com/PC/Result/TitleList/1,2,0-a-0-0-b-1,00.html.

Here's how to change icons:

1. Right-click the item whose icon you want to change.

2. Select Properties from the right-click menu.

3. Click the Internet Shortcut tab.

4. Click the Change Icon button at the bottom of the dialog box.

5. When the Change Icon dialog box appears, shown in Figure 23.8, choose an alternative from the Current Icon field, or click the Browse button to find an icon in another file or folder.

Skill 23

FIGURE 23.7: Internet Explorer places new shortcuts on the Windows Desktop.

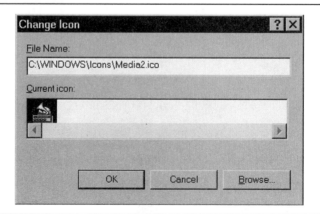

FIGURE 23.8: Use the Change Icon dialog box to assign a new icon to an item in your Favorites list.

6. Click the specific icon you want from the Current Icon field in the Change Icon dialog box. If necessary, use the slider bar at the bottom of the icon display to see additional choices.

7. To use the currently selected icon, click the OK button.

8. In the Properties dialog box, click the OK button.

Creating a Web Shortcuts Folder

If you have more than three or four Web shortcuts on your Desktop, you might want to place them in a separate Web Shortcuts folder, with a shortcut to the folder on the Desktop. Follow these steps to create a new folder:

1. Move your cursor to a blank spot on your Desktop.

2. Click the right mouse button and select the New ➤ Folder command. A folder icon like the one shown in Figure 23.9 will appear.

FIGURE 23.9: Windows assigns an icon like this one to new folders.

3. Type **Web Shortcuts** as the new name for this folder.

4. Drag the icons for each of the Web shortcuts you want to place in this folder from the Desktop to the folder icon.

Unfortunately, Windows won't let you change a folder icon to something more interesting, so you're stuck with the boring old file folder.

Adding a Web Shortcut to the Start Menu

As you know, you can use the Windows Start menu to open programs, folders, and files. If you don't want to see a bunch of shortcuts on your Desktop every time you turn on the computer, the Start menu is another convenient place to hide them.

Start menu commands may be on the main menu that appears when you click the Start button or on submenus that open when you select a folder on the main menu. In the example here, I've added shortcuts to the main Start menu for the Folk Music Home Page and The Well, along with a folder of shortcuts to Internet client programs.

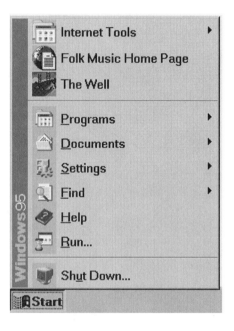

 NOTE   The Well is an online conferencing service based near San Francisco. I changed the icon that connects me to The Well to a picture of the Golden Gate Bridge because The Well is based in the San Francisco area.

To add a Web shortcut (or other command) to the top-level Start menu, drag the icon for that command to the Start button.

Adding a Web Shortcut to a Start Submenu

To create a new submenu or to add a command to an existing submenu, follow these steps:

1. Open the Start menu and select Settings ➢ Taskbar.

2. Click the Start Menu Programs tab to display the dialog box shown in Figure 23.10.

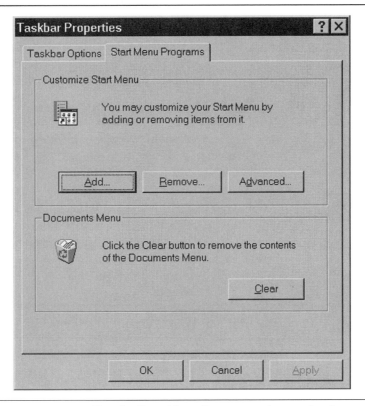

FIGURE 23.10: Use the Start Menu Programs tab to make changes to your Start menu.

3. Click the Add button to add new shortcuts to a menu or the Advanced button to move existing shortcuts to a different place in the Start menu structure.

Opening Shortcuts from the Keyboard

There's still another way to use a shortcut to start Internet Explorer and jump to a Web site. You can define a set of keystrokes as a keyboard shortcut. Keyboard shortcuts are especially convenient when you're using a word processor, spreadsheet, or other application, because you don't need to take your hands away from the keyboard.

Keyboard shortcuts are combinations of the Ctrl key, the Alt key, and almost any other key. When you press all three keys at the same time, Windows will automatically start Internet Explorer and open the Web page assigned to that key combination.

To create a keyboard shortcut, follow these steps:

1. Right-click the Web shortcut icon for which you want to create a keyboard shortcut.

2. Select Properties from the right-click menu.

3. When the Properties window opens, click the Internet Shortcut tab to display the dialog box shown in Figure 23.11.

4. Move your cursor to the Shortcut Key field.

5. Hold down the Ctrl or Alt key and the letter or other key you want to assign to this shortcut. Although you don't press both Ctrl and Alt, the keyboard shortcut will require both of those keys. If you plan to use this shortcut with Microsoft Word, don't use Ctrl+ Alt+ *a number key,* because those combinations are already assigned in Word.

6. While you have the Internet Shortcut dialog box open, make sure the Run field is set to Normal Window rather than Maximized. When you use the keyboard shortcut from a maximized application program, Internet Explorer will open in a less-than-full-screen window, so you'll be able to switch back to the application more easily when you're finished with the Web browser.

7. Click the OK button.

Sending a Shortcut to Another User

Unlike shortcuts to programs and data files located on your own system, the target addresses of Web shortcuts are universal; you can point to a URL from anywhere on the Internet. Therefore, you can embed a Web shortcut into a document or copy it to a floppy disk and send it to another user. For example, you might want to send a daily or weekly "best of the Web" bulletin to friends and customers, with shortcuts to new or otherwise important Web sites that you want them to see. The recipients can jump to the sites you describe by clicking the shortcuts within the bulletin. If you and the person receiving your messages are both using an e-mail client that can handle Rich Text Format (RTF), you can include your shortcuts in a message.

FIGURE 23.11: Use the Internet Shortcut tab to assign a keyboard shortcut.

To attach a shortcut to an existing document, follow this procedure:

1. Open the document in a word processor, such as WordPad or Word for Windows.

2. Drag and drop the shortcut icon into the open application window.

3. Use the formatting tools in the application program to control the placement of the icon in the document.

In general, you can treat a Web shortcut just like any other embedded object in a Windows 95 application program. If you haven't worked with embedded objects before, consult the manual and online help for your application.

Changing the Default Browser: A Warning

If Internet Explorer is your only Web browser, you can skip this section. But if you have both Internet Explorer and Netscape Navigator or some other browser loaded on your computer, only one program at a time can be your default browser.

When you open a browser that is not your current default, it will display a message like the one in Figure 23.12, asking if you want to change the default. As you read the rest of this section, you'll understand why you should always make the current browser the default.

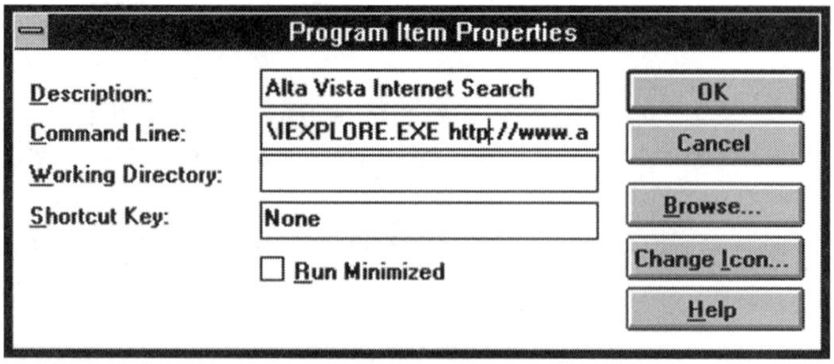

FIGURE 23.12: When you start a browser that is not your default browser, you'll be asked if you want to change the default.

The default browser is the program that Windows associates with HTM and HTML files. In other words, the default program is the one that starts when you use a shortcut to a Web page. Just because you used Internet Explorer to create a shortcut doesn't mean Internet Explorer will start when you select that shortcut. To make things even more confusing, Windows uses the default browser to open Web sites in the Internet Explorer Favorites and History folders.

If the current browser is not the default when you start it, things can get extremely messy. If Internet Explorer is not the default, it will open the default browser when you try to jump to a new Web site. If you open the Favorites folder, you'll see an icon for the current default browser next to each item. And in general, things won't always work the way you expect them to work.

The only way to avoid this confusion is to answer "Yes" whenever a browser asks if you want to make that program the default. Just because that browser is not your favorite, you should still make it the default, at least for the moment. This is really not a big deal because it's so easy to change defaults. Using a non-default browser is just not worth the trouble.

In the next skill, you will find information about using Internet Explorer to transfer programs, documents, pictures, sound recordings, and other data files across the Internet.

Are You Experienced?

Now you can...

- ☑ **build a list of favorite Web pages**
- ☑ **manage your Favorites list**
- ☑ **create a hot list page**
- ☑ **create shortcuts to Web pages**

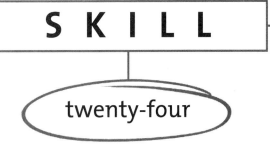

S K I L L

twenty-four

24

Downloading Internet Files

- ❏ Changing and adding MIME file associations

- ❏ Saving Web pages to view offline

- ❏ Downloading files from Web pages

- ❏ Getting files from FTP archives

- ❏ Downloading files from gopher servers

There's more to using Internet Explorer than just visiting Web pages. You can also use the program to transfer programs, documents, and data files from Web sites and other servers to your own computer. Some of these files are accessible through links from Web pages, but many more are available from file servers all over the world. In this skill, you can learn how to find files and download them through Internet Explorer.

When you jump to a new Web page, Internet Explorer downloads a copy of a text file encoded in Hypertext Markup Language (HTML). As the Web page arrives at your computer, Internet Explorer uses the HTML codes to figure out how to display the page on your monitor. If the page incorporates pictures or other graphic elements, Internet Explorer downloads them as separate files and places them in the location specified in the HTML document. If the page includes sounds, video clips, or other special files, Internet Explorer plays or displays them along with the text and graphics.

But Web pages are just one type of file found on computers connected to the Internet. When you download a file that isn't part of a Web page, Internet Explorer can either store that file on your hard drive or immediately open the file in another application program. For example, if you download a document in Microsoft Word format, you can read it in Word as soon as the download is complete or store it to review later. When you download an executable program file, Internet Explorer offers you the choice of running the program immediately or storing it.

Associating MIME Types with Application Programs

Internet Explorer uses the same list of registered file types (in Windows 95) or file associations (in Windows 3.1) that Windows uses to handle local files. It combines the MIME (Multipurpose Internet Mail Extensions) method used by most Web browsers with the file-handling system that Windows uses for local files.

As you know, when you open a file, Windows uses the file name extension to identify the program that can open the contents of that file. For example, if you open a .txt file, Windows will run a text editor such as Write or WordPad; if you open an .xls file, it will load that file into Microsoft Excel.

The MIME protocol extends that same approach to the Internet. When you download a file, the server identifies the MIME type to Internet Explorer. As with file name extensions for local files, each MIME type has an application program associated with it. If you download a file that does not have a MIME type attached to it, Internet Explorer will use the application associated with the file's extension.

When you download a program or a data file from the Internet, Internet Explorer offers you several choices:

- You can save the file on your hard drive or a floppy disk.

- You can load the contents of the file into the application program associated with its MIME type or file name extension.

- If the file is an executable program (with a .exe or .com file name extension), you can run the program now.

- If no application is attached to this MIME type or file name extension, you can select an application now, either for this download only or for all files with the same MIME type or file name extension.

When you install Internet Explorer, you also add a long list of MIME types to your Windows file associations. The defaults are a good start, but if you add new file viewer applications (such as audio or video players) to your system, you may want to attach those applications to specific MIME types or file name extensions.

For example, you might install a graphic file viewer program such as Paint Shop Pro or LView to display and print pictures in formats that Microsoft Paint can't recognize. To automatically open the file viewer when you download an image, you should associate the standard file name extensions for those formats with the viewer program.

Many Windows 95 application programs automatically set up file associations when you install them. Unfortunately, many program developers operate on the assumption that theirs is the latest and greatest, and *of course* you will always want to use their shiny new program rather than one from their competition. If the program is working with a unique format (such as a specialized type of multimedia), this is not a problem. However, if it overwrites an existing file association, manually reset the file association to use the program it used before you installed the new program.

Changing an Existing File Association

If you have a favorite file viewer, associate it with the appropriate MIME types, even if it's not the original default.

To change a file association, follow these steps:

1. Select the Options command from the Internet Explorer View menu, or the menu that appears when you right-click the Internet icon on your Desktop.

2. When the Options window appears, select the Programs tab and click the File Types button to display the dialog box shown in Figure 24.1.

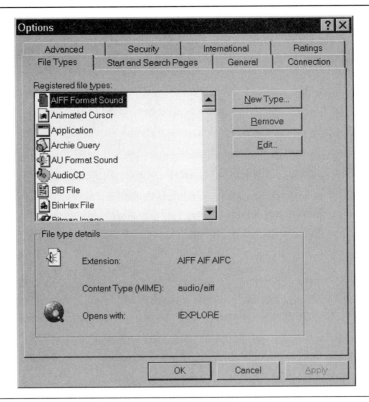

FIGURE 24.1: Use the File Types tab to link applications to files.

3. Select the file type whose association you want to change and click the Edit button. File types are listed in alphabetical order by description rather than by file name extension.

4. When the Edit File Type dialog box, shown in Figure 24.2, appears, select Open from the list of actions, and then click the Edit button. You'll see the Editing Action for Type dialog box.

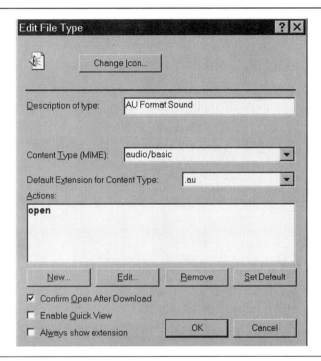

FIGURE 24.2: Use the Edit File Type dialog box to attach an application to a file type.

5. Use the Browse button to open a file browser where you can select the program to open this type of file. Then click the Open button to close the browser.

6. Confirm that the program you just selected is named in the Application Used to Perform Action field, and then click the OK button.

7. If you want to change the description that appears in the list of file types, enter the new text in the Description of Type field in the Edit File Type dialog box.

8. If there's already a MIME type associated with this file type, the MIME will be named in the Content Type (MIME) field. Don't change it. If no type is specified, look for that MIME type in the drop-down list in the Content Type (MIME) field. If you can't find the MIME type you want in the list, type it directly into the field. Make sure you have the name of the MIME type exactly as it will come from the server. The manual or readme file that came with the program should include information about the MIME type the program expects.

9. If you want Internet Explorer to automatically open every file of this type immediately after it downloads the file, remove the check mark next to Confirm Open After Download. If you want Internet Explorer to offer a choice of either opening the file right away or saving it to disk, place a check in the box. Don't worry about the other two check box options; they don't apply to downloaded files.

10. Click the OK buttons in the Edit File Type dialog box and the Options dialog box.

Adding a New File Association

In general, it's easier to wait until you download a new file type before you create a file association for that type. When Internet Explorer doesn't recognize the MIME type of a file, it will offer you a choice of either saving the file to a disk or opening the file now. If you instruct Internet Explorer to open the file, you'll need to specify an application program.

Follow this procedure to attach a new file association to a downloaded file:

1. When you download a file for which there's no association, Internet Explorer will first ask if you want to open the file or save it to disk, as shown in Figure 24.3.

2. Click the Open It button. The Open With dialog box, shown in Figure 24.4, will appear.

3. Type a description of the file type in the Description field.

4. If you want to open this file type with the same application you use for other files, select that program from the list. If the application is not on the list, click the Other button and choose the program from the file browser.

5. To use the same application program for all files of this type, make the Always Use This Program option active.

6. Click the OK button to close the dialog box.

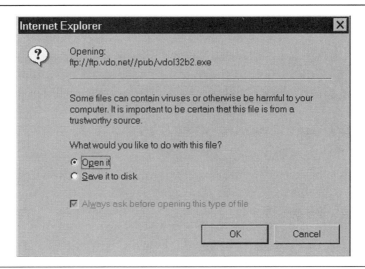

FIGURE 24.3: Click the Open It radio button to see the contents of a down-loaded file.

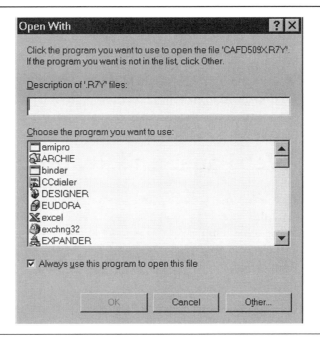

FIGURE 24.4: Use the Open With dialog box to attach an application to a file type.

When the download is complete, Internet Explorer will load the file into the viewer program you specified. If you know the MIME type used for files with this extension, open the View menu, select Options, and then choose the File Types tab. Click the Edit button, and type the MIME type in the Content Type (MIME) field. If you don't know the MIME type, look in the documentation (such as the user's guide or readme file) supplied with the program.

Finding New File Viewers

When you encounter a file in a new format, you may not discover that you don't have a tool for reading that format until after you have downloaded it. When that happens, you should save the data file and then find a program that recognizes the format.

The first place to look for a program that can read a strange format is on the Web page where you found the file. If there's a link or a graphic that says, "Click here to download the WhoopieMatic player," go ahead and do it. It will probably take you to the application developer's home page, where you can find instructions for obtaining and installing the program. If you don't see any obvious link to a source for an application program, use one of the Web search services described in Skill 21 to find what you need.

Pictures and other graphic images are a special case. Internet Explorer includes a built-in viewer for some of the most commonly used graphic formats, but if you find a picture in a more obscure format, you will need an external viewer. Two of the best general-purpose shareware image viewers are Paint Shop Pro, available for download from `ftp.jasc.com`, and LView, which you can find through the shareware search service at shareware.com (`http://www.shareware.com`).

Saving Web Pages and Reading Them Offline

If your Internet service provider charges you for the time you spend online, downloading and saving files and Web pages rather than taking the time to read them while you're connected can help reduce your monthly bill. Reading Web pages offline may be a little awkward when you want to follow a series of links, but it's ideal for reading articles from magazines, newspapers, and other online information sources.

Saving a Web Page

Follow these steps to save a Web page:

1. Jump to the Web page you want to save.

2. Open the File menu and select the Save As File command.

3. Find the folder in which you want to place a copy of this page, or click the Create New Folder button to place the page in a new subfolder within the current folder.

4. If you created a new folder, change the name of the folder to something that describes the pages you plan to save.

5. Type a file name for this page. Use the file name extension .htm.

6. Click the Save button.

7. Repeat the process for each additional page you want to save.

8. Disconnect your computer from the Internet.

Viewing a Saved Web Page

To read a Web page that you saved earlier, follow these steps:

1. Open the folder where you saved the Web page.

2. Double-click the icon for the first page you want to see.

Internet Explorer will open and load the local Web page you requested. If you click a link in the local Web page, Internet Explorer will reconnect to the Internet through your Winsock stack and jump to the destination you requested, just as it would jump from a "live" Web page.

To jump to another local page, type the path and file name in Internet Explorer's address field.

Downloading Files from Web Pages

A link to a downloadable file in a Web page can look exactly like a link to another Web page. Of course, this should not be surprising, because a Web page is really just a specialized type of file.

When you click a link in a Web page, Internet Explorer uses the MIME type or other file association to determine the action that it will take when the download is complete. Therefore, when you transfer a Web page (which is a text file with an .htm or .html extension), the page opens in Internet Explorer. When you download an audio or video file, Internet Explorer will use an add-on program that may either embed the audio player within the Internet Explorer window or open a separate window with specific controls for this type of file.

Skill 24

But when you want to transfer a file that you don't want to use right away, you must instruct Internet Explorer to save the file someplace on your hard drive rather than loading it into a program. In most cases, these files will be things like documents, pictures, and executable program files. These file types should have the Confirm Open After Download option active.

For example, this is what happens when you download a program file:

1. During the file transfer, you will see the same kind of window that appears when you copy a local file in Windows 95.

2. While the transfer is in progress, Internet Explorer displays the Confirm File Open window shown in Figure 24.5. Click the Open It radio button to open the file now, or the Save It to Disk button to save the file for later use.

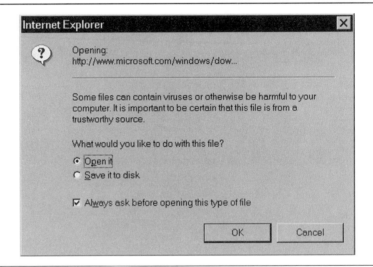

FIGURE 24.5: The Confirm File Open window provides the choice of either opening or saving a downloaded file.

Downloading Files from FTP Archives

Web pages aren't the only online resources that Internet Explorer can recognize. Among other things, you can also use the program to obtain files from FTP servers. Some Web pages contain links to FTP servers, but you can also reach them directly by typing the server's URL into Internet Explorer's address field. The standard URL format for FTP servers is *ftp://address*.

To move to a different directory or download a file, click the link to that directory or file, just as you would click a link in a Web page.

 TIP If you download a lot of files from FTP archives, you should consider using a dedicated FTP client program instead of Internet Explorer, because FTP clients can be faster and easier to use.

Moving around an FTP Archive

Internet Explorer displays the contents of an FTP archive as a list of links to subdirectories and individual files, as shown in Figure 24.6. FTP archives are organized very much like the files-and-folders structure of your own hard drive. If you start at the top-level directory, you will probably see a list of subdirectories, and possibly a file called readme, readme.txt, or something similar. It's always a good idea to download and open a readme file, especially in the top-level directory, because it probably contains a guide to the way the archive is organized, along with descriptions of the other files in the same directory.

Another useful file that shows up in many directories is called index or maybe index.txt. The index file is usually a list of all the files in the current directory, with a brief description of each one. If the title of a file doesn't give you enough information about its contents, you might find more information in the index.

Although it's not as common as a readme file or index file, some FTP servers also contain a file called ls-lR in their top-level directories. An ls-lR file contains a complete list of all the directories and files on the server.

Some FTP servers are dedicated computers that do nothing else, but their owners frequently use FTP servers for other purposes, so the servers refuse access to some files and directories. It's common practice to place the files that are available for public access in the /pub/ directory. If you don't see a directory name that describes the type of files you're looking for, /pub/ is always a good place to start your search.

When you display the contents of a subdirectory, you will see a link at the top of the list with two periods (..) instead of a name. Click that link to move up one level in the directory structure. If there's no .. in the directory, you're already at the top-level directory.

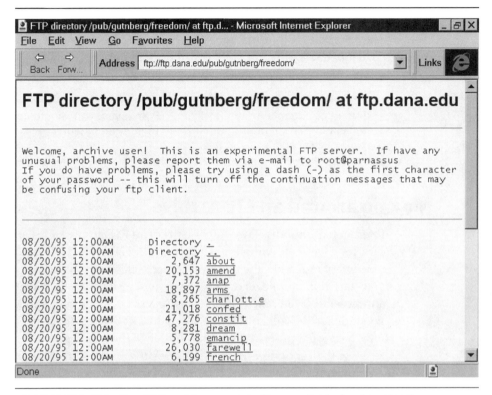

FIGURE 24.6: FTP archives contain files available for download.

Finding Files with Archie

There are almost two and a half million files in more than 1,500 FTP servers around the world. In other words, there's a huge amount of stuff out there, and you'll need help from a trained native guide in order to find a specific file. If you know the name of the file you want, you can use Archie to locate it.

Archie is a database that contains directories for almost every public FTP archive in the world. Once a month, the master Archie server in Montreal contacts each FTP server and downloads a copy of that server's directory. As it updates the file directory, the master server sends copies to each of the other Archie servers around the world.

To locate a file, you can enter a complete or partial name or keyword into a client program, which will send your request to an Archie server. When the server finds matching file names or descriptions in its database, it returns a list of archives that contain files that match your search terms.

You can find Archie Web pages at http://www-ns.rutgers.edu/htbin/archie, and at http://hoohoo.ncsa.uiuc.edu/archie.html. There's a list of other Archie gateways at http://web.nexor.co.uk/archie.html.

As an example, let's try a search through a site that uses ArchiePlex, the most common Web-based Archie search engine, as shown in Figure 24.7. Other Archie forms may look a bit different, but they all ask for the same information.

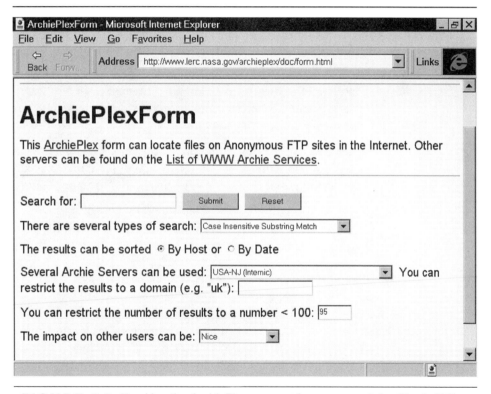

FIGURE 24.7: Use the ArchiePlex request form to search for files in FTP archives.

The ArchiePlex form includes these fields:

- **Search For**   You can use Archie to search for a specific file name, for a partial name, or for a string of characters within a name. You can also use UNIX regular expressions to search for matching patterns (such as *name.** for a file called name with any file name extension).

- **Type of Search**   Choose the search type from the drop-down list. If you don't know the exact name of the file you want, choose Case Insensitive Substring Match.

- **Sort By**   Choose Sort by Date if you're looking for the most recent version of a file that might be available from more than one site; otherwise, choose Sort by Host so you can download the file from the nearest host.

- **Choose an Archie Server**   Use the drop-down list of servers to select the one you want to search.

- **Restrict the Results to a Domain**   In most cases, you should leave this field blank. It's hard to think of any good reason to limit a search to FTP servers with specific domains.

- **Restrict the Number of Results**   If you're looking for a specific file, you will probably find it within the first 50 to 100 items. If you're looking for everything that includes a keyword in the file name, leave this field blank.

- **Impact on Other Users**   This is a goofy way of setting the search priority. Other Archie search forms use a Priority field with Urgent, Standard, Medium, and Low options. Use the Nice or Standard option.

After you've filled in all the fields in the search form, click the Submit button to send the search request to an Archie server. After a few minutes, you should receive a list of matching files like the one in Figure 24.8. In this case, a search for *oyster* produced pointers to a handful of recipe files located on a server at Columbia University. To download a file, click the link.

Notice that the list also includes direct links to the directories and hosts that contain the files that match your search terms. This can make it easy to find other files that are related to the one you originally searched for. For example, if you jump to the shellfish directory, you'll find recipes for shrimp, scallops, crab, and other types of shellfish along with the oysters, as shown in Figure 24.9.

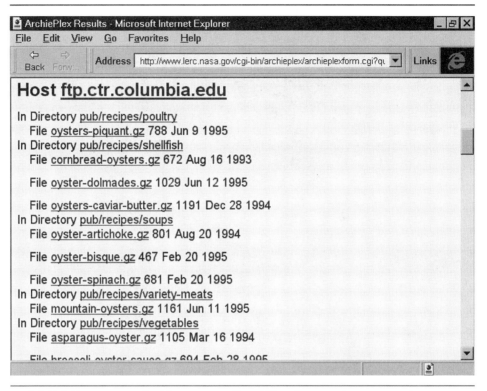

FIGURE 24.8: Archie returns a list of files that match your search terms, with a link to each file.

Working with Compressed Files

In order to save space on the server and reduce the amount of time needed to transfer files through the Internet, many FTP archives contain files stored in compressed form. Software developers often combine all of the files needed to install and run a program into a single compressed file.

Before you can read a compressed data file or run a compressed program file, you must "uncompress" the file. The most widely used compression format for DOS and Windows files is called zip. However, many files on FTP servers were originally created on computers that use other operating systems, so you may find many other compression formats in FTP archives. For example, the shellfish recipes in the FTP archive at Columbia (shown in Figure 24.9) have a .gz file name extension, which shows that they use the gnu zip compression format.

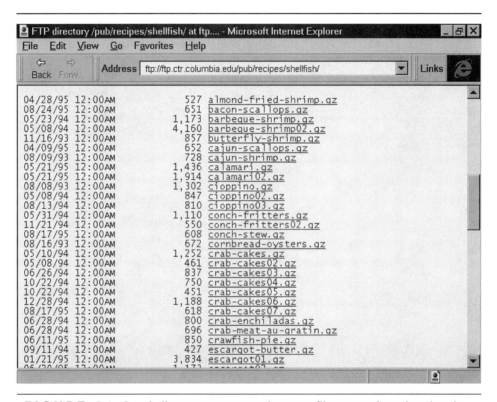

FIGURE 24.9: A directory may contain many files on topics related to the one you originally requested.

To uncompress a compressed file, you must use a utility program such as Stuffit Expander or WinZip. Both of these programs can handle most common formats, including .zip, .arj, .gz, and .lzh. You can find a shareware version of WinZip at http://www.winzip.com, and Stuffit Expander (freeware) at http://www.aladdinsys.com.

 TIP   Stuffit and WinZip each has some features that the other lacks. Stuffit Expander can work with some file formats that WinZip doesn't recognize, but it's a little easier to view the contents of a compressed file with WinZip. In the end, either of these programs will probably meet most of your requirements. Your best bet is to download copies of both and see which one you prefer.

When you install WinZip in Windows 95, it will automatically set up associations for .zip and other file name extensions. If you decide to use Stuffit as your default, you should use the File Types dialog box in either Windows or Internet Explorer to associate Stuffit with .zip and the other file name extensions listed in the About Stuffit Expander window.

If you discover a file compressed with a more obscure format, you may need to find some other way to open it. David Lemson's list of more than 60 different compression formats provides sources for programs that can decode each one. You can download the most recent version of the list from `ftp://ftp.cso .uiuc.edu/pub/doc/pcnet/compression`.

Downloading Files from Gopher Servers

The first gopher server was established at the University of Minnesota in 1991. Minnesota is the Gopher State, and the University's teams are known as the Golden Gophers, but that's not the only reason the folks in Minneapolis used that name. Like the small furry rodent of the same name, the Internet Gopher tunnels through the Internet to "go fer" files and services on distant computers. The World Wide Web has overshadowed gopher, but it's still a useful tool for exploring the Internet and finding files and other resources related to specific topics.

Working through Gopher Menus

Each item on a gopher menu is a direct link to another menu or to a specific file, Web page, Telnet host, directory, database search tool, or other server. Some gopher servers arrange menus by topic; others list all the services within a specific geographic area. Most gopher menus also include one or more links to a higher-level geographic or subject-based menu, so it's usually possible to move from one menu to any other menu within no more than four or five steps. As with links on Web pages, you can spend hours following gopher threads and examining interesting-sounding files and services.

There are half a dozen or more separate gopher clients for Windows, but you can also use Internet Explorer (or any other Web browser) to move around gopherspace. Figure 24.10 shows a gopher menu in Internet Explorer.

Internet Explorer displays items in gopher menus as links. To move to a different menu, or to open a file, click the link. Gopher servers identify files with MIME types, so Internet Explorer should automatically load data files into viewer programs for you.

Skill 24

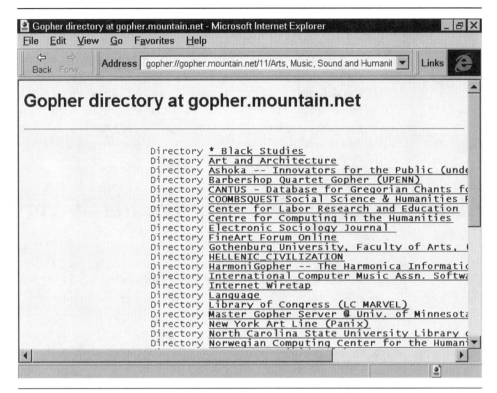

FIGURE 24.10:   Gopher menus are organized by topic and geographic location.

Exploring Gopherspace

The original point of the gopher design was to permit anybody with a server to create pointers to resources that visitors might find interesting, entertaining, or useful, regardless of their location. Like Web pages, many gopher menus reflect the interests and prejudices of their creators. Here are some good starting places for exploring gopherspace:

gopher://gopher.tc.umn.edu   Minnesota is the "Mother Gopher" that
gopher://gopher2.tc.umn.edu   includes links to every other gopher server
                                     in the world.

`gopher://gopher.mountain.net`	The gopher server at MountainNet includes a large list of interesting sites, organized by topic.
`gopher://cwis.usc.edu`	Gopher Jewels is a catalog of more that 2,000 links to specific items, arranged by subjects.
`gopher://gopher.well.com`	The Well is an online conferencing service based near San Francisco that attracts participants from all over the English-speaking world. The regulars are about evenly split among journalists, techies, and Deadheads. Most of the items on the Well gopher are a couple of years old, but many are still interesting. The Internet Outbound topic is an especially good list of links.

The skills you've read so far contain just about all the information you need to use Internet Explorer. In the next skill, you can find a complete explanation of Internet Explorer commands and a guide to using them.

Are You Experienced?

Now you can...

- ☑ add and change MIME file associations
- ☑ save Web pages to view offline
- ☑ download files from Web pages
- ☑ retrieve files from FTP archives
- ☑ explore gopher servers

Skill 24

S K I L L

twenty-five

25

A Guide to Internet Explorer Commands

❑ Learning menu bar commands

❑ Using right-click menu commands

❑ Mastering toolbar button commands

This skill contains explanations of all the Internet Explorer menu and toolbar commands. You've seen some of this information organized differently earlier in this book, but it's all here for your convenient reference.

Learning File Menu Commands

The File menu contains commands that control the way Internet Explorer works with HTML documents and other files.

New Window

Use the New Window command to open a second Internet Explorer window with the same Web page visible as in the current window. This can be convenient when you want to move quickly between two Web sites, or if you want to move to other Web sites while you download a large file.

Open

Use the Open command to load a local Web page or other file into the currently active Internet Explorer window. When the Open dialog box in Figure 25.1 appears, type the path and name of the file you want to see, or use the Browse button to find the file in a browser.

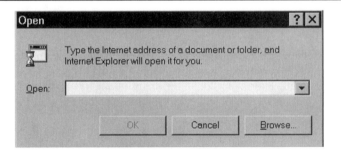

FIGURE 25.1: The Open dialog box specifies the local file you want to load into Internet Explorer.

Save

The Save command is a standard command in many Windows applications. It instructs the program to save the changes to the current file. However, since you can't use Internet Explorer to change a Web page, the command does nothing. The fact that it's included in the program suggests that a future version of Internet Explorer may offer some kind of Web page–editing function.

Save As File

Use the Save As File command to store a copy of a Web page or other HTML document on your own system. The Save As File command opens a file browser, which you can use to specify the location where you want to save the local file.

When you use this command, the only thing you actually save is the text and layout information in the HTML document. The pictures and other artwork, as well as any embedded audio or video, are all in separate files, so they won't show up when you open the saved file. Figure 25.2 shows a saved file as it appears in Internet Explorer.

One more potential problem may occur when you try to view a saved file. If the original Web page designer used links that identify addresses relative to the current page, rather than full URLs, Internet Explorer will treat those addresses as if they were on the same computer as the saved file. When this happens, the destination address will appear in the status bar as a shortcut to a local file, as shown in Figure 25.3. Notice that the target address begins with "C:\" because Internet Explorer is reading the current page from your C: drive. Since the target file doesn't exist on your hard drive, nothing will happen when you click one of those links.

So saving a Web page as a file doesn't store the pictures on a page, and the links in a saved page may not work. What good is this command? It's an easy way to save the text of a Web page, but that's about it. If you're using somebody else's page as a starting point for a page of your own, the Save As command is a good way to capture the HTML code in a text file.

To save a picture or other graphic element embedded in a page, you must use the Save Picture As command that appears when you move your cursor over the artwork and click with the right mouse button.

MSN Welcomes You To The Internet! - Microsoft Internet Explorer
File Edit View Go Favorites Help
Back Forward Stop Refresh Home Search Favorites Print
Address Quick Links
Clickable Map Image
Customize This Page
See the latest sports scores, stock prices, comics, and more.
Welcome to MSN's web site. Try the Microsoft Internet Explorer 3.0 beta. Peruse Slate. Take a whimsical look at how a better mix of NBA players could have made the U.S. Olympic Dream Team blowout wins more interesting. Beta test MSN Investor - our new financial information site. Chat with Carmen Electra tonight on ET ONLINE! See our sponsors! And stop by 475 Madison Avenue.
Watch Baseball LIVE on your PC!

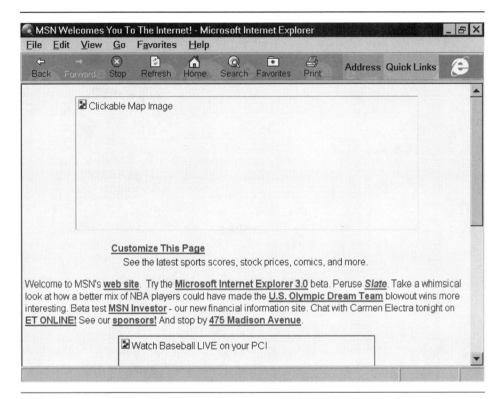

FIGURE 25.2: The Save As File command doesn't capture pictures along with the text.

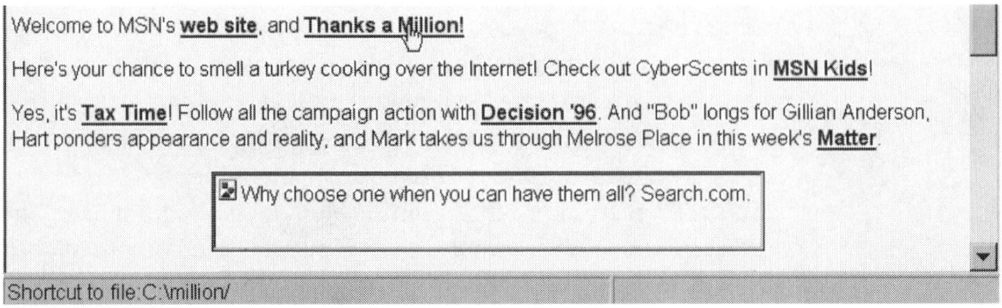

Welcome to MSN's web site, and Thanks a Million!
Here's your chance to smell a turkey cooking over the Internet! Check out CyberScents in MSN Kids!
Yes, it's Tax Time! Follow all the campaign action with Decision '96. And "Bob" longs for Gillian Anderson, Hart ponders appearance and reality, and Mark takes us through Melrose Place in this week's Matter.
Why choose one when you can have them all? Search.com.
Shortcut to file:C:\million/

FIGURE 25.3: A relative link assumes that the target file is on the same computer as the current page.

Send To

The Send To command is the same command that appears in Windows Explorer and in the right-click menu that appears when you select an icon on your Desktop. To send a copy of the current Web page or other HTML file to a floppy disk, or any of the other destinations in the submenu, click the destination.

Page Setup

Page Setup is a Windows 95 command that controls the way Internet Explorer places text or other data on a printed page. The Page Setup dialog box uses the current printer properties for page size, orientation, and paper source as defaults. In most cases, you won't want to change them. Figure 25.4 shows the Page Setup dialog box. The options in the dialog box are described in the following sections.

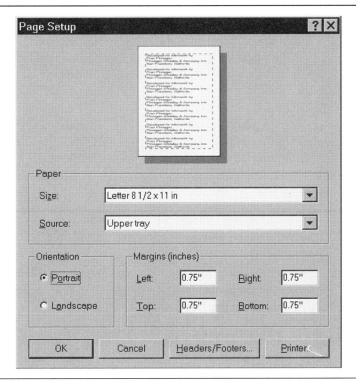

FIGURE 25.4: The Page Setup dialog box controls the layout of a printed page.

Paper Size

The Paper Size field contains a drop-down list of standard sheet and envelope dimensions. In North America, the most common page size is 8½ x 11 inches. In most other places, the standard is A4 210 x 297 mm. If you're trying to print to a sheet size that isn't on the drop-down list, choose the User-Defined Size option.

Paper Source

The Paper Source option tells your printer where to obtain blank sheets of paper. The drop-down list of options includes all possible paper sources for the current printer type.

Orientation

The Orientation option specifies the layout of text and artwork on the page. When the Portrait option is active, the narrow edges of the page are at the top and bottom. When the Landscape option is active, the narrow edges are at the sides, and the wider edges are at the top and bottom. The orientation of the picture in the dialog box shows the current setting.

Margins

The Margins settings control the amount of white space around the sides of your page.

Headers/Footers

Click the Headers/Footers button to open the dialog box shown in Figure 25.5, which provides space for standard headers and footers that will appear on each printed page.

In addition to plain text, you can also use variables to substitute specific information about the current page for the variable codes in the Headers and Footers fields. Internet Explorer recognizes these variable codes:

&w	Window title
&u	URL or local path of the current Web page
&d	Date in short format (M/D/Y—10/1/96)
&D	Date in long format (Month D, Year—October 1, 1996)
&t	Time of day

&T	Time in 24-hour format
&p	Page number
&P	Total number of pages

To print a single ampersand (&) in a header or footer, type two ampersands (&&).

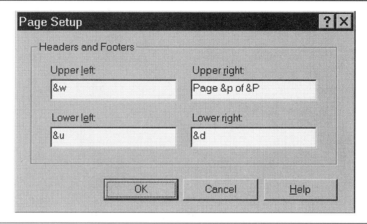

FIGURE 25.5: The Headers and Footers fields contain the text you want printed on every page.

Printer

Click the Printer button to instruct Internet Explorer to use a different printer.

Print

Use the Print command to send a copy of the current Web page to your printer. When you enter the Print command, you will see the Windows 95 Print dialog box, with one additional option, as shown in Figure 25.6.

Choose an option in the Print Range box to specify which parts of the Web page you want to print: all of the document, a range of pages, or just the selected text. To print more than one copy of the current Web page, change the Number of Copies setting.

The Shortcuts option adds a table to the printed page that lists the target URLs of each link in the current document. This is a nice feature when you're printing a Web page to send by fax or postal mail, or to save as a hard copy.

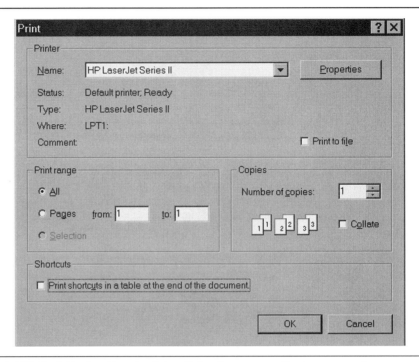

FIGURE 25.6: Use the Print dialog box to specify the range of pages, and the number of copies you want to print.

Create Shortcut

The Create Shortcut command produces a Windows shortcut to the current Web page and places it on your Desktop. You can move the shortcut to a folder or to your Start menu by dragging and dropping the shortcut icon. To change the name of the shortcut icon, use the Rename command from the right-click menu.

Properties

Like the command in other Windows applications, the Properties command in Internet Explorer opens a Properties window, as shown in Figure 25.7.

The only really useful information in the Properties window is the URL of the current page.

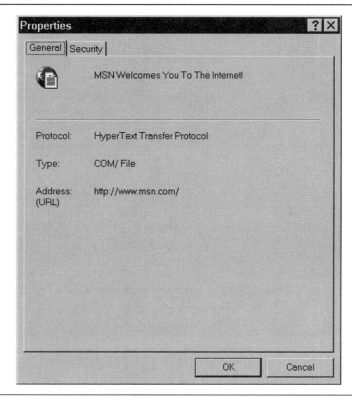

FIGURE 25.7: The Properties window supplies additional information about the current Web page.

Close

The Close command shuts down Internet Explorer and returns you to the Windows Desktop.

Using Edit Menu Commands

If you've used any other Windows programs, the commands in the Edit menu will be familiar. These commands allow you to move text or pictures to other documents through the Windows Clipboard and to search for words or other character strings in the current Web page.

To select text for the Cut or Copy command, move the cursor to the beginning of the text string you want to select, hold down the left mouse button, and drag the mouse to the end of the text you want to select. To select the entire text of the current page, use the Select All command. Internet Explorer displays selected text with reversed colors.

Cut

Use the Cut command to remove the currently selected text or other elements from a text field and place the deleted material in the Windows Clipboard. The Cut command does not work with body text in Web pages.

Copy

Use the Copy command to place a copy of the currently selected text or other items in the Windows Clipboard without removing it from the current document. From the Clipboard, you can paste the text to a text editor, word processor, or any other Windows application program.

Paste

Use the Paste command to place the contents of the Windows Clipboard into a text field.

Select All

Use the Select All command to select the whole text of the current Web page. As Figure 25.8 shows, selected text includes descriptions of embedded pictures, but it does not include the pictures themselves.

Find (on This Page)

Use the Find (on This Page) command to search for a word, phrase, or character string in the current Web page, including portions of the page that are not currently visible within the Internet Explorer window.

When the Find window shown in Figure 25.9 appears, type the word or phrase you want to locate in the Find field. To search through the whole document, place a check mark next to Start from Top of Page. If there's no check mark in the box, the search will start at the current cursor position.

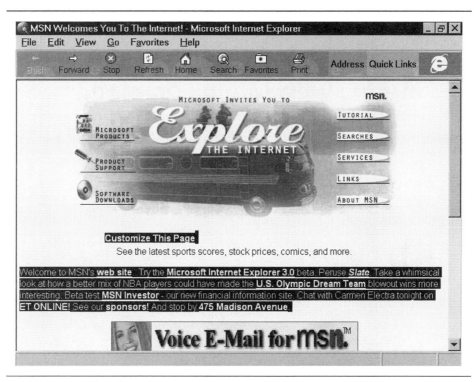

FIGURE 25.8: The Select All command selects only text, not pictures.

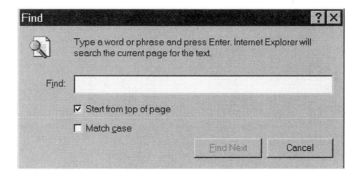

FIGURE 25.9: To search for a text string, type the text in the Find field.

When Match Case is active, the search will be limited to an exact match with the contents of the Find field. If it's not active, the program will find any similar character string, even if it has lowercase letters instead of capitals.

Mastering View Menu Commands

The View menu contains commands that control the appearance of the Internet Explorer window.

Toolbar

Use the Toolbar command to hide or display the Internet Explorer toolbar, the Address field, and the Quick Links toolbar.

Status Bar

Use the Status Bar command to display or hide the status bar at the bottom of the Internet Explorer window.

Fonts

The Fonts command controls the size of text in Web pages, if the page designer did not specify font sizes. To change the font size, select the Fonts command, and choose the size you want from the submenu.

When you change font sizes, you may also change the overall size of the page and the relative position of text and some pictures. If you want to come as close as possible to the designer's original intent, use Medium fonts. Figure 25.10 shows the same Web page with both medium and large fonts.

 NOTE The Fonts command controls the size of display text, but has no effect on the typeface. To change the typeface, open the International tab with the Options command.

Stop

The Stop command interrupts a download in progress and cancels your request to open a new page or file. When a page seems to be taking too long to load, or if you click a link by mistake, you can use the Stop command (or the Stop button in the toolbar) to cut off the current download.

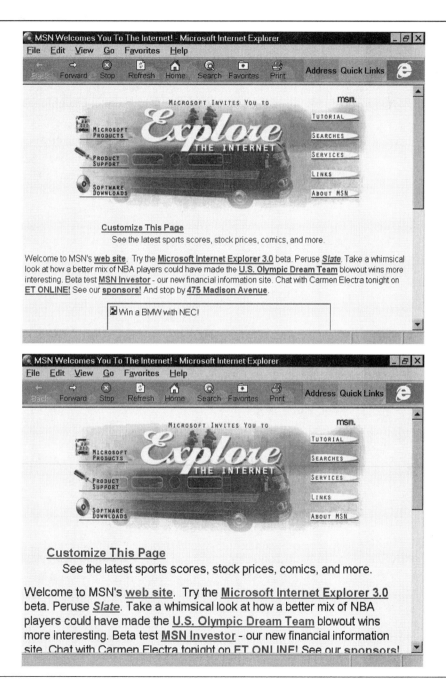

FIGURE 25.10: The Fonts command changes the size of text in Web pages.

Refresh

The Refresh command instructs Internet Explorer to start downloading the current Web page again from the beginning.

When you're looking at a page that is frequently updated (such as a news bulletin or a picture from a video camera), or if Internet Explorer loads a copy of a page from the local cache on your computer or your ISP's server, the Refresh command may get you a more recent version of the page than the one already on your screen.

Refresh may also be useful when a page seems to stop before the download is complete. A slow or interrupted download can happen when the file server is sending data to many clients at the same time, or when there's a lot of traffic on the backbone between the server and your Internet access point.

If you don't see any change in the progress bar at the bottom of the Internet Explorer window, or if the RD light on your modem (or the modem icon in the Windows Taskbar) stays dark for more than about a minute, the Refresh command can sometimes get the download moving again. It doesn't always work, but it's worth a try.

Source

Select the Source command to display the HTML source code for the current Web page. When you enter the Source command, Internet Explorer loads the code into the Notepad text editor.

If you know something about HTML code, you can use the Source command to give yourself a better idea of how and why the current page looks the way it does, or even to make some changes to the appearance of the page. If you're creating your own Web pages, you might want to use code from an existing page as a model for your own design.

Options

The Options command opens the Internet Properties dialog box, which controls a variety of Internet Explorer features and functions. You can also set these options from the Internet Properties dialog box in the Windows Control Panel or by using the Properties command in the Internet icon's right-click menu.

General Tab

The General tab, shown in Figure 25.11, contains commands that change the way Internet Explorer displays Web pages and other documents. The General tab options are described next.

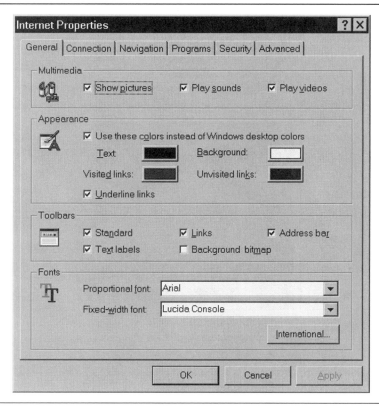

FIGURE 25.11: Use the General tab to change the appearance of Web pages in Internet Explorer.

Multimedia

Multimedia options specify whether Internet Explorer includes imbedded pictures, sounds, and video clips when it downloads Web pages.

Show Pictures   When the Pictures option is active, Internet Explorer will automatically download all pictures and other graphic elements embedded in Web pages. When it is not active, Internet Explorer leaves spaces in Web pages for pictures, as shown in Figure 25.12. To see an image when Show Pictures is turned off, click the icon within the picture frame.

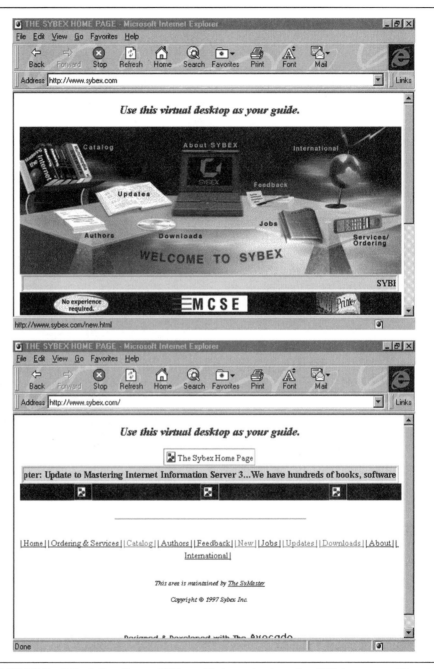

FIGURE 25.12: Turn off Show Pictures to download Web pages without graphic images.

> **TIP**   Turning off pictures can make a huge difference in the amount of time needed to download a new Web page, especially when the page contains large or complex images. The same page might take less than 10 seconds to download without pictures, but more than a minute or two when all of the pictures and other graphic devices come along with the text. Therefore, many people browse with pictures turned off in order to move more quickly from one page to the next.

Play Sounds   A growing number of Web pages include audio clips that download along with the text and pictures. If your computer has a sound board and speakers, the audio plays automatically when the download is complete.

The vast majority of these embedded sounds are, choose one or more: irritating, dumb, and irrelevant to the visual content of the page. After the first three or four times you hear them, fanfares, frog sound effects, synthesizer riffs, and crickets are not particularly entertaining. And a hearty disembodied voice crying, "Welcome to the Hoo-Hah Enterprises Web Page!" can be enough to make you drop your coffee cup into your lap.

Audio takes even longer to download than images, so you may want to seriously consider turning sounds off. If your computer doesn't have a sound board, it's a no brainer—don't waste your time downloading sounds you can't play.

Play Videos   Animation in Web pages can be short video clips, cartoons, moving text, and animated icons. They all take extra time to download, so you can instruct Internet Explorer to ignore them when it opens new Web pages.

If you omit video when you open a Web page, you can download and view an animation later by clicking the icon that replaces it.

Appearance

Use These Colors Instead of Windows Desktop Colors   The Custom Colors options control the default text and background colors that Internet Explorer uses for Web pages that don't include their own background and text color attributes.

When the Use These Colors option is not checked, Internet Explorer will use the Window text and background colors specified in the Windows Display Properties dialog box. To open the Windows Display Properties dialog box, open the Control Panel and click the Display icon, or place your cursor over a blank spot on your Desktop and click the right mouse button.

To use different colors for Web pages, place a check mark in the Use Custom Colors check box and click the Text or Background button to choose a new color.

As a general rule, black and other dark colors work best for text, and white and other light colors make the best backgrounds.

Links   The Links options control the way Internet Explorer identifies hypertext links in Web pages. As you know, shortcuts appear in Internet Explorer in a different color from other text. After you visit a Web page, Internet Explorer keeps that page's URL in its History list, so it can distinguish between new sites and the ones you've already seen.

   A Web page can specify the colors for links within their pages. If no color is specified, Internet Explorer will use the default settings. The Visited Links button sets the default colors for links to URLs that you have visited before. The Unvisited Links button controls the default color for links to new URLs. To change the color of either kind of link, click the button and select a new color from the choices in the Color dialog box.

Underline Links   When the Underline Links option is active, Internet Explorer displays hypertext links as underlined text. When the option is not active, links appear in the same type style as other text, but they're in the colors specified by the Visited and Unvisited Links options (or the colors specified by the designer).

Toolbars

The Toolbars options specify which toolbars will be visible in the Internet Explorer screen. When an option is not active, the toolbar controlled by that option is hidden.

Standard   The Standard toolbar contains icon buttons that duplicate some of the most frequently used menu commands.

Text Labels   When the Text Labels option is active, the Standard toolbar includes captions that identify the functions of each command button. When it is not active, no captions are visible, but a tooltip appears when you move your cursor over a command button.

Links   The Links toolbar contains five quick links to URLs specified in the Navigation Options tab.

Address Bar   The Address bar shows the URL of the current Web page.

Background Bitmap   When the Background Bitmap option is active, all visible toolbars include a pattern under the text and icons. When the option is not active, the background is a solid color.

Fonts

Some Web pages include font attributes that instruct Internet Explorer to use a particular typeface for text and headlines, but many other pages leave the choice of a font to the browser. If a Web page does not include font attributes, Internet Explorer will use the typefaces specified in the Fonts fields.

Proportional Font   Internet Explorer uses the typeface specified in the Proportional Font field for most headlines and body text in Web pages. These fonts are called "proportional" because some letters (like m and w) are wider than others (like i and f).

The default proportional font is Times Roman—an excellent typeface on paper, but not as good as other fonts on a computer screen. Arial is a good choice, but experiment with other typefaces before you decide to permanently change your default.

Fixed-Width Font   Web pages use fixed-width fonts for text with characters that must maintain a constant width, such as tables or columns of numbers. The default fixed-width font is Courier, which looks like the output of a typewriter, but Lucida Console is a better choice for on-screen reading.

If the list of installed languages includes more than one character set, you can change to a different set by selecting the one you want and clicking the Apply button. To install a new character set, click the Add button.

International   The International button opens a dialog box that specifies the character set that Internet Explorer uses to display text in Web pages. In most cases, you won't want to change the character set unless you're trying to download Web pages in foreign languages.

Connection Tab

Figure 25.13 shows the Connection tab. Windows automatically configures the options in this tab when you use the techniques described in Chapter 17 to set up Dial-Up Networking. When AutoDial is active, Internet Explorer (and every other 32-bit Winsock-compliant application program) will automatically set up a dial-up networking connection the first time the application tries to send or receive data through the Internet. The Connection tab options are described next.

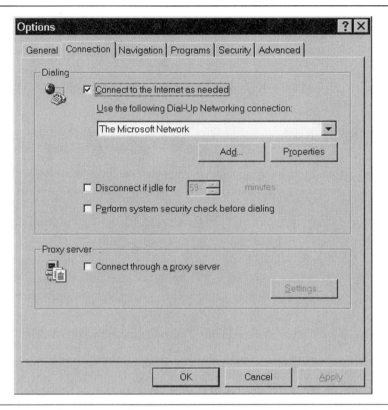

FIGURE 25.13: The Connection tab controls connections to the Internet through a modern and telephone line.

Connect to the Internet As Needed   If you're connecting to the Internet through a modem and a dial telephone line, the Connect As Needed... option should be active. If you connect to the Internet through a LAN or a direct high-speed network connection, the Connect As Needed... option should be turned off.

Use the Following Dial-Up Networking Connection   If you have more than one Internet access account, or if you have created separate Dial-Up Networking connection profiles for different locations, you can use the drop-down list in this field to set one of these connection profiles as your default.

You don't need to change your default to use a different connection, but you must configure the connection profile before you start Internet Explorer or any other application program. To use a different connection profile, follow these steps:

1. Open the Dial-Up Networking folder from the My Computer window.

2. Double-click the connection profile you want to use.

3. When the Connect To dialog box appears, enter your user name and password, and then click the Connect button.

Add   Click the Add button to create a new Dial-Up Networking profile.

Properties   Click the Properties button to change the telephone number, modem configuration, or server configuration in the current Dial-Up Networking profile. The Connection Properties dialog box that appears when you click the Properties button is shown in Figure 25.14. This dialog box is identical to one that appears when you select the Properties command from the right-click menu in the Dial-Up Networking window.

Disconnect If Idle   If the Disconnect If Idle option is active, Dial-Up Networking will hang up the modem connection if you don't send or receive any data for the number of minutes in the Disconnect If Idle field.

When the connection has been idle for the period specified, the information window in Figure 25.15 will appear, and your computer will beep once. After another 30 seconds, you will lose your connection unless you click the Cancel button.

It's a good idea to keep Auto Disconnect turned on, especially if you're using an Internet service provider that charges by the hour (or minute) for connect time. There's no good reason to pay for a connection when you're not using it. Even if you have unlimited access, you should disconnect when you're not using the link, because you're tying up an incoming telephone line and a modem at the ISP. If you're not using the line, it's a courtesy to other users to let them get to it.

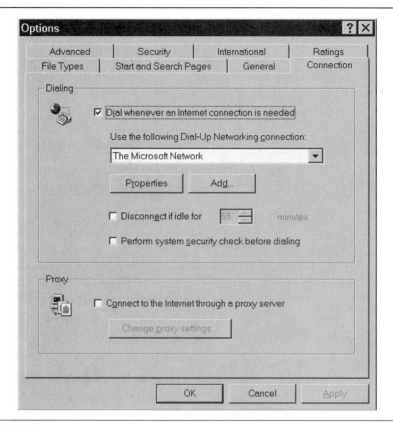

FIGURE 25.14: Use the Connection Properties dialog box to change the characteristics of a Dial-Up Networking profile.

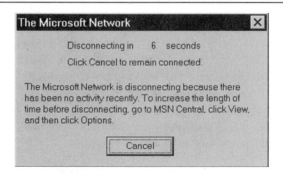

FIGURE 25.15: Click the Cancel button to interrupt Auto Disconnect.

> **NOTE**   The idle time counter does not reset itself when you send or receive data through Netscape Navigator, Winsock FTP, and many other Internet application programs, so you might see the Disconnecting in xx Seconds warning, even if your connection hasn't been idle. If that happens, just click the Cancel button and go on with what you're doing. If you expect to do any large FTP file transfers, you should turn off Auto Disconnect, so you don't lose the link when you leave your desk to get a cup of coffee.

Perform System Security Check Before Dialing   If your computer is connected to a LAN, it might be possible for unauthorized users to obtain access to files, printers, and other network resources through your Dial-Up Networking connection to the Internet at the same time that you're using Internet Explorer or some other Internet client program. It's not likely that anybody will try to break into your network this way, but it's possible. You can protect your network from unauthorized access by using the Advanced tab (described later) to add a proxy server to your Internet connection.

When the Perform Security Check option is active, Dial-Up Networking looks for unprotected LAN access, and issues a warning before it connects you to the Internet.

Connect through a Proxy Server   When you connect your PC to the Internet, you also connect all the other computers on the same LAN as yours. Without some kind of protection, somebody outside your LAN could upload copies of private files without permission. A proxy server is a computer that acts as a filter (sometimes called a "firewall") between your LAN and an Internet connection. When the Connect through a Proxy Server option is active, all incoming and outgoing Internet commands and data pass through the proxy server on their way to or from the Internet, rather than going directly to their ultimate destination. If your computer is not connected to a LAN, you don't need to worry about a proxy server.

Change Proxy Settings   When the Connect through a Proxy Server option is active, you can click the Settings button to open the dialog box shown in Figure 25.16. The Servers fields identify the addresses and port numbers that your network uses as proxy servers for each type of address. You can obtain the information you need for these fields from your network administrator.

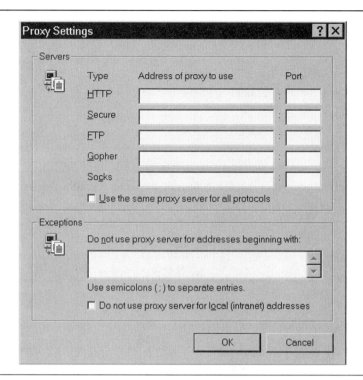

FIGURE 25.16: Use the Proxy Settings dialog box to connect to the Internet through proxy servers.

If you want to connect directly to certain computers on the Internet without going through the proxy server, type the addresses of those computers in the Exceptions field, separated with commas. You can also bypass complete domains (such as .edu) or port numbers.

Again, talk to your network administrator or help desk before you try to set up your system to work with a proxy server. You're probably not the first person on the LAN to try to do this, so the network experts can tell you exactly what you need to do to make this work properly.

Navigation Tab

The Navigation tab contains options that control permanent links to Web pages and other URLs. Figure 25.17 shows the Navigation Options dialog box.

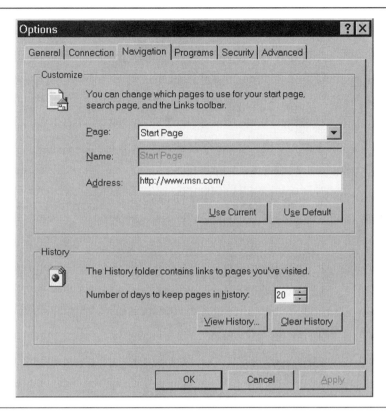

FIGURE 25.17: Use the Navigation options to change your Start Page, Search Page, and Quick Links.

Start Page   The Start Page is the Web page that Internet Explorer loads automatically when you start the program and when you click the Home command button in the toolbar.

Search Page   The Search Page is the page that loads when you select the Search button. You can use the Start and Search Pages dialog box to define the current Web page as either the Start Page or the Search page.

Quick Links   Quick Links are commands in the Links toolbar that take you directly to a specified Web page or other URL.

Changing a Destination   To define a new Start Page or Search page, or to create a new Quick link, follow these steps:

1. Jump to the page you want to specify as the new Start Page, Search Page, or Quick Link.

2. Open the Options dialog box, and choose the Navigation tab.

3. Select the type of page you want to change from the drop-down list in the Page field.

4. Click the Use Current button.

5. If you're changing one of your Quick Links, look at the Name field to confirm that the name (which will appear in the Links toolbar) clearly identifies the new Web page.

History   When you visit a Web page, Internet Explorer places a shortcut to that page in the History folder. You can open your History folder from the Go menu. You can control the size of the History folder with the Number of Days to Keep Pages option. To delete all shortcuts from the History folder, click the Clear History button.

Programs Tab

The Programs tab, shown in Figure 25.18, specifies the default Mail and News applications and provides a link to the Windows file register.

Mail and News   Internet Explorer does not include a built-in e-mail manager or newsreader. Therefore, if a Web page contains a link to mail or news, Internet Explorer must open a separate program to handle the link. You can use Microsoft's own Internet News and Internet Mail programs, or client programs supplied by other software developers. To link an external Mail or News program to Internet Explorer, choose the program from the drop-down list of available programs.

Viewers   Internet Explorer uses the Windows 95 file register to open files after it downloads them. The File Types button opens the same dialog box as the one that appears when you open the File Types tab in a Windows folder, as shown in Figure 25.19. Skill 24 explains how to associate file types with MIME types and application programs.

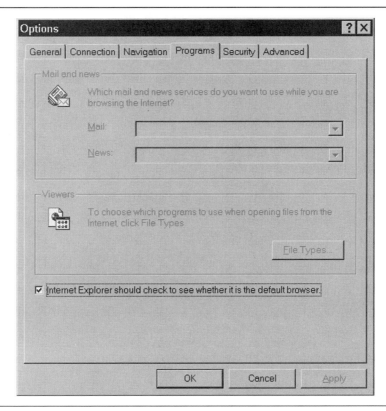

FIGURE 25.18: Use the Programs tab to control links between Internet Explorer and other programs.

Internet Explorer Should Check to See Whether It Is the Default Browser

The default Web browser is the program that Windows uses to load and display Web pages from shortcuts in folders and menus. If you double-click a shortcut to a Web page in a window, a menu, or your Desktop, Internet Explorer will start the default browser.

If Internet Explorer is your only Web browser, it's automatically the default. But if you have more than one Web browser on your PC, such as Internet Explorer and Netscape Navigator, things can get confusing, because both programs use

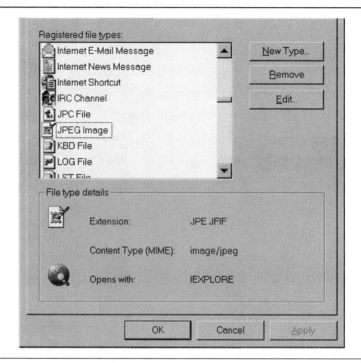

FIGURE 25.19: Use the File Types dialog box to change file and MIME type associations.

the default browser to open Web pages from the list of favorites (Netscape calls them bookmarks). Therefore, if the current browser is not the default, you might unexpectedly start some other browser rather than loading the page you want in the current browser.

To avoid this kind of confusion, the Check for Default option should always be active, and you should always make the current browser the default.

Security Tab

The path between your PC and a server may pass through a dozen or more intermediate computers. In theory, every one of those computers offers an opportunity for somebody to read the commands and data you're sending and receiving.

Theft of data doesn't happen that often. Sending your credit card number through the Internet is probably less dangerous than giving a card to the cashier in an all-night gas station. But if the idea makes you nervous, be sure to use a secure connection.

Theft of data is not the only potential risk you face when you use the Internet. It's also possible—though unlikely—for content providers to download viruses to your system. Many providers want to store "cookies" on your system that provide specific information that they can use to personalize the data that they return to you. The Security tab, shown in Figure 25.20, allows you to see warnings before Internet Explorer sends or receives data that might be a security problem or an invasion of your privacy.

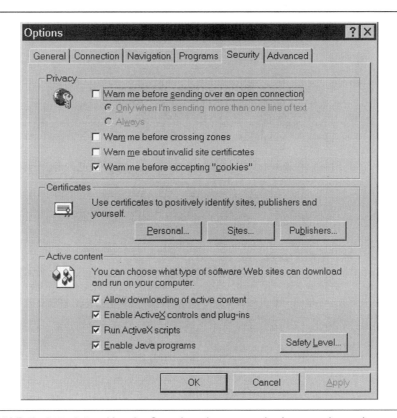

FIGURE 25.20: Use the Security tab to control privacy and security warnings.

Privacy   To reduce the danger of unauthorized access to valuable information, some Internet servers use security protocols that transmit data in encrypted form. When you connect to one of those servers with Internet Explorer, you will see a padlock in the status bar, like the one in Figure 25.21.

FIGURE 25.21: A padlock in the status bar indicates that Internet Explorer has received the current Web page from a secure server.

The options in the Security Options dialog box don't have much to do with secure servers, but they do allow you to hide or display warning messages when you send or receive data from a site that is not secure. These options control the warning messages, but they don't make any difference in the security of the actual transmission.

Warn Me Before Sending Over an Open Connection

The Warn Me Before Sending options determine if and how often Internet Explorer displays a warning message before you send data to a site that doesn't use security protocols.

Warn Me Before Crossing Zones

When the Warn Me Before Crossing Zones option is active, Internet Explorer displays a warning message before it receives data from a Web page located on a secure server.

Warn Me About Invalid Site Certificates

One part of the security protocol is an authentication certificate that includes several pieces of information that identify the server, including its address. When a Check Security option is turned on, Internet Explorer compares the address in the certificate to the address to which you instruct it to send data. When the Warn Me About Invalid Site Certificates option is active, Internet Explorer will display a warning message if the two addresses don't match.

Warn Me Before Accepting "Cookies"

Cookies are blocks of information that a Web server stores on a client system to personalize the data that it sends to that system. If you prefer not to allow a server to use a cookie, you can instruct Internet Explorer to display a warning before it stores the cookie on your hard drive.

Certificates   Use the Certificates options to specify the types of security certificates that Internet Explorer will accept.

Active Content   Some Web pages can automatically download and run programs that will run on your PC. This feature is intended to enhance performance by adding animation, interactivity, and other special functions to otherwise static words and pictures, but it also opens up a possible way for viruses or other damaging programs to enter your computer. Use the Active Content options to display a warning about possible problems before a doubtful page downloads or to automatically reject pages that might contain a security problem.

Click the Safety Level button to restrict access to Web sites that might have a potential security problem.

Unless you receive warnings about possible security problems from your system administrator, you should make all of the Active Content options active, and choose the Normal safety level.

Advanced Tab

The Advanced tab, shown in Figure 25.22, is a catch-all for options that don't fit any of the other tabs.

Ratings   A few Web pages include content that contains language or pictures of unsurpassed vulgarity. Because the Web population includes everyone from Nobel Prize winners down to as low as you can go, Internet Explorer contains a set of tools that you can use to reject pages that contain certain types of material.

The Ratings options allow you to set the specific levels of sex, violence, and other material that you want to filter, and to turn the filter function on and off.

Internet Explorer includes a rating system created by the Recreational Software Advisory Council (RSAC) that many Web site developers include in their pages. Different users may have different personal standards for what they consider objectionable. For example, some parents might not want their children to see Web pages that disagree with their religious or political beliefs. To replace the RSAC ratings with some other set of acceptable options, click the Properties button. When the Content Advisor dialog box appears, select the Advanced tab and click the Rating Systems button.

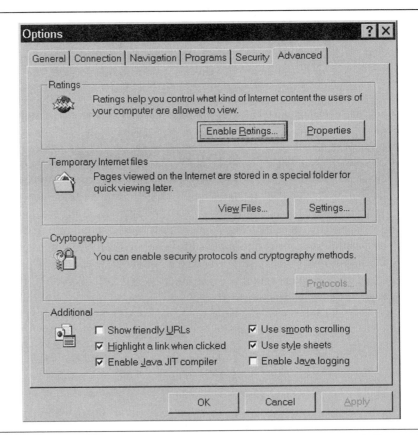

FIGURE 25.22: The Advanced tab contains options that don't fit any of the other tabs.

To set the acceptable levels of content, click the Ratings tab and move the sliders to set the ratings, as shown in Figure 25.23.

Temporary Internet Files   Every time you view a Web page in Internet Explorer, the program stores a copy of that page on your hard drive as a temporary file. When you return to a page you've recently seen, Internet Explorer will try to load the page from the temporary local file rather than downloading another copy through the Internet. Therefore, it generally takes a lot less time to reload a page than to download a new page. However, the version of a page in a temporary file remains the same, even if the original has changed. The Temporary

Internet Files options allows you to instruct Internet Explorer to download a new copy of every Web page that you view at least once during your Internet Explorer session.

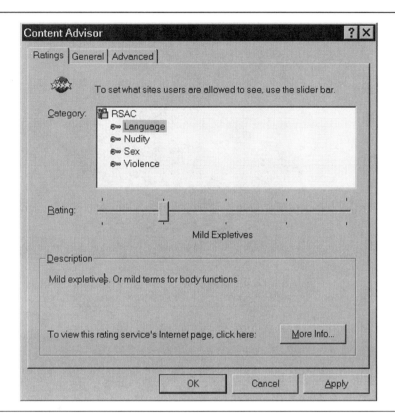

FIGURE 25.23: Move the sliders to change each content rating.

View Files

Click the View Files button to open the Temporary Internet Files folder.

Settings

Click the Settings button to open the dialog box shown in Figure 25.24.

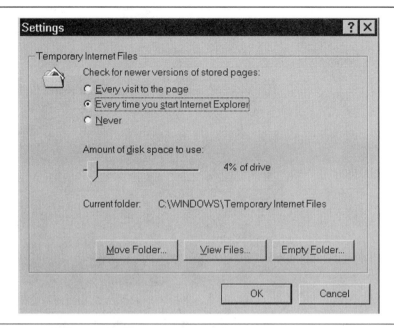

It's a good idea to select the Every Time You Start Internet Explorer option so that you won't miss updates to familiar Web pages. To download a new version of a page at any time, click the Reload button in the Internet Explorer toolbar.

The Amount of Disk Space slider sets the maximum size of the folder that contains your temporary Internet files, expressed as a percentage of the total size of your hard drive. If you increase the amount of space available, you may reduce the amount of time needed to view Web pages, but you won't have as much space available on your hard drive for other files and programs.

Cryptography   When they become available, cryptography methods and protocols will allow you send or receive secure data through Internet Explorer. Click the Protocols button to specify the cryptography protocols you want to use.

Additional   The additional area of the Advanced tab contains miscellaneous options.

Show Friendly URLs

The Show Friendly URLs option controls the format that Internet Explorer uses to display addresses in the status bar when you move your cursor over a link. When Show Friendly URLs is active, the program shows the address of the destination in this form: `www.name.com/path.htm`, or possibly just `path.htm` if the link points to another file in the same directory or folder as the current page. When the option is turned off, you will see the complete URL in the status bar, like this: `http://www.name.com/path.htm`.

Highlight a Link When Clicked

When Highlight a Link When Clicked is active, you will see a dotted-line box around a text or graphic link when you click it once.

Enable Java JIT Compiler

Java is a programming language that downloads simple application programs along with data. When you download a Java file through Internet Explorer, the JIT (Just In Time) compiler creates the necessary Java program if the Enable Compiler option is active.

Use Smooth Scrolling

When Smooth Scrolling is active, Internet Explorer scrolls the content of a Web page at a defined speed.

Use Style Sheets

If a Web page includes an HTML style sheet, Internet Explorer will use the style sheet if this option is active.

Enable Java Logging

When the Enable Java Logging option is active, Internet Explorer will create a log of Java activity.

Using Go Menu Commands

The commands in the Go menu instruct Internet Explorer to move to a different Web page.

Back

Use the Back command to return to the page that was visible immediately before the current page.

Forward

After you use the Back command, you can use the Forward command to return to the next page in the current series.

The Back and Forward commands are easier to use than to describe. If you start at Page A and jump to Page B, you can use the Back command to return to Page A, and then use the Forward command to go to Page B again.

Start Page

The Start Page is the Web page that Internet Explorer automatically opens when you start the program. Use the Start Page command to return to that page.

Search the Web

The Search Page is generally a Web page that provides access to one or more Internet search tools. To jump to your Search Page, select the Search the Web command.

Today's Links

The Today's Links command is a link to a Microsoft Web page that contains pointers to other new and interesting Web sites.

History List

The Go menu includes a list of Web pages that you have recently visited, as shown in Figure 25.25. To return to one of the pages in the History list, select the description of that page.

Open History Folder

The Open History Folder command loads the History folder into Internet Explorer and changes the commands in the menu bar and toolbar. As Figure 25.26 shows, the command set in the History folder window looks more like a Windows folder window than an Internet Explorer Web page. Each item in the History folder is a shortcut to a Web page. To jump to a page, double-click the shortcut.

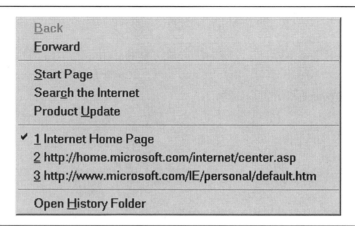

FIGURE 25.25: The Go menu includes a list of recently visited Web pages.

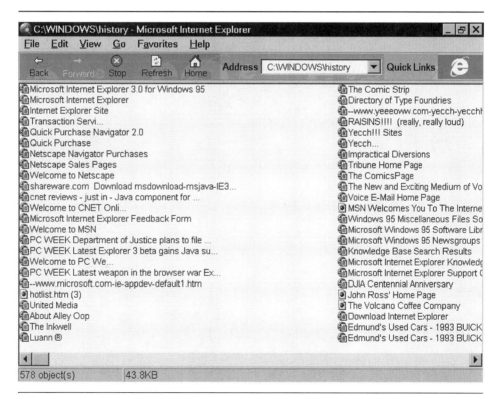

FIGURE 25.26: The History folder contains shortcuts to the last couple of hundred Web pages you've visited.

The default arrangement of shortcuts in the History folder shows the names of Web pages in alphabetical order, with items displayed as list entries. You can change the order of the list. However, since all the shortcuts are the same type and size, the only other arrangement that makes any sense is Arrange by Date, which places the shortcuts in chronological order, with the most recent items at the top of the list.

You can also replace the list with large or small icons, or by a detailed list that shows the date and time you visited each site.

Learning the Favorites Menu Commands

The Favorites menu contains just two commands, plus shortcuts to items on your list of favorite sites. Skill 23 contains detailed information about working with favorites.

Add to Favorites

Use the Add to Favorites command to place a shortcut to the current Web page in your Favorites folder and, if there's space, add the shortcut to the list in the Favorites menu.

Organize Favorites

Use the Organize Favorites command to open a dialog box that you want to use to move items in your Favorites list to subfolders.

Favorite Web Pages

As Figure 25.27 shows, the Favorites menu includes links to as many of the shortcuts in the Favorites folder as space allows (the exact number depends on the size of your monitor screen). To jump to one of the pages in the list, select it just as you would select any other command in a menu.

Accessing the Help Menu

The Help menu in Internet Explorer is like the Help menu in most other Windows programs. It contains a Help Topics command that provides access to Internet Explorer Help, and an About command that opens an information window with the version number and other information about the program.

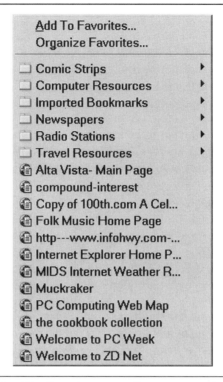

<u>A</u>dd To Favorites...
<u>O</u>rganize Favorites...
☐ Comic Strips ▶
☐ Computer Resources ▶
☐ Imported Bookmarks ▶
☐ Newspapers ▶
☐ Radio Stations ▶
☐ Travel Resources ▶
🗿 Alta Vista- Main Page
🗿 compound-interest
🗿 Copy of 100th.com A Cel...
🗿 Folk Music Home Page
🗿 http---www.infohwy.com-...
🗿 Internet Explorer Home P...
🗿 MIDS Internet Weather R...
🗿 Muckraker
🗿 PC Computing Web Map
🗿 the cookbook collection
🗿 Welcome to PC Week
🗿 Welcome to ZD Net

FIGURE 25.27: The Favorites menu lists as many shortcuts in the Favorites folder as space allows.

The Microsoft on the Web commands opens a submenu that contains links to a handful of Microsoft Web sites where you can obtain additional software, technical support, and additional information about Internet Explorer and other Microsoft products.

Activating Right Mouse Button Commands

Internet Explorer displays a context-sensitive command menu when you click the right mouse button. "Context-sensitive" means that the specific set of commands changes, depending on the exact location of the cursor. A few of these commands are duplicates of the ones in the menu bar, but most are available only from a right-click menu. Several of the right-click commands can make it easy to lift out individual elements of a Web page and use them for other purposes.

Save Background As

Many Web pages use pictures or textured patterns as a background. To save a copy of the background image as a file, move your cursor over the background and select the Save Background As command from the right-click menu.

Set As Wallpaper

If you *really* like a picture or a background image on a Web page, you can use it as your Windows Desktop wallpaper. The Set As Wallpaper command automatically saves the image in your \windows directory as a bitmap image file called Internet Explorer wallpaper.bmp, and defines that image as your current Desktop wallpaper.

If you decide to keep an image as your wallpaper, you should rename the file to something that describes its content rather than the source. Otherwise, you will overwrite the file image the next time you use the Set As Wallpaper command.

To change your wallpaper back to the original pattern or image, or to go back to a solid-color desktop background, follow these steps:

1. From the Windows Desktop, move your cursor over the wallpaper and click your right mouse button.

2. Select the Properties command from the right-click menu.

3. When the Display Properties window appears, choose the Background tab to display the dialog box shown in Figure 25.28.

4. Choose the image you want to use as wallpaper from the list in the Wallpaper field or click the Browse button to find an image in a different folder.

5. The picture of a monitor screen will show you how this image will appear as wallpaper. If you want many copies of the image to fill the screen, choose the Tile option. For one copy of the image in the center of the screen, choose Center.

6. Click the OK button to accept this wallpaper image and close the dialog box.

Copy Background

Use the Copy Background command to place a copy of the current Web page's background image in the Windows Clipboard. To load the image into another program, open the second program and use the Paste command.

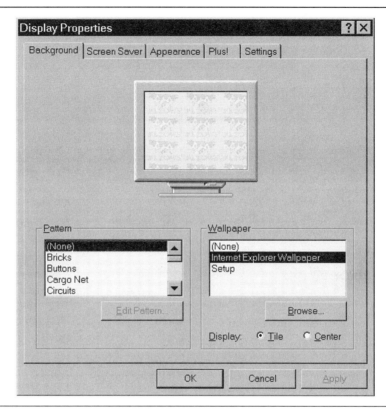

FIGURE 25.28: Use the Background tab to add or change your Desktop wallpaper.

Select All

The Select All command in the right-click menu is identical to the one in the Edit menu. Use this command to select all of the text in the current Web page. After you select the text, you can use the Copy command in the Edit menu to copy the text to the Windows Clipboard.

Create Shortcut

Use the Create Shortcut command to place a shortcut to the current Web page on your Desktop. This command also appears in the File menu.

Add to Favorites

Select the Add to Favorites command to include this Web page in your list of favorites.

View Source

The View Source command is identical to the Source command in the View menu. Use this command to load the HTML source code for the current Web page into a text editor.

Refresh

The Refresh command is a duplicate of the Refresh command in the View menu. Use this command to obtain a new copy of the current Web page from the server.

Properties

If your cursor is over text or background when you open the right-click menu, the Properties command opens a Properties window that contains information about the current Web page. If the cursor is over a picture or graphic image, the Properties window contains information about the image file. If the cursor is over a text link, the Properties window will provide information about the target URL for that link.

Open

The Open command appears in the right-click menu when your cursor is over a link. The Open command loads the destination of the current link into Internet Explorer, just as if you had clicked the link with your left mouse button.

Open in New Window

The Open in New Window command starts a second Internet Explorer window and loads the destination of the current link into that window. Loading a Web page into a new window can allow you to read the text of the current page while you wait for the next page to appear, or to compare the contents of several pages.

Save Target As

Use the Save Target As command to download the target of the current link and store a copy as a file without loading it into Internet Explorer.

Copy Shortcut

The Copy Shortcut command places a copy of the current link (the link itself, not the target Web page) on the Windows Clipboard. From there, you can use the Paste command to add a Web link to a document created with a word processor or another application program.

Save Picture As

The Save Picture As command appears in the right-click menu when the cursor is over a picture or other graphic image. To save the image as a bitmap file, select the command and use the browser to choose the folder where you want to store the file.

Show Picture

When you turn off Show Pictures on the Appearance tab of the dialog box, or if you interrupt a download before Internet Explorer has transferred all of the images in a Web page, you will see an empty box in place of each missing picture. The Show Picture command instructs Internet Explorer to download the image file for the current cursor location.

Employing Toolbar Commands

Most of the commands in Internet Explorer's Standard toolbar are duplicates of commands in the menus, but a few are not available anywhere else. The Standard toolbar is shown in Figure 25.29. The toolbar commands are described in the following sections.

When you move your cursor over a toolbar command button, the icon changes from black and white to color.

FIGURE 25.29: The Internet Explorer Standard toolbar includes many of the commands you will use most frequently.

Back

The Back button is an arrowhead pointing to the left. Click the Back button to return to the Web page that was visible immediately before you jumped to the current page. When the Back command tooltip appears, it includes the name of the previous Web page.

Forward

After you use the Back command to retrace your steps, you can use the Forward button to return to the next page in the current string. As with the Back button, the tooltip for the Forward button includes the name of the next page.

Stop

Use the Stop button to interrupt the current file transfer.

Refresh

When a download is in progress, the Refresh command instructs Internet Explorer to restart the file transfer from the beginning. When a download is not in progress, the Refresh command obtains a new copy of the current URL. Although Internet Explorer has placed a copy of the current Web page in the local cache, the program will get a new copy from the server.

Home

Click the Home button (with a picture of a house on it) to jump to your Start Page. To choose a different Web page as your Start Page, use the Options command in the View menu.

Search

The Search button opens your Search Page. The icon on the Search button is a magnifying glass suspended over the Earth. To change you Search Page, open the Explore menu and select Options.

Favorites

Click the Favorites button to open your Favorites menu. This menu includes the Open Favorites Folder command, the Add to Favorites command, and shortcuts to the sites in your list of favorites.

Print

Click the Print command button to print a copy of the current Web page.

Font

The Font command changes the size of the text in the current Web page. To step through several font sizes, click the Font command button several times. There are five font size steps from smallest to largest. Internet Explorer will continue to use the new font size until you change the font size again.

Address Field

The address field shows the URL of the current Web page. To jump to a new page, type a URL into the address field and press the Enter key.

If you're jumping to a Web page, you can type the address without the URL heading; Internet Explorer will add `http://` to the address to create a URL. When you want to move to any other kind of Internet resource, such as a gopher menu, an FTP archive, or any other file or server whose URL has some other type of code, you must type the complete URL.

The address field is also a drop-down list of Web pages that you have viewed during the current Internet Explorer session. To return to a Web page, open the drop-down list, select the URL you want to view, and press the Enter key.

Quick Links

Quick Links are links to the Web pages that have been specified in the Navigation Options dialog box.

Don't be intimidated by the many pages it takes to describe all of the commands in Internet Explorer. The basic structure of the World Wide Web and the architecture of Internet Explorer both make navigating the Web relatively easy. After you know how to click a link or type a URL in the Address field to jump to a new site, almost everything else is fine-tuning.

Are You Experienced?

Now you can...

- ☑ use the menu bar commands
- ☑ activate the right-click menu commands
- ☑ employ the toolbar button commands

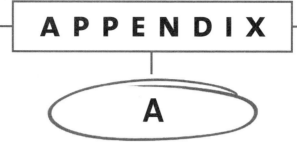

APPENDIX

A

File Allocation Table

The *File Allocation Table* (known by its attractive acronym as the FAT) is how the operating system keeps track of the files on your hard drive. In the FAT is each file's name, some useful information about the file such as its size and if it's been backed up, and the address where it is stored on the hard drive. This way when the operating system needs a file, it's not necessary to search the entire hard drive. Instead, the operating system goes to the FAT, finds the address for the file it wants and goes directly to its location.

Until now PCs using all versions of Windows (and DOS) had FAT-formatted drives. And FAT worked pretty well until a few years ago when hard drives started getting bigger and bigger. On hard drives bigger than 512MB, FAT utilized space in an extremely wasteful way. Every file, even the smallest, could take up 16KB worth of space. And FAT couldn't deal with partitions larger that 1GB at *all*.

NOTE The FAT32 option is available only on versions of Windows 95 that were installed on new computers first sold at the end of 1996. See the section "What FAT Do You Have?" to determine if you have FAT32.

A New Kind of FAT

This version of Windows 95 installed on your computer comes with a new type of FAT, namely FAT32. In almost all cases FAT32 will be installed (or not installed) by the computer's manufacturer.

NOTE Formatting described as just plain FAT always means FAT16 because it was the only kind of FAT for many years, so there was no need for a distinguishing name.

The advantage of FAT32 is that it will use your disk space in a very efficient way. A hard drive formatted as FAT32 will use 4KB of space for the same tiny file that uses 16KB in FAT16. It will also make it possible for you to have large hard drives that do not have to be broken up into partitions.

The down side of FAT32 is that it cannot even *see* drives with other types of formatting. In other words:

- All your hard drive space must be formatted with FAT32.

- If you're on a network, all drives that need to be shared must be FAT32 *or* FAT16. Not a mixture.

- If your Windows 95 hard drive space is FAT32, you will not be able to dual-boot with Windows NT.

What FAT Do You Have?

When you go to buy your computer, you may (in fact, you should) be asked how you want the hard drive formatted. If the hard drive you're getting is a single hard drive that's larger than 1GB and you'd like it to be a single partition, the choice will have to be FAT32. However, with other configurations—such as more than one physical hard drive, none larger than 1GB, or a hard drive that you don't mind dividing into multiple partitions, none larger than 512MB—you can decide.

If you don't know how your hard drive is formatted, here's how to find out:

1. Double-click the My Computer icon on your screen.

2. Right-click the drive you want to check and select Properties. This will open a window like the one shown in Figure A.1.

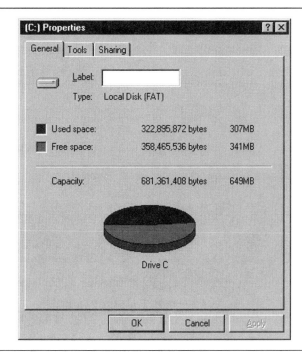

FIGURE A.1: Information about formatting, plus capacity and available space, can be garnered from checking a drive's properties.

Next to Type, you'll see how the drive is formatted.

 NOTE   You won't have the Sharing tab on the properties sheet unless you're on a network.

Switching from One Type to Another

Transforming hard drives from FAT32 to FAT16 or vice versa is best left to experts. It's neither simple nor easy, but if you feel at home with hard drives or your Cousin Vinnie is a genius at this kind of thing, it can be done.

From FAT16 to FAT32

Switching from FAT16 to FAT32 isn't even possible unless your computer's manufacturer did a setup that allows you to make a backup set of Windows 95 disks and you in fact actually made those Windows 95 disks. This is necessary because you'll have to reinstall Windows 95 after reformatting the hard drive(s).

 WARNING   Disks from a copy of Windows 95 sold in stores *will not work.*

First, everything must be backed up from the hard drive(s). Understand that everything on the hard drive will be *deleted and you will have to reinstall all your programs,* so make sure you have the original disks for all programs. Then follow these steps:

1. Make a Windows 95 Start Up disk.

2. Go to the Control Panel and select Add/Remove Programs. Click the Startup Disk tab and follow the instructions.

3. When the Startup Disk is completed, leave it in the floppy drive and click the Start button and select Shut Down.

4. Select Shut Down the Computer (as shown in Figure A.2) and let the computer shut down normally. Turn the computer off.

5. After a few seconds, turn the computer back on. It will boot from the floppy disk and stop at an unadorned A:\ prompt.

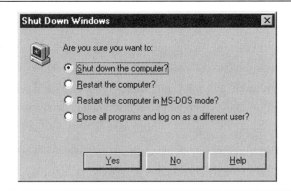

FIGURE A.2: Select Shut Down the Computer and click the OK button.

6. Type in **Fdisk** and press Enter.

7. You will see a fairly large and detailed warning. Read it carefully. If you want to proceed with the conversion to FAT32, type the letter **Y** in the space where you're asked if you want to enable large disk support and press Enter.

8. Use Fdisk to set the partition(s) you want.

9. Exit Fdisk, which takes you back to the A:\ prompt.

10. Type in **Format** followed by the drive letter. For example,

   Format C: /S

   The /S instructs the computer to transfer system files from the floppy to the hard drive. If you have additional partitions, format them as well. At the end of each format operation you'll see the Format Results which should list each allocation unit as having 4096 bytes. That's shows you have FAT32 on that partition.

NOTE   Only partitions *larger* than 512MB can be formatted with FAT32.

Reinstall Windows 95 and your other applications. Restore backed up data files.

Appendix A

From FAT32 to FAT16

Like the change from FAT16 to FAT32, going in the opposite direction is a complicated process. Again, you must have disks for the version of Windows 95 installed on your computer.

 NOTE Disks from a copy of Windows 95 sold in stores *will* let you change to FAT16, but if you reinstall Windows 95 from those disks you will lose your Internet Explorer, Microsoft Network, and other features.

First, everything must be backed up from the hard drive(s). Understand that everything on the hard drive will be *deleted and you will have to reinstall all your programs,* so make sure you have the original disks for all programs. Then follow these steps:

1. Make a Windows 95 Start Up disk.

2. Go to the Control Panel and select Add/Remove Programs. Click the Startup Disk tab and follow the instructions.

3. When the Startup Disk is completed, leave it in the floppy drive and click the Start button and select Shut Down.

4. Select Shut Down the Computer. Let the computer shut down normally and then turn the computer off.

5. Wait a few seconds then turn the computer back on. It will boot from the floppy disk and stop at an A:\ prompt.

6. Type in **Fdisk** and press Enter.

7. You will see a fairly large and detailed warning. Read it carefully. If you want to proceed with the conversion to FAT16, type the letter **N** in the space where you're asked if you want to enable large disk support and press Enter.

8. Use Fdisk to set the partition(s) you want. The partitions will have to be 1GB or smaller. However, try to limit partitions to 512MB if it's feasible because that will limit each storage unit to 8192 bytes.

9. Exit Fdisk, which takes you back to the A:\ prompt.

10. Type in **Format** followed by the drive letter. For example,

 Format C: /S

 The /S instructs the computer to transfer system files from the floppy to the hard drive. Format the additional partitions.

 Reinstall Windows 95 and all other applications. Restore data files.

A Final Note

In this appendix, I purposely don't explain what I think are prerequisites to fooling around with FAT tables. For example, you should have a knowledge of system files or the program Fdisk. If you don't know how to use Fdisk (one of the oldest DOS programs) you are probably in over your head and should get help.

It's certainly no disgrace not to know Fdisk, but it's another reason you should get the hard disks on your machine set up the way you want them before software is installed and you have something to lose.

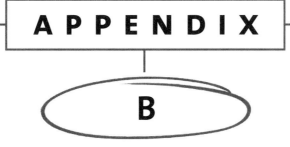

A P P E N D I X

B

B

Installing and Configuring Internet Explorer

Before you start to use Internet Explorer, you must install the program onto your PC. The installation process is fairly painless, but it does ask you to make a handful of decisions while the program loads. After installation is complete, some other possible tweaks can make Internet Explorer easier to use.

In this appendix, you can find explanations of all the installation options and instructions for configuring the program after installation is complete. While it's entirely possible to simply install the program and start using it, the suggestions found here will help you make the most of some of Internet Explorer's less obvious features.

Installing Internet Explorer in Windows 95

Microsoft has designed Internet Explorer to be easy to install. For the most part, they've succeeded. When you run the msienn.exe program, it automatically extracts the compressed files from the distribution file and places them in the appropriate folders or directories.

Some download methods automatically offer to install the program after they copy the distribution file to your hard drive. If it's not automatic, follow these steps to install Internet Explorer:

1. Copy the distribution file to a temporary folder.

2. Open the folder that contains the distribution file and double-click the icon for that file. If you're installing Internet Explorer as part of the Plus! package, or upgrading from an earlier version of the program, the installation routine will automatically decide where to place the program files. If you're loading the program for the first time, you must specify a location. It doesn't really matter where you put the files, but there are a couple of logical choices:

   - **The hard drive (C:) root folder**: Subfolders and files in the root folder are easy to find, but they contribute to a cluttered window, and there's always a chance that you might have a conflict among files with the same name that belong to different programs. You may never actually open the Microsoft Internet folder (because you'll use a shortcut from the Desktop or Start menu to start the program) so there's no reason to make it a top-level folder.

- **The Program Files folder**: In Windows 95, many well-behaved application programs place their files in subfolders within the Program Files folder. This seems like an entirely logical place for Internet Explorer.

- **A new top-level folder or directory called Internet Tools**: If you decide to use other Internet tools along with Internet Explorer, it makes sense to store them in subfolders within the same top-level folder. If you prefer, you might want to consider placing the Internet Tools folder in the Program Files folder.

In practice, if Internet Explorer recommends a destination folder during installation, it's probably a good idea to accept that suggestion.

The first time you click the Internet icon or select the Internet Explorer command from the Start menu after you load the software, Internet Explorer will step you through the Setup Wizard. The Wizard will ask if you want to use the Microsoft Network or some other service provider to connect to the Internet, as shown in Figure B.1.

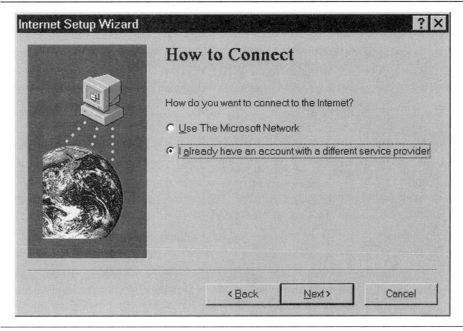

FIGURE B.1: The Internet Setup Wizard offers you the choice of connecting through MSN or another Internet service provider.

If you choose MSN as your connection to the Internet, the Wizard will find the closest telephone number for dial-in access and help you set up a new account if you don't already have one. If you choose a different service provider, the Wizard will ask for additional information that Internet Explorer will use to process mail and directory services. If you haven't already configured a Dial-Up Networking connection profile for your ISP (as described in Skill 17), the Wizard will use this information to create one for you.

Using the Desktop Internet Icon

When installation and setup are complete, you will see the Internet icon on your Windows 95 Desktop, as shown in Figure B.2, and an Internet Explorer command in the Start menu's Programs submenu. When you double-click the icon (or choose the menu command), Internet Explorer will automatically connect your computer to the Internet and display the Start Page. You can find information in Skill 21 about customizing the default Microsoft Start Page or substituting a different page.

F I G U R E   B . 2 :   Internet Explorer adds an Internet icon to the Windows 95 Desktop.

Using the Internet Properties Dialog Box

Like all other Windows 95 icons, the Internet has a Properties command in the menu that appears when you click the Internet icon with your right mouse button. You can also open the Properties dialog boxes with the Options command in the View menu within Internet Explorer.

Figure B.3 shows the Connection tab in the Internet Properties dialog box. If you're using Dial-Up Networking to connect to the Internet, make sure there's a check mark next to the Connect to the Internet as Needed option, and choose your default connection in the drop-down list. If you're connected to the Internet through a LAN or a direct high-speed link, you can remove the check mark from the Connect as Needed option.

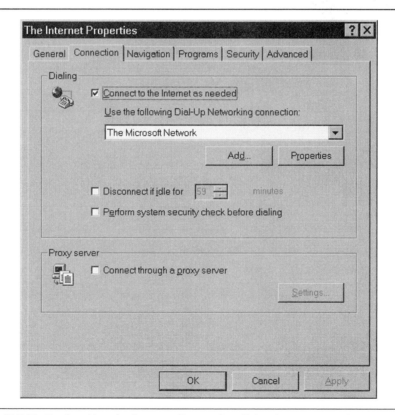

FIGURE B.3: Use the Internet Properties dialog box to control automatic connection to the Internet.

You can use the Properties button to change an existing connection profile, or the Add button to create a new profile. The Disconnect If Idle option breaks your connection to the Internet and hangs up the telephone line if there's no activity for the specified number of minutes. Unfortunately, the program does not monitor third-party application programs like Netscape Navigator or Winsock FTP, so you might see a "Disconnecting in 30 Seconds" message in the middle of an active session. This is a nuisance, because it means that you can't go away from your computer and do something else during a long file transfer. You may want to disable this option if you expect to use other Internet programs along with Internet Explorer.

The Perform System Security Check Before Dialing option limits access to shared printers and files through the Internet. If your PC is not on a LAN, you can safely turn off this option.

The Proxy option turns access to a proxy server on or off. If you're using Dial-Up Networking, this option should be off. If you connect through a LAN that has a "firewall" to protect against unauthorized outside access to your local network, you may need to use a proxy server. Your LAN administrator or help desk can supply the information you need to use Internet Explorer through a firewall.

All of the other tabs in the Internet Properties dialog box control Internet Explorer options. There are explanations of these options later in this appendix.

Removing the Icon from Your Desktop

Unlike shortcuts to programs and data files, you can't remove the Internet icon from your Desktop by dragging it to the Recycle Bin. If you don't want to use the icon, there are two ways to eliminate it:

- Use the Delete command in the right-click menu.

- Use a free program called Tweak UI (available as part of the Windows 95 Power Toys collection from Microsoft's Web site at http:// www.microsoft .com/windows/software/powertoy.htm).

Tweak UI is the better choice, because it allows you to restore the icon to the desktop if you change your mind about removing it, and because it controls other Desktop icons, as shown in Figure B.4.

Changing the Name of the Icon

If you keep the the Internet icon on your Desktop, you might want to rename it to "Internet Explorer", especially if you also use other Internet application programs.

There's a Rename command in the menu that appears when you move the cursor over the icon and press the right mouse button.

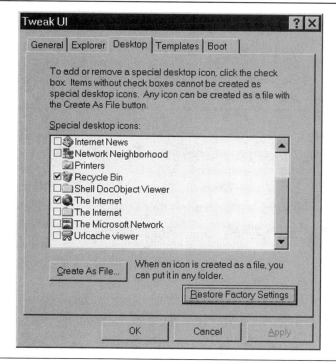

FIGURE B.4: Use Microsoft's free Tweak UI program to hide or display special Desktop icons, including the one for the Internet.

Changing Internet Explorer's Appearance and Performance

As you work with Internet Explorer (or any other Web browser), it's useful to understand that a Web page or other HTML document does not always include information about the specific colors and type fonts that appear on your screen. The Web browser program receives the page as text with embedded formatting commands, and it performs the formatting when it displays the page.

Therefore, you can change the way Internet Explorer formats a page by choosing different colors and typefaces. The wrong choices can make a page completely unreadable, but other options might actually improve the way a page looks.

It's also possible to reduce the amount of time needed to download a page by skipping artwork, sounds, and animation. This is especially useful if you're using a slow modem.

NOTE   For many users, Internet Explorer's default configuration will do everything they need. "If it's not broke, don't fix it" is a completely acceptable working philosophy for installing and using the program. If you're happy with the type-face and other appearance options, and if you don't mind waiting for graphic images and sound files to download, you don't have to make any changes.

Options in the General Tab

To control the appearance of pages in Internet Explorer, follow these steps:

1. If it's not already running, start Internet Explorer.

2. Open the View menu and select the Options command.

3. If it's not visible, click the General tab to display the dialog box shown in Figure B.5.

Working with Multimedia Elements in Web Pages

The Multimedia section of the General tab includes these options:

- **Show Pictures**   When Show Pictures is not checked, Internet Explorer does not automatically download pictures and other graphic elements embedded in Web pages. Hiding the pictures can reduce the amount of time needed to download a page, but it may also eliminate much of the information contained in a Web site. If you don't show pictures when you download Web pages, you can click on an image icon to download an individual picture later. If the page includes graphic links or an image map, you won't be able to use any of the links until you download the picture. Figure B.6 shows the same Web page with and without pictures.

- **Play Sounds**   Some Web pages are accompanied by audio recordings of background music, sound effects, or voice narration. If your computer has a sound board, Internet Explorer will automatically play these sounds when you download a page, but like everything else in a Web page, sounds take time to download. If you don't have a sound board, or if you're not interested in hearing anything, turn off the Play Sounds option.

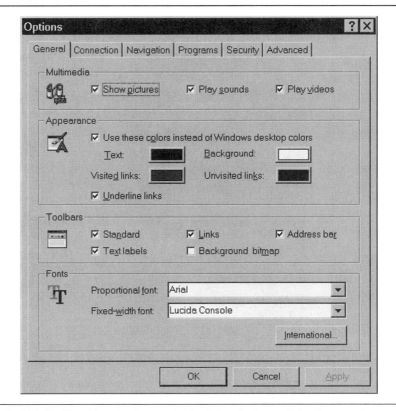

FIGURE B.5: Use the General tab of the Options dialog box to change the fonts and colors of Web pages.

- **Play Videos**   Animated images and other moving pictures require extremely large files. To avoid waiting for them to load, remove the check mark from the Play Videos option.

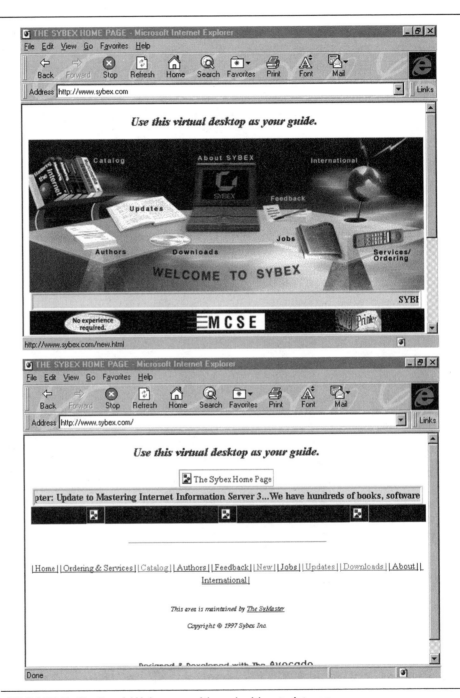

FIGURE B.6: A Web page with and without pictures

Controlling the Colors of Web Pages

The Use These Colors Instead of Windows Desktop Colors options specify the colors that Internet Explorer uses to display text, background, and links in Web pages. When there is no check mark next to Use These Colors, Internet Explorer will use the color settings defined in the Windows Display Properties dialog box, unless a Web page specifies a text or background color. To change the default colors, place a check mark in the box next to Use These Colors and click the Text or Background buttons to select a new color. As a rule, you should use a dark color for text and a light color for background to make your pages as easy to read as possible.

Changing the Appearance of Text Links

Internet Explorer maintains a history file that contains a list of URLs that you have recently downloaded. When a Web page contains a shortcut to one of the URLs in your history file, it will display the shortcut in the color shown on the Viewed Links button. Click the button to choose a different color. When a Web page contains a shortcut to a URL that is not in your history file, Internet Explorer will display the shortcut in the color shown on the Unvisited button. Click the button to choose a different color.

 NOTE   When you click a link, Internet Explorer downloads the file identified in that link. If the target is another Web page or other URL. Internet Explorer loads and displays it; if it's another type of file, it uses the association for the file name extension to decide how to handle the file.

When Underline Links is active, Internet Explorer displays links in Web pages with a single underline. When this option is not active, you will see links in the colors specified by the Visited Links and Unvisited Links options.

Configuring the Internet Explorer Toolbars

The Toolbars section of the General tab hides or displays portions of the toolbars that appear just above the main window, as shown in Figure B.7.
It includes these options:

- **Standard**   The Standard toolbar contains command buttons that duplicate important menu commands.

- **Text Labels**   When the Text Labels option is active, the Standard toolbar includes a caption under each command icon that identifies the function of that command.

- **Links** The Links toolbar is a set of five quick links to Web pages that you visit frequently. Use the Navigation tab to specify the destinations of your quick links.

- **Address Bar** The Address bar shows the URL of the current Web page.

- **Background Bitmap** When the Background Bitmap option is active, there's a pattern under the icons and text in all visible toolbars. When this option is not active, the background is a light solid color.

FIGURE B.7: You can hide or display one or more toolbars from the General tab.

Changing Type Fonts

The HTML code for most Web pages does not include an instruction to use a specific typeface for headlines or body text. Instead, the Web page designer leaves the choice of a font to the browser. In Internet Explorer, the options that specify your default font are in the General tab of the Options dialog box.

To change a font, click the arrow at the left of the option field and choose the font you want to use from the drop-down list.

Use the Proportional Font field to change the typeface that Internet Explorer will use to display headlines and body text in Web pages. It's called "proportional" because some letters are wider than others—for example, compare an I with an M. The default proportional font is Times New Roman, which was originally designed for ink on paper. Some other fonts, such as Arial, are better choices for on-screen reading. To select a different font, open the drop-down list and select the one you want to use.

Use the Fixed-Width Font field to change the typeface used for tables and other text elements that must maintain a constant width. The default fixed-width font is Courier New, which looks like the print from an old-fashioned typewriter. Lucida Console is a better choice, because it's easier to read and it looks more like real print.

Using a Foreign Character Set

Different languages may use different character sets, so you can configure Internet Explorer to recognize the one you use most often by clicking on the International button. In most cases, the International dialog box shown in Figure B.8 will list the home language for the version of Internet Explorer that you're using. If your version of the program supports more than one character set, or if you've added support for another language after installation, you can set different default fonts for each language.

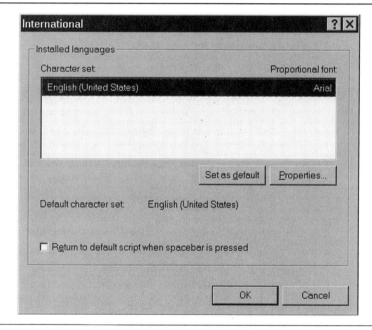

FIGURE B.8: Use the International dialog box to use a different character set.

To change to a different character set, follow these steps:

1. In Internet Explorer, open the View menu and select the Options command.

2. Click the General tab.

3. Click the International button to open the International dialog box.

4. Select the character set you want to use.

Changing the Address Format in the Status Bar

The Show Friendly URLs option in the Advanced Options tab controls the format that Internet Explorer uses to display addresses in the status bar. When Show Friendly URLs is active, the status bar shows the address without the extra URL information, like this:

```
www.destination.com
```

When the option is not active, the status bar shows the address with all the URL coding, like this:

```
http://www.destination.com/
```

Connecting File Types with Programs

As mentioned in Skill 4, when you open a file from the Windows 95 Desktop or Explorer, Windows uses the file name extension to identify an application or utility that can read the file. For example, if you select a text file called report.doc, Windows might load the file into Microsoft Word. If you choose an HTML file called picture.htm, Windows might use Internet Explorer to display the contents of the file. The installation routines for Windows and many application programs automatically assign file associations to the particular file name extensions that are normally used with those programs.

Internet Explorer adds MIMEs (Multipurpose Internet Mail Extensions) to the list of file associations used with other Windows programs. Therefore, when you select a file for download through the Internet, Internet Explorer looks for the file name extension in the list of registered file types, and takes the action specified for that type. Depending on the file type, Internet Explorer might open and display the file within its own window, start another program to display or run the file, or store the file in a directory or folder.

 NOTE There's a very good chance that you will never have to worry about associating a MIME with a program, because the default associations will do everything you ever need.

When you download a new file type, Internet Explorer will offer you several choices:

- Open this file, but don't permanently associate the file name extension with an application program or utility.

- Associate the file name extension with a MIME, so all future files of this type will automatically open.

- Store the file in a folder or directory.

If you prefer, you can create a new MIME type or change an existing MIME before you download a file. Follow these steps to add or change a file type:

1. In Internet Explorer, open the View menu and select the Options command.

2. Click the Programs tab.

3. Click the File Types tab to display the dialog box in Figure B.9.

4. To create a new file association, click on the New Type button. To change an existing association, select a description from the list of Registered File Types and click the Edit button. You'll see the New File Type or Edit File Type dialog box, which have similar fields.

5. To assign an application to a MIME, choose an existing item from the Actions field (for example, you might want to choose Open as an action) and click the Edit button, or click the New button to create a new action. You'll see the dialog box shown in Figure B.10 (which may be called Editing Action for Type or New Action).

6. Use the Browse button in the dialog box to select the program that you want to use with this file type. Then click the Open button to close the browser, and the OK button in the dialog box.

7. If you want Internet Explorer to offer you a choice of either opening a file as soon as it has downloaded that file or storing the file without opening it, place a check mark next to the Confirm Open After Download option in the New File Type or Edit File Type dialog box. Generally, this option should be active for executable files and for data files that you may not want to run or examine until after you have broken your connection to the Internet.

8. Click the OK buttons in the dialog boxes.

Once your installation and configuration are complete, you're ready to start using Internet Explorer.

Appendix B

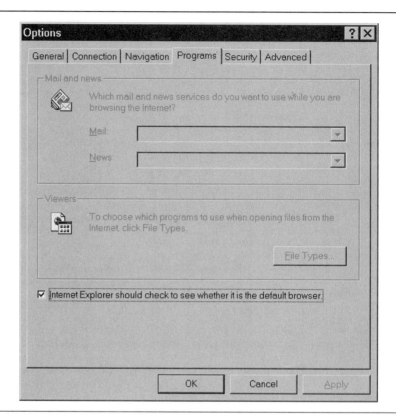

FIGURE B.9: Click the File Types button to assign programs to file name extensions.

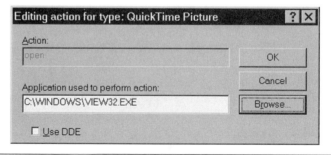

FIGURE B.10: Use one of the Action dialog boxes to attach an application program to a file type.

GLOSSARY

Glossary

16-bit, 32-bit

Refers to how certain programs address memory and other technical details. In general, 16-bit programs are those written for DOS or earlier versions of Windows or Windows NT. Windows 95 can use 32-bit programs that can do true multitasking (as opposed to task switching). If designed correctly, 32-bit programs can be faster than 16-bit programs but they are not inherently so.

active window

The window that keyboard or mouse movements act on. Many windows can be open, but only one is active at a time. You can spot the active window by its title bar, which is a different color than the title bar of other windows.

administrator/system administrator

The individual in charge of planning, setting up, and maintaining a network. This person is responsible for making sure that system resources are made available to users in an orderly and secure manner and he or she is the one to whom you'll inevitably go running whenever there's a problem.

anonymous FTP

A way to use the FTP program to log on to another computer when you don't have an account on that computer. When you log on, enter anonymous as the user name and your address as the password. This gives you access to all the publicly available files. (See also: *FTP*.)

application

An application is a collection of files that may include several programs. WordPerfect is an application that consists of any number of files constituting a single package. Applications are also grouped by type such as word processing applications, database applications, and so forth.

ASCII

Pronounced "AS-key." Stands for the American Standard Code for Information Interchange. Developed back in the '60s as a standard numerical code for characters used on all computers. Today, ASCII usually means normal text as opposed to code, unreadable by regular folk.

associate

To connect files having a particular extension to a specific program. When you double-click a file with the extension, the associated program is opened and the file you clicked is opened. In Windows 95, associated files are usually called *registered* files.

attribute

A bit of code in a file that determines an aspect of the file's status. The four file attributes are read-only, hidden, archive, and system. A file can have none or several of the attributes. You can modify these but only if you have a good reason. (This is a noun, pronounced with the accent on the first syllable, not the second.)

backbone

A high-speed line or series of connections that form a major pathway within a network. The term is relative, because a backbone in a small network will likely be much smaller than many non-backbone lines in a large network. On the Internet, the backbone consists of the very high-speed connections owned by the government, large communications companies, and some major Internet service providers.

background

All the screen area behind the active window. Can also mean a process that is going on other than in the active window.

baud

The speed at which data is transmitted over a communications line or cable. This is not *really* the same as bps (bits per second) but the terms are used interchangeably.

bit

Represents a single switch inside a computer set to 0 or 1. There are millions of them in every computer. Short for binary digit, 8 bits make up a byte, the basic unit of data storage.

bitmaps

Picture or image files that are made up of pixels. Pictures made in Paint are automatically saved as bitmaps (with a .BMP extension).

boot

A simple name for the complicated processes your computer goes through when starting up.

bootable disk

A disk containing the *system* files needed to start the computer. When your system starts up, it looks for a disk first in drive A: if none is there it goes to drive C:. When a disk is found, the computer examines the disk to see if it contains the system files. When a disk with system files is found, the computer uses that disk's information to start the system running. If a disk with system files is in drive A:, information on that disk will be used to tell the computer about itself. Computers can normally be booted only from drive A: or drive C:.

BPS

Bits per second. A unit of measurement for the communication speed of modems and fax modems.

browse

To examine a list of computers on a network. When you use Network Neighborhood and/or the Entire Network icons, you're browsing the network.

byte

The basic unit of data storage. A byte is 8 bits. For all intents and purposes, a byte equals a single character.

client

In a client/server network environment, a client is a computer that says "you have it, give it to me." In other words, a client accesses shared network resources (be they files, printers, or whatever) provided by a server.

client/server network

A network that consists of at least one server and one client, though usually many more. Client/server networking has many advantages, not the least of which is that it allows users to share system resources in an efficient, secure manner.

configuration

A set of values in a program or for a device such as a printer. The values will be things such as how menu options work or a particular size of paper for a printer to use.

DDE

Stands for Dynamic Data Exchange. An older standard for making information updated in one program available in another program. It's been replaced by OLE.

default

The configuration settings that a device or program will have without any intervention from you. Usually you can change the default settings, but care should be taken.

dialog box

A window that opens to ask you impertinent questions or request input. Windows 95 programs are knee-deep in dialog boxes.

DLL

Short for Dynamic Link Library. A file with information needed by one or more programs. Don't delete files with this extension willy-nilly because your programs will be dysfunctional without the DLL files they need.

DNS name servers

Servers that contain information about part of the Domain Name System database. These servers make computer names available for name resolution across the Internet. For example, when you type in www.microsoft.com, the name must be translated into a numerical address for the site to be found. DNS servers perform that service.

driver

A program made up of instructions to operate things that are added on to your computer such as a printer, modem, or mouse. Windows 95 includes most drivers you're likely to need, but there are rare times when you need to acquire a newer driver (and instructions on installing it) from the manufacturer of the device.

Dynamic Data Exchange (DDE)

Communication between processes. When programs that support DDE are running at the same time they can exchange data by means of conversations. Conversations are two way connections between two applications that transmit data alternately.

Dynamic Link Library (DLL)

A program module that contains executable code and data that can be used by various programs. The DLL is used by the program only when the program is active and is unloaded when the program closes.

Exchange

Microsoft's messaging application, which you can access by double-clicking the Inbox icon on your Desktop. With Microsoft Exchange, you can send and receive electronic mail using various services, including Microsoft Mail and Internet Mail. You send messages from and store all messages in Microsoft Exchange, so there's one convenient place to look for all your messages. (Also called Microsoft Messaging in some versions of Windows 95.)

FAT

An acronym for "File Access Table," the file system type used by DOS, Windows 3.x, and Windows 95, and one of the two file system types recognized by Windows NT.

FAT32

A new version of the file allocation table (FAT) available in Windows 95 OSR2. FAT32 reduces the size of each cluster on a hard drive to 4KB. Therefore, data is accessed more efficiently. FAT32 can support hard drives up to 2 terabytes in capacity.

file system

A set of files stored on a disk or one partition of a disk. Each file system contains files and folders that in turn may contain further folders. Each file system is also of a distinct type.

finger

A program that displays information about someone on the Internet. On most UNIX systems, this command tells you who is logged on right now. On most Internet hosts, it tells you the name (and possibly some other information based on the person's Internet address) and the last time that person logged on.

folder

A means of organizing files. Each installed program will make its own folder and perhaps several subfolders. The user can likewise make folders to organize programs and files. Folders are analogous to directories in Windows 3.1 and DOS.

FTP (File Transfer Protocol)

A method of transferring one or more files from one computer to another over a network or telephone line.

gateway/hub

A computer that connects two or more networks and relays messages and other communications from one network to another.

GIF (Graphic Interchange Format)

A file format commonly used to distribute graphics files on the Internet.

gopher

A system that lets you find information on remote systems by using menus. To use gopher, you usually Telnet to a gopher server and begin browsing through the menus.

gopherspace

Collectively, all the gopher servers on the Internet.

HTML (Hypertext Markup Language)

A system used for writing pages for the World Wide Web. HTML allows text to include codes that define fonts, layout, embedded graphics, and hypertext links.

HTTP (Hypertext Transfer Protocol)

The method by which World Wide Web pages are transferred over the Internet.

hypertext

A system of writing and displaying text that enables the text to be linked in multiple ways, available at several levels of detail. Hypertext documents can also contain links to related documents, such as those referred to in footnotes.

initialize

To prepare for use. With disks, this means to format the disk so it can be read. Programmers use this term to mean to get everything in the program to a known, beginning state.

IP (Internet Protocol)

The transport layer protocol used as a basis of the Internet. IP enables information to be routed from one network to another in packets and then reassembled when they reach their destination.

IP number

A four-part number separated by periods (for example, 165.113.245.2) that uniquely identifies a machine on the Internet. Every machine on the Internet has a unique IP number; if a machine does not have an IP number, it's not on the Internet. Most machines also have one or more domain names that are easier for people to remember.

Java

An advanced programming script similar to C and C++ used to design applets in Web pages to provide animation and other advanced features that make a Web page unique.

LAN (Local Area Network)

A group of connected computers, usually located close to one another (such as the same building or the same floor) so that data can be passed among them.

kilobyte

One thousand bytes (actually 1,024). Abbreviated as K and KB.

landscape

A printer setting in which the characters are printed sideways along the length of the page. The opposite setting is "portrait."

log on

Either a noun or a verb. As a noun, it's the account name used to gain access to a computer system. Unlike a password, the logon name is not a secret. As a verb, it means the act of entering into a computer system; for example, "Logon to CompuServe and then go to the Travel forum."

mapped drive

A folder or drive that is assigned its own drive letter and is made available to network users.

megabyte

One million bytes (or 1,048,576 bytes). Abbreviated as M or MB.

mirror

1. Two partitions on two hard drives configured so that each will contain identical data to the other. If one drive fails, the other can continue. 2. An FTP server that provides copies of the same files as another server. Some FTP servers are so popular that other servers have been set up to mirror them and spread the FTP load to more than one site.

modem

A contraction for MOdulator-DEModulator. A device that connects between a computer and a telephone line to allow the computer to talk to other computers through the system. Modems convert the computer's digital signals into analog waves that can be transmitted over standard voice telephone lines. Modem speeds are measured in bits per second (bps)—also sometimes expressed as kilobits (thousands of bits) per second (Kbps). For example, 28.8 Kbps and 28,800 BPS are the same thing—28,800 bits per second.

Multitasking

Using more than one application at a time. Most of the time in Windows 3.1 you were *task switching*, moving back and forth between applications, not actually using more than one at the same time. Windows 95 makes true multitasking possible, but to get the full effect you need to be running 32-bit programs.

NetBEUI (NetBIOS Extended User Interface)

A small and fast protocol that requires little memory but can't be routed. Remote locations linked by routers can't use NetBEUI to communicate.

network

A series of two or more computers that are linked together. In a LAN (Local Area Network), the computers are physically connected by means of network adapter cards and cables. In a WAN (Wide Area Network), computers may be connected in a variety of ways, using modems and telephone lines or satellite connections, just to name two examples.

network adapter

Also known as a network card, it's the piece of hardware that physically connects a computer to a network. Sometimes called a Network Interface Card (NIC).

Network Neighborhood

On a networked computer, Network Neighborhood is your key to sharing files, folders, and printers with other people. If you double-click the Network Neighborhood icon, you should see icons for all the computers currently connected to your network.

Network Protocol/Network Protocol Stack

The agreed-upon language that computers on a network use to communicate with one another. Three of the most common network protocols are IPX/SPX, NetBEUI, and TCP/IP.

newsgroup

On the Internet, a distributed bulletin board system about a particular topic. Usenet News (also known as Netnews) is a system that distributes thousands of newsgroups to all parts of the Internet.

node

A computer on the Internet, also called a host. Nodes that provide a service, such as FTP sites or places that run Gopher are also called servers.

OLE

Pronounced "O-lay." Short for Object Linking and Embedding. An automatic way for Windows programs to share data.

online

To be in a state of readiness. A printer is said to be online when it's ready to print. These days, online is mostly used to mean being connected to another computer via modem. The connection can be to a commercial service, an Internet provider, and so forth.

optimize

Computer jargon for "improve the performance of."

packet

A chunk of information sent over a network. Each packet contains the destination address, the sender's address, error-control information, and data.

page

A document, or collection of information, available via the World Wide Web. A page may contain text, graphics, video, and/or sound files.

paging

A virtual memory operation in which pages are transferred from memory to disk when memory becomes full. When a thread accesses a page that's not in memory, a page fault occurs and the memory manager uses page tables to find the page on disk and then loads the page into memory.

parallel

A port on your computer usually used to connect a cable to a printer. Can also be used to connect other devices, such as an external drive or network adapter, to your computer. Information transmitted through a parallel port travels through multiple side-by-side paths inside the cable.

password

A sequence of characters that a user types when logging in to verify his or her identity.

peer-to-peer network

A network scheme that is often contrasted with client/server networking. On a peer-to-peer network, there is no hierarchy of server vs. client; all the computers are equal. Each may provide services to others, if the appropriate permissions have been granted.

peripheral

A device attached to the outside of your computer. This includes the monitor, keyboard, mouse, and printer.

permission

A rule associated with an object (usually a directory, file, or printer) that regulates which users can have access to the object and in what manner.

Plug and Play

A recent standard for hardware. The user can install hardware that uses this standard on a Windows 95 computer with very little intervention. The hardware will be detected and configured by Windows 95 to run properly.

Manufacturers of disk drives, modems, network cards, and other devices have been rapidly adopting Plug and Play.

Point of Presence (POP)

A physical site in a geographic area where a network access provider, such as MCI, has equipment to which users connect. The local telephone company's central office in a particular area is also sometimes referred to as their POP for that area.

Post Office Protocol (POP)

A system by which a mail server on the Internet lets you grab your mail and download it to your PC or Macintosh. Most people refer to this protocol with its version number (POP2, POP3, and so on) to avoid confusing it with Point of Presence.

PPP (Point-to-Point Protocol)

A protocol that provides router-to-router and host-to-network connections over a telephone line (or a network link that acts like a telephone line). Similar to SLIP.

port

A connecting point on your computer for plugging in external devices. At a minimum, most computers have two serial ports and one parallel (printer) port. Computers also have a specialized port for the keyboard; some have a special mouse port, too.

portrait

The usual way a page of text is printed with lines running across the width of the sheet. The opposite setting is "landscape."

protocol

A set of rules that determine the flow of data and how it's used. The modems at either end of a communication line have to be using the same protocol to talk to each other. Likewise, computers on a network need to be speaking the same protocol in order to connect.

RAM

Short for Random Access Memory. In a nutshell, memory is where things happen in your computer. The processor (CPU) does the work but it can hold only so much information. Programs and files are retrieved from the hard disk and stored in RAM so that operations can proceed rapidly.

register

To tell Windows 95 what program to use to open files of a certain type (that is, files with a particular extension). If a file type is registered, a double-click of a file of that type will start the necessary application and open the file. For example, a file with the .DOC extension will automatically be opened in Word. A .TXT extension will cause a file to be opened in Notepad. Same as *associate*.

registry

A database that keeps track of the configuration for a Windows 95 computer. It is accessible only by using the Regedit program and is for experts only.

Remote Access Service (RAS)

Allows users to dial in from remote locations and access their networks for file and printer sharing, e-mail, scheduling, and database access.

resources

A general term for some of the items commonly shared over a network: disk space, printers, and network fax modems, and so on.

router

A special-purpose computer (or software package) that handles the connection between two or more networks. Routers look at the destination addresses of the packets passing through them and decide which route to use to send them.

serial

A particular type of port that transmits information one bit at a time. Mostly used by a modem or a mouse, and occasionally by a scanner.

server

In a client/server network environment, a server is a computer that says, "You want it, I've got it." In other words, a server is the machine that provides clients with access to shared network resources, be they files, printers, or whatever.

sharing

The process of making a resource (be it a file, directory, printer, fax modem, or whatever) available to network users.

shortcut

A tool that acts as a pointer to a file, folder, application, or device. Shortcuts are very small files you can place almost anywhere. When you double-click a shortcut, the object it points to will be opened. So you can have a shortcut to an object in various places without having to physically move or copy files.

SLIP (Serial Line Internet Protocol)

A protocol used to run IP over serial lines or telephone lines using modems. Rapidly being replaced by PPP (Point to Point Protocol).

SMTP (Simple Mail Transfer Protocol)

A protocol used to transfer e-mail messages between computers.

socket

An endpoint to a connection. Two sockets form a complete path for a bi-directional pipe for incoming and outgoing data between networked computers. The Windows Sockets API is a networking API for programmers writing for the Windows family of products.

swap file

Space on the hard disk that Windows 95 uses to increase the amount of memory available to Windows 95 programs. The swap file in Windows 95 is dynamic so it automatically grows larger or smaller based on current activity on the computer.

system resources

A finite portion of memory that is set aside for Windows 95 to keep track of all its pieces. In earlier versions of Windows, running out of resources is common even if you have a lot of memory because the amount available for system resources can't get larger or smaller. Windows 95 has more space for system resources and manages those resources much more intelligently, so you can have many more programs open at once.

TCP/IP

An abbreviation for Transport Control Protocol/Internet Protocol. Perhaps the most-used network protocol stack on the Internet and many other networks, large and small. TCP/IP is currently used to link all kinds of computers worldwide over a variety of media, from high-speed optical network cabling to regular phone lines.

Telnet

The command and program used to log on from one Internet site to another. The Telnet command/program gets you to the logon prompt of another host.

topology

A fancy term for the way a network is designed.

UNIX

A computer operating system designed to be used by many computer users at the same time (it is "multiuser") with TCP/IP built in. It is the most common operating system for servers on the Internet.

URL (Uniform Resource Locator)

The standard way to give the address of any resource on the Internet that is part of the World Wide Web. This is an example of a URL: `http://www.capecod.net/~fcollege/index.htm`. The most common way to use a URL is to launch a Web browser, such as Microsoft Internet Explorer or Netscape Navigator.

VRML (Virtual Reality Markup Language)

A system used for writing pages for the World Wide Web. VRML allows your Web Page to include codes that define animation and 3-D graphics.

virtual memory

Simulated RAM created by taking advantage of free space on the hard drive, also called a swap file. If you start more programs or processes than your RAM has room for, the programs actively doing something will be placed in RAM while the less-active or inactive ones will be moved to the swap file space on the hard drive. Windows 95 will automatically swap programs back and forth as needed. The swap file is dynamic in Windows 95, which means it will also automatically grow and shrink as necessary.

WAN (Wide Area Network)

Any Internet or network that covers an area larger than a single building or campus. (See also: *LAN* and *network*)

Windows Socket (WinSock)

Windows Sockets is a standard way for Windows-based programs to work with TCP/IP. You can use WinSock if you use SLIP to connect to the Internet.

WINS (Windows Internet Name Service)

A name resolutions service that converts computer names to IP addresses in a routed environment.

WWW (World Wide Web)

A hypermedia-based system for accessing information on the Internet.

W3C (World Wide Web Consortium)

The World Wide Web is the universe of network-accessible information. The World Wide Web Consortium exists to bring about the full potential of the Web. W3C works with the global community to produce specifications and reference software. Industrial members pay for it, but its products are freely available to all.

Index

Note to the Reader: Throughout this index **bold** page numbers indicate primary discussions of a topic. *Italic* page numbers indicate illustrations.

Q

R

SYBEX BOOKS ON THE WEB!

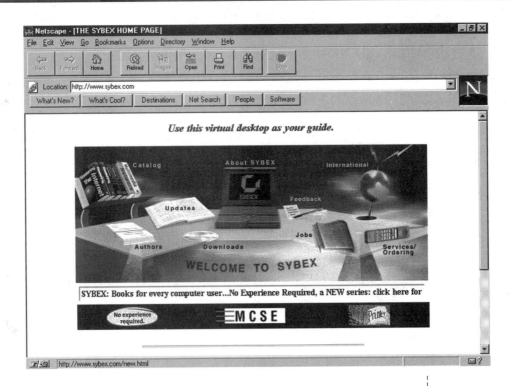

Presenting a truly dynamic environment
that is both fun and informative.

- access special book content
- view our complete online catalog
- preview a book you might want to own
- find out about job opportunities at Sybex
- order books online at special discount prices
- learn about Sybex
- what's new in the computer industry

http://www.sybex.com

SYBEX Inc. • 1151 Marina Village Parkway • Alameda, CA 94501 • 510-523-8233